Sourcebook in Late-Scholastic Monetary Theory

Studies in Ethics and Economics
Series Editor
Samuel Gregg, Acton Institute

Advisory Board
Michael Novak, American Enterprise Institute, United States
Edward Younkins, Wheeling Jesuit University, United States
Manfred Spieker, University of Osnabrück, Germany
Jean-Yves Naudet, University of Aix-Marseilles, France
Maximilian Torres, University of Navarre, Spain
Rodger Charles, S.J., University of Oxford, England
Leonard Liggio, George Mason University, United States

Economics as a discipline cannot be detached from a historical background that was, it is increasingly recognized, religious in nature. Adam Ferguson and Adam Smith drew on the work of sixteenth- and seventeenth-century Spanish theologians, who strove to understand the process of exchange and trade in order to better address the moral dilemmas they saw arising from the spread of commerce in the New World. After a long period in which economics became detached from theology and ethics, many economists and theologians now see the benefit of studying economic realities in their full cultural, often religious, context. This new series, Studies in Ethics and Economics, provides an international forum for exploring the difficult theological and economic questions that arise in the pursuit of this objective.

Titles in the Series
The Boundaries of Technique: Ordering Positive and Normative Concerns in Economic Research, by Andrew Yuengert

Within the Market Strife: American Economic Thought from Rerum Novarum *to Vatican II*, by Kevin E. Schmiesing

Natural Law: The Foundation of an Orderly Economic System, by Alberto M. Piedra

The Church and the Market: A Catholic Defense of the Free Economy, by Thomas E. Woods Jr.

The Constitution under Social Justice, by Antonio Rosmini, translated by Alberto Mingardi

Sourcebook in Late-Scholastic Monetary Theory

The Contributions of Martín de Azpilcueta, Luis de Molina, S.J., and Juan de Mariana, S.J.

Stephen J. Grabill

LEXINGTON BOOKS

A division of
ROWMAN & LITTLEFIELD PUBLISHERS, INC.
Lanham • Boulder • New York • Toronto • Plymouth, UK

LEXINGTON BOOKS

A division of Rowman & Littlefield Publishers, Inc.
A wholly owned subsidary of The Rowman & Littlefield Publishing Group, Inc.
4501 Forbes Boulevard, Suite 200
Lanham, MD 20706

Estover Road
Plymouth PL6 7PY
United Kingdom

British Library Cataloguing in Publication Information Available

Library of Congress Cataloging-in-Publication Data

Sourcebook in late-scholastic monetary theory: the contributions of Martín de
Azpilcueta, Luis de Molina, S.J., and Juan de Mariana, S.J. / [edited by] Stephen J.
Grabill.
    p. cm. — (Studies in ethics and economics)
  Includes bibliographical references and index.
  ISBN-13: 978-0-7391-1749-1 (cloth : alk. paper)
  ISBN-10: 0-7391-1749-1 (cloth : alk. paper)
  ISBN-13: 978-0-7391-1750-7 (pbk. : alk. paper)
  ISBN-10: 0-7391-1750-5 (pbk. : alk. paper)
  1. Economics—Moral and ethical aspects. 2. Money—Moral and ethical aspects. 3.
Azpilcueta, Martín de, 1492?–1586. 4. Molina, Luis de, 1535–1600. 5. Mariana, Juan
de, 1535–1624. I. Azpilcueta, Martín de, 1492?–1586. II. Molina, Luis de, 1535–1600.
III. Mariana, Juan de, 1535–1624. IV. Grabill, Stephen John.
  HB72.S624 2007
  332.401—dc22   2007029039

Printed in the United States of America
⊖™ The paper used in this publication meets the minimum requirements of American
National Standard for Information Sciences—Permanence of Paper for Printed Library
Materials, ANSI/NISO Z39.48–1992.

To Marjorie Grice-Hutchinson (1909–2003)

in memoriam

*for her pioneering and enduring research
in late-scholastic Spanish economic thought*

CONTENTS

PART TWO
Treatise on Money (1597) by *Luis de Molina, S.J.*
Translation by *Jeannine Emery*

PART THREE
A Treatise on the Alteration of Money (1609) by *Juan de Mariana, S.J.*
Translation by *Patrick T. Brannan, S.J.*

ABBREVIATIONS

BNP   *Brill's New Pauly: Encyclopaedia of the Ancient World*, mang. ed., English edition, Christine F. Salazar, 9 vols. (Leiden: Brill, 2002–)

BU   *Biographie Universelle, ancienne et moderne; ou Histoire, par ordre alphabétique, de la vie publique et privée de tous les hommes qui se sont fait remarquer par leurs écrits, leurs actions, leurs talents, leurs vertus our leurs crimes*, ed. J. Fr. Michaud and L. G. Michaud, 85 vols. (Paris: Michaud freres [etc.], 1811–1862)

CE   *The Catholic Encyclopedia: An International Work of Reference on the Constitution, Doctrine, Discipline, and History of the Catholic Church*, ed. Charles G. Herbermann et al., 17 vols. (New York: The Encyclopedia Press, 1840–1916)

DMA   *Dictionary of the Middle Ages*, ed. Joseph R. Strayer, 13 vols. (New York: Scribner, 1982–1986)

DNP   *Der neue Pauly: Enzyklopadie der Antike*, ed. Hubert Cancik and Helmut Schneider, 16 vols. (Stuttgart: J. B. Metzler, 1996–)

EB   *The Encyclopaedia Brittannica: A Dictionary of Arts, Sciences, Literature, and General Information*, ed. Hugh Chisholm, 11th edition, 32 vols. (New York: The Encyclopaedia Brittannica Company, 1910–1911)

ERE   *Encyclopedia of Religion and Ethics*, ed. James Hastings, 13 vols. (New York: Charles Scribner's Sons; Edinburgh, T. & T. Clark, 1911–1922)

EtR   *Encyclopedia of the Renaissance*, ed. Paul F. Grendler, 6 vols.
         (New York: Scribner's published in association with the
         Renaissance Society of America, 1999)

Nbg   *Nouvelle biographie générale depuis les temps les plus reculés
         jusqu'a nos jours, avec les renseignements bibliographiques et
         l'indication des sources a consulter; publiee par mm. Firmin
         Didot freres, sous la direction de m. le dr. Hoefer*, ed. M. Jean
         Chrétien Ferdinand Hoefer, 46 vols. (Copenhagen: Rosenkilde et
         Bagger, 1963, repr. of the 1857 ed.)

NCE   *New Catholic Encyclopedia*, prepared by an editorial staff at the
         Catholic University of America, 18 vols. (New York: McGraw-Hill,
         1967–1988)

NCIRE   *The New Century Italian Renaissance Encyclopedia*, ed.
         Catherine B. Avery (New York: Appleton-Century-Crofts, 1972)

OCD   *The Oxford Classical Dictionary*, ed. Simon Hornblower and
         Antony Spawforth, 3d edition (New York: Oxford University
         Press, 1996)

EDITOR'S INTRODUCTION

Precursors to Modern Economics: Retrieving the Scholastic Contribution to Economics Before Adam Smith

The Contested Place of Scholastic Economics in Economic Historiography

For the same underlying reasons that moral theology is held in disrepute by many Western intellectuals, modern economists tend to glibly dismiss or just simply ignore the economic ideas of the scholastics. For many intellectuals nowadays moral theology has come to signify a passé form of religious thinking that embraces irrationality and dogmatism, and economic historians—along with notable astrophysicists, geneticists, paleontologists, political analysts, philosophers, and ethicists—have all espoused this line of thought. Among the latter, in particular, the identification of scholastic economics (or, the "canonical concept of market behavior," as it is sometimes called) with Aristotelian metaphysics and ecclesiastical authority has made modern economic professionals reticent or, at the very least, unreceptive to acknowledging any sophisticated analytical contribution to monetary and value theory by the Schoolmen or the Doctors—their sixteenth and seventeenth-century heirs.

Among post-war historians Raymond de Roover,[1] Marjorie Grice-Hutchinson,[2] and Joseph Schumpeter[3] were the first to shed new light on the analytical significance of the scholastic contribution to price, money, and value—which, to some extent, built on the insights of previous commentators[4]—but they labored alone and their research was often assailed by positivist critics within the neoclassical mainstream. Undeterred, however, they persevered and their work has come to inspire a new generation of revisionist economists,[5] economic historians,[6] political economists,[7] philosophers,[8] and moral theologians,[9] who now write economic history from a broader, history of ideas perspective in contrast to the conventional positivist historiography of the neoclassical mainstream.

Mark Blaug, a prolific British economist, is typical of most mainstream historians with regard to his method and philosophical assumptions. For example, despite acknowledging that the scholastic tradition has been frequently misinterpreted concerning its utility-cum-scarcity understanding of value and the role of common estimation in determining a just price, Blaug repeats the standard criticism of the tradition on usury, namely, that "money capital is sterile."[10] For, as modern commentators commonly suppose, the scholastic understanding of *cambium* which closely parallels Aristotle's treatment in the *Politics*[11] and *Nicomachean Ethics*,[12] led ecclesiastical officials to prohibit interest from being taken on any loan—commercial or otherwise—since all interest was regarded as "a breed of barren metal."[13] But, as the medievalist Odd Langholm assesses the ecclesiastical debate over usury, a somewhat different evaluation emerges:

> It is not that usury is wrong because money *cannot* breed; it is rather that money *should not* be made to breed, because this is an unnatural use of money, such as in money-changing, usury, and debasement. . . . The only natural use of money is to serve as a medium of exchange. This is money's true end. But the end for which a thing is invented is subordinated to man's end, reinterpreted by the scholastics in Christian terms. Making money breed is wrong because it is inspired by cupidity, said Albert the Great.[14]

Cupidity, however, is neither a necessary nor a sufficient motivation of currency exchange; other less malicious, more pragmatic motivations are certainly possible, if not likely, as the Schoolmen and the Doctors themselves acknowledged.

Some Schoolmen (such as Henry of Ghent [ca. 1217–1293] and Guido Terrena [?–1342]), in fact, came to acknowledge the usefulness of money-changers, just as Albert the Great (ca. 1206–1280) and Thomas Aquinas (1225–1274) had acknowledged the need for professional merchants. In his *Genovese Sermon* (1243), Albertanus of Brescia (ca. 1190–?), a little known medieval jurist and representative of the emerging *podesta* (magistracy) literature,[15] taught that wealth creation and the intelligent use of one's acquisitions were virtuous activities. "Now we must consider the third exercise of virtue, as Cicero says. The third is the moderate and intelligent use of our acquistions. Here we should note that we ought always to win over to ourselves those who come for our advice and assistance and profit from them and make use of their friendship and riches with moderation and intelligence in keeping with the peculiar nature of virtue. For, as the same Cicero said, 'It is characteristic of virtue both to reconcile the spirits of men and to unite them for their usefulness, that is, their benefit.' We ought to derive, then, benefit, wealth, and advantages from them."[16]

The intelligent use of profit, derived from money (i.e., capital) risked in an entrepreneurial venture, is a formal aspect of the thought of the fifteenth-century casuists Saint Bernardine of Siena (1380–1444), a Franciscan, and Saint Antonine of Florence (1389–1459), a Dominican.[17] According to Bernardine, when a businessman lends from balances held for commercial purposes, he "gives not money in its simple character, but he also gives his capital."[18] Elsewhere, he writes: ". . . what, in the firm purpose of its owner, is ordained to some probable profit, has not only the character of mere money or a mere thing, but also beyond this, a certain seminal character of something profitable, which we commonly call capital. Therefore, not only must its simple value be returned, but a super-added value as well."[19] In describing how any loan may result in profit foregone (*lucrum cessans*) for the lender, or, in modern terms, the opportunity cost of liquid funds, Antonine likewise points to the productive potential of money: "I believe that anyone can claim compensation, not merely for the harm done him, but also the gain he might otherwise have obtained, if he be a merchant accustomed to engage his money in business. The same holds good even if he be not a merchant but have only the intention of investing the funds in lawful trade; but not if he be a man who hoards his wealth in his coffers."[20] Herbert Johnson has suggested that this premodern understanding of capital is an application of the Augustinian doctrine of *rationes seminales* to money.[21]

Yet, despite these important counterexamples to the scholastic-money-capital-is-sterile thesis, Blaug still doubts whether scholastic writing has anything substantive to offer modern economists on the topics of money and interest—largely, it would seem, because of the dogmatic and metaphysical base to its treatment of usury. "Ingenious apologists have found other nuggets in the literature," he quips, "but on the whole it is analytically sterile."[22] Ekelund and Hebert, along with numerous other mainstream historians, would concur with Blaug's assessment: "An absolutist position on economics would not accord medieval thought a high ranking. The scholastics' discussion of utility and value was fragmentary and mainly adventitious. Their views on price control and their general condemnation of monopoly and price discrimination, outside of the link with theology, were not original. Greek and Roman sources were often much clearer on the nature and effect of controlled prices. Most critically, their ideas on value were normatively oriented."[23]

Usury has been a favorite target of positivist, rationalist, and anti-Catholic polemicists. Three nineteenth-century critics, in particular, William Lecky,[24] Andrew Dickson White,[25] and Henry Charles Lea,[26] condemned the ecclesiastical prohibition against usury as a sulphurous residue of theological superstition and clerical oppression.[27] Under the labyrinthine edifice of scholastic casuistry, boomed Lea, competition withered, the flow of credit congealed, and interest rates soared.[28] In a similar vein, the economist C. E. Ayres complained that "a great deal of casuistry has gone into the formulation of the doctrine of capital, and we owe much of this to the master hand of the medieval church."[29] Chicago School economist Frank H. Knight assigned modern economics the accolade of being "the leading phase in the development of Liberty and Liberalism," which finally liberated economics "from its long confinement under priestly dictatorship."[30] And, finally, even such an eminent historian as Raymond de Roover, a pioneer himself in the revival of scholastic economic research, spoke of usury as the Achilles' heel of scholastic economics, which eventually led to its decline and fall:

> The great weakness of scholastic economics was the usury doctrine. Canon law, dating as it does back to the early Middle Ages when most loans were made for consumption purposes, defined usury as any increment demanded beyond the principal of a loan. Since this definition was part of Catholic dogma, the Schoolmen were unable to change it. As time went by, it became a source of increasing embarrassment. Tied to their definition, the Doctors were sucked deeper into a quagmire of contradictions.[31]

Usury is perhaps the most ridiculed, but least understood, idea in the history of economics.

The fundamental deficiency in almost every modern evaluation of usury is an insufficient understanding of and appreciation for the integrated nature of scholastic economics with metaphysics, dogmatics, and the traditions of both canon and civil law jurisprudence. Modern commentators tend to isolate and abstract narrower, more specialized topics such as usury from their context within larger, intellectual systems, which they then proceed to evaluate on the basis of anachronistically construed canons of rationality. Once a topic like usury is severed from its metaphysical schema and broader intellectual tradition, the verdict of its incoherence and obsolescence is already sealed in the court of modern opinion.

An adequate evaluation of any topic within scholastic economics must also acknowledge that this tradition, like the traditions of natural law and natural right, has been deeply affected by the "seismic" intellectual shift of the fourteenth and fifteenth centuries (essentialist/nominalist debates). "That shift involved changes in the understanding of both the nature of nature and of the essence of law," relates the learned medievalist Francis Oakley, "and it was concerned with the very metaphysical grounding of natural law. It ensured that not one but two principal traditions of natural law thinking would be transmitted to the thinkers of early modern Europe. And it is necessary to take into account the continuing dialectical interchange between those traditions if one is to make adequate sense of what was going on intellectually in the array of natural law theories framed during the sixteenth, seventeenth, and even eighteenth centuries."[32] If the import of Oakley's image of a "profound geologic fault"[33] running across and beneath the conflicted landscape of the Western intellectual tradition is fully grasped, it will be impossible to treat scholastic economics historically and philosophically as an undifferentiated and homogeneous tradition with respect to its metaphysics (essentialism/nominalism), anthropology (intellectualism/voluntarism), dogmatics (Protestant/Roman Catholic-Franciscan-Dominican-Jesuit), or epistemology (discursive/self-evidence). The clear implication is that modern commentators should be much more circumspect in the blanket evaluations they make of it because historical and philosophical outliers will always foil their caricatures and generalizations.

The Debate Over the Prehistory of Economics

The positivist severing of economic ideas from their original historical and metaphysical contexts becomes especially pronounced in the contemporary debate over the prehistory of economics. Invariably, most mainstream economic historians identify the birth of modern economics to be in Adam Smith, the mercantilists, and the physiocrats. For Blaug, the prehistory of economics begins with the seventeenth-century mercantilists and not, as the revisionists insist, with either the ancient Greeks or the thirteenth-century scholastics. He coins the term *pre-Adamite economics* to methodologically define and restrict the era of prehistory to Smith's immediate and direct historical precursors: the seventeenth-century mercantilists, the physiocrats, and the British free-trade writers of the eighteenth century.

The broader question of whether the prehistory of economics should start in the thirteenth century or much earlier is, in Blaug's estimation, "an afterthought."[34] An afterthought, we might infer, which could presumably surface information that would challenge positivist assumptions about human behavior and social cohesion, and one that will yield few, if any, new insights into quantitative methods and models. Where the scholastics analyzed economic and commercial transactions as either ethical or legal matters involving the application of natural law to civil contracts, "It was the mercantilists," contends Blaug, "who, long before Adam Smith, broke with the canonical conception of market behavior as a moral problem and fashioned the concept of 'economic man'. . . . They believed in the direct power of self-interest and in matters of domestic economic policy came near to advocating laissez-faire. Adam Smith was not the first to have confidence in the workings of the 'invisible hand.' Nor is it necessary to appeal to scholastic influences to account for his grasp of the determination of prices by demand and supply."[35]

Regardless of whether it is necessary to appeal to scholastic influences to explain how Smith, in particular, understood price and value to be determined, does not speak to the wider issue of whether such seminal figures in the history of economics as Bernardo Davanzati (1529–1606), Ferdinando Galiani (1728–1787), Hugo Grotius (1583–1645), Samuel von Pufendorf (1632–1694), Gershom Carmichael (1672–1729), Francis Hutcheson (1694–1746), Adam Ferguson (1723–1816), Jean-Jacques Burlamaqui (1694–1748), Auguste Walras (1801–1866), and Léon Walras (1834–1910) were influenced by scholastic treatments of price and value. Or even, for that matter, whether Smith's entire system of thought remains intelligible, if the role he assigns to teleology, final causes, divine design, and virtue is disregarded as merely ornamental.[36] In this wider respect, therefore, the modern quibble over scholastic influences in Smith is a red herring because, as Langholm attests,[37] it sidesteps serious historical investigation into the continuities and discontinuities between scholastic and modern economic ideas. And furthermore, it also has the convenient side effect of downplaying the importance of teleology and natural theology in the thought of Smith himself and other seventeenth-, eighteenth-, and nineteenth-century political economists.

In fairness to Blaug, he readily acknowledges that "scholastic doctrines were transmitted to Adam Smith by way of the seventeenth-century natural-law philosophers, Hugo Grotius and Samuel von Pufendorf. Moreover, the writings of the physiocrats with which Smith was acquainted are replete with scholastic influences: Quesnay often sounds like an eighteenth-century version of Thomas Aquinas."[38] His principal concern, however, is not to dispute the point that "the Schoolmen may have contributed ideas that passed through Grotius, Locke, and Pufendorf to Francis Hutcheson and Adam Smith," but rather to call into question "Schumpeter's reduction of mercantilism to a mere by-current in the forward march of economic analysis."[39]

So, with this in mind, let us assume that Blaug is correct about "Schumpeter's reduction," the question then becomes: What is lost or gained as far as the analytical contribution of scholastic economics is concerned? The answer, I think, is nothing. If Schumpeter did throw the proverbial baby out with the bathwater to make his point about scholastic influence, is it not also an overreaction to use his indiscretion like a club to overshadow the legitimate criticism he raises of positivist historiography? Even if Schumpeter's glib assessment of mercantilism were to be struck from the record out of simple respect for Blaug's extensive research in mercantilist literature, the methodological question still remains of where to begin the prehistory of economics. On what reasonable grounds should scholastic influence on modern economics be considered discontinuous, if evidence can be presented that demonstrates lines of continuity extending from Aristotle and Aquinas that run through the Salamancans and the seventeenth-century natural-law philosophers to Smith, Galiani, Walras, and beyond?

In light of the evidence revisionist historians have indeed surfaced, one is therefore justified in doubting whether recent work on mercantilism and the Scottish Enlightenment requires a reduction of the prehistory of economics to Smith's modern precursors. This position is the methodological converse of Blaug's historical starting point.[40] Moreover, as de Roover argues, "To consider scholastic economics as medieval doctrine is simply an error, and economists have bypassed a current of thought which runs parallel with mercantilism and reached out into the eighteenth century, connecting the *économistes* and even Adam Smith with Thomas Aquinas and the medieval Schoolmen. Traces of scholastic influence still permeate eighteenth century economic thinking and sometimes appear in unexpected places, such as the *Encyclopédie* of Diderot and d'Alembert."[41]

Scholastic Economics: The Boogey Man of Economic History

"Scholastic," according to almost any contemporary definition, means "arcane, abstruse, and dogmatic," and harkens back to an era when theological scholarship was allegedly tedious, opaque, and sterile. Scholars who subscribe to this viewpoint generally find confirmation of their suspicions in the debates over usury and the barrenness of money. Mark Blaug, as we have seen, is no exception here and neither was John Locke, the eighteenth-century British nominalist.[42] Locke dismissed the scholastics as "the great mintmasters" of useless and empty terms.[43] He lamented that "sects of philosophy and religion" routinely coin new terms to support strange opinions and cover weak hypotheses. The sophistry of the Schoolmen and Metaphysicians, he wrote, "remain empty sounds, with little or no signification, among those who think it enough to have them often in their mouths, as the distinguishing characters of their Church or School, without much troubling their heads to examine what are the precise ideas they stand for."[44]

Despite its apparent "emptiness" and "uselessness" as an intellectual movement, scholasticism (with its roots in Christian Aristotelian philosophy) extended from approximately 800 to 1700, with the twelfth and thirteenth centuries representing the high water mark in the development of scholastic method. Some of the most prominent names in medieval scholasticism are active in this span of time: Hugh of Saint Victor (1096–1141), Bernard of Clairvaux (1090–1153), Peter Lombard (ca. 1100–1160), Thomas Aquinas, Anselm of Canterbury (1033–1109), Roger Grosseteste (1168–1253), Roger Bacon (1214–1294), Bonaventure (1221–1274), Peter Abelard (1079–1142), John Duns Scotus (1265–1308), and William of Occam (ca. 1287–1347). From approximately 1150 to 1650 a modified Christian Aristotelianism dominated European educational curricula,[45] and was a vital current among Protestant and Roman Catholic theologians[46] until it was unseated by the new philosophies of Cartesianism, atomism, and rationalism that gained traction around the dawn of the eighteenth century.

Moderns attach diverse meanings to the term *scholasticism*. First used in a derogatory sense by humanists (e.g., Diderot said it "was one of the greatest plagues of the human mind") and historians of philosophy in the sixteenth century (e.g., C. A. Hermann described it as "philosophy brought into slavery to papist theology"), the term has come to be associated with a petrified and antiquated system of thought. Most commentators today mistakenly think that scholasticism refers to a body of doctrines, a philosophical system, or some theological result. This misinterpretation is as much of a problem in mainstream historical theology[47] as it is in the historiography of the social and natural sciences.[48] Originally, however, the term simply referred to teachers and authors who employed the scholastic method. According to J. A. Weisheipl,

> The scholastic method was essentially a rational investigation of every relevant problem in liberal arts, philosophy, theology, medicine, and law, examined from opposing points of view, in order to reach an intelligent, scientific solution that

would be consistent with accepted authorities, known facts, human reason, and Christian faith. Its ultimate goal was science (*scientia*), although frequently school-men had to be content with probable opinions and dialectical solutions. Its highest form, developed in the thirteenth century, was a positive contribution to education and research. In the sixteenth century the medieval method assumed the form of theses, proofs, and answers to objections to meet catechetical and apologetic exigencies.[4]

The ultimate goal of the Schoolmen and the Doctors was to use scholastic method in conjunction with the philosophy of Christian Aristotelianism to formulate a unified body of knowledge applicable to all areas of life.

Scholastic Economics Is a Normative (and a Descriptive) Science

One reason why mainstream historians tend to regard scholastic economics as "an afterthought" is to circumvent philosophical and historical counterexamples to the Enlightenment redefinition of economics along secular, descriptive, and rationalistic lines. It goes without saying that the Schoolmen and the Doctors, like the philosophers of antiquity, thought political economy had an inescapable anthro-pological (normative) dimension that was integrated seamlessly into discussions of private property, public finance, money and exchange relations, commercial ethics, value and price, distributive justice, wages, profits, and interest and bank-ing. Moreover, as Francisco Gómez Camacho shows in the case of the Spanish scholastics, in addition to the anthropological (normative) dimension of their thought there was also an intrinsic analytical (descriptive) dimension.[50]

The Spanish scholastics clearly distinguished between the normative first principles of morality, which are abstract and immutable, and the socioeconomic cases to which they were applied, which are contingent and mutable. "Abstract principles do not descend to the analysis of specific socioeconomic circumstances, and cannot be applied immediately and directly to the *case* defined by circum-stances. Mediation between general principles and singular cases became the task that Spanish doctors would commend to *recta ratio* [or natural law]."[51] This meant that it was essential for the Doctors to analyze and study the circumstances that define a specific case, and thus to the normative dimension of natural law was added an equally necessary analytical dimension. Likewise, as Schumpeter had discerned from his research, in late-scholastic thought "the normative natural law presupposes an explanatory natural law."[52]

This *recta ratio* approach still held currency in the eighteenth century when Adam Smith assumed the chair of moral philosophy from his predecessor Francis Hutcheson at the University of Glasgow. In fact, as economic historian James Alvey points out, "Even when [scholasticism] was replaced by more modern, natural law views (of Grotius and Pufendorf), the place of economics changed little. In the European universities of the 1700s economics was taught as part of moral philosophy."[53] This is an important recognition because it is possible to show the direct historical linkage of the late-scholastic theologians in Spain (e.g., Martín de Azpilcueta [1493–1586], Luis de Molina, S.J. [1535–1600], and Juan de Mariana, S.J. [1535–1624]) through Leonardo Lessio, S.J. (1554–1623) to Hugo Grotius and Samuel von Pufendorf and through them to Francis Hutcheson and Adam Smith. "In the case of Adam Smith," writes de Roover, "the ascendance which links him to scholasticism passes through his teacher, Francis Hutcheson, Samuel Pufendorf, and Hugo Grotius. Smith's library contained copies of both Grotius and Pufendorf. Moreover, there is evidence that Adam Smith read Grotius at the age of fifteen when he was a student at Glasgow College. At that time, his teacher was using as a textbook a translation of Pufendorf's *De officio hominis et civis* by Gershom Carmichael (d. 1729), Hutcheson's predecessor in the chair of Moral Philosophy."[54]

In his economic analysis of the values and prices of goods and services, Pufendorf followed Grotius (*De jure belli ac pacis libri tres*, II.12) very closely in fundamental outline, but added a great deal of detail in his *De jure naturae et gentium* (V.1–7). "More particularly," as Terence Hutchinson insists, "[Pufendorf's] chapter on value and price has a key position in the history of economic thought, not so much for its originality, but because it acted as authoritative transmitter of a long tradition of analysis of fundamental economic concepts concerned with value and price, the central element in which, the idea of scarcity, included the elements of the supply and demand framework, as well as a subjective concept of utility."[55] And it was through Gershom Carmichael and Francis Hutcheson in Glasgow that Pufendorf's version of the basic, natural-law doctrine of the values and prices of goods and services passed on to Adam Smith.[56]

Whereas, in Geneva, through Jean-Jacques Burlamaqui (a near contemporary of Hutcheson) Pufendorf's ideas passed to Auguste Walras, and so to his son Léon, who became the father of the general equilibrium theory and one of the leaders (along with William Stanley Jevons and Carl Menger) of the nineteenth-century marginal utility revolution. "Incidentally," observes Hutchinson, "Auguste Walras was amply justified in complaining how neglected the natural-law concept of scarcity had become in the nineteenth century. In any case, however, a writer [namely, Pufendorf] among whose intellectual grandchildren may be counted both Adam Smith and Léon Walras surely possesses a notable place in the history of the subject."[57]

Economic History Is Inseparable from the History of Ideas

By methodologically constricting the prehistory of economics to the mercantilists and the physiocrats, as positivist historiographers commend, economic history congeals around such characteristically "modern" concerns as the concept of "economic man," self-interest, and the emancipation of economics from the so-called "canonical conception of market behavior." This arbitrary limitation of who and what ideas carry weight in economic history only serves to bolster twentieth-century positivist assumptions, particularly those of value neutrality and *homo economicus*. *Homo economicus* is the assumption that humans act as rational and self-interested agents who desire wealth, avoid unnecessary labor, and seek to order their decision making exclusively around those goals. In the end, the modern reduction of the prehistory of economics to the seventeenth-century mercantilists can be put in the form of an Occam's razor-like question: Why appeal to scholastic influences to illumine modern notions of money, value, and price, when all the basic elements of classical economics are already embedded in mercantilism?

The most straightforward reply is that seminal ideas, which also encompass revolutionary economic ideas, never develop in intellectual, historical, religious, philosophical, or geographical vacuums. "Enlightened," secular reaction to the medieval Church's temporal jurisdiction and to theology's intellectual hegemony as the queen of the sciences has created a modern milieu where scholars are no longer even aware of the historical influence that fundamental Christian doctrines have exerted in Western culture and university life. From very early times, Christian theologians assumed that the application of patterns of discursive reasoning (as in scholastic method, which, as we have seen, was a twelfth-century invention by Christian theologians) could yield an increasingly accurate understanding not only of God's word and moral will but also of the created order itself.

This all makes sense within the Christian Aristotelian framework because, as Rodney Stark points out in *The Victory of Reason*, "The Christian image of God is that of a rational being who *believes in human progress*, more fully revealing himself as humans *gain* the capacity to better understand. Moreover, because God is a rational being and the universe is his personal creation, it necessarily has a rational, lawful, stable structure, *awaiting increased human comprehension*."[58] The dogmatic and essentialist underpinning to Christian Aristotelianism is succinctly expressed already in the writing of Quintus Tertullian (ca. 155–230), an early church father, who discerned the fundamental connection between the *imago Dei*, human reason, and the material world:

> For God is rational and Reason existed first with him, and from him extended to all things. That Reason is his own consciousness of himself. The Greeks call it *Logos*, which is the term we use for discourse; and thus our people usually translate it literally as, "Discourse was in the beginning with God," although it would be more correct to regard Reason as anterior to Discourse, because there was not Discourse with God from the beginning but there was Reason, even before the beginning, and because Discourse takes its origin from Reason and thus shows Reason to be prior to it, as the ground of its being. Yet even so there is no real difference. For although God had not yet uttered his Discourse, he had it in his own being, with and in his Reason, and he silently pondered and arranged in his thought those things which he was soon to say by his Discourse. For with his Reason he pondered and arranged his thought and thus made Reason into Discourse by dealing with it discursively. To understand this more easily, first observe in yourself (and you are "the image and likeness of God") that you also have reason in yourself, as a

rational creature; that is, a creature not merely made by a rational creature, but given life from his very being. Notice that when you silently engage in argument with yourselves in the exercise of reason, this same activity occurs within you; for reason is found expressed in discourse at every moment of thought, at every stirring of consciousness.[59]

According to the hallowed divine ideas tradition—of which Quintus Tertullian, Augustine (354–430), Aquinas, and a majority of the scholastics and natural-law philosophers were a part—there is an elementary correspondence between the archetypal knowledge God has in his own mind and the ectypal knowledge that is reproduced in human beings stamped in his image and that is, furthermore, insinuated into the very structure of the material world.

Christian divine ideas proponents held that God used the created order as the primary instrument through which to reveal this information to the human mind. In this sense, the world can be said to embody the very thoughts of God; but, as the Dutch Reformed theologian Herman Bavinck admonishes, that is only half of the equation. "We need eyes in order to see. 'If our eyes were not filled with sunshine, how could we see the light?' There just has to be correspondence or kinship between object and subject. The Logos who shines in the world must also let his light shine in our consciousness. That is the light of reason, the intellect, which, itself originating in the Logos, discovers and recognizes the Logos in things. . . . Just as knowledge within us is the imprint of things upon our souls, so, in turn, forms do not exist except by a kind of imprint of the divine knowledge in things."[60]

The systematic application of reason to a variety of intellectual undertakings, including economic problems, led to increased understanding of the world and human affairs, and spurred efforts to formulate logical explanations of regular occurrences in nature. "All things whatsoever observe a mutual order; and this is the form that maketh the universe like unto God," wrote Dante in the *Divine Comedy*.[61] It can be argued that the specific application of scholastic method to economic problems became the seedbed for innovative ideas that, after much dialectical refinement, came to shape the world of modern economics. The truth of this statement does not rest on modernity's own understanding of its birth, development, or future trajectory, but rather on the demonstrable "internal interconnections and affinities among ideas, their dynamism or 'particular go' (Lovejoy's phrase), and the logical pressures they are capable of exerting on the minds of those that think them."[62]

Assent to this claim, however, will require the positivist historian to reconsider not only the relationship between metaphysical schemata and intellectual traditions, which, in turn, will require an acknowledgement of the indispensable role of theological doctrines in the history of ideas,[63] but it will also require an admission that the recent detachment of economics from morality is an aberration from a long-standing tradition within political economy itself.[64] In Alvey's judgment, "There are two major reasons why economics has become detached from moral concerns. First, the natural sciences came to be seen as successful, and the attempt was made to emulate that success in economics by applying natural science methods, including mathematics, to economic phenomena. Second, the self-styled economic science came to adopt positivism, which ruled out moral issues from science itself."[65] It is the latter recognition, perhaps more than any other, that squares the revisionists off against the positivists in the debate over the prehistory of economics.

Discovery of the School of Salamanca:
The Tipping Point in the Revision of Economic History

In the sixteenth and early seventeenth centuries, a small but influential group of theologians and jurists centered in Spain attempted to synthesize the Roman legal texts with Aristotelian and Thomistic moral philosophy. The movement began with the revival of Thomistic philosophy in Paris, where, as Camacho recounts, "Pierre Crockaert underwent an intellectual conversion from nominalist philosophy to the philosophy of Thomas Aquinas."[66]

Shortly before 1225, the year of Aquinas's birth, Aristotle's works on metaphysics, physics, politics, and ethics became available in the West, and within the span of a generation Aristotelianism, which had been brought to Europe by Arabic scholars, would be a serious contender in medieval thought. Thomas sought a rapprochement between the Greek philosophical tradition that Aristotle represented and the Christian divine ideas tradition that Quintus Tertullian, Augustine, and Bonaventure articulated. In 1512 Crockaert published his commentary on the last part of Thomas's *Summa theologicae* with the help of a student Francisco de Vitoria (ca. 1483–1546).[67]

Approximately two hundred years before Thomas was born, the *Corpus juris civilis* of Justinian had been rediscovered and had become the object of academic disputation. But the traditions of Roman law and Aristotelian and Thomistic philosophy existed in relative isolation from one another, at least until the early sixteenth century in Spain. "In the sixteenth and early seventeenth centuries," states Camacho, "a synthesis was finally achieved by that group of theologians and jurists known to historians of law as the 'late scholastics' or the 'Spanish natural law school.'"[68] Schumpeter concurs with this judgment and adds: "It is within their systems of moral theology and law that economics gained definite if not separate existence, and it is they who come nearer than does any other group to having been the 'founders' of scientific economics."[69]

As a school of economic thought, these late Spanish scholastics are commonly referred to as the "School of Salamanca." This term has a distinguished history and attempts to designate that group of moral philosophers, moral theologians, and jurists who either attended or lectured at the University of Salamanca and had been students of or colleagues with Francisco de Vitoria.[70] But not all historians accept the validity of the Salamancan designation and it is regarded as a "point of dispute" in the literature.[71] Even Schumpeter himself expressed some doubt about the claim that a school of thought centering on a single intellectual leader had been found in Spain, but admitted there was "some justification" for it in his *History of Economic Analysis*.[72] More than any other commentator, however, it was Marjorie Grice-Hutchinson who after decades of painstaking research convinced fair-minded observers that "a definite group of theologians associated with the University of Salamanca wrote about issues of value theory and money with insight and originality. In addition, she applied her skills as a translator and linguist to present the world with the evidence required."[73] Her translations of short excerpts from the Latin and Spanish texts of this group appeared in 1952 as part of her first monograph, *The School of Salamanca: Readings in Spanish Monetary Theory, 1544–1605.*[74]

For over half a century, Grice-Hutchinson ably defended her thesis that, in the area of value and monetary economics, a genuine and incipient school of thought existed at Salamanca. This tradition began with Vitoria who brought Thomas's teachings to Salamanca from Paris, which he used to purge the curriculum of nominalist influence and to develop a great legal and philosophical system that addressed matters of international law, moral theology, politics, economics, and business practices. His insights about money, markets, and prices, reasoned Grice-Hutchinson, "spawned a network of 'colleagues ... disciples and ... principal continuators' such as Luís Saravia de la Calle, Domingo de Soto, Martín de Azpilcueta, Tomás de Mercado, Francisco García, Martín Gonzalez de Cellorigo, Luis de Molina, and Pedro de Valencia, who carried out Vitoria's 'research programme,' with dedication and accomplishment."[75] Over time Grice-Hutchinson has been successful in persuading unbiased observers within the economics profession, intellectual history, and moral theology that "something critically important to understanding the development of economic reasoning did happen in Salamanca in the sixteenth century."[76]

This *Sourcebook in Late-Scholastic Monetary Theory* is the latest installment in the Grice-Hutchinson-inspired excavation of the mines of late-scholastic Spanish thought on economics. The aim of this book is to offer economists, intellectual historians, moral theologians, and graduate students in the fields of economics, economic ethics, economic history, banking history, political economy, and moral theology, a useful collection of some of the most important late-scholastic Spanish texts on *cambium* (money and exchange relations). Now, for the first time, the unabridged texts of Martín de Azpilcueta's *Commentary on the Resolution of Money* (1556), Luis de Molina's *Treatise on Money* (1597), and Juan de Mariana's *Treatise on the Alteration of Money* (1609) will be available in English translation and with scholarly annotations. The publication of these primary texts under a single cover, it is hoped, will help to facilitate exploration of the continuities and discontinuities, agreements and disagreements, innovations and ruptures within the Salamancan tradition of commercial ethics during the latter half of the sixteenth century and the early seventeenth century. A close reading of these documents will likewise reveal that the Salamancans were involved not only in an internal conversation within Spain concerning inflation, usury, rates of currency exchange, currency debasement, subjective value, just prices, and so on, but they were also critical interlocutors in a wider conversation spanning centuries that included prominent canonists, jurists, philosophers, and theologians.

The translations (in conjunction with the introductions by leading authorities) will show the sophistication with which the Spanish doctors examined the new process of using bills of exchange (*cambium per litteras*) to replace the cumbersome and dangerous transportation of metallic coins between commercial fairs, which led not only to new scholastic insights on interest, credit, and international trade, but also to a much more comprehensive analysis of monetary exchange and banking practices than had been undertaken before. The texts will also address the question of why the same currency was worth more in one region than another area's currency and, moreover, why the rate of exchange fluctuated between one area and the next. The Salamancans, writes Moss, "were as interested in a general theory of how exchange rates between different currencies are formed as in explaining why a bill of exchange is worth more in one region of Spain than in another region. Was the *agio* or exchange premium evidence of usury and therefore immoral behavior on the part of merchants and traders, or rather something 'natural' governed by the basic laws of supply and demand?"[77] These moral and economic concerns, along with many others, will be addressed in fine scholastic detail throughout the course of the documents.

A Parting Word on Source Documents

Wherever possible the source documents used for translation have been the modern Spanish critical editions,[78] except in the case of Mariana's *Treatise on the Alteration of Money*. In this instance, Father Brannan translated from the Latin text of *De monetae mutatione* (1609), which John Laures, S.J. faithfully reproduced and published in an appendix to *The Political Economy of Juan de Mariana* (New York: Fordham University Press, 1928), 241–303. Father Laures based his reproduction on the first and only available edition of *De monetae mutatione* found in *Tractatus VII*, Coloniae Agrippinae, sumptibus Antonii Hierati, 1609, 189–221. Since the initial appearance of the translations as scholia installments in the *Journal of Markets & Morality*, several significant emendations have been made to them, not the least of which is the addition of annotations. In the case of Mariana's text, in particular, I have made extensive refinements to Father Brannan's translation, specifically in paragraph breaks and the spelling of names, places, and book titles, which I conformed to Josef Falzberger's recent (1996) critical edition of *De monetae* in Latin and German.[79]

In *Economic Thought before Adam Smith*, Murray Rothbard recounts the fascinating saga surrounding Mariana's *De monetae mutatione*,[80] which I have reproduced here. Mariana's tract, which attacked King Philip II's debasement of the currency, led the monarch to haul the aged (73-year-old) scholar-priest into prison, charging him with the high crime of treason against the king. Mariana was convicted of the crime, but the pope refused to punish him. He was released from prison after four months on the condition that he would remove the offensive passages in the work, and would promise to be more careful in the future.

King Philip, however, was not satisfied with the pope's punishment. So the king ordered his officials to buy up every copy they could find and to destroy them. After Mariana's death, the Spanish Inquisition expurgated the remaining copies, deleted many sentences and smeared entire pages with ink. All non-expurgated copies were put on the Spanish *Index*, and these in turn were expurgated during the seventeenth century. As a result of Philip's censorship, the existence of the Latin text remained unknown for 250 years, and was rediscovered only because the Spanish edition,[81] which Mariana himself had translated into Spanish, was incorporated into a nineteenth century collection of classical Spanish essays. Hence, few complete copies of the original survive, of which the only one in the United States can be found in the Boston Public Library.

—Stephen J. Grabill

Notes

1. Raymond A. de Roover, *Money, Banking and Credit in Mediaeval Bruges; Italian Merchant Bankers, Lombards and Money-Changers: A Study in the Origins of Banking* (Cambridge, Mass.: Mediaeval Academy of America, 1948); de Roover, *Gresham on Foreign Exchange: An Essay on Early English Mercantilism with the Text of Sir Thomas Gresham's Memorandum: For the Understanding of the Exchange* (Cambridge, Mass.: Harvard University Press, 1949); de Roover, *The Rise and Decline of the Medici Bank, 1397–1494* (Cambridge, Mass.: Harvard University Press, 1963); de Roover, *San Bernardino of Siena and Sant' Antonino of Florence: The Two Great Economic Thinkers of the Middle Ages* (Boston: Baker Library/Harvard Graduate School of Business Administration, 1967); de Roover, *Leonardus Lessius als economist: De economische leerstellingen van de latere scholastiek in de Zuidelijke Nederlanden* (Brussels: Paleis de Academiën, 1969); de Roover, *La pensée économique des scholastiques: doctrines et méthodes* (Montréal: Institute for Medieval Studies, 1971); and de Roover, *Business, Banking, and Economic Thought in Late Medieval and Early Modern Europe: Selected Studies of Raymond de Roover*, ed. Julius Kirshner (Chicago and London: University of Chicago Press, 1974).

2. Marjorie Grice-Hutchinson, *The School of Salamanca: Readings in Spanish Monetary Theory, 1544–1605* (Oxford: Clarendon Press, 1952); Grice-Hutchinson, *Early Economic Thought in Spain, 1177–1740* (London: G. Allen & Unwin, 1978); Grice-Hutchinson, *Aproximación al pensamiento económico en Andalucía: de Séneca a finales del siglo XVIII* (Málaga: Editorial Librería Agora, 1990); and Grice-Hutchinson, *Economic Thought in Spain: Selected Essays of Marjorie Grice-Hutchinson*, ed. Laurence S. Moss and Christopher K. Ryan (Brookfield, Vt.: Edward Elgar Publishing Company, 1993).

3. Joseph A. Schumpeter, *History of Economic Analysis*, ed. Elizabeth Boody Schumpeter (New York: Oxford University Press, 1954), 73–142.

4. Wilhelm Endemann, *Studien in der romanisch-kanonistischen Wirtschafts- und Rechtslehre: bis gegen Ende des siebenzehnten Jahrhunderts*, 2 vols. (Berlin: J. Guttentag, 1874–1883); John Laures, S.J., *The Political Economy of Juan de Mariana* (New York: Fordham University Press, 1928); Bernard W. Dempsey, S.J., "The Historical Emergence of Quantity Theory," *The Quarterly Journal of Economics* 50, no. 1 (November 1935): 174–84; Dempsey, *Interest and Usury* (Washington, D.C.: American Council on Public Affairs, 1943); and José Larraz, *La época del mercantilismo en Castilla, 1500–1700* (Madrid: Aguilar, 1943).

5. James E. Alvey, "A Short History of Economics as a Moral Science," *Journal of Markets & Morality* 2, no. 1 (Spring 1999): 53–73; Alvey, "The Secret, Natural Theological Foundation of Adam Smith's Work," *Journal of Markets & Morality* 7, no. 2 (Fall 2004): 335–61; Robert A. Black, "What Did Adam Smith Say About Self-Love?" *Journal of Markets & Morality* 9, no. 1 (Spring 2006): 7–34; and Andrew Yuengert, *The Boundaries of Technique: Ordering Positive and Normative Concerns in Economic Research* (Lanham and New York: Lexington Books, 2004).

6. José Luís Abellán, *Historia Crítica Del Pensamiento Español*, 5 vols. (Madrid: Espasa-Calpe, 1979), Tomo II and III; Roger E. Backhouse, *The Ordinary Business of Life: A History of Economics from the Ancient World to the Twenty-First Century* (Princeton and Oxford: Princeton University Press, 2002), 11–65; Francisco Gómez Camacho, S.J., *Economía y filosofía moral: la formación del pensameinto económico europeo en la Escolástica Española* (Madrid: Síntesis, 1998); Camacho, "El triángulo Glasgow, París, Salamanca y los orígenes de la ciencia económica," *Miscelánea Comillas* 48 (1990): 231–55; Camacho, "Later Scholastics: Spanish Economic Thought in the XVIth and XVIIth Centuries," in *Ancient and Medieval Economic Ideas and Concepts of Social Justice*, ed. S. Todd Lowry and Barry Gordon (Leiden and New York: Brill, 1998), 503–61; Camacho, "Luis de Molina y la metodología de la ley natural," *Miscelánea Comillas* 43, no. 82 (January–June 1985): 155–94; Alejandro A. Chafuen, *Faith and Liberty: The Economic Thought of the Late Scholastics* (Lanham and New York: Lexington Books, 2003); Jesús Huerta de Soto, "New Light on the Prehistory of the Theory of Banking and the School of Salamanca," *The Review of Austrian Economics* 9, no. 2 (1996): 59–81; Barry Gordon, *Economic Analysis Before Adam Smith: Hesiod to Lessius* (New York: Macmillan, 1975), 187–243; Odd Langholm, *Price and Value in the Aristotelian Tradition: A Study in Scholastic Economic Sources* (Bergen: Universitetsforlaget, 1979); Langholm, *Wealth and Money in the Aristotelian Tradition: A Study in Scholastic Economic Sources* (Bergen: Universitetsforlaget, 1983); Langholm, *The Aristotelian Analysis of Usury* (Bergen: Universitetsforlaget, 1984); Langholm, "Scholastic Economics," in *Pre-Classical Economic Thought: From the Greeks to the Scottish Enlightenment*, ed. S. Todd Lowry (Boston/Dordrecht/Lancaster: Kluwer Academic Publishers, 1987), 115–35; Langholm, *Economics in the Medieval Schools: Wealth, Exchange, Value, Money, and Usury According to the Paris Theological Tradition, 1200–1350* (Leiden and New York: Brill, 1992); Langholm, *The Legacy of Scholasticism in Economic Thought: Antecedents of Choice and Power* (Cambridge and New York: Cambridge University Press, 1998); Langholm, *The Merchant in the Confessional: Trade and Price in the Pre-Reformation Penitential Handbooks* (Leiden and New York: Brill, 2003); S. Todd Lowry, "Aristotle's Mathematical Analysis of Exchange," *History of Political Economy* 1 (1969): 44–66; Lowry, *The Archeology of Economic Ideas: The Classical Greek Tradition* (Durham, N.C.: Duke University Press, 1987); Lowry, ed., *Pre-Classical Economic Thought: From the Greeks to the Scottish Enlightenment* (Boston/Dordrecht/Lancaster: Kluwer Academic Publishers, 1987);

S. Todd Lowry and Barry Gordon, ed., *Ancient and Medieval Economic Ideas and Concepts of Social Justice* (Leiden and New York: Brill, 1998); John T. Noonan, *The Scholastic Analysis of Usury* (Cambridge, Mass.: Harvard University Press, 1957); Oscar Nuccio, *Il pensiero economico italiano*, 5 vols. (Sassari: Gallizzi, 1984–1991); Nuccio, *Economisti italiani del XVII secolo: Ferdinando Galiani, Antonio Genovesi, Pietro Verri, Francesco Mengotti* (Rome: Mengotti, 1974); Karl Pribram, *A History of Economic Reasoning* (Baltimore and London: The Johns Hopkins University Press, 1983), 20–30; Murray N. Rothbard, *Economic Thought before Adam Smith: An Austrian Perspective on the History of Economic Thought*, vol. 1 (Brookfield, Vt.: Edward Elgar Publishing Company, 1995): 99–133; Jacob Viner, *Religious Thought and Economic Society: Four Chapters of an Unfinished Work by Jacob Viner*, ed. Jacques Melitz and Donald Winch (Durham, N.C.: Duke University Press, 1978), 46–113; and Jeffrey T. Young and Barry Gordon, "Economic Justice in the Natural Law Tradition: Thomas Aquinas to Francis Hutcheson," *Journal of the History of Economic Thought* 14 (Spring 1992): 1–17.

7. Samuel Gregg, *The Commercial Society: Foundations and Challenges in a Global Age* (Lanham and New York: Lexington Books, 2007); Terence Hutchinson, *Before Adam Smith: The Emergence of Political Economy, 1662–1776* (Oxford: Basil Blackwell, 1988); Oscar Nuccio, *Scrittori classici italiani di economia politica* (Rome: Bizzari, 1965); Alberto M. Piedra, *Natural Law: The Foundation of an Orderly Economic System* (Lanham and New York: Lexington Books, 2004); and Jeffrey T. Young, *Economics as a Moral Science: The Political Economy of Adam Smith* (Cheltenham, U.K.: Edward Elgar Publishing Limited, 1997).

8. Robert I. Mochrie, "Justice in Exchange: The Economic Philosophy of John Duns Scotus," *Journal of Markets & Morality* 9, no. 1 (Spring 2006): 35–56; and Juan Antonio Widow, "The Economic Teachings of the Spanish Scholastics," in *Hispanic Philosophy in the Age of Discovery*, ed. Kevin White (Washington, D.C.: Catholic University of America Press, 1997), 130–44.

9. Rodrigo Muñoz de Juana, *Moral y Economía en la Obra de Martín de Azpilcueta* (Pamplona: Eunsa, 1998); Muñoz, "Scholastic Morality and the Birth of Economics: The Thought of Martín de Azpilcueta," *Journal of Markets & Morality* 4, no. 1 (Spring 2001): 14–42; and Robert A. Sirico, "The Economics of the Late Scholastics," *Journal of Markets & Morality* 1, no. 2 (Fall 1998): 122–29.

10. Mark Blaug, *Economic Theory in Retrospect*, 5th ed. (Cambridge: Cambridge University Press, 1997), 30.

11. In criticizing the trade of the petty usurer (i.e., money-changer), Aristotle penned these immortal words, words that have shaped the development of Western commercial, legal, religious, and ethical institutions since their inception: "The natural form, therefore, of the art of acquisition is always, and in all cases, acquisition from fruits and animals. That art, as we have said, has two forms: one which is connected with retail trade, and another which is connected with the management of the household. Of these two forms, the latter is necessary and laudable; the former is a method of exchange which is justly censured, because the gain in which it results is not naturally made [from plants and animals], but is made at the expense of other men. The trade of the petty usurer [the extreme example of that form of the art of acquisition which is connected with retail trade] is hated most, and with most reason: it makes a profit from currency itself, instead of making it from the process [i.e., of exchange] which currency was meant to serve. Currency came into existence merely as a means of exchange; usury tries to make it increase [as though it were an end

in itself]. This is the reason why usury is called by the word we commonly use [the word *tokos*, which in Greek also means 'breed' or 'offspring']; for as the offspring resembles its parent, so the interest bred by money is like the principal which breeds it, and [as a son is styled by his father's name, so] it may be called 'currency the son of currency.' Hence we can understand why, of all modes of acquisition, usury is the most unnatural." Aristotle, *The Politics of Aristotle*, trans. Ernest Barker (Oxford: Clarendon Press, 1948), I.x.4–5. For Aristotle's fuller treatment of exchange and the origin, nature, and purpose of currency (money), see I.ix-xi.

12. Aristotle's account of money (complementary to that found in the *Politics*), wherein he examines the proportion of reciprocity that must obtain in exchanges for them to be just, can be found in *Nicomachean Ethics*, trans. Martin Ostwald (Indianapolis and New York: Bobbs-Merrill Company, 1962), V.5.

13. Roger Backhouse provides an explanation of how the sterility idea informed the discussion of usury: "The fundamental idea underlying all discussions of usury was that money is sterile. Making money from money is unnatural. Thus, if a borrower makes a profit using money he or she has borrowed, this is because of his or her efforts, not because the money itself is productive. This idea of the sterility of money was reinforced by the legal concept of a loan. In law, most loans took the form of a *mutuum*, in which ownership of the thing lent passes to the borrower, who subsequently repays in kind. The original goods are not returned to the lender. This can apply only to fungible goods, such as gold, silver, wine, oil, or grain, that are interchangeable with each other and can be measured or counted. Because ownership passed to the borrower, it followed that any profit made using the goods belonged to the borrower, and that the lender was not entitled to a share." *The Ordinary Business of Life*, 46.

14. Langholm, "Scholastic Economics," 128–29, cf. 126–32.

15. For more on this point and Albertanus in general, see Flavio Felice, "Introduction to Albertanus of Brescia's *Genovese Sermon* (1243)," *Journal of Markets & Morality* 7, no. 2 (Fall 2004): 606, 603–22; and Oscar Nuccio, *Epistemologia della "azione umana" e razionalismo economico nel Duecento italiano: Il caso Albertano da Brescia* (Torino: Effatà Editrice, 2005).

16. Albertanus of Brescia, "Genovese Sermon (1243)," trans. Patrick T. Brannan, S.J., *Journal of Markets & Morality* 7, no. 2 (Fall 2004): 632–33, 623–38.

17. For important treatments of the thought of Saint Bernardine of Siena (1380–1444) and Saint Antonine of Florence (1389–1459), which serve as counterexamples to Blaug's thesis, see de Roover, *San Bernardino of Siena and Sant'Antonino of Florence*; and Gordon, *Economic Analysis Before Adam Smith*, 195–200. For a general statement of the monastic contribution to the concept that money is capital, see Rodney Stark, *The Victory of Reason: How Christianity Led to Freedom, Capitalism, and Western Success* (New York: Random House, 2005), 59–61.

18. As quoted by Gordon, *Economic Analysis Before Adam Smith*, 197; Bernardine, *De evangelio aeterno*, Sermo 42:2:2.

19. As quoted by Gordon, *Economic Analysis Before Adam Smith*, 198; Bernardine, *De evangelio aeterno*, Sermo 34:2.

20. As quoted by Gordon, *Economic Analysis Before Adam Smith*, 198; Antonine, *Summa*, 2:1:7.

21. Herbert L. Johnson, "Some Medieval Doctrines on Extrinsic Titles to Interest," in *An Etienne Gilson Tribute*, ed. C. J. O'Neil (Milwaukee: Marquette University Press, 1959), 96–98.

22. According to him, "The bulk of scholastic writing on the subject dealt with the legal distinction between a loan and a partnership. To demand interest from a partner was never justified. A loan, however, was a voluntary contract and interest on loans could be demanded under certain conditions extraneous to the circumstances of the borrower. Two of these conditions were losses suffered by the lender as a result of the loan (*damnum emergens*) and a gain foregone by the lender on an alternative investment (*lucrum cessans*); this equates interest to the opportunity cost of liquid funds, an idea which must be put down as a genuine analytical insight. Ingenious apologists have found other nuggets in the literature but on the whole it is analytically sterile." Blaug, *Economic Theory in Retrospect*, 30–31.

23. Robert B. Ekelund Jr. and Robert F. Hebert, *A History of Economic Theory and Method* (New York: McGraw-Hill, Inc., 1975), 28, 19–28.

24. William Edward Hartpole Lecky, *History of the Rise and Influence of the Spirit of Rationalism in Europe*, Rev. ed., 2 vols. (London: Longmans, Green, & Co., 1887–1890), 2:250–70. In this work, a classic of nineteenth-century liberalism, Lecky writes: "A radical misconception of the nature of interest ran through all the writings of the Fathers, of the medieval theologians, and of the theologians of the time of the Reformation, and produced a code of commercial morality that appears with equal clearness in the Patristic invectives, in the decrees of the Councils, and in nearly every book that has been written in Canon Law" (255). It was this radical misconception, a product of dogmatic superstition, opines Lecky, which was finally routed by the new rationalism in Europe.

25. Andrew Dickson White, *A History of the Warfare of Science with Theology in Christendom*, 2 vols. (New York and London: D. Appleton and Company, 1896), 2:264–87. In this work, another classic of nineteenth-century liberalism, White states: "Among questions on which the supporters of right reason in political and social science have only conquered theological opposition after centuries of war, is the taking of interest on loans. In hardly any struggle has rigid adherence to the letter of our sacred books been more prolonged and injurious" (264).

26. Henry Charles Lea, "The Ecclesiastical Treatment of Usury," *Yale Review* II (February 1894): 375–85.

27. Noonan, *The Scholastic Analysis of Usury*, 398–400.

28. Lea, "The Ecclesiastical Treatment of Usury," 384–85.

29. Clarence Edwin Ayres, *The Theory of Economic Progress: A Study of the Fundamentals of Economic Development and Cultural Change* (Chapel Hill: North Carolina University Press, 1955), 46.

30. Frank H. Knight, "Schumpeter's History of Economics," *Southern Economic Journal* 21, no. 3 (January 1955): 264, 261–72.

31. Raymond de Roover, "Scholastic Economics: Survival and Lasting Influence from the Sixteenth Century to Adam Smith," in *Business, Banking, and Economic Thought in Late Medieval and Early Modern Europe*, 318. Julius Kirshner, a friend and intellectual collaborator, thinks de Roover's suggestion that the scholastics would have jettisoned the ban against usury if they had not been confined by the straightjacket of dogma is "a purposeful anachronism." Regardless of whether de Roover's strategy of reconciling the scholastics' "procrustean faith in a doctrine that moderns find ludicrous and irrational with their precocious generalizations about value and price" was ill-fated from the outset, concludes Kirshner, "the portrait of the scholastics as repressed intellectuals in some instances and astute theoreticians in others cannot be sustained from an analysis of their texts." Julius Kirshner, "Raymond de Roover on Scholastic Economic Thought," in *Business, Banking, and Economic Thought in Late Medieval and Early Modern Europe*, 27.

32. Francis Oakley, *Natural Law, Laws of Nature, Natural Rights: Continuity and Discontinuity in the History of Ideas* (New York and London: Continuum International Publishing Group, 2005), 25–26; and Stephen J. Grabill, *Rediscovering the Natural Law in Reformed Theological Ethics* (Grand Rapids, Mich.: Wm. B. Eerdmans Publishing Company, 2006), 54–69.

33. Oakley, *Natural Law, Laws of Nature, Natural Rights*, 26–27. "Along that subterranean and long-forgotten fault, periodic bursts of seismic activity are inevitably to be expected: the bumping, the grinding, the subduction, if you will, of those great tectonic plates of disparate Greek and biblical origin which long ago collided to form the unstable continent of our *mentalité*. And the later Middle Ages, I would suggest, can be helpfully understood as a period distinguished, intellectually speaking, by a recrudesence of precisely such seismic activity leading to, among other things, a reconceptualization of the metaphysical grounding of the law of nature in both the moral/juridical order and the order of physical nature."

34. Blaug, *Economic Theory in Retrospect*, 29.

35. Blaug, *Economic Theory in Retrospect*, 31.

36. Alvey, "The Secret, Natural Theological Foundation of Adam Smith's Work," 335–61.

37. "From an analytical and terminological point of view," writes Langholm, "there is much of scholastic teaching that can be seen to have survived into modern economics. This is not surprising, since (at least if this observation is limited to our Western civilization) it was in the high Middle Ages that the foundations were laid for the kind of systematic reasoning about social relationships that has run on continually to the present day. Sometimes, as in the case of the fairness of the market price, it was deemed pertinent above to point out a subtle shift in the moral basis which supported an apparently unaltered doctrine. Elsewhere, where doctrines have changed as radically as in the case of lending at interest, the scholastics can still be credited with posing the terms of an ongoing argument. So it would seem that much of the old vessel remained to receive new content. The question is how completely it was ever emptied of the ferment prepared for it in the medieval schools. This is a subject which requires a book rather than a few lines. In fact, it has been the subject of many books, some of them provoked or inspired by Max Weber's ideas about religion and capitalism. For simplicity, let us recall that scholastic economics rested on three intellectual traditions. The first support was the tradition of the Bible and the Church Fathers with its emphasis on individual duty. The second was the tradition of the recently rediscovered Roman law with its emphasis on individual rights. The two traditions were made to balance briefly and precariously in the Thomist synthesis by means of a third support in Aristotelian social philosophy." Langholm, "Scholastic Economics," 132–33.

38. Blaug, *Economic Theory in Retrospect*, 30.

39. Blaug, *Economic Theory in Retrospect*, 31.

40. Blaug states: "One may doubt, therefore, whether recent work on scholastic economics required a revision of the history of economic thought prior to Adam Smith. The Schoolmen may have contributed ideas that passed through Grotius, Locke, and Pufendorf to Francis Hutcheson and Adam Smith, but we are hardly justified for that reason in following Schumpeter's reduction of mercantilism to a mere by-current in the forward march of economic analysis." *Economic Theory in Retrospect*, 31.

41. De Roover, "Scholastic Economics," 333.

42. J. R. Milton, "John Locke and the Nominalist Tradition," in *John Locke: Symposium Wolfenbüttel 1979*, ed. Reinhard Brandt (Berlin and New York: Walter de Gruyter, 1981),

128–45; and Francis Oakley, "Locke, Natural Law, and God: Again," in *Politics and Eternity: Studies in the History of Medieval and Early-Modern Political Thought* (Leiden: Brill, 1999), 217–48.

43. John Locke, *An Essay Concerning Human Understanding* (London: Awnsham, John Churchill, and Samuel Mansbip, 1690), Book III, chap. 10, para. 2.

44. Locke, *An Essay Concerning Human Understanding*, Book III, chap. 10, para. 2.

45. Joseph S. Freedman, "Aristotle and the Content of Philosophy Instruction at Central European Schools and Universities during the Reformation Era (1500–1650)," in *Proceedings of the American Philosophical Society* 137, no. 2 (1993): 213–53; Freedman, "Philosophy Instruction within the Institutional Framework of Central European Schools and Universities during the Reformation Era," *History of Universities* 5 (1985): 117–66; Charles B. Schmitt, *Aristotle and the Renaissance* (Cambridge, Mass.: Harvard University Press, 1983); Schmitt, "Towards a Reassessment of Renaissance Aristotelianism," *History of Science* 11 (1973): 159–93; Paul Oskar Kristeller, "Renaissance Aristotelianism," *Greek, Roman, and Byzantine Studies* 6, no. 2 (1965): 157–74; and Fernand Van Steenberghen, *Aristotle in the West: The Origins of Latin Aristotelianism*, trans. Leonard Johnston (Louvain: E. Nauwelaerts, 1955).

46. Schmitt, *Aristotle and the Renaissance*, 26; and Richard A. Muller, *Post-Reformation Reformed Dogmatics: The Rise and Development of Reformed Orthodoxy, ca. 1520 to ca. 1725*, 4 vols. (Grand Rapids, Mich.: Baker Academic, 2003), 1:360–405.

47. For an abbreviated list of seminal contributions to the growing body of revisionist historical theology, consult the following sources: Richard A. Muller, *Post-Reformation Reformed Dogmatics*, 1:37; Muller, *After Calvin: Studies in the Development of a Theological Tradition* (New York: Oxford University Press, 2003); Muller, "The Problem of Protestant Scholasticism—A Review and Definition," in *Reformation and Scholasticism: An Ecumenical Enterprise*, ed. Willem J. van Asselt and Eef Dekker (Grand Rapids, Mich.: Baker Book House, 2001), 45–64; Muller, *The Unaccommodated Calvin: Studies in the Foundation of a Theological Tradition* (New York: Oxford University Press, 2000); Carl R. Trueman and R. S. Clark, ed., *Protestant Scholasticism: Essays in Reassessment* (Carlisle, U.K.: Paternoster Press, 1999); and Willem J. van Asselt and Eef Dekker, ed., *Reformation and Scholasticism: An Ecumenical Enterprise* (Grand Rapids, Mich.: Baker Book House, 2001).

48. S. Drakopoulos and G. N. Gotsis, "A Meta-Theoretical Assessment of the Decline of Scholastic Economics," *History of Economics Review* 40 (Summer 2004): 19–45; and F. A. Hayek, *The Counter-Revolution of Science: Studies on the Abuse of Reason* (Indianapolis: Liberty Fund, 1979), 17–60.

49. *New Catholic Encyclopedia*, s.v. "Scholastic Method."

50. Camacho, "Later Scholastics: Spanish Economic Thought in the XVIth and XVIIth Centuries," 506–14.

51. Camacho, "Later Scholastics: Spanish Economic Thought in the XVIth and XVIIth Centuries," 509. For more on *recta ratio*, see Grabill, *Rediscovering the Natural Law in Reformed Theological Ethics*, 217, n. 40; and Louis I. Bredvold, "The Meaning of the Concept of Right Reason in the Natural-Law Tradition," *University of Detroit Law Journal* 36 (December 1959): 120–29.

52. Schumpeter, *History of Economic Analysis*, 111.

53. Alvey, "A Short History of Economics as a Moral Science," 55.

54. De Roover, "Scholastic Economics," 333.

55. Hutchinson, *Before Adam Smith: The Emergence of Political Economy, 1662–1776*, 99–100.

56. Alejandro Chafuen supports this judgment: "In Germany, the Hispanic Scholastics had a great impact on the writings of Samuel von Pufendorf (1632–1694). Through Grotius, Pufendorf, and the Physiocrats, many late-scholastic ideas influenced Anglo-Saxon economic economic thought, especially the "Scottish School" consisting of Ferguson (1723–1816), Hutcheson (1694–1746), and Smith (c. 1723–1790)." *Faith and Liberty*, 15–16.

57. Hutchinson, *Before Adam Smith: The Emergence of Political Economy, 1662–1776*, 100.

58. Stark, *The Victory of Reason*, 11–12.

59. See *The Early Christian Fathers: A Selection from the Writings of the Fathers from St. Clement of Rome to St. Athanasius*, ed. and trans. Henry Bettenson (London and New York: Oxford University Press, 1956), 162–63 (cf. *Adversus Praxean*, 5–7).

60. Herman Bavinck, *Reformed Dogmatics*, vol. 1, *Prolegomena*, ed. John Bolt, trans. John Vriend (Grand Rapids, Mich.: Baker Academic, 2003), 233.

61. As quoted in Edwin Arthur Burtt, *The Metaphysical Foundations of Modern Science* (Garden City, N.J.: Doubleday Anchor Books, 1954), 20.

62. Oakley, *Natural Law, Laws of Nature, Natural Rights*, 9.

63. Oakley, *Natural Law, Laws of Nature, Natural Rights*, 13–34. See also the various essays in Oakley's *Politics and Eternity*; Oakley, *Omnipotence, Covenant, and Order: An Excursion in the History of Ideas from Abelard to Leibniz* (Ithaca: Cornell University Press, 1984); Oakley, *Kingship: The Politics of Enchantment* (Oxford: Blackwell Publishing, 2006); and William J. Courtenay, *Covenant and Causality in Medieval Thought: Studies in Philosophy, Theology, and Economic Practice* (London: Variorum Reprints, 1984).

64. See Young, *Economics as a Moral Science*; Alvey, "A Short History of Economics as a Moral Science," 53–73; Ricardo F. Crespo, "Is Economics a Moral Science?" *Journal of Markets & Morality* 1, no. 2 (Fall 1998): 201–11; Peter J. Boettke, "Is Economics a Moral Science? A Response to Ricardo F. Crespo," *Journal of Markets & Morality* 1, no. 2 (Fall 1998): 212–19; and Crespo, "Is Economics a Moral Science? A Response to Peter J. Boettke," *Journal of Markets & Morality* 1, no. 2 (Fall 1998): 220–25.

65. Alvey, "A Short History of Economics as a Moral Science," 53.

66. Camacho, "Later Scholastics: Spanish Economic Thought in the XVIth and XVIIth Centuries," 503.

67. Camacho, "Later Scholastics: Spanish Economic Thought in the XVIth and XVIIth Centuries," 503.

68. Camacho, "Later Scholastics: Spanish Economic Thought in the XVIth and XVIIth Centuries," 503.

69. Schumpeter, *History of Economic Analysis*, 97. "And not only that," he continues in the next sentence, "it will appear, even, that the bases they laid for a servicable and well-integrated body of analytic tools and propositions were sounder than was much subsequent work, in the sense that a considerable part of the economics of the later nineteenth century might have been developed from those bases more quickly and with less trouble than it actually cost to develop it, and that some of that subsequent work was therefore in the nature of a time- and labor-consuming detour."

70. I accept the broad outline of Grice-Hutchinson's thesis regarding the School of Salamanca, but I prefer a more generic designation such as "late-Spanish scholastics" precisely because its elasticity can better distinguish and still unify the later writers such

as Luis de Molina, Leonardus Lessius, and Juan de Mariana who are farther removed from Vitoria. Karl Pribram has noted some important differences between Molina and the Jesuits from the rest of the largely Dominican Salamancan group. He opted to segregate Molina, in particular, from the rest of the Salamancans, while still affirming a large degree of consensus on economic ideas between them. See Pribram, *A History of Economic Reasoning*, 27–30. This makes sense, as Laurence Moss points out, "because Molina, like his eminent contemporary Francisco Suarez, had comparatively weaker ties with Salamanca and the teachings of Vitoria. Their studies at Salamanca occurred well after the death of Vitoria and both had their longest tenures at the Universities of Coimbra and Evora." Laurence S. Moss, "Introduction," in Grice-Hutchinson, *Economic Thought in Spain*, xi.

71. Moss, "Introduction," x–xxii.

72. Schumpeter, *History of Economic Analysis*, 165.

73. Moss, "Introduction," vii. Cf. Marjorie Grice-Hutchinson, "The Concept of the School of Salamanca: Its Origins and Development," in *Economic Thought in Spain*, 23–29.

74. This text was published by the Clarendon Press of Oxford University. Those same translations have been reprinted as the Appendix: "Translations by Marjorie Grice-Hutchinson of Texts by Spanish Authors," in *Economic Thought in Spain*, 143–68.

75. Moss, "Introduction," viii.

76. Moss, "Introduction," viii.

77. Moss, "Introduction," xv.

78. Martín de Azpilcueta, *Comentario Resolutorio de Cambios*, introducción y texto critico por Alberto Ullastres, José M. Perez Prendes y Luciano Pereña (Madrid: Consejo Superior de Investigaciones Cientificas, 1965); and Luis de Molina, S.J., *Tratado sobre los cambios*, edición, introducción, y notas por Francisco Gómez Camacho, S.J. (Madrid: Instituto de Estudios Fiscales, 1990).

79. Ioannes Mariana, S.J., *De monetae mutatione (MDCIX)* = *Über die Münzveränderung (1609)*, herausgegeben, übersetzt und mit Einzelerklärungen versehen von Josef Falzberger (Heidelberg: Manutius, 1996).

80. Rothbard, *Economic Thought before Adam Smith*, 121.

81. Juan de Mariana, S.J., *Tratado y discurso sobre la moneda de vellón*, estudio introductorio por Lucas Beltrán (Madrid: Instituto de Estudios Fiscales, 1987). Mariana's original Spanish title was *Tratado y discurso sobre la moneda de vellón que al presente se labra en Castilla y de algunos desórdenes y abusos*.

Part One

Commentary on the Resolution of Money (1556)

Martín de Azpilcueta

INTRODUCTION

Martín de Azpilcueta: Biographical and Scientific Profile

Martín de Azpilcueta y Jaureguizar (1492–1586),[1] known as Doctor Navarrus, earned a bachelor in theology degree at Alcalá University. Later, he completed his training in Toulouse, the most renowned center for juridical studies in France, where he received the degree of doctor in canon law (1518) and gained his first teaching experiences.

As of 1524, he had served in several Canon law chairs at the University of Salamanca, and, together with Francisco de Vitoria, he renovated the juridical and theological thought of the day.[2] Some years later, in 1538, he was invited by the kings of Portugal and Spain to transfer to Coimbra University for a brief period, which extended until 1556 when he returned to Spain to devote himself entirely to his writings.

In June 1561, Martín was appointed defense counsel in the criminal proceedings brought against the Toledo archbishop Bartolomé de Carranza, a case that took him to Rome in August 1567, where, together with his work as defense counsel, he was appointed advisor in the Supreme Penitentiary Tribunal then Major Penitentiary, on the initiative of Pius V and Charles Borromeo. He died there at the age of ninety-three.

Although he worked in numerous disciplines, his most important doctrinal contribution was in the field of canon law and morality. Among his numerous written works the most important is the *Manual de confesores y penitentes*[3] because of its significance and influence with a complex writing process that originated in a chance happening (1549) and developed in consecutive stages until it achieved its final form (Salamanca, 1556). It was an immense publishing success: In the second half of the sixteenth century and first quarter of the seventeenth, it ran to eighty-one editions, with ninety-two more in revisions, versions, and abridgments. First written in Portuguese, then in Spanish, and finally in Latin, it was translated several times into Italian and French.[4]

As its title suggests, the *Manual* is a work directed to the pastoral aspect of penance. It deals with issues considered necessary for the administration of the sacrament. However, the most important work by Doctor Navarrus extends beyond the genre of the *Sumas de penitencia*, which originated at the end of the thirteenth century and was based on the precedent of the *libri poenitentiales* of the late Middle Ages with few doctrinal developments and was organized alphabetically according to terms, much like a dictionary. Because of its systematic structure and doctrinal vigor, Azpilcueta's *Manual de confesores y penitentes* is considered a milestone in the emergence of moral theology as an autonomous discipline[5] at the beginning of the seventeenth century.

The *Commentary on the Resolution of Money* (CRM) is one of four appendices to this *Manual* and as such belongs to Navarrus's group of moral writings. In them, the author recommends guiding criteria for pastors and penitents and indirectly offers acute observations and an analysis of the economic reality of his time, which has recently attracted the attention of economic historians.

The Scholastics and the Historiography of Economic Thought

The historiography of economic thought has become increasingly interested in the moral literature of the second Scholastic period, which looks into the economic practices of sixteenth-century commercial capitalism. Although such interest regards the whole of scholasticism, it especially considers the authors of the late Scholastic or second Scholastic period, which peaked during the Spanish *Siglo de Oro*[6] with the so-called School of Salamanca.[7]

During the sixteenth century, there was a theological renaissance driven by the changes that gave way to a new social and cultural life that put an end to the medieval model. Together with specifically theological matters—the need for renovation and the later Protestant reforms that were the immediate antecedents to the Council of Trent—other factors were the new idea of man and society; the demographic expansion in Europe; the surge of modern national states; and the discovery of the New World, with a massive affluence of precious metals and new markets in the Indies. Both circumstances soon had an effect on Spanish prices.

These phenomena, together with the development of banking activities and new forms of payment, gave way to an increasing capital flow and to the growth of credit and speculative activity, all of which became a formidable challenge for moral theology.

The new theological genres included the works of the penitential pastoral and *De iustitia et iure* treatises, along with more specific ones such as Azpilcueta's CRM. In them, we find observations on monopolies, just pricing, taxes, banking or credit practices, currency markets, and so forth. The publishing of new essays and Joseph Schumpeter's *History of Economic Analysis* (1954), devoted largely to the Scholastic doctors, have made some historiographers defend the Scholastic literature as an important precedent for the specifically scientific analysis of the economy and have even led them to think of its authors as founders of modern economics.[8]

In this context, Azpilcueta's work plays a singular role. Perhaps the greatest originality of Doctor Navarrus and the issue that has most attracted economists is precisely the quality of his analysis regarding the value of money, as is reflected in the CRM.

The development of monetary doctrines had been driven by the expansion of commerce in the last centuries of the Middle Ages, the evolution of currency and alternative means of payment, the commercial fairs of Castile, and the consecutive consolidation and improvement of banking and financial activities.[9] In Navarrus's case in particular, the price revolution in Castile precipitated his writing.

In fact, one of the first consequences for the Castilian economy of the sixteenth century caused by the supply of precious metals from America was steady price increases. E. J. Hamilton tried to quantify this flux and to examine its effects on prices, salaries, and economic welfare.[10] He concluded that the importation of metal was the cause for prices to triple between 1501 and 1600. Other authors have toned down Hamilton's statements (correcting calculations and adding other factors with inflationary effects and complementary information), but the critics have not offered other alternatives to the quantitative theory he espoused. Although there is not a univocal correspondence between the arrival of massive amounts of precious metals and the price increases, it is impossible to deny a causal relationship between these two elements.[11] In attempting to devise contemporary explanations for this phenomenon, Hamilton underestimated Scholastic reflection:

> Few Spaniards had sufficient education to compose a mercantilist tract and the clergy had little inclination for economic speculation. The vast majority of outstanding Spanish mercantilists before 1700 were ecclesiastics, little acquainted with either the economic literature or life of financially advanced nations. Their profession afforded them scant opportunity to acquire the intricate economic knowledge requisite to fathom foreign exchange.[12]

However, other studies following Hamilton's showed the merits of the School of Salamanca's analysis (Azpilcueta among them) on the phenomenon of Castilian inflation. First, Dempsey, Ullastres, and Larraz, and some years later Marjorie Grice-Hutchinson, defended Navarrus's role as precursor and encouraged a closer examination of his formulation of the quantitative theory of money.[13]

With some precedents in Aristotle and the medieval tradition, Jean Bodin (1568) was considered the first to demonstrate the principal cause of inflation. Larraz, however, pointed out how little space Bodin assigned to this issue and defended Salamanca's primacy, proving two things: first, that Bodin was preceded by the Spanish natural lawyers and moralists; and, second, that the Spanish school was broader than the French because the latter only linked monetary mass to price level, while the Spanish considered, too, a third interdependent factor, namely, foreign exchange.[14]

The issue here is not merely concerned with establishing precedence in the formulation of the quantitative theory of money. Grice-Hutchinson has said from a more general perspective that it was Schumpeter who realized that the origins of economic analysis lay in moral philosophy more than in mercantilism, as the majority of economic historians before had thought. Regarding the School of Salamanca, Grice-Hutchinson notes its consistent originality in a triple contribution to monetary theory: its formulation, in the first place, of a psychological theory of value that may be applied both to goods as well as to money; in the second place, of a quantitative theory; and, finally, its formulation of a theory of foreign exchanges similar to the modern theory of the parity of buying power that we do not usually associate with the sixteenth century.[15]

The Commentary on the Resolution of Money

We have already alluded to the historical context of the CRM by referencing the economic evolution of the sixteenth century. From an intellectual point of view, therefore, it is important to refer now to the problem of usury.

Doctrinal Context

The theory of usury is in many respects autonomous and of great significance for the Scholastics' commercial ethics. The reason is that doctrinal developments—perhaps here more than in any other aspect of economic ethics—have a multisecular tradition: The biblical writings and Roman law texts were developed for the first time in the writings of the church fathers and shaped into the canonical legislation on usury, which extends for more than a thousand years. Often they are judged too hastily, and the medieval approach to the problem of usury is ruled out without paying too much attention to the economic reality of each period and to the arguments for why usury practices were considered unjust. As it is not possible to go into them in detail here, only a summary of their conceptual framework will be provided.[16]

Usury is applied to the loan of things whose use is their consumption (*mutuum*), such as wheat, wine, money, and so forth. Usurious was any retribution that was demanded for the use of a consumable good. The reason was that in such cases, because the use of the thing was inseparable to its consumption, the contract transferred the property, and the one who received it agreed to not give back the same thing—which was impossible—but an equivalent quantity and genre of what had been received. For this reason, demanding anything more than the loaned capital (*ultra sortem*) was considered usury. Some of the arguments used were that it was illicit to sell time; that money, unlike other things, did not deteriorate with use; and that there was an absence of risk for the lender, who turned the interest into a profit that did not compensate for the work or risk and was therefore unjustified. Renting a house or a field was different because they were not consumed by use and had to be restituted themselves together with their fruits, that is, they allowed for the payment of a rent. The profit gained from the use of consumable goods was a fruit not of the goods but of the work applied to them; a retribution for what was deemed "mere lapse of time" (*inter esse*) was not allowed. Saint Thomas Aquinas's example is instructive: He opposed giving money as a loan to giving money to a merchant or artisan in order to constitute a society. In the first case, there is a transference of ownership and risk for the loss of the thing, and, because of this, the lender should not ask for more. But the one who gives money to a merchant retains the property and risk, and may thus ask, as a fruit of the thing that belongs to him, a part of the profit gained.[17]

In addition to this consideration, which was the essence of the Scholastic doctrine on usury, there was a doctrine on *external titles*, that is, cases where payment was justified for extrinsic reasons to the *mutuum* contract. It was generally licit to pay a sum not as interest but for damage or loss to the lender (*damnum emergens*), as for example, a delay in fulfilling the contract. *Lucrum cessans* posed a more complex problem, and there were different opinions. In some authors, it is difficult to establish a clear distinction between the limits of a damage and the end of a profit or benefice. The development of this argument in the sixteenth century is interesting, finally justifying the payment of an interest only when the money is lent by a merchant, that is, by the one who gives money a productive use and undergoes an economic loss when lending. This is, for example, Azpilcueta's case: "More is owed to the merchant for the money he deals with than to another who does not deal with anything. The consequence of which is that money pays better in the hands of merchants and money chargers who invest it 'actively' than in other hands in which it may end up being hoarded."[18]

Finally, among the extrinsic titles is risk (*periculum sortis*), considered not as the possibility of the borrower's insolvency so much as the risk of the possessions' loss. In many cases, the risk was related to the danger of a long voyage: pirates, theft, shipwreck, and so forth. In any case, *periculum sortis* was unanimously rejected as a title to compensation.

Following Aristotle, the early Scholastics had already reflected on money, but the morality of exchange operations became important with Saint Antonino de Florencia's work and was officially approved in the sixteenth century with the publishing of Cajetan's (1499) *De cambiis* ("On Money"). Later, the subject matter of *de cambiis* became independent from the study of usury. Azpilcueta himself wrote a treatise about each one of those issues, and published them as appendices to the *Manual*: The *Comentario Resolutorio de Usuras* and the *Comentario Resolutorio de Cambios* (Salamanca, 1556). Such differences have more to do with juridical criteria than with doctrinal criteria, as money exchange operations were considered as long as they had a financing element and, thus by extension, were given the same moral treatment as usury.

As strange as the handling of this issue seems today, this is the formal structure behind the Scholastic reflection when considering compensation for credit and other types of monetary exchange that are similar to it. We should remember the distance between the economic reality of those days—deficiencies in the monetary system, the lack of a productive destiny for capital, credit, and so forth—and today's economic realities.

The Economic Ideas of the CRM[19]

The Concept of Exchange

The word *exchange* had two meanings for Navarrus. A general one, which the Romans called *permuta*, referred to the exchange of one thing for another or of money for money. In a restricted sense, it applied to the exchange of money for money or to other contracts that did not fit into the Roman law classification: some types of acquisition, rentals, and so forth. Thus, *exchange* meant "any contract of money for money that was not gratuitous," be it acquisition, deposit, or any other (CRM, par. 10).

The Different Uses of Money

Azpilcueta had no doubt about the need for money, which was based on eight uses (cf. CRM, pars. 11–12):

1. as a means of payment,
2. as a measure of the value of things,
3. as an employment in exchanges between coins of different metal, different value, or different places,
4. to display one's riches to others,
5. as an ornamental element in dress,
6. "to enliven with its presence,"
7. "to cure with its broth some illnesses" (the broth of gold was thought to have therapeutic properties), and
8. as pawn for a debt.

Obviously, some of these uses did not have an economic content. Regarding its use in exchanges (cf. par. 3), the author confronted Aristotle's negative opinion on the *crematistic* (the lucrative commerce with no limits, different from the exchanges made to satisfy domestic needs), which was, according to the philosopher, unnatural. The profit-based economy was for Aristotle a consequence of the invention of money. He illustrated it with an example: It was possible to give a double use to shoes: a natural one, as footwear, and an improper one as an object of exchange. Navarrus softened Aristotle's harsh opinion: As well as using shoes to trade with, using money in exchanges is not unnatural, even if it is a secondary use compared to the principal one. With this observation, the author put money on the same level as any other merchandise, and, consequently, established that the morality of exchanges did not depend on money as their object but on an equitable exchange (cf. CRM, par. 13).

Types of Exchange

Taking into account the earlier classifications (Silvestre, Cajetan), Azpilcueta offered seven types of exchange, some of which were in these precedents.

Exchanging as a Professional

More than a type of exchange, the author analyzed the licitness of the exchanger's occupation and his remuneration. He tended to accept it for the following reasons: (1) There is no usury if the payment rewards the work of the exchanger instead of the loan; (2) such profession is a service to the republic (common good), and the employees may receive a salary; and (3) if the money exchanger carries out a public function, it is just that he receive a retribution for it, and he may also receive payment by practicing the profession in private, although in this case, there is a possibility of fraud.

Exchanging for Small Coinage

In regard to the exchange of large denomination coins for small denomination ones, or the opposite, the author considered it licit to charge something for the service, even if such activity might be prohibited to private exchangers for reasons of monetary policy.

Exchanging for Bills of Exchange

The increase of commerce together with the coin scarcity forced the creation of alternative means of payment and the use of paper. The commercial fairs of Castile played an important role in this process.[20] Azpilcueta referred to it as the "virtual transference of money" to another place by means of a bill of exchange. The author thought that this form of exchange could be licitly rewarded, under the condition that the nominal price was equivalent to the sum rendered, as such payment compensated for the service rendered (the physical transportation of the money or the work involved to keep the money in a distant place) and not for the credit, in which case it would be an usurious practice (cf. CRM, par. 23). The exchanges made for reasons of place (*ratione loci*) were admitted unanimously. This was not the case with those made for reasons of time lapse (*ratione temporis*) because they were considered usurious.

Exchanging by True Transference

This expression referred to the physical transference of money, as opposed to its *virtual transfer*. The author referred to the acquisition of money in a certain place where it could be devalued for a certain reason, to take it where it would be exchanged for a higher price in order to obtain a profit in the two successive exchanges. This may be a primary form of what we know today as currency swapping. He believed that this type of exchange was licit, as long as it was carried out for a just price and more or less money was not given for advancing or postponing the payment.

Exchanging for Interest

The previously mentioned doctrine about extrinsic titles may apply here. The exchanger who by lending was harmed because of profit, loss, or damage could ask for compensation for the benefits that he renounced or for the damages suffered. The author adds: Merchants may charge more if the debt is due to the second fairs than if it is due to the first ones because the *lucrum cessans* is greater: "The exchanger who is prevented from exchanging for two fairs with his money, more is prevented from earning than if he is prevented from exchanging for one" (CRM, par. 34). However, he goes on to condemn the person who removed his money from the deal and transferred it from fair to fair for an interest that was equivalent to the amount he was used to gaining through commerce (CRM, par. 35). The reason for condemning this practice was the previous abandonment of commerce, which eliminated the possibility of *lucrum cessans*.

Azpilcueta considered time lapse relevant as long as it affected the amount of the damage or profit/loss and, with it, the compensation owed to the lender. However, setting aside the issues pertaining to interest, the term for the credit could not be taken into consideration to establish a retribution for the capital, as this was a reprehensible moral activity.

Exchanging for Safekeeping

This form of exchange consisted of the actual visible bank deposit, whereby the bank committed to making payments on behalf of the depositor. He believed it was a useful enterprise for the republic by which the exchanger could licitly be paid a salary because he "works in receiving, keeping, and preparing the money of so many merchants, and in writing, giving, and keeping accounts with everyone" (CRM, par. 36). The author cleverly condemned those who deposited with the exchanger and "do not want to pay anything saying that what they earn with their money ... is enough for a salary ... and if the exchangers ask them for something, they leave them and go deal with others, and so that they are not left, they let them keep the salary owed to them, and take it from someone who does not owe it to them."

Exchanging by Buying, Bartering, or Innominate Contract

It is described as if someone gave one hundred in Medina to receive one hundred ten in Flanders or the other way around. Then, with a great deal of realism, Azpilcueta sets himself apart from the juridical-formal structure of contracts, stating that there were actually two things that could make an exchange unjust: "the inequality of what is given and of what is to be taken," and "taking for oneself more or less for advancing or postponing [the payment], or for giving a longer or shorter deadline for returning the money" (CRM, par. 41). Once rid of the formal juridical requirements (pars. 42–43), he tackled the main issue: "The difficulty is in declaring how a profit may be made justly by commutation of money."

The Value of Money: The Quantitative Element

Navarrus thought it was possible to establish the value of money by deciding when and how a currency, which was apparently equal to another, was worth more or less for a certain reason. He described eight factors that affected the value of money. It is worth noting that the author had an unstructured idea of money, tied to the monetary unit, whether in its nominal aspect or in the materiality of the metal, even if he went beyond the rigid notion of giving an immutable value to it. However, when evaluating his position, one should take into account the deficiencies of the monetary system in sixteenth-century Europe.

The eight factors that affected the value of money were

1. the nonexistence of coins of the same metal;
2. metals of a different value;
3. the different shape and weight;
4. the diversity of the land in which they circulated;
5. decisions made by the authority relative to the context where the coin circulated or changes in the relationship between the legal value and the intrinsic value;
6. the diversity of time;
7. the lack and need of money; and
8. the presence or absence of different coins.

The first five factors of price variation address money's fluctuation between its purely metallic dimension and the nominal one. As for the time factor, the author admitted it was a purely accidental consideration, but one that had a relationship with other factors that affected money's value.

The quantitative aspect is more interesting. Azpilcueta noted that money changed its value in relationship with its quantity. If goods got costlier because of the great need for them and their scarcity, that is, because of supply and demand, money was not an exception to this rule. Navarrus's words are sufficiently explicit:

The rest being the same, in the countries where there is a great lack of money, less money is given for marketable goods and even for the hands and work of men than where there is an abundance of it; as we can see from experience in France, where there is less money than in Spain bread, wine, wool, hands, and work cost less; and even in Spain, when there was less money, much less was given for marketable goods, the hands and work of men than later when the discoveries of the Indies covered it in silver and gold. The cause of which is that money is worth more where and when there is lack of it, than where and when there is an abundance, and what some say, that the lack of money reduces the price of everything, is born of the fact that their more than sufficient rise makes everything appear much lower, just as a small man next to a very tall man appears smaller than if he were next to his equal. (CRM, par. 51)

Azpilcueta transcended a notion of money based on the nominal and metallic aspects and established its value based on its relationship with goods. In other words, money derived its value from its buying power. Also, given a certain moment in time and without the influence of other factors, there was a proportional quantitative relationship between the total amount of money available and the volume of merchandise—including the "work of men"—that could be bought with that amount of money. The author's ideas may be summed up in three conclusions.

The first is that the abundance or scarcity of money affected the relationships that diverse sectors of the monetary system had among them, as well as the system itself considered in its totality—that is, the goods that could be acquired with these monetary units or with units of another system.

The second is that the value of money could rise or fall, not only because it was metal but also because it was a price for other things (CRM, par. 57). Money was considered something fixed when taken as a unit for counting, but its value was variable when considering the utility it brought to its possessor (CRM, par. 58).

The third is that Azpilcueta's clarity and his notion of money related to its buying power set him apart from the medieval theory that considered money as an invariable mass. After observing the phenomenon of Castilian inflation, Navarrus could no longer remain in that position. His observations were published twelve years before Jean Bodin's.

The Critical Text

The CRM's text, whose English version follows, appeared as an appendix to the cited principal edition of the *Manual de confesores y penitentes* and was dedicated to the prince Don Carlos, son of Philip II.[21] The treatise—which followed another one on usury—extends from page 48 to page 104. The paragraphs are numbered, and each chapter is preceded by a summary of subjects. The Castilian text presents a difficult orthography, with marginal notes in Latin and abundant abbreviations. The version used by the Spanish editors corresponds to the one existing at the Madrid

National Library (R/18063), signed by Miguel de Azpilcueta, which suggests that the exemplar may have belonged to the author.

The maturity of Azpilcueta's ideas should be situated around 1530, when he was professor at Salamanca and engaged in commentary on the *Decreto* and the *Decretales* (on usuries and exchanges). Indeed, the CRM appeared, according to its title and continuing with the genre developed in the field of canon law, as a commentary on the first part of the well-known decretal *Naviganti*. However, the CRM was actually a genuine treatise on exchanges that widely exceeded its function of gloss on the decretal. After dealing successfully in its first pages with the problems raised in the decretal on the contract of maritime insurance, the author offered a detailed analysis of the main points regarding the matter *de cambiis*.

The CRM extended quickly. The last edition in Spanish, the tenth, is the one from Valladolid, 1569. Already there were translations into Portuguese (1560), Italian (1568), Latin by an unknown author (1569), and into French (1601). In the Latin edition of the *Manual de confesores y penitentes* (Rome, 1573), the author disavowed that particular translation because it contained "many things contrary to my thoughts." He did not, however, introduce a translation of the CRM into the Latin edition but rather provided a synthesis with some references to the Spanish edition (chap. 17 in the *Manual*), which he authorized as an interpretation of the 1556 original. The Spanish text was not edited again, while the Latin edition was reproduced many times in the editorial centers of Europe. The response of the author to five inquiries on the subject, published in another volume in 1583, are also of value, as they examine the application of these principles to tangible situations.

—Rodrigo Muñoz de Juana

Notes

1. The classical biographers are M. Arigita y Lasa, *El Doctor Navarrus Don Martín de Azpilcueta y sus obras: Estudio histórico-crítico* (Pamplona: J. Ezquerro, 1895); H. De Olóriz, *Nueva biografía del Doctor Navarrus D. Martín de Azpilcueta y enumeración de sus obras* (Pamplona: N. Aramburu, 1916). E. Tejero gathers information of biographical writings on Azpilcueta: "Los escritos sobre el Doctor Navarrus," in *Estudios sobre el Doctor Navarrus: En el IV centenario de la muerte de Martín de Azpilcueta*, ed. Gobierno de Navarra (Pamplona: Universidad de Navarra, 1988), 22–34.

2. In a work that contains many autobiographical notes, Azpilcueta himself says: "Nobody denies that I brought from Tolosa, in France, to the University of Salamanca ... the solid and useful science of Canon Law. The same as, a year later, Francisco de Vitoria, as wise as he is pious, introduced an elaborate theology, studied at the University of Paris." "Apologetic Letter from Martín de Azpilcueta to don Gabriel de la Cueva, Duque de Alburquerque," in *Comentario Resolutorio de Cambios*, introducción y texto crítico de A. Ullastres, L. Pereña, and J. Pérez Prendes (Madrid: Consejo Superior de Investigaciones Científicas, 1965), 43–44.

3. *Handbook for Confessors and Penitents.*

4. An almost exhaustive catalogue of the editions appears in E. Dunoyer, *L'Enchiridion confessariorum del Navarrus: Dissertatio ad lauream in facultate S. Theologiae apud Pontificium Institutum "Angelicum" de Urbe* (Pamplona: Gurrea, 1957).

5. Cf. Rodrigo Muñoz de Juana, *Moral y economía en la obra de Martín de Azpilcueta* (Pamplona: Ediciones Universidad de Navarra, 1998), 111–22; J. Theiner, *Die Entwicklung der Moral-theologie zur eigenständigen Diszpilin* (Regensburg: F. Pustet, 1970).

6. *Siglo de Oro*: A period of great prosperity, happiness, and achievement in Spain (1555).

7. Among the recent bibliography, Odd Langholm may be consulted: *Economics in the Medieval Schools: Wealth, Exchange, Value, Money, and Usury According to the Paris Theological Tradition, 1200–1350* (Leiden and New York: Brill, 1992); Murray N. Rothbard, *Economic Thought before Adam Smith: An Austrian Perspective in the History of Economic Thought*, vol. 1 (Brookfield, Vt.: Edward Elgar Publishing Company, 1995); A. del Vigo Gutiérrez, *Cambistas mercaderes y banqueros en el Siglo de Oro español* (Madrid: BAC, 1997); F. Gómez Camacho, S.J., *Economía y filosofía moral: la formación del pensameinto económico europeo en la Escolástica Española* (Madrid: Síntesis, 1998).

8. A study of the main views in the debate may be seen in Muñoz, *Moral y Economía en la obra de Martín de Azpilcueta*, 22–69. For an English summary, see Muñoz, "Scholastic Morality and the Birth of Economics: The Thought of Martín de Azpilcueta," *Journal of Markets & Morality* 4, no. 1 (2001): 14–42.

9. For monetary aspects, banking activity, and commercial fairs, see H. Lapeyre, *Une famille de merchands: les Ruiz* (Paris: Colin, 1955), 241–71 and 475–501; R. Carande, *Carlos V y sus banqueros: La vida económica en Castilla (1516–1556)* (Madrid: Sociedad de Estudios y Publicaciones, 1965), 223–53 and 295–349; F. Ruiz Martín, "La banca en España hasta 1782," in *El Banco de España: Una historia económica*, ed. A. Moreno Redondo (Madrid: Banco de España, 1970), 1–196; and P. Spufford, *Money and Its Use in Medieval Europe* (Cambridge: Cambridge University Press, 1989).

10. Cf. E. J. Hamilton, "Spanish Mercantilism before 1700," in *Facts and Factors in Economic History: Articles by Former Students*, ed. E. F. Gay (Cambridge, Mass.: Harvard University Press, 1932), 214–39; E. F. Gay, *American Treasure and the Price Revolution in Spain, 1501–1650* (Cambridge, Mass.: Harvard University Press, 1934).

11. Cf. J. Nadal Oller, "La revolución de los precios españoles en el XVI: Estado actual de la cuestión," *Hispania* 19 (1959): 503–29.

12. Hamilton, "Spanish Mercantilism Before 1700," 230.

13. B. W. Dempsey, S.J. "The Historical Emergence of Quantity Theory," *The Quarterly Journal of Economics* 50, no. 1 (November 1935): 174–84; A. Ullastres, "Martín de Azpilcueta y su comentario resolutorio de cambios: Las ideas económicas de un moralista español del siglo XVI," *Anales de Economía* 3–4 (1941): 375–409; and 5 (1942): 51–95; J. Larraz López, *La época del mercantilismo en Castilla, 1500–1700* (Madrid: Atlas, 1943); Marjorie Grice-Hutchinson, *The School of Salamanca: Readings in Spanish Monetary Theory, 1544–1605* (Oxford: Clarendon Press, 1952). The work by Ullastres, which was published in two parts in *Anales de Economía*, is reproduced as an introduction to the critical edition of the CRM, 42–117.

14. J. Larraz, *La época del mercantilismo en Castilla* (Madrid: Aguilar, 1963), 86.

15. Grice-Hutchinson, *The School of Salamanca*, 47ff.

16. I have written on the evolution of usury in the Scholastics with some degree of thoroughness, focusing especially on Azpilcueta, in Muñoz, *Moral y economia en la obra de Martín de Azpilcueta*, 203–337. For a synthesis of the biblical perspectives, see A. Bernard, "Usure. I. La formation de la doctrine ecclésiastique sur l'usure," *Dictionnaire de Théologie Catholique* 15, no. 2 (1950), 2317; Bernard, "Usure. I.," 2365–67; and H. Lesetre, "Pret," *Dictionnaire de la Bible* 5 (1912): 617. For a general perspective, see G. Le Bras, "Usure. II. La doctrine ecclésiastique de l'usure a l'époque clasique (XII–XV siecle)," *Dictionnaire de Théologie Catholique* 15, no. 2 (1950): 2336–72; the study by T. P. McLaughlin is magnificent, "The Teaching of the Canonist on Usury (XII, XIII, and XIV Centuries)," *Mediaeval Studies* 1 (1939): 81–147; and 2 (1940): 1–22. Even if guided by a debatable presupposition, J. T. Noonan's work is a classic, *The Scholastic Analysis of Usury* (Cambridge, Mass.: Harvard University Press, 1957).

17. Cf. *Summa theologicae*, II-II, q. 78, a.2 ad 5.

18. Martín de Azpilcueta, *Comentario Resolutorio de Usuras* (Salamanca: Andrea de Portonarijs, 1556), 25, n. 52.

19. A thorough analysis of the CRM may be found in Ullastres (cf. note 13) and in Muñoz, *Moral y economía en la obra de Martín de Azpilcueta*, 281–337. See also Bernard and Michele Gazier, *Or et monnaie chez Martín de Azpilcueta* (Paris: Economica, 1978).

20. Cf. Carande, *Carlos V y sus banqueros*, 338; B. Aguilera Barchet, *Historia de la letra de cambio en España, seis siglos de práctica trayecticia* (Madrid: Tecnos, 1988).

21. Cf. L. Pereña, "El comentario de cambios," in *Comentario Resolutorio de Cambios*, 15–27.

Commentary on the Resolution of Money (1556)

Martín de Azpilcueta

Translation by Jeannine Emery

PREFACE

On the Beginning of the Final Chapter of *de usuris*

In order to understand what we intend to say about exchanges in our time, we state the beginning of the last chapter of *de usuris*, whose words are the following:

Gregory IX,[1] in the final chapter of *de usuris*:

> *Nauiganti, vel eunti ad nundinas certam mutuans pecuniae quantitatem, eo quod suscepit in se periculum, recepturus aliquid ultra sortem, usurarius est censendus.*

One lending a certain quantity of money to someone sailing or going to a fair, in order to receive something beyond the capital for this that he takes upon himself the peril, is to be thought a usurer.

1

Text Interpretation

Summary

If the person who takes upon himself the peril lends money to someone about to sail or transfers the money somewhere else is a usurer, and when he is such . . . **1, 2**

And what will happen if he lends something that is not money . . . **6**

This chapter has two interpretations, and which is the best one . . . **1, 2**

The example does not restrict the rule . . . **2**

If there is an affirmation about something, no denial is made of similar or contrary issues . . . **2**

Gregory IX proves to be methodical, beneficial,[1] and concise[2] . . . **2**

He often embarks upon uncertain issues . . . **3**

This means it is the truth and should be considered . . . **3**

What nautical usury is . . . **3**

Nautical usury is prohibited today . . . **4**

[Nautical usury is prohibited] in the following way . . . **6**

1. The first thing we say regarding this principle is that it has two interpretations. One belongs to the ancient doctors,[4] according to whom the words *Eo quod periculum in se suscepit: because he took on the danger*, should be joined to the participle *recepturus: hoping to receive*. Thus, the wording should be arranged as follows: *Mutuans certam pecuniae quantitatem naviganti, vel eunti ad nundinas recepturus aliquid ultra sortem, eo quod suscepit in se periculum, usurarius est censendus*. Meaning what Panormitanus's[5] summary says; that is, that the person who receives more than what he lent is a usurer even if he assumes the risk.

The other interpretation belongs to some newer authors, which we, too, followed when we read them at this most distinguished University of Salamanca in the year 1530, according to whom the words: *eo quod periculum in se suscepit: because he took on the danger* should go next to the participle *Mutuans*: the person who lends. The result of which is: *Mutuans certam pecuniae quantitatem, eo quod periculum in se suscepit, naviganti, vel eunti ad nundinas recepturus aliquid ultra sortem, usurarious est censendus*. Meaning that the person who lends money to whomever is about to head to dangerous places, under the condition that he insures it with the lender and gives him something more than the amount lent for the insurance, is a usurer.

Such is the way John Major[6] understands it, saying the gloss here is inaccurate. Such is the way Silvestre[7] also understands it, saying the Supplement did not analyze this text.

Such is the way it seems that Cajetan,[8] Medina,[9] and Soto[10] understand it.

This way of considering things makes it seem from the ancient doctors' interpretation that whoever insures a piece of merchandise that is to go through dangerous places is a usurer if he takes something for it, a practice that goes against all Christian custom, against a law that allows setting a price on insurance,[11] and against the general opinion.[12]

2. In the second place, we state that even if in the past we held this [second] interpretation because of this argument, now, however, that God allows us to judge the texts more maturely, we think the first interpretation that the gloss received given by everyone to it, is better, according to which the result is somewhat more judicious than that of the others,[13] and is as follows: The person who lends money to take it elsewhere (even if he takes the danger upon himself), should be judged a usurer if he takes for himself more than what he lent.

This is [supposed to be] a general summary, because even if the text only refers to the person who lends to the merchant or to the one who goes to the fairs the summary [refers to] him and to whomever lends to anyone who will take it elsewhere. The text does not refer to the person who lends to the merchant or to the one who goes to the fairs to indicate that this does not occur with other lenders but as a mere example or to say that it occurs with them for more important reasons.[14] If someone who lends to a person who is to undergo a sea voyage (where there are generally more dangers) is not excused of usury even if he assumes the dangers, there is less excusing the person who assumes the dangers and lends to someone who will undergo fewer perils.

If the lender of the person who goes to the fairs, often a merchant who borrows in order to make a bigger profit when he goes to the fairs by buying merchandise, is not excused, then he is even less excused if he lends to someone who is in more unfortunate circumstances.

Third, this summary and this interpretation confirm the following:

— This is the way it has been interpreted by all those who have explained it here.

— The structured text of this principle is very clear on this and cannot say what others would like to interpret without constructing it in a way that is obviously forcing the argument, as would probably happen if a person reconstructs it according to the two interpretations in an impartial way.

— This text is structured by Gregory IX, and, as such, is methodical, beneficial, concise, and well analyzed, without inaccuracies or strange constructions, and out of one hundred learned men in Latin composition who read this text—without taking into consideration whether the insurance granted by the merchants is licit or not—it would be difficult to find three who said that this text does not refer to the person who takes for himself more than what he lent for lending and insuring.

— If Gregory IX had wanted to say what is meant by those who hold the second interpretation, he would not have said: *Eo quod suscepit in se periculum: because he took on the danger*, but he said *ut susciperet in se periculum: so that he would take on the danger*. Those who hold the second interpretation say he refers to the one who lends with the agreement that the borrower will take an insurance from the lender.

— According to the construction and order that the others [the ones who hold the second interpretation] give to it, the text refers to the one who insures before lending, because it says *Mutuans eo quod suscepit in se periculum: the person who lends because he took on the danger*, and the same people who thus order the text say it refers to the one who lends under agreement that what is lent is insured with him, and consequently they presuppose what he is talking about when the loan precedes the insurance, thus contradicting themselves without realizing it. If anyone said that in some newer books not *suscepit* in the past but *suscipit* in the present appears, let him look into the old and most of the new books where *suscepit* appears, and it matters little here, as the same meaning will be found after close scrutiny.

3. Gregory IX seldom analyzes issues that are not uncertain, and there is no doubt at all that there is usury in lending to someone under an agreement that forces him to pay not only what he receives but to do something that is convenient to the lender.[15] There is no doubt that this is carried out when the borrower is forced to insure with the lender. One other thing that few notice is that Gregory IX did not say that he was referring to the usurer but to the one presumed to be a usurer, as he does not say *usurarius est*:[16] *He is a usurer*, but *usurarius est censendus*: *He should be presumed to be a usurer*, meaning that it may be possible that before God the person he is talking about may sometimes not be a usurer, but the Church should consider him such, and according to the other interpretation [the second one] it would have meant that he is a true usurer before God and the people.

According to this interpretation [the true one], there may be good reasons to disbelieve and arrive at a conclusion that, once heard, everyone will say is the truth. Because the reason for disbelieving (according to everyone's and our opinion) was that no canon text forbade usury, known as nautical or traiecticia,[17] as is practiced when one lends and insures, assuming the dangers of the trip and of getting lost at sea, which is permitted by civil law for much greater reasons than the others because of the danger that the lender takes on.[18] So, it seemed this would also be licit, according to the canons.

The reason why Gregory IX decided the opposite (even though there was disbelief) was not the reason put forth by the gloss (by Panormitanus and the others) but by the need to put an end to veiled or covert usuries carried out as insurances because many, in seeing that canon law forbade usuries in general but did not prohibit nautical ones (and this one seemed licit because of the danger that the lender took on), took to lending by assuming the risk whether there was danger or not and whether what was lent went through sea or land.

Many borrowed saying they did so to carry it for themselves or for others across the sea, or across such and such mountains, or beyond the kingdom, and so forth, in order to find someone who would lend them money interested in what they would gain for the feigned insurance. Even others, who really wanted to borrow to go through those places and did not want to insure it, were forced to insure because the lenders did not want to lend without a profit. Because they could not obtain a profit for lending, they wanted to cover it up and conceal it as insurance. This is the reason why Gregory IX ordered that whoever lent money and obtained more for it (even if he insured it) was to be judged a usurer, even if he said that the money he gave and took was on account of the insurance. This was certainly a very prudent ruling because if the nautical usury were allowed to someone who lent with an insurance, then everyone would give and borrow with an insurance—some saying truthfully and some falsely—that they were borrowing to carry it by sea or through dangerous lands.

4. By the same ruling, it has been ordered not long ago in these kingdoms and in those of Portugal that there shall be no exchange from one city in the kingdom to another because it is presumed that there are veiled usuries, as we will explain later.[19] By this same ruling, it is determined that when someone buys something for a price inferior to what it is worth, under agreement that he will give it back for the same price whenever he feels like it, it be considered a loan and pawn and not a sale in the external jurisdiction.[20]

Also, not only are the other usuries forbidden today by canon law, but even those known as nautical[21] (as the ones mentioned above such as Hostiensis[22] stated), which here nobody contradicts, with which Saliceto[23] agrees, and which saying Ioannes Annanias[24] declares he shares, concluded that this text corrects a chapter of civil law.[25]

Yet, if we took into account the other interpretation [the second one], we should then declare that they [nautical usuries] are [more] licit than illicit because this text would not prove them to be illicit, and there is not another in the world that proves them to be so—at least outwardly. Finally, it is compelling to hold that the principle of this most solemn chapter would not insist in attaining an uncertain resolution, which would be useless and superfluous, as there is no student with three years of canon study who doubts that it is usury to lend money to another under the obligation of insuring it with him. Saying this of Gregory IX's text is irreverent and insolent temerity.

5. Fourth, we say that it does not contradict at all the argument that we noted earlier and one day seemed to us impossible to work out, as it seemed to the aforementioned, who moved away from this common interpretation, that is, that from our common understanding follows that whoever insures merchandise that will pass through dangerous places is a usurer if he takes something for it. This practice goes against all of Christianity's customs, against a law[26] that sets a price for insuring, and against the general opinion.[27]

We say that it does not contradict this [argument] because we deny that this reasoning derives from this interpretation. The only reasoning that originated [from the first interpretation] is that whoever lends money and takes more than what he lent (even if he insures it) must be considered a usurer. Our interpretation differs from what the argument implies in three aspects:

— The first: It does not include the person who insures without lending, and the other does.
— The second: It does not include the person who lends something that is not money, and the other does.
— The third: Stating this [that the usurer is the one who lends money and takes more than what he lends, even if he insures] is not stating that that person is a usurer but that he should be presumed a usurer, and holding the other view is saying that he is a usurer.

If you should reply with what Saint Antonino stated—that someone who helps others by lending should not be judged as a more inferior human being than someone who does not lend, and, thus, there is no reason why he should not insure and receive something for insuring such as another—we answer, conceding that before God and in one's own conscience (where only truth is seen and the penitent is believed), that it is licit for the lender and insurer to take an amount of money as much as another who does not lend but insures for the insurance. However, in the external jurisdiction, he is worse off, presuming that the insurance is carried out to cover and conceal the usury and to screen under goodness what in truth means that he is taking more for lending than for insuring. Because of this, Gregory did not say here that he is a usurer but that he should be presumed a usurer. This was also Adrian VI's[28] opinion (if I am not mistaken).

All this means that if the merchant who sells a piece of cloth on credit for the fair highest price to someone who later sells it for less to the same merchant who pays less money for it by giving a fair lower price does not commit usury nor sin before God, he would easily be presumed a usurer before men for what we explained in the *Manual*.[29] This would be so even if in selling it on credit for a fair price he helped out more than another who did not sell it. Accordingly, if someone else who did not sell it to him nor did him any good, bought it from him, even for a lower price than what the merchant bought it from him, he would not be, nor presumed to be, a usurer.

The tutor and guardian cannot buy[30] such things from their subordinates, just as the other people nor the temporal judges can buy those things belonging to their subjects.[31] This would be so even if they do more good than the others, and are legally in a worse off condition than the rest, in order to avoid frauds, at least in the external jurisdiction.

6. The fifth thing we state is that from all this we conclude that if the penitent confesses that he lent money to someone who wanted to insure it to carry it across the sea or through other dangerous places, and with no other agreement or force he insured it for what others would insure it, the penitent should not be forced to restitute anything. However, if he were to confess that he took a larger amount for having lent the money or an amount for having lent the money with the insurance, he should restitute the part he took for the loan. This would also be so if he did not want to lend unless the money was insured with another with whom he shared the profit, as this same chapter proves according to the second interpretation, which, as far as these issues are concerned, is judged to be true.

Another conclusion is that this text does not refer to the person who lends and insures other merchandise. One reason is because it only refers to the person lending money, as the pope used the Latin word *pecunia*, which, even if in its general sense means money and any other goods,[32] according to the particular sense, it means only money.[33] In order to indicate that he was using the special meaning in this chapter, the pope did not leave it alone but added some words to it, saying, *certam pecuniae quantitatem*, meaning that he only wanted to apply this rule to those lending an amount of money and not to those lending other goods.

Also, this text—which is far-reaching and deviates from the right road inasmuch as it proposes a new interpretation (they call it *iuris et de iure*) whose opposite cannot be proved[34] (that the person who lends and insures and takes more than what he lent is presumed to take it for lending and thus should be considered a usurer)—should be narrowed[35] and not broadened.

It should also be narrowed because the same reason cannot be found for the one who lends money as for the one who lends other things. This is generally because these other things are appraised, sold, and not lent. This is partly because it is difficult to do as much fraud with goods as with money because there are few to whom they can be given and few who can take them and do fraud without shameful defamation. Only the dealers (and not all of them but only those who deal at sea or in different kingdoms) can take hold of them without it seeming to be fraud. Yet money can be taken by the big, the small, and the medium sized, pretending they will send it to Flanders or out of the kingdom for relatives, friends, business, or their own or someone else's fortune. There is no reason why fraud should be done with these other things because if an unfair profit is wanted, they can increase their price.

7. The sixth issue is that which we said earlier should be interpreted: Nautical usuries are forbidden today by the canon law in this distinct text. It should be understood that they are completely forbidden in the external jurisdiction, if they are carried out for a loan of money, and also in one's own conscience, if and as long as they are carried out for lending money or any other thing. This does not hold true as long as they are carried out only for insuring, providing one charges what another charges only for insuring, which is a new and extraordinary resolution.

Against Molinaeus,[36] this most extraordinary text, which we again praise, declares that it is not only a sin to lend with usury to the needy who take it to sustain themselves but also to lend to the rich and merchants who use it to make a bigger profit, because it is evident that those who borrow to take it across the sea or to fairs are not usually poor people who borrow to support themselves. Concerning this, Gregory IX says that not even with these can those who lend money carry out usury, even if they insure it.

It follows, too, that the guarantor[37] may collect something for guaranting, because he does not lend money and does what the insurer does, although the insurer collects from the person who is insured [the lender], and the guarantor collects what is owed to him from the person against whom the insurance is taken [the person representing the risk or borrower].

Even if Laurencio[38] is not too sure of this, there is nothing to worry about—except when there is fraud. This would be the case if I did not want to lend you any money and if you did not give me *N* for guarantor with whom I have agreed that he take from you a certain amount that we will divide by two or that he transfer the amount to me; thus releasing himself from the guaranty. Or, this would be the case if I did not want to lend to you without a profit, and then I send my brother or someone else to whom I have sent money so that he lends it to you under agreement that you take me for guarantor, but then I do not want to give a guarantee if you do not pay me an amount.

8. It is true what Ioannes Annanias[39] says that exchanges are illicit because to give in Rome 100 hard-and-fast *ducats* that are picked up here is a manner of insurance. All exchanges should not be considered illicit because of some that are illicit. Therefore, it is very difficult to set apart these from the others[40] [the licit ones] about which we have not said anything either in the *Manual* or anywhere else. We will now work with the required[41] assistance in the beginning of the other *Commentary*, trying to be as resolute and brief as in the others, adding: (1) what exchanging is, (2) how it is divided, and (3) what types are licit.

2

Concept and Types of Exchanges

Summary

What does it mean to exchange? What is not selling or buying? What happens with all saleable goods, even with money? . . . **9**

What exchanges are licit . . . **9**

The common people in Spain refer to exchanging both in a stricter sense and in a wider sense than what the law does . . . **10**

Exchanging may be divided into the exchanging of money and the exchanging of other goods . . . **9**

What is the exchanging of money in dry exchange and real exchange; in fair, unfair, and doubtful exchange; and in pure and impure exchange, according to some? . . . **10**

Exchanging can be divided better into seven categories: to exchange for small coinage, for bills of exchange, by transference, by buying, by bartering, for an interest, and by safekeeping . . . **10**

9. The eighth thing we add, then, is that to exchange, also called *Cambium* in Latin, is to change one thing for another, which the jurisconsults commonly call barter.[1]

The first point is that, strictly speaking, exchanging is not buying[2] or selling or depositing or lending—*Mutuum* in Latin. Nor is it what is called *Commodatum*, or renting or leasing. It is more of an *innominate* contract, which in many things differs from the above mentioned.[3]

Second, strictly speaking, exchanging is generally divided into the exchanging of money and the exchanging of other goods. Even if it seems more natural to exchange one natural thing for another natural thing—as when a coin is exchanged for another coin or something else and not as price or money but as a piece of gold, silver, or metal—exchanging can also be considered when one changes coins for coins as long as one is not given for the price of the other but in exchange of it. All things that can be sold can also be exchanged,[4] and money can be sold as we will see later.[5] This happens every day with coins of different value or metal, as everyone confesses, and even (according to those who study this) with coins of the same metal and value when one is in one land and the other elsewhere. This happens even when they are both in the same place, but one is near and the other is not. It also happens when one seems better because it is beautiful, because it is antique, or because of some other reason that motivates the person who wants to obtain it by barter, as every day it is evident that a *real*,[6] a *ducat*,[7] a *doubloon*,[8] and an *angelot*[9] seem lovelier than another of these.

10. The third issue is that the vernacular language from Spain and the vernacular Latin of some Scholastics today do not use the word *exchange* in as wide a sense as its original meaning. Instead, they use another more frequently. According to the original meaning, every barter is exchange and every exchange is barter. However, the vernacular does not call every barter exchange but only the barter of money for money. It also uses the word *exchange* to refer to many contracts, which are not specifically exchanges but are, rather, buying, renting, and other innominate contracts. So, to exchange (as the vernacular understands it) is every kind of contract of money for money, which is not gratuitous, be it a barter, a purchase, a deposit, or anything else. It is also important to differentiate between the Spanish vernacular and the Code of Law,[10] which considers all and only barter and permutation an exchange.[11]

Thus, exchanging, as the vernacular understands it, can be divided, according to Saint Antonino[12] (whom the theologians who have later written about the subject have followed), into real exchange and dry exchange. According to them, dry exchange is an imaginary kind of exchange, which in fact is no exchange at all. Laurencio who has also addressed[13] this issue is more accurate when he says that dry exchange is when the exchanger gives before receiving, and because he does not receive but gives it is called dry. According to Cajetan,[14] it can also be divided into clearly fair exchange and clearly unfair and dubious exchange. According to others, it can be divided into pure and impure exchange. Some, such as Medina,[15] call those [exchanges] that do not have elements of other contracts, pure exchange. Soto,[16] however, calls them pure when there is no mixture of unfairness and impure when there is. Yet all these categories are not very useful and are very confusing. That is why it seems more useful to say that there are seven categories, species, or methods of exchange:

1. by profession or work to be offered[17]
2. for small coinage[18]
3. by bills of exchange[19]
4. by true transference[20]
5. with an interest[21]
6. by safekeeping[22]
7. by buying,[23] bartering, or any other innominate contract

These categories are easier to understand, and they make the subject broader. This is what the real and dry, the clearly fair and clearly unfair and dubious, and the pure and impure come down to. We will explain each one so that by their motives and rules everyone's questions may be answered.

3

The Origin and Functions of Money

Summary

Exchanging is prior to buying and selling . . . **11**

What was money created for? What is its main purpose and
use? . . . **11**

What is the art of exchanging? When and why is it licit?
. . . **11**

Money is useful for many contracts, and it has eight
purposes and uses . . . **12**

A simulated contract is judged by what it is, and not for what
is feigned . . . **12**

11. Regarding [paragraph] nine, we state that the exchange or barter of goods
that are not money (as was said most correctly by Paul,[1] the jurisconsult) is a much
earlier operation than buying and selling, which began after money was introduced.
Before money came into existence, if someone owned a good and was in need of
another, he looked for someone who had it and wanted to exchange it for his possession. This was the case, for example, when someone had wine and wool, but
not wheat nor shoes, and looked for someone with wheat and shoes who wanted
to exchange them for his wine and wool. This is the case even today with some
foreigners with whom the Spanish and others deal.

After a time, money was discovered, which was certainly a very necessary discovery on the one hand. On the other, I am not sure if today it destroys souls because of greed; bodies because of wars, travels, and terrifying pilgrimages; and even itself and the fleets where it travels because of horrifying storms and shipwrecks. The main use and purpose in creating money was as a means of payment in order to buy and sell with it the necessary things for human life,[2] so that it would become a public measure [common standard] of goods to be sold.[3] After this, coins of a metal or value started being bartered for coins of another metal or another value, such as the thick one for the thin one and the thin one for the thick one. Later, because the currency of a land was worth less there than somewhere else (as today almost all the gold and silver currency from Spain is worth less there than in Flanders and France), the art of exchanging started, which is the art of dealing with currency. By giving and taking one for another, money started getting transferred from where it was worth least to where it was worth most. As happens in our time, many people have increased their fortune, taking to Flanders and France *ducats* in groups of two, four, and ten, some in small barrels, pretending they are olives, some in wine barrels, making a big profit with each one. In turn, they brought from those places merchandise that was worth little over there but had great value over here, thus helping with one but hurting us much with the other.

Aristotle[4] thought it was wrong to exchange and trade with money because he did not think this third use of money was natural nor brought any benefit to the republic nor had any other purpose but that of profit, which is an end without an end. Saint Thomas[5] said that any art of exchange whose main purpose was only to obtain profit was illicit. Saint Thomas[6] himself, however, declares that the art of exchange is licit if its purpose is a moderate profit to support oneself and one's home and if the art of exchange brings about some benefit to the republic. We say that if it is exercised as it should be and the purpose of the profit is directed to honestly and moderately support oneself and one's home, then it is licit. It is not true that using money to obtain a profit by exchanging it goes against its very nature because, even if it is a different use than the first and main one for which it was created, it is still apt for a less principal and secondary use. This happens, for example, when shoes are used to make a profit, which, although is a different use than the primary one for which they were created (which was to wear on feet), does not go against their very nature.

12. Money has eight different purposes. The first three are the ones already mentioned.[7] The fourth is to display one's riches,[8] showing it to everyone or putting it in the marketplace where it is dealt with or exchanged. The fifth is to use it as medals and clothing decorations. The sixth use is to cheer with its presence.[9] The seventh use is to cure some illnesses with its broth as, they say,[10] is one of the properties of gold powder. The eighth use is as security for a debt. For these last five purposes, it is possible not only to lend and exchange money but even to rent it out. Thus, money may be given by way of many contracts: by way of price for a purchased good; by way of merchandise sold for another money; by way of innominate contract of barter or other, exchanging it for something else or for money; by way of lending called *Mutuum*, when something else is given back and not the same thing; by way of lending called *Commodatum*, in order to get back the same thing given; by way of security for what is owed; and by way of rental of a sum so that the same amount that was given is returned, after the person who borrows it takes advantage of its use, by showing his riches, or enjoying its presence, or using its broth, or giving it as security, and so forth.

It can be taken[11] by as many ways as it can be given. Because the nature of the above-mentioned contracts, by which it is possible to give and take money, is diverse, so there are diverse law regulations that determine if and when they are licit or not. If money is given by way of buying and selling, it cannot be given but for what something else is worth.[12] The same goes for when it is given by way of exchange or barter.[13]

If it is given by way of loan or if it is given as security for one's own loan (whether the same or another is given back), neither a small nor a big sum can be charged.[14] If rented out to enliven or honor with its presence or to cure with its broth or to use as security for someone else's debt, an honest rent may be taken[15] because the nature of this contract is not to transfer the ownership but only the appraised use of money according to the amount of time for which it was taken. It is important to understand what truly happens than what is feigned to happen.[16] Every time one of these contracts is carried out truthfully and another is feigned, one should judge not by the rules of the feigned one but by the [rules of the] true one. Thus, if the exchanger truly lends his money, he cannot take anything for this operation, even if he feigns he is exchanging it or renting it out.

4

Just and Licit Exchange

Summary

Exchanging, bartering money, or other things of dissimilar
value is illicit . . . **13**

The exchanger as exchanger may not take more than what
he gives but only what is regulated . . . **13**

The exchanger or barterer, for just being [exchanger or
barterer], cannot take more than what he should because
of his profession, et cetera. However, he can certainly
barter what he does not have yet for something the other
person has . . . **14**

The contract where more or less is given or taken for
advancing or selling on credit is usurious . . . **14**

13. We go on to add that in order to make buying and selling just activities,
it is necessary that what is bought is worth an equal price to what is being paid
for it, and, conversely, that the price paid for it is equal to the goods' worth.[1] For
any rental to be just, it is necessary that the use of the item that is rented out is
worth the price given for it, and, conversely, that the price paid for it corresponds
to what it is worth. So, too,[2] in order for the exchange or barter to be just and licit,

it is necessary that what one party gives to the other has the same value as what is being received.

From this it follows that if the purchase of a mule worth 100 *ducats* for 80 or 120 is unfair, as is the renting of a house, the use of which is worth 50 *ducats* a year, for 40 or 60, so the barter of a beast that is not worth 6 *ducats* for another worth 10 is not just. Nor is the exchange or barter of 10 *ducats* in *reales* for 12 *tarjas*[3] licit.

The logical outcome of this is that every time the exchangers carry out a true exchange and barter of money for money, they cannot take more than what the [money] they give is worth for the barter and exchange, and some little thing that is usually offered for bartering one currency for another after it is counted. It may happen though that on some occasion, for other factors that interfere in making it a less pure type of exchange, something may be taken, as we will explain later. If the inequality of bartered things makes illicit the exchange and barter of natural things—among which the barter is more legitimate or at least more natural[4]—more so will [the inequality of the bartered things] make illicit the barter of money, which being money is something artificial, not created in the first place to exchange one [piece of money] for another, but as price[5] [unit of measure of the value of things] that, wherever one went, might be taken in order to buy whatever was needed.

14. No money exchanger may take for himself more than what he otherwise could for giving his money before the other person gives him his and waiting to be paid a month or two, or more, or until the next fair.[6] Nor can the opposite happen. Another can licitly give the exchanger some money under agreement that in a year, or in three months, or when the next fair takes place, he gets back that money and an added amount, or he gets something done [by him] that by its very nature is worth money. Whenever more than the principal is given or taken for reason of the time elapsed, or for waiting, or for advancing the payment, it becomes a veiled loan and contains a veiled usury, as we have already said elsewhere.[7] Just as the person who gives a mule today so that another that is worth much more is given to him in three, four, or six months, is a usurer, so also the person who gives some money today so that in three, four, or six months a larger sum is bestowed on him, is a usurer.

It is not necessary to do what some people[8] require, which is that the goods that one will barter or exchange with someone else's be produced now and belong now to the person who wants to barter them. First, there are no documents or motives that prove this to be necessary. Second, just as it is possible to buy,[9] pawn,[10] promise,[11] and send[12] what is yet to be born, so it is possible to barter in this way, at least the general barter, which in this is the same as the special one.

Silvestre[13] himself confesses that if I want to licitly barter and exchange 10 *ducats* in Lisbon with 10 *ducats* paid here, it is not necessary that when you give me the 10 *ducats* here that I have them in Lisbon. It is sufficient that I can borrow them over there with an interest, or in some other way, when the time comes to give them to you over there.

Also, if I barter with you 100 pounds of oil that I have here for the same amount or more of oil that you give me in Lisbon, it is not necessary that I give them to you at the same time as you have them there. It is enough that you have them when it is time to give them to me. There is no truth in saying that in order for a barter to take place, it is necessary to barter a specific thing for another specific thing. In the first place, even if this is required for the special barter, it is not for the general one. Second, if this were necessary, almost no merchant who took money in Medina to send to Flanders, or the other way around in Flanders to send to Medina, would do a true exchange,[14] as neither one (even if he had a lot of money where he is supposed to give it) hands those *ducats*, *reales*, or *tostones*[15] over.

Although it is true that in order for the barter to be completed on both sides, and neither side to be sorry for having carried it out, it is not only necessary to give the other party what they want but also that both parties have rendered the delivery, as bartering is an innominate contract. It is not necessary for both parties to have rendered the delivery in order for the bartering contract to be valid, as the other contracts that are not innominate are valid before the delivery is made either on both parts or on one side.[16]

5

Exchanging as a Profession

Summary

Can the person who devotes himself to exchanging as a profession and lending as a job take something for himself? There are seven arguments defending this action . . . **15**

And others against it . . . **16**

Conclusion with other arguments in defense, under certain circumstances, and so forth . . . **17, 18**

The business of lending gratuitously may be established by the republic . . . **15**

The judge, priest, and witness may not receive for the following, but for these other reasons, and so forth . . . **15**

The priest for going to say mass elsewhere or being there to say it today may take something . . . **15, 16**

The business of lending moderate usuries is illicit . . . **16**

When Mounts of Piety[1] and the business of lending turn out to be different . . . **16**

An argument that is based on what it wants to conclude is
   not sound . . . **15**

The one who is forced to lend to the republic deserves a
   salary, and what this implies . . . **17**

There are licit businesses that may not be practiced privately
   but may be done so publicly . . . **18**

15. There is great doubt as to whether it is licit to practice the first type of exchange as a profession and to work as a lender. Cajetan[2] says he had a few cases where the exchanger, as long as he was a lender who offered to lend to those who needed money, could receive an amount of money for a certain amount lent for a certain period of time (according to the virtuous man's free will) for the work and diligence put into looking for, keeping, and taking care of a large amount of money, which are necessary for carrying all this out and then for keeping account, taking guaranties, and assuming dangers and anxiety. This is what Durando[3] and Medina[4] agree on too. They believe in the first place that the so-called lender does not get anything for lending but for the work he offers to do, which is undeniably great, and it is true that there is no usury when a greater amount than what was lent is taken for another just and different reason from lending.[5] In the second place, [they believe that] the person who is in charge of exchanging one currency for another that will be paid at a later date, may be given something for that business and work,[6] and the same reason seems to apply in this case.

In the third place, according to Scotus,[7] the republic may determine the existence of a money lender who lends for a certain amount and for a certain period of time. This is licit if it is ordered by the republic. If it is licit, and not forbidden, anyone can borrow and take advantage of him, paying a fair amount for it, according to Scotus[8] himself.

The fourth issue is that the judge, priest, and witness who may not receive anything for their rulings,[9] sacraments, and testimony may receive something for their sustenance and the work they carry out. Fifth, when the exchanger lends to someone, he is prevented from dealing, and thus, he may take for himself an interest for profit as we state in another commentary[10] and down below.[11] Sixth, the clergyman may take more for going to say mass some miles[12] away, or for going today, than if he said it here or by chance.[13] Seventh, as we have seen in another commentary[14] that the Mounts of Piety are licit, and in them the poor people who borrow money are allowed to give a certain amount according to the amount borrowed so that every month there is money to pay for the salary of those carrying the burden of caring for the money, keeping accounts, and standing ready to loan.

16. Others[15] hold the opposite view because it seems that it is the same to say this as to say that it may be ordered and even without ordinance carry out the art and business of lending under moderate usuries, which seems to go against the Gospel's spirit, as well as the natural and canon law, and against all the interpreters and doctors of them. For this consideration alone, they say all reasons said against this can be settled. If the profession is not licit, neither will it be licit to take a salary for it, or for the work needed to carry it out, or for preparing everything that is needed.

Nor can anything be deduced from the profession of judge, witness, ecclesiastic, and chaplain for this, because those are licit, but this is not. That is why it does not follow that if for the responsibility, work, and maintenance of these something must be given, so, too, should something be given for lenders. Additionally, because they hold that the Mounts of Piety are not licit, they do not have to reply to the seventh argument, which seems one of the strongest. Even if we consider that they are licit, there is still a big difference between [lending] and the Mounts of Piety, because in lending there is a profit that is looked for and wanted, whereas it is not there where only compensation for the one in charge of it [is sought for] so that he does not have to offer gratuitously from his house his valued work, care, and industriousness. In a loan, the money belongs to the lender, and to him belongs its safekeeping; in the Mounts of Piety the money belongs to the poor or to someone else who gives it to the poor, and they are the safe keepers. What they give or pay is very small, and is brought together with a donation or just contribution and according to the profit obtained by the one who takes [money]. Because of this and other reasons, one may not infer this [i.e., that it is licit to carry out the art and business of lending under moderate usuries] from that [i.e., the Mounts of Piety].

The other opinion [i.e., it is licit to take moderate usuries for the profession of lending] does not sound to us as insubstantial as they suggest. First, their opinion is based on assuming as certain what is precisely in doubt. What is in doubt (at least implicitly) is if that profession is licit or not. The opposing viewpoint holds it is licit, but they hold it is not.[16] Also, they do not respond to the first argument: that there is no usury when more is not taken than what is given for lending, although something more can be taken for a good and just reason. Soto himself confesses somewhere else[17] that one can licitly take a salary when one is forced to lend to the republic every time it is in need.

17. From Soto's opinion[18] what cannot be denied (to our way of thinking) is that the republic might give a certain salary to someone required to collect money and have a certain amount ready to lend to those in need of it once a year and to collect it from someone else to lend it in turn to others. Thus, a person who was forced to do all this would take that salary every year, not essentially for lending, but for being required to own the amount of money to lend and to suffer the above mentioned troubles and worries.

Additionally, it should be established that it is licit and useful that the republic have someone forced to gratuitously lend a certain amount every year, and it cannot be denied that the republic may give a just salary to the person in charge of that business, as Doctor Scotus's excellent words[19] advocate.

Also, if the business of gratuitously lending to the poor is licit, and if for the licit business the republic may make a salary mandatory, it may order a salary for this business and thus charge a sum from those who take advantage of that business and position. Consequently, it may order that they pay the republic a salary in proportion to their loan or a wage that is part (according to the extent to which they profited) of that salary. Consequently, in order not to waste any time or have extra expenses, those who took advantage of this would pay that amount to the person in that position, depending on the amount they took, and on the length of time for which they borrowed.

Also, the reasons and authority of the Holy See—because of which in another commentary[20] we concluded that the Mounts of Piety were licit, holy, and worthy of praise—conclude this, too, to be licit.

Therefore, if there may be licitly someone appointed to be in charge of the exchange for small coinage because it is licit and useful (according to what will be said later) and he may licitly take a salary from the republic or from those who profit from the position according to the profit they gain, as is carried out, [then] for the same reason will the above mentioned be licit.

18. For these reasons (except the due correction) we bring into agreement both opinions in the following manner: The first determines that the republic set up with its authority the mentioned profession, and we even dare to hope kings and princes provide their republics with such lenders that are made to do what we said above and be forbidden under heavy penalties to take more than what is determined by your Highnesses. However, the habit of wrongly earning too much money will make it difficult to find someone who wants to earn a just salary.

The second should be applied to the person who assumes the profession of lending without having permission to carry it out by private authority. It does not follow that because the profession is in itself licit, each one may take hold of it with no other authority and take for his sustenance whatever would be reasonable for the republic or for its prince, according to Scotus's[21] excellent presumptions. Consequently, in everything, Durando's[22] and Medina's[23] opinions are correct. So we say that it should not follow. First, because Durando and Medina refer also to the one who has not been allowed [to carry out the profession] [and] who has other motives than the one who has permission to do so. This is the main argument behind our belief that this profession is licit and a salary may be taken for it. Also, if these reasons ever proved that it would be licit before God and in one's own conscience to practice this profession with a holy purpose (even without the permission) and to take advantage of it, taking less money than the person forced to practice it, before men and in the external jurisdiction, he should be judged a usurer to avoid greater frauds, which would be committed under cover of piety according to what we have said above[24] about the lender and insurer.

6

Exchange for Small Coinage[1]

Summary

Exchanging for small coinage is licit and is useful for the
republic. A public officer may be appointed for it, with a
salary . . . **19**

The difference between his position and the exchanger's
. . . **19**

Someone may be in charge of exchanging, and not be a
public officer . . . **19**

Money may be exchanged according to its intrinsic value,
even if it is not worth that amount by law . . . **20**

Money that is appreciated by law is worth more for its
exceptional utility . . . **20**

Exchanging for small coinage is illicit in certain
circumstances . . . **20**

19. According to everyone,[2] it is licit to exchange for small coinage, which
is exchanging large for small currency and small for large, such as 1 *ducat* for 11
reales or 375 *maravedis*, or the other way around, exchanging 11 *reales* or 375
maravedis for a *ducat*. Because the republic would benefit greatly from having a

public officer in this position, it may order a just salary to that person.[3] The republic would take his payment from the public income or order that those who make use of the service of exchanging or bartering hand over a percentage to him. As it is ordered in these kingdoms,[4] for the exchange of 1 *Castilian*,[5] 4 *maravedis* may be taken; and for the *ducat* and *dobla*,[6] 3; and for the *florin*,[7] 2.

According to the law of these regions,[8] this position may go to any exchanger as by its name, too, it is suggested. The law though, establishes a difference between the public officer and the exchanger. The exchanger's job is to weigh[9] all currency in gold and silver, to say what each is worth, and to settle the amount between the parties who are taking and giving the money. In Seville, this person may not be an exchanger, nor have any money to barter, nor take any remuneration for weighing it. Instead, he should own a house, scales, and receive a salary from the republic.[10] There was a person who was employed in both positions (I do not know what his fee was) in this very renowned Salamanca in those very rich days of gold, and, when I was university professor in Canon Law. He [the exchanger], for the trade of a 24-carat gold *doubloon* took 2 *maravedis* that remained from the 22 *reales*, and for 22 *reales* and 4 *maravedis* he gave a *doubloon* from those same ones.

Cajetan says[11] that no other person who is not in that public position may take this excess licitly. We disagree, as do Medina and Soto disagree for their own reasons because of the trouble and work that go into [this type of barter]—going to the chamber, opening the safe box, counting once and again, and putting the money away, all of which are activities that may be assessed in monetary terms.[12]

However, some say[13] that it is forbidden in these kingdoms for any private individual to take anything more for exchanging small coinage, although we do not think so. In the first place, these people do not claim any law that bans this. Second, the laws that refer to these matters only forbid[14] anyone from taking on the position of exchanger to publicly exercise the business of exchanger without public authorization. Nor can he be a foreigner, even if this person owns the citizenship.[15] Third, the Pragmática[16] clearly states three times that the exchanger and any other person may take an extra amount for making the exchange.

20. However, it might be possible to prohibit—if it were convenient—that the price of money not be altered so much and that the large currency not be taken out of the country. In order for someone to barter his large pieces of money for small ones with a profit, we have seen foreigners in Portugal give to the natives in private much more than what the gold coins were worth in order to take them to another kingdom; thus bringing about great damage to the first one.

We also believe that the person who has some very fine gold coins may sell them or exchange them as coins and pieces of gold. He may take for himself something more of what they are worth (according to what the law establishes) from the person who wants them to gild something, or use it for medicines and other things, as long as they are really worth more because of what they are made of, or, if by giving them, he loses the advantages he was enjoying that are worth the same or more than what is being paid in excess.[17]

This was a frequent practice in Toulouse, France, in our time, whereby those who had the gold coins sold them for gilding to the knife owners, who bought the *cruzados*[18] in Portugal (no longer found there) at an even higher price than the *ducats* with two faces from these kingdoms, which no longer appear on them. Medina[19] does not agree with this and goes against the norm without a good solid reason for doing it. This opinion (also held by Soto)[20] is based on the fact that even if the republic has increased the value of that coin in a certain amount for its principal use (that of being a price for things), and if no one can sell wheat (justly appreciated) for more than that fixed price, and if nobody can be forced to give the money for more than what it is appraised, there are other uses for it for other particular reasons, which the law calls exceptional utility.[21] The one who owns the coins may take from the one to whom he gives them an extra amount.[22]

However, this exchange, which in itself is the most natural of all, may turn illicit if the exchanger takes more for himself than what for just law or custom is owed to him; if he gives false money, a mistaken percentage, or is delayed in giving his part to the person who is requiring the exchange; if he is deceiving as far as the value of the gold piece is concerned when the one who barters ignores what the Pragmática in these kingdoms[23] has determined; and finally, if the person who receives the exchange does not pay the exchanger what is owed to him.[24]

7

Exchanging for Bills of Exchange

Summary

Exchanging for bills of exchange is licit. How to do it and the reason for its name . . . **21**

It is a contract but without a name . . . **22**

It is an innominate contract: Sometimes I give to you so that you give me something back; other times I give to you so that you do something for me . . . **22**

Contracts with a name and that are to receive a name are all similar in that they require equality . . . **23**

Exchanging for bills of exchange is illicit when more than the fair salary is taken or less than the fair salary is given for lending on credit or advancing, and restitution is required . . . **24**

Worse is the contract that is feigned for a later date and is really for today . . . **25**

Contracts where there is no equality, or more is given or taken for lending on credit or advancing, are unjust . . . **24**

21. It is also licit, according to everyone, to practice the third type of exchange, which is to exchange for bills of exchange. This is a virtual transference of money by which if someone wants an amount of money in another land, he gives it in this one or does something that is worth that amount, or partly does and partly gives to the exchanger or to anyone else who has money or credit in the other place. He then receives bills of exchange for which an amount of money is given to him over there that is equal to the amount he gave or what he did over here. He will also give a sum as profit for arranging that the money be given over there in exchange for the bills of exchange.

This is called "exchange for bills of exchange" because it is usually carried out with these certificates, although it is also practiced through a messenger or the person himself who goes to that other place and gives the amount.

This contract is just and much praised by Baldo,[1] although he does not give a special name to it, nor do we believe it has one, as it greatly conforms to Calderini's,[2] and to that of the wisest jurists' opinions. However, if we had to come up with a name for this type of exchange, it would be that of a purchase or sale agreement; exchange or barter; loan or rent of work, labor, industry; and credit to or from another in order to hand over the money where it is needed. However, it is none of these properly and purely. First, none of the substantial things of any of these is completely or by itself included in this type of exchange [we are referring to]. Second, out of one hundred people who exchange in this way, there are not four who think they are buying or selling, lending or borrowing money, bartering, or renting work and labor from the exchanger in order to receive it someplace else. Contracts, after all, depend on the contracting parties' intention.[3]

22. If it were any of the above-mentioned [kinds of contracts], it would be that of [a contract] renting the work and industry of transferring something from one place to another from another [person]. This, however, is not so. In this case, the ownership of the thing to be transferred[4] is not passed on to the person who is to transfer it, and in this one [the new type of exchange we are referring to] it is—the ownership of the money that is to be transferred and is given to the exchanger is bestowed on him. However, it is the kind of contract that does not have a special name, which the jurisconsults call[5] innominate. It can consist of (1) giving so that you give to me, (2) giving so that you do something for me, and (3) giving so that you give and do[6] [for me]. In other cases, (1) I do so that you give or do, or (2)

I do and give so that you give and do, and so forth. I give you the money here so that you give me bills of exchange or do something so that they give them to me, or you yourself give me the same amount [of money] in that other place, for which I pay you a just salary on account of your work,[7] industry, and credit, which you have already offered and now will offer again and make others offer so that I receive in that other place.

23. When contracts with a special name differ in other things from contracts without a specific name,[8] they do agree with them in that in order [for both types of contract] to be just, they also require that what is given or done by one of the parties is worth as much as what is given or done by the other party. According to Scotus's solemn rule:[9] In every contract that is properly such where one party gives to another and there is not an intention to do it for free, there must be equality between what one party gives or does and what the other gives or does. Consequently, in order for this contract to be licit, it is necessary that what is given to the exchanger for conferring a document that makes someone else give money to its holder in another place is a just salary, and he not take more than what is due.[10] In order to know which salary is just and which one is unjust for being too great or too small, one must appeal to the law, and if there is none and then to custom if there is one. If both are lacking, then to the good and prudent man's free will.[11]

24. Consequently, in the first place, unjust exchanges that are mortally evil are those where the exchanger takes more than his fair salary, even if he sells on credit to the person who does not have any money and will give it back at a later date. The more he takes for having to wait for longer periods of repayment, the worse [these exchanges] are. Also [unjust and evil] are those [exchanges] where the exchanger takes more than his fair salary if he orders that the money be given right away in that other place for where it is required, even if he is satisfied with him for having the money returned three or four months later.

[Unjust and mortally evil are] also those exchanges where, on the contrary, those who give the money a year or half a year before [do it] under agreement that the exchanger will not take a fair salary later for giving it to them over there. We see many religious and wise men making mistakes on this issue, and there is proof of such contracts. In all these cases, either the just salary is not paid, or too much is paid, or for giving or taking the money sooner or later more or less is taken from the just price. The reason they are wrong is because of the already[12] stated rule: All contracts that are unequal are unjust. This is also true because of another stated[13] rule in this commentary as well as in another:[14] All contracts where more than the highest fair price is taken in ready money, or less than the lowest fair price is taken in ready money are formally or visually usurious.

25. In the second place, there is another evil type of exchange according to everyone and especially unjust, according to Cajetan.[15] It is those exchanges that we see every day carried out with kings, noblemen, dealers, and others who take money from the exchangers and give them documents so that they are paid in Rome, Lisbon, León, Flanders, Venice, or other places in a certain amount of time or at a certain fair. Both parties know that the person who is taking it does not have, in that other place, the money, credit, agent, nor intention to pay over there but rather here, where they take it for the price that it is worth in that other fair for which they supposedly took it. The exchanges are worse if the person who takes the money here promises to pay for the exchange in the other place, and then for a new exchange back here if the documents are not valid over there, whereupon the exchanger sends his documents over there, and they return back here notified to whom they are sent with their response that they ignore who is sending the documents, or that they do not want to fulfill their obligations. In the first type of these two exchanges a usury is paid; in the second, two usuries are paid.

26. Also [illicit] are the exchanges where someone gives money to another party who promises to pay when the fairs of Flanders or of someplace else take place at the rate of what the money is worth there. Carrying out these types of exchanges, looking for ways to deceive God, and showing unfaithfulness is forgetting or not remembering that the divine wisdom sees all our acts with our good and bad thoughts much more clearly than we ourselves. Only in one of these types of the three exchanges can the person be saved from mortal sin and the obligation to restitute. That is when the exchanger finds someone who wants to take his money for a true exchange, and, because he wants to help someone else, he does not give the money to the first person, thus depriving himself from gaining for the just exchange as much as he gains for reasons of the feigned[16] exchange. The reason being is that it is not for his own personal gain.[17]

27. It is worth noting that even if there is a statute where the documents of exchange are naturally enforceable, the documents of feigned exchanges are not, as Annanias[18] said it was stated in Bononia. If instead, the exchange contained in the document were partly true and partly feigned, only the part that is real could be enforced, and the adversary would have to confess what was true regarding the document.[19]

In the third place, it is also illicit if I give you 1000 *ducats* right now under agreement that you will have them given to me in Rome in a year's time, unchanged in their amount, for the advantage you took of them in the time you had them. It is usury on my part if for giving the payment in advance I earn the salary that I should have given you if you had had them given to me immediately.[20]

28. In the fourth place, even if Doctor Soto[21] determined in some place that nothing could be taken for this type of exchange when the bills of exchange were given in one city of the kingdom for another in the same kingdom, such as from Medina to Toledo or Seville, in another place[22] he approved and said it was allowed. Soto had two reasons. First, because of the reasons we talked about earlier that justify this contract from here to Rome, also justify the contract from here to León, and from here to Pamplona, Burgos, Seville, and Toledo—as long as the exchange is carried out sincerely and without fraud and as long as one takes less when there is a shorter distance and fewer dangers, work, and coastlines involved through which to pass, take, keep, and safeguard the money than when farther places are involved. Second, because the motives that determine that documents for another kingdom that are feigned usuries are illicit conclude, on the contrary, that documents that are destined to another city in this kingdom are licit if they are genuinely, without fraud or deception, given for an honest salary.[23]

Some say, however, that exchanges from one part of the kingdom to another are banned by new prohibitions both here as well as in Portugal because these were generally carried out to cover usuries. However, we consider that they should be limited and not [be banned] if the exchanger receives before giving or having someone else give. The first reason is because it is difficult to feign usury when the exchanger receives before giving, as it is commonly done with this type of exchange. Usuries are feigned when it is the other way around and the exchanger gives first and receives later, a type of exchange that the Bononienses call dry, as was said earlier,[24] invoking Laurencio.[25]

The second reason is because this type of exchange has a law unto itself and respects the divine, canon, and civil law; and laws should not be changed unless the usefulness and goodness sought after are evident.[26] This does not seem to be the case with this prohibition. Moreover, if it were banned, students, pilgrims, and many other dealers would be bereft of a good way to transfer (almost without expenses and danger) the supplies and money from Seville and other similar cities to Salamanca, Burgos, and other parts; and from Burgos and other such cities to Seville and other far away places between which there are dangerous roads.

29. However, there is great cause to forbid the exchange within the kingdom when the exchanger gives before in order to receive more now or some other time because it is probable that many usuries would be covered with this [type of exchange]. To my weak understanding, however, there is little usefulness in this, because it does not remove from the usurers who want to go ahead with veiled exchanges the instruments to veil their profit. In fact, it gives them the opportunity to do what they did before with fear and shame and less profit for one of the kingdom's cities, now without fear and much more profit for another city outside the kingdom. It would be a much better solution to have honest judges examine the past and present exchanges and, if they were to find from the people's situations that they are veiled, punish those who did them for wherever it was, carrying out the old laws that have not been revoked by this new ban,[27] which is not contrary to them.

Another reason [why there is little usefulness in forbidding this type of exchange] is because it conceals and almost forgives past actions, which is an unjust mercy,[28] because, when past actions are concealed and future actions are banned, there is opportunity of doing what is banned, in hopes that the actions are once again concealed, and going against clement justice, which by means of punishing past actions stops evil people from [commiting] future ones.[29] However, it makes it easier to learn about the feigned exchanges because it is easier to see that this Spanish person who takes money to pay it in Flanders does not have money there, as it was possible to see that he does not have it in Seville. Although we have already seen frauds against this in Lisbon, where a gentleman who needed money did not take it himself for Medina but asked a dealer to take it for himself, promising to pay them there with the exchange. So true is what the Italian said: *Fata la lege trobata la fraude.*[30]

30. In the fifth place, His Majesty's past intention to prevent the disorder caused by taking an exorbitant profit for this type of exchange was a holy one, and he ordered that for the exchange from these kingdoms to Rome no more than 400 *maravedis* per Chamber *ducat*[31] could be taken, nor from Rome to here more than 420. Nor from these kingdoms to Naples could be taken per long *ducat* more than 400, nor for Besancon for the *mark's*[32] *escudo*[33] more than 375. Nor could be taken from Besancon to here for *escudo* more than 390, nor from here to Flanders for an *escudo* of six salaries[34] of 60 *maravedis*, more than 370, nor from Flanders to here for *escudo*, less than 70 great ones. Nor could be taken from here to Valencia for a gold *Castilian*, more than 380, nor from Valencia to here, more than 510 for *Castilian*. Nor could be taken from here to Zaragoza for an *escudo*, more than another *ducat* over there, nor from Zaragoza to here more than 400. Nor could be taken from here to Barcelona but what has been given up to here, nor from here to Portugal for *ducat* more than 370, which are worth over there 400 *reales*, nor from Portugal to here for *ducat* more than 385.[35]

After this moderating provision, His Royal Majesty forbade exchanges in all Spain. That is, it was forbidden from the kingdoms of Castile to those of Aragón, Cataluña, and Valencia, and even to those of Castile,[36] with some small limitations that would make the exchanges possible, and those are that the exchanger receive the money before giving it for the reasons already mentioned.[37]

Let us hope everything is carried out with as much watchfulness, integrity, and perseverance as the good intentions that have been displayed. Although I fear this will not be so, at least as far as exchanges are concerned, I hope this will be so from the kingdoms where money is worth more and there is more merchandise to these here. Those who have money there will not want to give their money before, so that they are paid less here than what it is worth in those other parts, as we have noted down below in the exchange from Flanders and Portugal to here.

8

Exchanging by Transference

Summary

What exchanging by true transference is. Used for buying
and selling or pure barter . . . **31**

It is just to retain equality . . . **31**

And not otherwise, as long as the just laws are adhered to
. . . **32**

Money may be sold under many forms, except as price
. . . **32**

31. Everyone agrees that it is licit to practice the fourth type of exchange, by true transference, carried out by buying, bartering, or using another innominate contract to give currency that is worth less in one land than in another because it is not used there; because its metal is not worth as much there as in the other place; or because it is broken, disfigured, dented, worn out, or weightless and take it to the other land where it is worth more because it is not weighed there or because it is more used there. It can then be exchanged for another currency that is worth more where the other was worth less as long as due equality is maintained, as all this is buying, selling, bartering, or another innominate contract where I give so that you give, as we will see below.[1] All of these are licit if they are equal.[2]

55

This does not mean that something less was given for one thing in one land, then something more is taken for that same thing in another land. The reason why less is given in one land is because it is worth less there; and the reason why more is taken for it in another land is because it is worth more there. So, what was bought for less in this land may be sold for more in another one; and what was bartered in this land for something of less value, may be bartered somewhere else for something of more value. This applies to all merchandise, as long as much less in one place is not given, nor much more is taken in another that the just price is not honored to the prudent man's own free will.

32. Consequently, money may be bought and sold, even if Soto holds the contrary opinion,[3] which is a very true thing when it is not considered as money but as a piece of metal, and as gold, silver, or broken copper. Even when it is considered as money, under any one of the eight aspects, which we will describe below, it can be worth more or less than the price that the law establishes as long as it is offered as merchandise and not as price of other merchandise,[4] if this were to be thoroughly analyzed.[5] Every time that it is considered according to one of these aspects, and not [according to the fact] that it is the price of other things, it is merchandise that may increase in value more or less and consequently be bought.[6] The Arcediano[7] does not hold the contrary opinion, which some try to influence on him.[8] Although he ponders it, he does not say that money cannot be sold, but rather that its use cannot be sold inasmuch as it is money without selling [money] itself. The law[9] determines that everything that may be exchanged may be sold and everything that may be sold may be exchanged, excepting spiritual things, which may be exchanged but not sold. Everyone confesses that money may be exchanged.

33. It follows, too, that this type of exchange would be unjust if for example what is worth less is a piece of land, and the exchanger buys it or exchanges it for even less than what it is worth and that which is worth more he buys or exchanges for even more than what it is worth, especially when this is done for advancing the price or selling on credit. This principle may be easily proven by the two rules mentioned above.[10] It would also be unjust if money that is forbidden is transferred in such a way that to the others it is unjust to transfer it.[11]

9

Exchanging for an Interest

Summary

Exchanging for an interest is licit, and something may be
    taken for the interest . . . **34**

If for exchanging a person gets out of a deal in which he
    was engaged, he should be stopped, which should not
    happen if he has not . . . **35**

Defense of Doctors Antonio and Luys Coronel . . . **34**

34. The fifth type of exchange, exchanging for an interest, is also licit. This means that if the exchanger deals with merchandise and for lending to whom it is convenient he stops dealing, he may take an interest both for the profit as well as [for] the loss. As we have proved extensively elsewhere,[1] any merchant may take an interest under certain conditions. We add again that even if he does not deal with other merchandise apart from his exchanges, but if for lending he stops dealing with them (if they are licit), he may take an interest for the profit that for lending he is deprived of earning in his occupation of just exchanger.[2] Cajetan's[3] above-mentioned[4] decision may be applied here, which is the one referring to the person who stops dealing in true exchanges for helping someone else with a feigned exchange. He may earn what he would earn with the true one. Woe to the one who for this reason does not stop dealing or doing so many true exchanges as

57

before and takes feigned interest without there being a real or probable one,[5] as if God did not exist (who not only sees our acts but even our hearts).

This type of exchange can correct the doctors of Paris—among whom were those two renowned brothers Antonio Coronel and Luys Coronel (whose works and advice we benefited from for some time) and whom Saint Doctor Soto[6] admonishes. Merchants may take more if they have to wait for their payment until the second fairs than if they wait until the first ones. They can take even more if they wait until the third ones than if they wait until the second ones. Because the exchange of the interest is larger the longer the period, in all probability the person is not earning. It is certain that the dealer who stops dealing and the exchanger who stops exchanging with his money for two fairs is prevented from earning more than if he stopped for one fair, as is the case with the person who does not deal in two more than the person in one [fair]. It is hard to believe that such renowned doctors belonging to such a great university analyzed this other type of exchange regarding buying or bartering. Even students with few years of study know that buying or bartering for a higher price when there is a longer term is usury. This subject, though, is not talked about in schools, according to what Saint Doctor Soto[7] says. It was never discussed until him, although we believe that Gaspar Calderini,[8] Laurencio Rodulfo,[9] Saint Antonino,[10] Ioannes Annanias,[11] Silvestre,[12] Cajetan,[13] Medina,[14] and others studied this subject extensively, even if they did not explain its concepts as much as we did.

35. As far as this exchange is concerned, the exchanger who stops being a merchant to become an exchanger once he has gotten his money out of the deal and devotes all his money to exchange from fair to fair for a certain or uncertain interest, is mortally sinning and must pay restitution. That means [that he exchanges] under agreement that those who take his money pay him as much as what those who deal in what he used to deal earn, or a certain amount of probable interest [that is equal to what] he would earn if he were dealing. Because he has already removed his money from the deal and does not want to deal, there is no true nor probable interest, as was said in the *Manual*[15] and in another commentary.[16] Also sins the exchanger who in order to exchange his money does not stop dealing with the money he has destined for that purpose. He should pay restitution on what he has earned for the same reason. Therefore, there are many penitents who have enriched themselves in these ways, and many confessors who listen and have listened to them in confession, absolving them without ordering them to stop doing it or to pay restitution on what they have earned or ordering thus and not being obeyed, which condemns both one side as well as the other.[17]

10

Exchanging by Safekeeping

Summary

To exchange by safekeeping is licit . . . **36**

When something may be taken for it . . . **37**

The exchanger receives and pays in cash and with treasury notes.[1] Can he receive something more for paying in cash? . . . **37**

Paying five per thousand for cash is illicit, except in three cases . . . **37, 38**

It is better to earn a small amount justly than to earn a big amount and to commit a sin . . . **39**

The person who does not pay the exchanger or [the person] who takes him cash and leaves [this cash] with him, sins [as well as the exchanger] . . . **40**

36. The sixth type of exchange, by safekeeping, is also just because there is a law,[2] custom, or statute that makes the exchanger a safekeeper, depositary, and guarantor of the money that is given to him or exchanged for something needed by those who give it or send it. This makes him [i.e., the exchanger] pay the merchants or the people that the depositors choose in a particular way, and, because of this, it is licit that they take a just salary from the republic or from the depositing parties. Because this profession and work is useful to the republic and does not possess any iniquity whatsoever, it is just that someone who works earn his wage.[3]

This exchanger's occupation is to receive the money from the merchants; to deposit it; to have it ready; and also to write, keep the books, give an account of the money to everyone with great difficulty, and to run the risk of making a mistake with the accounts and other things. The same thing could be carried out with a contract[4] by which one of the parties commits himself to some people to receive and keep money under deposit, giving, paying, and keeping the books with the people according to the way they tell him to because this is the kind of contract where the activity and work of one is rented out to someone else. Such a contract is specifically provided for by the law and is just and holy.[5]

What the salary should be for this type of work has not been resolved by law. It is worth noting that the exchanger has two ways of taking money: in cash by actually taking the money, and in treasury notes by accepting documents of other exchanges or from other people with which they promise or deposit in his bank the payment of what they remit to him so that he forwards it to his account. There are also two ways in which the exchanger pays: by actually giving the money, or in treasury notes by forwarding the payment to other exchanges.

37. Some[6] believe that it is ordered and established in this kingdom that when the exchanger pays someone in cash, he should receive 5 per every 1,000, and when [he pays] with a document, remitting to another exchange, he should receive nothing. We have found quite the opposite in the laws[7] of these kingdoms. In one[8] of them, it says that the Catholic Sovereigns ordered, in Seville in the year 1491, that the exchanger could pay those who had treasury notes and others with coins that are defective, broken, and crushed, paying for the defective ones. If someone were to fancy his payment in sound, healthy, and chosen coins, [the exchanger] would be able to take 5 per every 1,000 for paying it thus, and not any more, even if the other party wanted to give more.

In another [law],[9] it says that the Catholic Sovereigns themselves found out that the exchangers took advantage of such a law to not only take for themselves those 5 per every 1,000 in those situations but also in all those cases where cash was paid in any coin, whether it was chosen or not. They reviewed that law in 1513, invalidating what pertained to this [issue] and establishing that the exchangers not pay in broken or crushed money nor take anything for themselves from those to whom something was deposited in their accounts or who owed them money, under great penalties. This provision was very holy and necessary.

38. It is against all natural, divine, and human reason[10] that you take from me and others 1, 5, or 10 per 1,000 of what our debtors or others have deposited for us in your bank or exchange, without doing anything else for us than paying what was deposited in [your bank]. It is not just[11] that we pay for the work you put into taking care of the money from our debtors or from those who deposited with you in our favor or in keeping their accounts. Even if some say there is great effort that

deserves the said 5 per 1,000, I do not believe so because it would be unjust unless it is one of the three cases that we will discuss later.

Consequently, not only are the said 5 per 1,000 (when cash is paid) not his salary, but they become his theft and unjust extortion, which drive him to hell or restitution and a complete contrition to deliver himself[12] from [these sins], except in three cases. The first is when the payment goes to the same people who deposited and gave their money in cash for the exchange, and they pay thus to get a discount on the work and care that the exchanger has in receiving and taking care of their money and do it for the above-mentioned [persons]. The second is when the depositors sold their merchandise for a higher price that depended on the higher amount they had to pay for receiving the exchange in cash for the discount and discharge of what the depositors owe the exchanger. The third is when, by their own free will, those who receive the payment give it to exchange it [for cash] so that they do not have to wait for the payment eight or ten days until [the payments are due] in order to transfer the payment to the exchanger so that they do not have to leave anything for cashing in, as it has happened to us. Those [who receive the payment and give it to exchange] are very few because [the payment is not theirs yet] even if [the depositors] have left it [in deposit]. Their will to do this is as unnatural as the will of the one who pays usuries to the usurer, which does not excuse from sin or restitution.[13]

39. Others say that their salary is 2, 3, or 4 percent, according to whether the money belonging to the lenders is more or less expensive or whether they give in cash to some and to others until the next fair. All of this is usury and mortal sin, with the obligation of restitution, and cannot be denied in any way.[14]

That is why we say that the salary is what each dealer gives or should give according to each virtuous man's[15] free will in each fair, once the accounting has been finished according to what is given for it until such conclusion, which is something that is not determined. They tell us that some give them 1 or 1½ per 1,000 apart from what they get for exchanging coins.

If you say that today (when there are no gold pieces to barter) the second is little or nothing and the first is little to make so many rich, so quickly, and in such a big measure, we will answer that (according to what they say) they have been a great part of the cause. There are no gold pieces in the kingdom, nor are they bartered, because of their having taken the money out by means of much skill and dexterity, although I believe that there has been a greater cause. We also say that the exchanges were not invented to enrich the exchanger but to make deals more useful and easier so that there is more merchandise and it is cheaper, which would be the case if they carried out their job honestly and would content themselves with a just salary. This just salary would be the result of receiving it from those who owe it to them, whose money they hold and whose accounts they keep and not from those who do not owe it to them, remembering what that great King and prophet said:[16] "It is better to gain little with justice, than many riches with sin." Also remembering what the author of the prophets said:[17] "What is the use of gaining the whole world, and losing the soul for it?" and not wanting [against the Psalm's[18] precept] to imitate the evil ones who gained their riches illicitly.

40. Regarding this type of exchange, not only do the exchangers sin and have to pay restitution but also those who give them money to keep and do what we saw earlier and then do not want to pay anything, saying that what [the exchangers] earn with their money and receive from those who pay in cash is enough as salary. Then if the exchangers ask for something, they leave them and go deal with someone else, and so, in order to avoid this, they [the exchangers] decide not to take a salary owed to them but take it from someone who does not owe it to them.

Those who sin, too, are the ones who give the exchangers some money in cash and then if they take it in treasury notes for themselves or for others and not in cash when the accounts are done with, they make [the exchangers] offer the payment for having given to them in cash, which is at least at 2 percent. This profit they cannot take for anything in the world as something owed to them, but for the advantage the exchanger takes or will take from that money that he was paid in cash. Thus it is clear usury because the exchanger who takes money works in order to receive it, store it, keep accounts, and have it ready for when it is needed or deposited, and the one who gave it or gives it does none of these things.

The exchangers commit another kind of usury regarding this matter when they receive money in cash in their hands, bank, or operating table from a merchant and immediately deposit an additional sum of money in another bank for whatever he wants for as long as they keep his money and for as long as [the merchant] leaves with [the exchangers] the revenue that they would have had to pay because of the cash payment. All this, at least in its intentions, is evident usury because the dealer leaves the revenue to the exchangers that he thinks he has earned for the cash payment, so that the exchangers lend him by way of deposit another amount, or a sum until the next fairs, and the exchangers lend it so that they do not [have to] pay that which they owe the depositor. All this is great misfortune and should be grieved for.

11

Exchange by Buying, Bartering, or Innominate Contract

Summary

To exchange by buying, and by bartering or another innominate contract do not differ as far as this purpose is concerned . . . **41**

Thus the name is of no importance. It requires two things to be just . . . **41**

Differences between the contract specifically provided for by the law[1] and an innominate contract, and similarities as far as this purpose is concerned . . . **41**

Substituting this word to include all contracts . . . **41**

Dealing with money results in a profit, as when dealing with other things . . . **43**

Money is worth more or less for these eight different motives . . . **43**

Fourth of which . . . **44**

The fifth . . . **45**

The sixth . . . **46**

The seventh . . . **51**

41. We declare that the same set of scales and measurements should be used to weigh and measure the justice of the exchange by buying as the exchange by bartering, which is another innominate contract. Buying, on the one hand, and bartering—which is an innominate contract[3]—and the other innominate contracts on the other, are different because buying is a contract specifically provided for by the law,[4] while the others are not. Consequently, in everything, contracts that are specifically provided for by the law for having a specific name[5] differ under the law from those that are not and because of such are called innominate.[6] There is no difference as far as our purpose is concerned, which is to see how it is possible to make a profit in a just way by buying, selling, or bartering money. Regarding this, it is the same to say it is a purchase as to say it is a barter or to say it is a contract where I give so that you give me, or I give or do so that you do, or so that you make someone else give me, or you do.

The contract by which one person gives to another in Medina 100 for 110 that the other person gives or has someone give him in Flanders; or gives him in Flanders 100 for having 120 given to him in Medina, becomes illicit for one or two reasons:

1. the inequality of what is given and what is to be received, and
2. taking more or less for advancing or postponing, or for giving a long or short term [to pay it back].

It is certain that these two things and each one of them make the bartering contract and any other contract specifically provided for by the law, such as the buying one, illicit, and also the opposite to the buying one, as with these others, for what was said above.[7]

42. The first conclusion is that there is no need to spend any time nor think any more about which opinion is truer: if the one that says that the next contract [we talk about] is a buying one, which is Cajetan's[8] opinion, and also Calderini[9] and Laurencio's,[10] or a bartering one, as Soto[11] says, and before him Calderini and

Laurencio,[12] or if it is an innominate contract: I give so that you give me, et cetera, which could perhaps be considered for what we said earlier[13] about exchange involving bills of exchange, and for other reasons that we could add.

The second conclusion is that in order to satisfy all opinions, we must use the word *commuting*,[14] which is common to all of the above operations and any other contract where one thing passes from one person to another.

The third conclusion is that said exchange (whatever it is called) is licit if it is carried out justly, and not if it is not. It is just when two things happen: One, that for the money commuted, the just value is given; and two, that its value is not lowered for repaying it at a later date, as Cajetan[15] noted and, before him and best of all, Silvestre.[16] These reasons, even if they or others had not noted them down, are proved by the two rules established above.[17]

43. The fourth conclusion is that the difficulty is in declaring how a profit can be made by commuting money by giving the just value for it. To which we respond that it may be done as with other merchandise, collecting it through exchange of its just value where or when it is worth less to exchange it where and when it is worth more. Saint Thomas[18] believes, and we have already said above,[19] that money (even insofar as it is money) may be commuted for money in order to gain a profit with it.

The fifth conclusion is that the solution of the aforementioned difficulty depends on knowing how and when a unit of money, which is equal to another according to the common price set by the law or custom at the time of coining it, is worth more or less for whatever reason than another [unit of money]. There is no way of knowing if the exchange of a certain amount of money for another is just without knowing the value of both, because, as we explained earlier, in order for the exchange to be just, [money] should be bought for what it is worth.

This uncertainty [regarding how and when a unit of money is worth more or less than another] has eight causes:

1. for being of different metals
2. for being of a different carat
3. for being of a different weight and shape
4. for the diversity of the land in which they [circulate]
5. for the disapproval or doubt of disapproval regarding the increase or decrease of one of them
6. for the diversity of time
7. for the lack or need of it
8. for the absence of one and presence of the other

44. Regarding the first cause, which is the difference in metal, sometimes a gold *ducat* is worth more to the one who has it than a silver or metal one because he can keep it better or take it far away; and the other way around, sometimes it is worth more to have a silver or another metal *ducat* than a gold one for the lack of small coinage to spend.[20]

Regarding the second cause, which is when the two coins are not the same carat metal, it happens that out of two *ducats*, which by law are appraised at the same value as the *ducats* from Castile, Portugal, Ungria, and Florence, one may be worth more than another, even if they are both in the same land.

Regarding the third, when they are a different weight and shape, sometimes a *ducat* with the same impression as another is worth more if it has an extra gram and a good shape, while the other lacks another gram or is broken, chipped, or disfigured.

Regarding the fourth, when they are in different lands, the same coin is worth more in one land than in another, according to Calderini's[21] words. This is because the metal in one land is worth more than in the other, such as gold is worth more in Spain than in the Indies, and more in France than in Spain because the king or one land's custom sets it at a higher price than the king or the custom in the other. This was the case when I studied in Toulouse, France. The king in that land manifestly raised the prices of his sun *ducats*[22] and those of the Spanish *ducats*, and they say he has gone on to raise them even more, with which most everyone agrees.[23]

45. Regarding the fifth cause, when there is disapproval regarding the value's increase, decrease, or doubt of disapproval, we have seen in past years that the *tarjas* worth 10 had a lower value for some time than the one they had had before. In other lands, where there are many who mint coins, many times some of them order that the coins of their fellow towns do not circulate in their town. Others lower their price, and just as when after they order that it does not circulate any more it is commuted for much less than before, so when they try to disapprove or lower the value and there is doubt regarding this, if it is done, it is commuted for something less. Just as after it rises, it is worth more, so when it is dealt with and there is doubt, it starts being commuted for something more. As certainly as the price rises for raising the value, and as certainly as it falls because of lowering the value, so when there is doubt regarding one or the other, there is an uncertain[24] increase and decrease. Because commuting money that is worth more or less according to these five reasons is exchanging by true transference (which we discussed earlier),[25] I refer to the above.

46. The eighth cause is the diversity of time because of which the value of money may rise or fall. Sometimes 100 gold *ducats* are worth more and sometimes less. The same is true for 100 silver *ducats* or 100 metal *ducats* or 100 [*units*] in absolute terms than what they would be worth in one year's time. They would be worth more (for what was said earlier),[26] for any of the many reasons that there may be for this; for example, if for taking it from the ground to buy food, go to war, or help friends who go to war there were now a lack of some or all of them and then in a year there were abundance for having sold the fruits and other merchandise from the ground or because the king has sufficiently paid his soldiers and servants, or for other similar causes. They would be worth less if there were now an abundance and, in one year's time, there were scarcity, just as a measure of wheat is not worth as much in August when there is great abundance of it, as in May, when there is scarcity of wheat, or less[27] amount of it.

47. But money is never said to be worth more or less for giving it before or after, or for a longer or shorter period of time, if any of the other eight reasons that make it increase or decrease is not attached to the time factor, according to almost everyone's common opinion.[28]

The conclusion is that in the first place all the exchangers, merchants, and any other who believe it is licit for them to take more than what they lent for having others keep their money for a longer period of time, without making use of it, and taking advantage of it, are wrong. Thus, the exchangers make a mistake when they measure and count the time there is until the next fair, or until the payment day, when they are to be paid, in order to take more or less for the exchange.

48. In the second place, the person who lends 100 pieces of gold to another and then the price of the pieces increases, may licitly ask for the greater value [they have] when he collects than when he lends them. He does not take a profit for the time lapse but for the increase of value—set by the king or by custom as time goes by—of what was owed to him. This is a conclusion that in many parts is taken from Bartolo,[29] who is widely accepted.[30] There is no doubt regarding this, if he intended to keep the money until then, as this chapter proves it,[31] as do Juan Calderini and, in other parts, Gaspar Calderini[32] and Laurencio Rodulfo[33] and Silvestre,[34] whom Soto[35] reprimands, without quoting anyone for it, although Francisco Curcio Senior[36] and others make reference to have held this opinion before him. Silvestre, however, does not deserve a reprimand because he refers to the person who lends the *ducats* that he was going to keep and because Soto's comparison (to our way of thinking) does not resolve [the issue]. Just as the person who lends a measure of wheat of 12 *celemines*[37] should not be repaid later a whole measure of 13[38] (even if it is ordered that the measure hold that amount), so the person who lends a *ducat* worth 11 *reales* should not receive a *ducat* worth 12 if it is ordered that it is worth this amount before.

49. We believe this comparison is not irrefutable, because when the measure of wheat of 12 *celemines* is increased to 13, it changes its form and substance and stops being the same measure that it was before. Instead, when the *ducat* increases from 11 *reales* to 12 by order of the prince, it does not change its substance or form nor stops being the same *ducat* it was at the beginning. What changes in it is something extrinsic and accidental, and does not belong to its essence, as Bartolo[39] holds, who is widely accepted.[40]

Because wheat does not stop being the same wheat as it was before, even if its appraisal grows or decreases, the person who borrows a measure of wheat has to give back another measure as good in its essence, even if it is worth more or less as far as price goes, which is something extrinsic to it. The metaphysical argument saying that price corresponds to the essence of the *ducat*, as *ducat* and coin, can be responded to with Bartolo's words, widely accepted: Even as coin, its essence is based more on its natural being than on its artificial one, as we have already stated.

We also say that such a lender may take that additional amount even if he had not intended on keeping the money, if he arranged that he would get back as many pieces and as various as the ones he had lent, whether they were worth more, less, or the same—at least if he did not have a greater certainty that its price would increase than that it would decrease, according to this chapter. This was like an adventure, a wager on what could happen, as everything is possible.[41]

50. We go on to say that according to Bartolo's[42] common and widely accepted opinion,[43] the person who lends 100 gold *ducats* must receive them in the same quality of gold, without discounting anything from the price even if the value increases and he had not intended on keeping them, nor he expressly plans that they should be given back in such and so many pieces as he has given, whether they increase or decrease. The person who lends something should receive something of equal substance as what was lent, as good as it is (as far as the intrinsic goodness of it).[44] The intrinsic goodness of money does not issue from the price the republic sets on it but from the quality and goodness of the substance it is made of, according to Bartolo's[45] true and accepted opinion.

Even if this accepted opinion could easily be held in all cases, we think it should be applied only in three of them:

— The first, when the person who lent them was going to put them away until the price went up.
— The second, when he expressly ordered such and so many pieces be returned as the ones he gave, whether they increased or decreased the value, assuming the danger of losing, as well as the hope of winning.
— The third, when the money's value increased so quickly, that even the person who borrowed it had not spent them, and was able to spend them and take advantage of them at the increased price.

Apart from these three cases, it is sufficient to pay the lender in the same pieces or other similar ones, or in the same metal as the ones he borrowed, and as many as there were at the time of the loan, giving the value they have at the time of the repayment. We hold these truths partly because of what Bartolo and the common[46] opinion holds, partly because of what Molinaeus says, and partly because of the great justice that[47] Baldo[48] wrote about, who declares it rightly.[49] We are not allowed any more (not even as much as we have said) because of the brevity that we desire.

12

The Value of Money

Summary

How money increases or decreases its value for the abundance or the lack of it . . . **51**

Merchandise increases or decreases its value for abundance or lack thereof . . . **51**

Money is merchandise . . . **51**

Its increase drags the rest down. The value of each metal rises when there is a shortage of metal in general . . . **52, 54, 56**

What [money's] main purpose is, what the others [are] . . . **55**

The *ducats* belonging to merchants and to people seem diverse . . . **53**

But they are not . . . **54, 56**

Money is the price of the rest of things. Something else may be its price . . . **55**

How it rises . . . **57**

Its value . . . **58**

51. The twentieth thing that we say regards the seventh motive of why money increases or decreases its value. That happens when there is great lack or need (or an abundance of it). It is worth more where and when there is a great lack of it than where there is a great abundance, as declare Calderini,[3] Laurencio Rodulfo,[4] and Silvestre,[5] with whom Cajetan[6] and Soto[7] agree.

From them follow several opinions:

In the first place, this is what most of the good and evil men of Christianity think, and thus it seems to be the voice of God and nature.[8]

Second, and very obviously, all merchandise becomes more expensive when there is a great need and small quantity of it.[9] Money, inasmuch as it is a thing that may be sold, bartered, or commuted by means of another contract, is merchandise for what we said above[10] and may also become more expensive when there is great need of it and not very much to satisfy this need.

Third, the rest being the same, in those countries where there is a great lack of money, less money is given for marketable goods, and even for the hands and work of men than where there is an abundance of it. This we can see from experience in France where there is less money than in Spain. Bread, wine, wool, hands, and work cost less. Even in Spain, when there was less money, much less was given for saleable goods, and the hands and work of men, than later when the discoveries of the Indies covered it in silver and gold. The cause for this is that money is worth more where and when there is a lack of it than where and when there is an abundance. That which some say, that the lack of money reduces the price of everything, is born of the fact[11] that its more than sufficient increase makes everything appear much lower, just as a small man next to a very tall man appears smaller than if he were next to his equal.

52. Fourth, the lack of gold coins may surely increase their value, so that more silver coins, or coins of another metal, have to be offered for the [gold coins],[12] as we see now that because of the lack of gold coins, some give 22 and even 23 and 25 *reales* for a *doubloon*, which by the kingdom's price and law is not worth more than 22.

We have even seen in Portugal 11½ silver *ducats*, and even 12 offered for 1 of 10. The shortage of silver coins may increase their value so that more gold coins or metal coins have to be given than before for the silver ones. Even the shortage of small copper coins or other cheap metals may have their value increase so that more gold or silver has to be given than before for them. This we have seen in Portugal where, when there was an abundance of *cetis*, 106 *maravedis* in *cetis* were given for 1 *teston*,[13] which is not worth more than 100. Then, when there was a shortage of *cetis*, we gave 1 *teston* for 94 in *cetis*. So, it seems that when money in general is scarce, the price of [the different coins] in general increases.[14]

In the fifth place, there is a law[15] that establishes this because, after saying that the reason why there is arbitrary action[16] in asking in one place for something that must be paid somewhere else is because something is worth more in one place than in another (mainly if it is bread, wine, or oil), it goes on to say about money the following words: *Pecuniarum quoque, licet videatur una et eadem potestas ubique esse, tamen allis locis facilius, et levioribus usuries invenintur, aliis, difficilius, et gravioribus usuries.*

53. There are many arguments against this opinion, and, because of which, one day we decided it was unreasonable. The first, that no matter how much or how scarce money is, never a *ducat* is worth more or less than 11 *reales* and 1 *maravedi* here or in Rome, Flanders, or León, as what the pope, the king, or custom has appraised it for. Nor will it be taken for a higher value from the person who sells you something.[17] Also, that in holding this opinion, we must say what some people[18] believe that there are two types of *ducats* and *escudos*: The first is the one used by merchants for their exchanges, which rises or falls according to the abundance or shortage of money. Consequently, many or few want to give or to take in exchange. The other [type] are those *ducats* and *escudos* intended to be spent by the population and even by the merchants themselves in their expenses that are not exchanges, which always have a fixed price. This seems a tenuous belief because the Roman, ecclesiastical, or secular jurisdiction never considered it.[19] Because merchants do not have the power to increase or decrease public money,[20] it sounds like something fleeting—a trap, a veil, and cover of usuries to feign *ducats* or *escudos*—to give them an imagined value so that no one who sells bread, wine, meat, fish, cloth, or any other thing will take them but by way of exchange to pay them back in another fair or place. There does not seem to be a solid reason why, except for lack of money in general, that a greater quantity of *ducats* and *escudos* are imagined only for exchanging them without there being another use for spending them. Thus, in exchanging them, a cloud is formed covering the loan that with usury is carried out under it. Also against [the earlier] opinion is the fact that money considered as money seems to be the price of all other merchandise[21] but is not merchandise, and its price is not appraised[22] in each kingdom, and thus, may not increase more than wheat when it is appraised by the republic.

54. Regardless of this and Doctor Medina's[23] contrary opinion (which, at one time, we thought was better), we hold the first opinion because of the new reasons and considerations in favor of it. To the first argument, which seems insoluble, we may respond that even if or when there is a shortage of money in general, a *ducat* should not be worth more *reales* than when there is an abundance of [money], nor the *real* more *quartos*, nor the *quartos*[24] more *maravedis*. All money is worth more because more saleable goods may be found for a fraction of what they were worth before, all else being the same.[25] This is not to say that [the increase in the price of money] is due to the decrease in the other thing's [prices] because [it is] this [decrease] that follows the increase in the [price] of money, as we have considered in the third argument.

To the second argument, which seems insoluble, we may respond by denying that it is necessary in order to defend this [first opinion] to introduce imagined and chimerical *ducats* and *escudos*, which as Plato's ideas, find themselves in specie and genre, and not individually, as the arguments rightly conclude. It is confirmed effectively with the consideration that whoever says this must confess that almost as many imaginary *ducats* must be fabricated as places money is given and taken for in the fair. There is almost a different price for each place: one for Flanders, another for Rome, another for León, another for Lisbon, another for Valencia, another for Zaragoza, and so forth. A comical thing, adding to this consideration is that it seems it has not been said enough that the *ducat* or *escudo* are not worth as much in the fair if they are not worth as much for such and such a place. Even those who say this mean that the *ducat* is given for such and such a place for the barter or price that is given for it in one place.

55. To the third argument, we answer by denying that money considered as money should always be considered as the price of things, because, even considered as money, it may be commuted by buying, bartering, or with a contract specifically provided for by the law or an innominate contract, as was said above.[26] Although it is true that its main and principal use and end for which it was created was as price and measure of saleable goods,[27] its secondary and less principal use and end, which is that of making a profit with it by dealing money for money, is not to be price but merchandise, just as the principal use and end of shoes is to put them on and wear them, but the secondary one is to make a profit by dealing with them through buying and selling them. As far as the value is concerned, we will respond to it below.[28]

56. The following conclusions are derived from the above:

First, that the gold coin, because of the specific shortage of it, may be worth more than it would be worth if there were an abundance of it; and the silver coin, because of the specific shortage of it, as well as the metal one, for its shortage, and all coins in general for their general shortage.

Second, there is no need to feign merchants' imaginary *ducats* or *escudos* that are different from those the population uses. Without them, it is still possible to clearly set a price for a *ducat* or *escudo* for one party and for the other. Moreover, it is more advisable not to feign them so that those who lend and give money unjustly do not have the chance to be repaid at the value they decide to fix, as Saint Doctor Soto[29] tacitly expressed.

Third, the exchange that many carry out is usury, who [according to them] give to some people *ducats* or *escudos* from one fair to the next to be paid at the price that they are worth when they are given, or [at the price that the merchants' ones are worth in the market] when they are to be paid, because there are no such *ducats* nor *escudos* in the world, and because, if they existed, they would be of such diverse values as the cities for where they are exchanged. For some cities, they are exchanged for an equal value, such as many times happens from Medina to Lisbon. For others, at 10 or 20 *maravedis*; for others at 30; and for others at 40 and 50. They even give them sometimes at the price they get for exchanging them in the city where they are worth the most. Moreover, the reason that justifies the commutation of a sum of money that has to be given in a far away city does not justify the commutation of a similar amount that has to be given in the same city, for the reason we will say below.[30] Although it should be confessed that whoever finds someone who takes his money for a true exchange and does not gain a profit with him because of giving it to his neighbor or another close person who much needs it, may in such manner earn with it what he is prevented from earning with the other person, for the reason we said above.[31]

57. Fourth, the value of money may not only increase or decrease inasmuch as it is a piece of metal, but even inasmuch as it is money and price of the rest of things:[32] The majority of the eight motives because of which money increases or decreases are motives that pertain to money as money and price of saleable goods and conclude that inasmuch as it is money and price, it is worth more in one land than in another, and even in one land more at one time than in another.

Fifth, there is a need to explain that compelling argument that against this is based on the price, whose solution above we reinstate down here. [The argument] is that money is appraised, and things appraised, as wheat is usually, do not increase for a lack of it. Some of the aforementioned[33] respond that even it is appraised inasmuch as it is price. It is not [appraised] inasmuch as it is merchandise. This is not satisfactory; however, for the reasons stated before, it is evident that even inasmuch as it is money and price, it [may] increase or decrease. Silvestre[34] declares that [money] is appraised inasmuch as it is price of other saleable goods but not inasmuch as it is price of money itself. He does not explain why there is such difference. Others[35] believe that money should never be sold, and thus some would say that there is not a higher price in its commutation. On the one hand, this goes against the common practice,[36] which refers to buying and selling money. On the other hand, it is not convenient to them at all. If they confess that there is barter and that you cannot barter but for what something is worth, that its value increases for its [greater] worth due to its great lack, and that more should be given the more it is worth,[37] they have to forcefully confess that its value increases regardless of its price, and thus have the same need of explaining the argument based on [its price] as have those who say you can buy it.

58. Thus, we answer again, conceding that money is appraised for one end and not for another. It is appraised in order to compel the person who sells something or to whom something is owed to take the money for said price so that he cannot be compelled to take it for more. It is not appraised in order that the person who has it cannot take less for it if he so wants to, nor in order that he cannot take more if he gains an advantage with this. This solution cannot reassure the consciences of those who commute it for a higher price for the shortage of it without there being an advantage in keeping it, even if the person with whom one is commuting it obtains [an advantage] in getting paid. The seller cannot sell the thing more expensively for the personal gain that this may bring to the buyer, although [he may sell it more expensively] for the benefit he loses in selling it, according to what Saint Thomas[38] and Scotus[39] said. We see every day the dealers whom few times do not obtain a benefit[40] from saving their money when there is great lack of it (even if it means only buying some things at a cheaper price). We see even those who are not dealers commute at present the *doubloons* for 24 and 25 *reales* when they are actually appraised at 22, for the great lack of them that there is. Though it might be said that they [the *doubloons*] are worth more for the intrinsic value of their gold, which is much higher than that of the *coronas*,[41] we would not be able to say the same of the rest of the other coins, though they increase or decrease every day as Bartolo[42] and Panormitanus[43] say, whom no one contradicts. Therefore, it seems safer to respond that money is appraised so that, all else being the same, it is not worth more in one place but not so that when it changes so much that there is great lack and need of that appraised money it cannot be worth more,[44] which seems so to wise and good men, at least in order to commute it for other money, as Silvestre says.

59. Sixth, it is not unusual that money (even inasmuch as it is money) is worth more in one fair than in another and more in one part of the same fair than in another part. It may be that in one part it is worth less because few people want to take it for true exchange, and many want to give it; and in another part, because of there being many who want to take it for true exchange and few who want to give it, it may be worth more. The price of money increases for great need or lack of it.[45] We say "true exchange" because we believe that the price of money should not be increased when there are a great many people who want to take it for feigned and illicit exchanges, as deception and fraud should not bring profit to the one who commits them.[46] No merchandise becomes more expensive when there are many who want to steal it or illicitly usurp it, although it does [become more expensive] when there are many who want to justly buy it or barter it.[47] As Saint Doctor Soto[48] stated wisely, money should not be more expensive at the fair for a lack of it or for an absence of people who want to give it when this lack is born of the illicit conspiracy of those who have to give it and of the exchangers who openly or covertly decide not to give it until it is more expensive.[49] Money should not be more expensive for their having taken some of them at the beginning of the fair most of [the money] at a cheaper [price] for other places, and then, as they are in possession of most of it, do not want to give it but as they please. In this case, those who are not guilty may give it in good conscience according to its lack, but not those who are guilty[50]—something that happens more often than it should.

60. Seventh, it would be [even] less surprising if the *ducat* were worth more in Portugal than in Castile, although there is doubt if it is. First, because the person who in Portugal owes 400 *reales* may pay them with a *ducat* worth 11 *reales*, and the person who owes and to whom is owed 400 *maravedis* here cannot pay them here or there with 1 *ducat*. This means that the *maravedis* from here are worth more than the *reales* from over there, but the *ducat* is worth the same here as there and there as here. In His Majesty's provision to moderate exchanges, whose content we referred to earlier,[51] it is established that 370 *maravedis* from here are worth 400 *reales* over there.

We think the opposite is truer, that is, that the *ducat* from here and from there is worth more there than here; also that the *real* from here is worth more there than here because the *ducat* is worth 400 *reales* from there and the *real* 36, and here the *ducat* is not worth but 375 *maravedis* and the *real* 34. That the *reales* from there and *maravedis* from here are equal is inferred from the fact that as a *real* is worth in Portugal 6 *cetis*, so the *maravedi* (now in use) is worth 6 *cornados*, which apparently are equal to the *cetis*, as seems to prove efficiently the Saint Archbishop Don Diego de Leyva y Covarrubias.[52] Today, in the kingdom of Galicia (where there are *cetis* as in Portugal) 6 [*cetis*] are worth 1 *maravedi*. In Portugal, too, they are worth 1 *real*. Also, what the contrary part alleges is not pertinent.[53] We deny that the person who owes in Portugal 400 *reales* does just payment here with 1 *ducat* if he is not satisfied with it, nor even [that there is just payment] when the one to whom you owe there 11 *reales* receives another 11 that you pay him here. We also deny that the person who owes here 400 *maravedis* [does just payment] there with 400 *reales*.

Also, it is possible to respond to the provision to moderate exchanges that such words were included there by accident.[54] If you reply that its determination[55] is based on it, we will say that it is based on someone else's acts and that the opposite[56] may be proved. We believe that even if this is accepted in these kingdoms for their benefit, it will be not be [accepted] in the foreign ones, even if [those kingdoms] belong to Your Majesty, because it will harm them.

61. Eighth, it is extremely important that whoever lends in Portugal 100 *ducats* is able to take for them in Medina more than 100 for the only reason that they are worth more there than here.[57]

Ninth, whoever lends 100 *ducats* in Medina should not receive 100 in Lisbon because they are worth more there than here,[58] and whoever lends may not take more than what he lent.[59]

Tenth, what has been said about Medina and Lisbon in these two last conclusions should also be said of any other two cities where the same currency is worth more in one of them than in the other. Thus, the person who lends 100 *ducats* in Flanders, Rome, or León (where the *ducats* are worth more than in Castile) should be paid more than 100 there [i.e., in Castile]. So also the other way around: The person who lends 100 in Castile should not get paid 100 in Rome, as Saint Doctor Soto presumes in a notable way.[60] Just as it would be usury to lend you a load[61] of wheat in Salamanca (where it is worth 2 *ducats*) so that you pay it to me in Galizia where it is worth 4; so it would be [usury] to lend you here a *ducat* worth 375 *maravedis* so that you pay it back to me somewhere else where it is worth 400. Just as [it is injustice] (although it is not usury, but injustice) that for a load of wheat that I lent to you in Galizia where it was worth 4 *ducats* you pay me with another one here in Salamanca where it is not worth more than 2; so it is injustice that for 100 *ducats* that you lent me in Rome or Lisbon where they are worth 400 I give you but 100 in Medina where they are not worth more than 375.

Eleventh, he who lends a certain quantity of wheat, wine, and oil where it is worth more should get back a greater amount if he is paid where they are worth less, [depending on] how much more it is worth where he lends than where he is being paid.[62] He who lends where something is worth less, should receive a smaller quantity if he is paid where it is worth more, depending on how much more it is worth where he is getting paid than where he lends. Thus, he who lends *ducats* where they are worth more, should receive so much more if he is paid where they are worth less as the greater value of those *ducats* amounts to. So, too, the other way around: He who lends *ducats* where they are worth less, should receive so much less if he is paid where they are worth more as that greater value amounts to.

Twelfth, because of this, it may seem to some that there is no doubt in Saint Doctor Soto's conclusion[63] that he who gives for exchange in Spain a *ducat*, which is not worth but 11 *reales*, so that he gets paid back in Rome another worth 12 or 13 *carlines*[64]—which are equal to our *reales*, or are worth more than 11, commits usury because he wants to take more than what he gives and gain an extra amount. This conclusion, however, nor the ones that follow from it, cannot be inferred from our deductions. Nor do we believe they are indisputable. They do not infer [from the above] because the said three deductions refer to the one who lends money and to the loan that in Latin is called *Mutuum*, whose very nature is gratuitous. By virtue of it, nothing more than what was loaned should be taken, as we said in another commentary.[65] His conclusion talks about the one who gives in exchange, whose nature is not gratuitous, and that is why it cannot be inferred from them; they both refer to different things.[66] This is not a true doctrine because everyday the opposite is done from Medina to Lisbon and Flanders and from there to Medina, the practice of which is licit whether by way of real purchase or by way of barter or other innominate contracts, as we go on to prove below.[67]

13

Money That Is Present and Money That Is Absent

Summary

Why money that is absent is worth less than money that is present . . . **62**

The rest being the same . . . **63**

The money that is more absent is worth less . . . **64**

When the payment will not happen in the same place . . . **67**

Jobs have a price even if some do them for free . . . **62**

The money from Alexandria is worth less in Genoa for the person in this city, and the [money] from Seville [is worth less] for the person who is in Burgos than the [money] in Burgos . . . **64**

Why the money from Flanders that is absent is generally worth more than the [money from Medina] that is present . . . **65**

Why to exchange is cheaper from here to Flanders, than from there to here . . . **65**

Why it is cheaper from Medina to Lisbon than from there to Medina . . . **66**

62. As for the eighth motive explaining why the value of money increases or decreases, which is that of its absence, Silvestre[1] believes more absolutely than anyone else that only its [absence] lowers its price in the place where it is absent from. Even if some may believe something else, Cajetan[2] agrees with us, and before all of them Calderini[3] and Laurencio Rodulfo,[4] and we think it juridical.

On the one hand, all merchandise that is absent and is purchased [to bring to the place] where one is, considered in its entirety, requires by its very nature expenses and work, estimated in monetary terms,[5] to retrieve and bring [it]. Despite the possibility that the merchant may have relatives, friends, or agents to retrieve it in the absent place, without any expense or work on his part, all [these] end up getting paid in one way or another, and for this [the merchant] is indebted to do the same for them, at least under the obligation to make compensation.[6] A job does not stop having a price even if someone does it gratuitously.[7] By justice one cannot take away what has been promised to someone for going from here to Rome by saying that on the way he found someone to pay for his expenses and even to give him money to accompany him.

On the other hand, no one will say that a mule that is in Seville is not worth less for the person who is here than another [mule] that is present of the same quality and price, even if by some accidental case or because of his skill he may bring it here without expenses or it may cost more over there than here. It is true that if no skill, custom, or provision of merchants were involved in this, much less would money from Flanders be worth here than what it is worth, and it is unfair that their [i.e., the merchants'] activity hurt anyone.[8]

63. Also, Doctor Medina's words[9] saying that the money's absence from the place is not enough on its own to make it worth less are not an impediment. The absence together with the dangers that occur and the expenses incurred to recover the absent money are sufficient cause to make it worth less than the [money] that is present. Because our words follow his, the expenses and work involved are as joined to its absence as we state and prove, even if some [of these expenses and work] accidentally detach themselves from [the absence].

Also, it is not an impediment either that Saint Doctor Soto[10] holds that neither the absence on its own (as Medina says) makes it worth less, nor the dangers and expenses, as they are not present today among merchants. From the logic of his saying, we arrive at our conclusion. He confesses *a contrario sensu* that if they existed, [money] would be worth more, and with the first reasoning we prove they exist, given the nature of the business, and even considering the expenses of the agents and representatives whom the merchant has over there for where they take it.

There is no impediment in his argument stating that if this were true, the money from Flanders in Medina would be worth less than the [money] from Medina itself, which is false, because according to what he says, a *ducat* from Flanders is worth more in Medina for which more than 400 *maravedis* are given [in Medina], than a *ducat* from Medina itself obtained for 375. We say, thus, that it is no impediment because we deny what is inferred. We do not mean to say that all absent money is always worth less than the present one, but that it is worth less when all else is the same; that is when the [money] that is present is worth the same where it happens to be as the [money] that is absent where it happens to be and not any other way.

A load of wheat in Toro is worth less to the one who is here than another that is present if all else is equal. This is true if both are the same quality, and the one over there is equal in worth to the one that is here, but it is not true if the [load of wheat] in Toro is worth 4 *ducats* over there and here no more than 2 and if he could have it brought securely for 1. Then it would be worth more, but a little less than the 4 *ducats*, for being absent. Thus, if the *ducat* from Flanders were not worth more in Flanders than the one from Medina in Medina, [the *ducat*] from Flanders would be worth less in Medina than another [*ducat*] from [this city]. It is worth so much more in Flanders than in Medina that even if for its absence its price might be diminished, it will not be so [diminished] that it still is not worth more than the one from Medina.

64. From which follows:

First, Calderini[11] did well in advising that a good purchase was that of one who bought from another in Genoa for 100 *ducats* 106 [*ducats*] from Alexandria in Egypt, because the 100 present [*ducats*] from Genoa were worth more for the person who was here than 100 that were absent, in Alexandria.

Second, if the exchanges from one part of the kingdom to another in the same [kingdom] were not, as they say they are, forbidden, one would be able to buy from a Sevillian in Burgos, Medina, or here with 100 *ducats* more than 100 [*ducats*] that had to be given in Seville. The *ducat* is worth as much here as there, and no more, and the absence lowers the price of money that is over there.

Third, the farther away the money, the lower its price, and the more dangers and expenses to recover it and pay for its transportation. Thus, more will cost in Salamanca the money that is in Medina than the one in Burgos; and more the [money] in Burgos than the one in Seville, and more the one in Seville than the one in Alexandria, Rome, Flanders, or León. So much more difficult is it to collect and greater the cost of transporting [its nature], the farther it is, and so much easier and lesser the closer it is. We said [its nature] because it may happen accidentally that something that is farther away may be easier to collect, it is important to take notice more of the nature[12] than of the accident of the business.

65. Fourth, the absence of money that is in Flanders makes it worth less in Medina to the one who is there and buys it there than it would be worth in Flanders to the person who is there and buys it there. It is frequently not worth so much less that it is not worth more in Medina than the *ducat* from Medina. Even if its absence (all else being the same) makes that which is absent worth less than that which is present, it should not be so much given that the *ducat* is worth more there than in Medina.

Fifth, the reason why the *ducats* from Flanders are frequently worth more in Medina than those same in Medina is that the *ducats* are worth so much more there than here. Even if the absence takes something away from its price, it does not take away so much that it is not always worth much more.

Sixth, the reason why the exchange is cheaper from here to Flanders than from Flanders to here is that 100 *ducats* from Medina cost less in Flanders than 100 from Flanders in Medina. The reason for this is that the price of 100 *ducats* from Medina proposed to be sold in Flanders diminishes for two reasons: one, because of their absence, and two, because the *ducat* is worth less in Medina than in Flanders, and the price of the *ducats* from Flanders proposed to be sold in Medina do not diminish except for one reason: their absence, which even if it makes them worth somewhat less is not so much given that they are worth more over there than here.

66. Seventh is the reason why from Medina to Lisbon many times there is a par exchange, that is, as many *ducats* [are exchanged] for as many others: 100 in Medina for another 100 given in Lisbon and no more or less. The reason for this is that the price of money from Lisbon proposed to be sold in Medina is lower than in Lisbon for being absent and outside of the kingdom. The reason why never, or very few times, the exchange to Flanders is equal (even if it is absent and outside of the kingdom) is that it is worth more in Flanders than in Lisbon, and even if the absence and being outside of the kingdom are sufficient to equal the money from Lisbon with that of Medina in Medina, not even the absence nor being outside of the kingdom are sufficient to equal the price of the [money] from Medina with that of Flanders.

67. Eighth, the above said does not apply to the exchange carried out in such a way that in one same place the money is given from one person to another and from the other to the first, whether the place where the agreement is to occur is determined for this or another that is farther away or nearer to it. So it only applies when it is agreed in such a way that the money belonging to one is given in one place to another, and in another place [the money] belonging to another [is given] to the other, as Cajetan[13] clearly wrote down. This had already been noted down abundantly with no additional help because the reason for expenses, work, and dangers on which the diminishment of the value of absent money is based cannot be applied when in one same place the delivery of both parts is carried out, but in order to pay (when there are many places involved) so much for the money as is paid in the exchange for small coinage, to which we referred above.[14]

14

International Credit and Exchange

Summary

If the exchanges carried out now from Medina to Lisbon are licit . . . **68**

Only on four conditions . . . **76**

Unequal exchanges, purchases, and bartering are illicit . . . **69, 70**

They are carried out with future things . . . **75**

Usurious is every commutation in which for reasons of time more or less is taken . . . **71**

To reprove commonly used exchanges is to condemn many good people . . . **72**

How they are saved by way of buying . . . **73**

By way of barter, not as they say to some people. When the thing that is bartered is required . . . **74**

If it is licit for the second fair . . . **76**

The time from fair to fair is considered as one day . . . **75**

It is regarded with a good and a bad eye . . . **75, 76**

68. The twenty-second and last thing we say is that there is doubt among the
learned men whether the dealings that are now carried out from Medina to Lisbon,
Flanders, León, and other similar cities, and from these to Seville, Medina, and
other such [cities], which many survive on (whom I know) without any another
[activity], are licit. These [dealings] work in the following way (as I have learned
at my expense): One who has money gives it at the end of the May fair in Medina
del Campo (which ends at the end of July) for Lisbon, to be paid within a month,
sometimes for an equal sum—that is, so many *ducats* for an equal sum, sometimes
at 1 percent. Then in Lisbon, he gives it again for the fair of Medina in the month
of October for 5 percent, 7 percent, or more for the fair of October. At the end
of this [fair] (which is at the end of December), he gives it again for Lisbon and
the twentieth of January, sometimes for an equal sum, sometimes at 1 percent or
more. Then, at the end of January, he gives it again for the fair of Villalon or of
Medina de Rio Seco at 5 or 7 percent. Almost the same thing is done in other fairs
of other cities and kingdoms for the [kingdoms] from here or others. Others give
(according to Saint Doctor Soto)[1] their money in Medina for Flanders, handing
over 410 *maravedis* per *ducat* here to receive [over there] 360 [per *ducat*], and
there they give them again for Medina, giving there a *ducat* worth 300 *maravedis*,
to receive here one of 375.

69. Against this deal:

First, it seems impossible to defend by way of buying or selling money because
all purchase of something of a higher price for a lower one is illicit, according to
Saint Thomas[2] and Scotus,[3] well-known by everyone as we said above.[4] In this
deal, 100 *ducats* from Medina are bought in Lisbon for less than 95 and in Flanders
for less than 90.

Second, it seems that inevitably it must be confessed that the purchase you
do in Medina for Flanders or Lisbon, or in Lisbon and Flanders for Medina is a
[purchase] of things of a greater price for a lower one. If it is a just price [that you

pay me] 100 *ducats* in Medina for 100 or 101 that I should give you in Lisbon in one month, it shall be an unjust price if I give you 107 for the fair of October for only 100 that you give me in Lisbon. It seems that the 100 one that I gave in Lisbon were not worth but 100 of yours in Medina, so your 100 from Lisbon cannot now be worth 107 of mine in Medina. If you have justly sold to me in past years in Lisbon 400 *maravedis* from Rome for 475, unjustly you have bought 400 [*maravedis*] from Lisbon for 400 that you give me in Rome. If for 410 that I give you in Medina, you justly sell me 360 that you have in Flanders, unjustly you sell me in Flanders 300 that you have there for 375 that I will give you here.

70. Third, it cannot be admitted for what Saint Doctor Soto[5] wants to admit for it: by way of pure exchange and barter, considering that a lower sum of money in the land where there is great lack of it is worth more than another larger sum from a land where there is greater abundance. I say, then, that it cannot be admitted by this way. The mentioned Doctor Soto expressly affirms that one cannot exchange licitly except what something is worth in one land for what something with the same value is worth in another land, and no more. The money that is given in Spain has to be worth as much and no more at the time when it is given as the money that for it will be given in Flanders is worth at that same time—whether it is given in eight days, or in a month, or in four, or in a year. Also, Soto himself says that there is no argument [to explain the fact that] you may licitly take in Spain, by sole way of exchange and barter, 410 *maravedis* for 360 that you will give me in Flanders, and then over there you give me 300 for 375 that I will give you here, because the exchange or barter from here to there, or from there to here, is unequal.

71. The fourth argument (against this kind of deal), a well-studied conclusion of Saint Thomas,[6] Scotus,[7] and all of them is that any deal where more is taken for reason of a longer period of waiting and delay is usury. It seems that in this deal more is taken for reasons of time and delay. The person who gives his *ducats* in Medina for Lisbon for a period of one month, gives them on equal terms, or at 1 percent. If he gives them for two months, he takes more; and for three, more. If he gives them in Lisbon for Medina when there are four months left for the fair, he takes more than if there were only three; if there were three, more than if there were not more than two; and if there were two, more than if there were no more than one. The person who gives money in Spain so that he gets paid back in Rome, gets [the money] cheaper if it is meant to be given back in three months than later. For these reasons, we once thought that this deal was not possible.

72. In spite of all of these, we believe it is licit:

First, because, as Calderini says,[8] it seems absurd to condemn so many good merchants who carry this out, and by [condemning them] to hurt everyone.

Second, without this kind of deal, the deals with foreign kingdoms would disappear, and one's own kingdom would impoverish itself.

Third, the whole basis for this deal is that money that is absent is not worth as much as money that is present, as proved above,[9] nor is it worth as much when there is abundance and a great quantity of it than when there is lack and need of it, as was also proved above.[10] It is possible for the person who has money in Medina to buy or try getting by way of barter and exchange other money that is in Flanders for less than what it is worth over there, and then obtain it there, and buy or try getting by barter and other innominate contracts with it other money that is in Medina for less than what it is worth there and in this way increase his assets. Also, someone who has money or credit in Flanders may buy or try to acquire by barter money in Medina outside of the fair, or at the beginning of [the fair] (if there is an abundance of it) for a cheaper price. Then [he may] buy or exchange it for a higher price at the fair, or at the end of it (if there is a greater lack) as long as he gives the just price for the absent money in present money and for the present [money] in absent money.

73. The fourth point is that for this third reason [we may] settle the first two arguments of the opposing part, as from this follows that admitting that there is no just purchase when there is no equality between the price and the merchandise, we should and must deny that, all else being the same, 100 that are present are not worth more than 100 that are absent. [And] we must deny that 100 that are absent cannot be bought for less than 100 that are present when the money from one place is worth the same as the money in the other place.

[We must] deny, too, the reason on which the arguments are based: that the just price for 100 *ducats* from Seville that are absent in Medina are 99 [that are] present, also 100 *ducats* [that are] present in Seville shall be in Seville the just price of 99 that are absent from Medina because rather 99 that are present in Seville shall be in Seville the just price for 100 that are absent from Medina.

We said, all else being the same, one amount in its place [of origin] is worth as much as the other in its [place of origin] as is worth the [money] from Seville in Seville and the one from Medina in Medina. If one amount is worth more where it is than the others where they are, it may happen what happens every day: The absent amount is worth more than the present [one], as have commonly been worth in our days more the absent ones from Flanders in Medina than the present ones from Medina in [this city], and many times, the absent ones from Lisbon in Medina than the present ones from Medina in [this city]. This is the reason why we deny that if the price of 100 *ducats* that are absent from Lisbon are in Medina 100 present ones, then 100 present ones in Lisbon shall be there the just price of 100 absent ones from Medina. This is because the *ducats* from Lisbon are worth more in Lisbon than the [*ducats*] from Medina in Medina, as we said above.[11] That is why the *ducat* from Lisbon that is present is worth more in Lisbon than the absent [*ducat*] from Medina for two reasons: for being present, and for being worth more over there by its very nature. So it is possible that the 100 that are present in Lisbon are worth much more than the 100 that are absent in Medina, although the very absence of the ones from Lisbon does not make them worth less in Medina than those of Medina for the compensation of the greatest value that the *ducats* have in Lisbon, as we have stated above.[12]

74. The fifth argument justifying this [kind] of deal is that for the said third reason the third argument of the contrary part is also resolved. From it follows that this deal may be admitted also by way of barter and by way of another innominate contract, as in I give so that you give me because from this follows that less money present is just barter, exchange, and equivalent to more money [that is] absent,[13] deducing everything much as the [issue] about buying has been worked out. We declare, however, that Saint Doctor Soto's manner of arguing cannot justify the deal that involves [sending] from one part to another, and from the other to another, as every day [people] deal for what we argued in the said fourth argument against his manner of justifying. It assumes three things from which its total destruction is concluded.

First, the barter or exchange of money may not be carried out justly but between the money that already truly belongs to the two [people] who will carry out the exchange. Second, the absent money is not worth less than the present one. Third, from these two follows that the present money may not be bartered nor exchanged for the absent money but giving an amount for the present [one] that is worth where it is as much as the absent [one] is worth where it is.

From these three things follows necessarily a fourth one. If 100 *ducats* are just barter and exchange in Medina for 90 from Flanders, no more, no less, then, too, 90 from Flanders, no more, no less, shall be just price for 100 from Medina. From this follows a fifth, that is, that for this kind of deal, nobody may increase his money nor even keep it, except with great danger, expense, and care, which nobody cares about without some kind of profit. Consequently this deal would die off. Those who until now have practiced it would be forced to restitute what they have gained [by carrying it out]. Because we concluded earlier[14] that none of these three said things may be proved by the law—rather, the opposite of them is in accordance with [the law]—we say that this deal, no more, no less, may be admitted by way of exchange, barter, or other innominate contract, as we have said earlier that it could be admitted by way of buying and selling.

75. The sixth argument that justifies this deal is that the fourth argument of the contrary party may be retorted by denying that in this deal (when it is carried out as it should be) something is taken for waiting or for a delay. First, between just merchants, the time that there is between payment and payment is considered as if it were one day and the present time in order to send the documents, get the payments ready, and carry them out, as Saint Doctor Soto declared favorably,[15] although he did not give the reason for this, which seems to be the following. By law, some time must be given to carry out these things, and since it is not determined by [law], it had to be determined by the good man's free will or law,[16] and custom has determined it, which becomes law where [law] is absent,[17] and has been induced by will of prudent merchants that it be as we just said, although sometimes less is enough and sometimes more is needed. The same argument [the fourth one] may also be retorted, considering that a different thing is buying or selling something for its just price, even if benign, that must be delivered from today in three months, which is licit. It is licit to sell on credit,[18] and to sell what has to be born yet,[19] and even to barter[20] as has been said above, which is what is done in this kind of deal. A different one is buying it for less than the just price (even if benign) for reason of advancing the money, or selling it for more than the severe just price for giving it on credit, which are illicit, as the argument proves and we declare.

Just as one can justly buy or collect by barter before Christmas the yarn and herbs of the year later for their just price, so one may buy or collect by barter at the fair of Medina the money from Flanders for its just price so that it is paid in the first, and even second, and even third fair, as long as one does not take more than the rigorous just price for getting it back at a later date than what one would take for getting it in the first fairs. We concede, however, that every time that something significant is taken that is more than what is just, for the waiting and delay, the person sins and has the obligation to restitution.

76. We conclude, thus, that said deal is licit, as long as these provisions are kept:

First, that the exchange not be feigned. That is, that the one who gives the money is willing and has the intention[21] of collecting it there for where it is taken, and he believes with reason that the one who takes it has or will have the money, extending a certificate or warrant to give it back there from where he takes it and [promising] that he will give it there.

Second, that for the absent money as much present money is given as is supposed to be just, and the price is not lowered too much for its absence. All of this should be estimated by the good man's own free will.[22]

Third, no more [money] be taken for reason of a longer period of time until the moment in which the delivery or payments must be handed over than if it were to be delivered immediately where the payment is due.

The fourth derives from this one: that he not sell, barter, or give for more [money] when selling, bartering, or giving it for the second or third fair, than if he gave it for the first. We said [more] because if he decided to give it for the second and even for the third fair for what he would justly take until the payments of the first, then he can rightly do it, and it shall be a deed of charity and friendship; he would not be able to take more because [even if] what is given by way of true exchange or true interest may be given more expensively for two fairs than for one, and more expensively for three than for two, as was said above,[23] [this is not so] with the exchange by buying, bartering, or other innominate contract, which we refer to here.

77. From this we understand:

First, there are reasons to be uncertain regarding a case that they asked us about in Lisbon, in which a Castilian who wanted to give there a certain [quantity] of *ducats* to a Portuguese merchant so that they were paid back to him with a certain profit in the first fair of Medina del Campo, which was to be held from that day in three or four months, saw great advantage in having the money brought back to him in Castile. On the one hand, it seemed it [was not possible] because there did not seem to be any reason for which he would be able to take [the profit].[24] Rather, it seemed that he had to give it to the merchant, as it suited the Castilian to bring his money from there to here, and the merchant was putting the skill and work of giving it to him here, according to what we said about the justice of exchange by bills of exchange.

On the other hand, there seems to be inequality and injustice in the merchant's giving as much here as he takes over there and, on top of that, giving of his skill and work and giving a profit[25] [to the Castilian]. The merchant did not want to give a profit if he had to give [the money] back soon after in Medina, but rather only if he had to give it from that time to three or four months, enjoying it in that time in between, and consequently was paying [the profit] for the delay in time, which is usury for what was said above[26] and elsewhere,[27] and Cajetan[28] seems to agree with this part.

78. Some however will be convinced by Saint Doctor Soto to hold the opposite view, saying that if the merchant found it convenient to bring his money from Medina to Lisbon, as the other found it convenient to bring his to Medina, he could well take the profit that is taken for the exchange of bills of exchange. In this case Cajetan[29] also holds this, even if he does not argue it. We, however, believe there are five different ways by which the said Castilian may give the said *ducats*, which are four without deliberations regarding a longer or shorter period of time until the next fair, at least as a principal issue, and one with this deliberation.

The first, without said consideration, is [by way] of loan. The second, by exchange of bills of exchange with which the merchant may transfer his *ducats* over here. The third, by way of his passing to the merchant his [*ducats*] from Medina over there. The fourth, [by way] of buying, bartering, or any other innominate commutation of the merchant's absent *ducats* in Medina for his present ones in Lisbon. The fifth is with principal consideration of the time and deadline until the fair, by any of the said ways, taking from him more or less according to the greater or lesser time that there was until them.

In the first case—wanting to give them by way of loan and with a pact or principal intention of having them paid in Medina—he was a usurer because, by loaning, he wanted to gain a benefit, that is, the obligation of making him pay in Medina with a profit, having lent them in Lisbon—which is a benefit estimated in money.[30] If, instead, he wanted to lend them to him without such pact and intention of making him pay unavoidably in Medina, but there in Lisbon, so much for so much, or in Medina with that profit as a reward for what the money was worth in excess over there than in Medina, he could then licitly take that extra amount if the *ducats* were worth so much more over there than here, for what we said above.[31]

In the second case, if he wanted to give them by way of exchange of bills of exchange so that the merchant transferred his money to Medina, the Castilian was forced to give the other a reward for this, for what we said earlier. This is true even if in the contract it were possible to agree that for his salary he take the excess of what the money was worth over there in relation to here or a part of it, whatever was just, for what we said above.[32]

In the third case, if he wanted to give them by way of transferring the money from here to there, the merchant could take the salary corresponding to what the banker would take justly for transferring them for him.

In the fourth case, if he wanted to give them by way of buying, bartering, or other innominate contract of "I give so you give me," he would be able to take more for two reasons: because the merchant's money was absent and thus was worth less, and because the money was worth over there more than the money over here, as we have said above.[33]

In the fifth case, if he wanted to give [the *ducats*] by any one of the ways described above, with principal consideration of the time that remained until the payment, wanting to take more or less according to the longer or shorter period of time there was, we say undoubtedly that this was illicit for him. We have concluded above[34] that not only the contract for lending but all other [contracts] in which more or less is taken for a longer or shorter period until the payment, are formal or virtual usury.

79. The second thing follows that proportionately this distinction should be set apart when someone else wants to give money in Medina, where it is worth less, for Lisbon, or for Flanders, where it is worth more; or in Seville for Medina, where it is worth the same, which to avoid extending ourselves, we shall not explain.

The third thing follows and is what should be said about Saint Antonino's[35] principle. The usurer is the exchanger or banker who gives someone in Rome 100 or 1,000 *ducats* for his commercial dealings, to be paid from today in six months in Paris with a pact that he pay him there 5 or 8 percent more. This is understood, too, by Silvestre[36] and both are approved by the most learned academic Gregorio Lopez,[37] who is satisfied with this name, [in spite of] belonging to the Council of the Indies,[38] and deserving, too, that of doctor as is manifest in the great work and erudition with which he has composed the very apt, discreet, and beneficial glosses on all the Seven Certifications[39] that he published and printed last year with great benefit to the republic while he was in this same cell as we are, although not as invisible as us.

And this is what should be said about this [principle]:

First, that it is true because in that contract, according to what it stipulates, 5 or 8 percent is taken for the delay and consideration of the time that there is between the loan and the payment, which is obvious usury.

Second, that such a contract could not be carried out licitly by way of loan to Paris—even if the time and delay were not taken into account—but could [be carried out] to Spain because, as nothing is to be desired for a loan and money is worth more in France than in Rome, it is illicit for two reasons: More is taken due to the place where [the money] is to be paid, and an extra 5 or 8 [percent] are taken. For Spain, it would be possible by not taking those extra 5 or 8 percent, inasmuch as money from here is worth less than money from there to be paid promptly here.

Third, that such a contract may be carried out licitly by way of buying, bartering, or another innominate contract by giving there, considering the time factor, those 100 present *ducats* for another similar amount and some more absent ones, as long as the said[40] four conditions are kept. He would be able to take more if he gave them for Spain than if he gave them for France because Spain is farther away from Rome than France and, for this reason, less are worth the absent ones from Spain in Rome than the absent ones from France, for what was said above,[41] and also because money is worth less in Spain than in Rome and in France more than in Rome and Spain. This was, according to our way of thinking, what Silvestre[42] meant when he said that said contract, as it was carried out, was usurious but that it was possible to carry it out properly.

80. Now follows the last issue: It is not exchange but usury under the name of exchange when those who, once the fair has started and the time of payment has arrived, give the debtors (who do not pay) a delay and more time until the next fair, as long as they pay an amount for the new exchange,[43] as Cajetan[44] notes well. It cannot be denied that by way of exchanging for an interest they could take from them [the amount that] for reason of them not paying [when they should] they stop from gaining with true exchanges that they would carry out if they had that money, for what was said above.[45]

This is what, with due correction, we have considered about exchanges with all honesty and without evil deception before God. This is the limit to where they can extend their profit. We have extended it as much as possible in order to justly defend the souls, honor, and fortune of so many important and honorable people. We hope that those who are not included in this deal do not feel any envy toward those who make a living from it, even if [they are] noble. We advise the confessors of those who live from [these kind of deals] to solemnly advise them against feigned exchanges and interests and persuade them that the temptations [that arise from them] make them walk toward Paradise through high and rocky grades from where the tumbles [that come] from the great love and attraction of great profits may easily hurl them down deep ravines of sins and such thick bramble patches of restitutions that late or never will they pick themselves up and get rid of them.

May the one who was crowned with a crown of brambles and thorns raise and rid those who have already fallen in them and those who as many times have fallen in others, and raise us all to the most boundless heights of the heavens for love of his very glorious mother queen of them all, the eighth day of whose most joyful visitation the Catholic Church today celebrates. Amen. *Salmanticae VIII Idus Iulias, Anno a partu eiusdem virginis matris 1556.*

NOTES

Preface

1. Gregory IX (1170–1241) was elected to the papacy in 1227. In addition to a strained relationship with Emperor Frederick II, Gregory's pontificate was marked by a continuous battle against heresy as indicated by the constitutions inserted into the *Corpus iuris canonici*, among which was included the ruling *Naviganti de usuries*. This famous ruling condemned all known forms of usury and became the starting point for subsequent learned discussion of the intricacies pertaining to usury doctrine throughout the medieval and early modern eras. (NCE, VI, 775–77, s.v. Gregory IX, Pope)

Chapter 1

1. In the original: "zumoso," meaning juicy.

2. In the original: "breviloquio," meaning concise.

3. A legal presumption that does not admit contrary proof.

4. Hostiensis, *Iur. utr. Monarchae celeberrimi in V Decretalium commentaria* (Venice, 1581); Ioannis Andreae, *In Decretalium Novella commentaria* (Venice, 1571); Panormitanus, *Panormitani prima in primum quintum Decretalium* (Lyons, 1555–1559), and company.

5. Nicolò de' Tudeschi (1386–1445), also known as "abbas modernus" or "recentior," "abbas Panormitanus" or "Siculus," was a Benedictine canonist. In 1400 he entered the Order of Saint Benedict; he was sent to the University of Bologna to study under Zabarella; in 1411 he became a doctor of canon law, and taught successively at Parma (1412–18), Siena (1419–30), and Bologna (1431–32). Meanwhile in 1425, he was made abbot of the monastery of Maniacio, near Massina, whence his title "abbas." In 1434 he placed himself at the service of Alfonso of Castile, King of Sicily, obtaining the See of Palermo in 1435, whence his name "Panormitanus." During the troubles that plagued the pontificate of Eugene IV, Nicolò at first followed the party of the pontiff but subsequently allied himself with the papal contender Felix V who, in 1440, named him cardinal. In his *Tractatus de concilio Basileensi* he upheld the doctrine of the superiority of a general council to the pope. It was

his canonical works, especially his commentary on the decretals of Pope Gregory IX that won him the title of *lucerna juris* ("lamp of the law") and insured him great authority; he also wrote *Consilia, Quaestiones, Repetitiones, Disputationes, disceptationes et allegationes*, and *Flores utriusque juris*. (CE, XI, 69, s.v. Nicolò de' Tudeschi)

6. John Major, *In quartum sententiarum quaestiones utilissimae* (Paris, 1521), dist. 15, quaest. 31, sub fine.

7. Silvestre de Prierias, *Sylvestrina suma, qua summa summarum merito nuncupatur* (Lyons, 1555), verbo *usura*, 3, quaest. 35.

8. Tomás de Vio Cajetan, *Summa Caietani* (Lyons, 1544), verbo usura exterior.

9. Juan de Medina, *Codex de Restitutione et Contractibus* (Compluti, 1546), tit. De usura restituenda, in principio [fol. 144] et postea in versic. *Inde*, fol. 145.

10. Domingo de Soto, *De iustitia et iure, libri decem* (Salamanca, 1553), lib. 6, quaest. 7, art. I.

11. Lex *Periculi pretium*, ff. De náutico foenore [Digesto 22, 2, 5].

12. Laurencio de Rodulfo, *Tractatus de usuris*, in can. *Consuluit* [Decretales 5, 19, 10], part. 3, quaest. I, no. 8; Antonino, *Summa theologicae* (Venice, 1503), part. 2, tit. I, cap. 7, s. 21; and Ioannes Annanias, *Commentaria super prima et secunda parte libri V Decretalium* (Bologna, 1480): [*De usuries Rubrica*: Decretales 5, 19, 19], no. 37.

13. Panormitamus, Ioannes Annanias, Petrus Ravena, nam Ioannem Andream ob brevitatem non sumam.

14. Argumentum ab illo loco: Si quid minus videtur inesse, inest, et id quod magis, et cetera. c. *cum in cunctis*, De electione: Authentico *multo magis*, c. De sacrosanctis [Codex I, 2, 14]. Et qui de uno dicit causa exempli, non negat de alio iuxta leg. *Damni infesti stipulatio*, ff. De damno infecto [Digesto 39, 2, 18], et glossam putatam singularem, cap. I, *Ne clerici vel monachi* [Decretales 3, 24, 127]. Et qui de uno dicit, non negat de alio simili, neque e conctrario, ut tradit Dominicus in causa *Qualis*, 25 dist. [Decretales I, 25, 4].

15. Argumentum, c. I, 14, q. 3 [Decreto II, 14, 3, I] et eorum quae ibi latius commenti sumus supra commetario proximo *Comentario Resolutorio de Usuras* sobre el capítulo primero, 14, q. 3.

16. Quod veritatem sonat, sicut et verbum *censendus* fictionem, aut praesumptionem, iuxta notata per Bartolum et Iosonem in lege *Si is* qui pro emptore, ff. De usucapionibus [Digesto 41, 3, 15].

17. *Trajecticius contractus*: The insurance taken from the insurer for the money that is to be taken across the sea.

18. Quod est quid aestimabile, leg. *Periculi praetium*, ff. De náutico foenore [Digesto 22, 2, 5].

19. See paragraph 30 below.

20. Iuxta glossam singularem, c. *Conquestus*, De usuris [Decretales 5, 19, 8] quam communiter receptam dixit Antonino Burgensis in capite *Ad nostram* [Decretales 5, 17, 3] col. 15, De emptione et venditione, et esse in usu ait Cassiodorus in decissione I, *De usuris*.

21. Ff. et C. de nautico foenore [Digesto 22, 2, 5; Cod. 4, 33].

22. Super hoc ipso capite [Decretales 5, 19, 19], per eius textum [De usuris Rubrica, cap. 19].

23. In Authentico, *Ad hoc*, C. de usuries, col. 3.

24. In praesenti [De usuris Rubrica, c. *Naviganti*], no. 3 citans Petrum ab Ancharano in lege *si*, C. De náutico foenore [Cod. 4, 33, I] reprobantem Iacobum Butrigam, qui contrarium tenuit in lege 1 Codicis de náutico foenore.

25. F. tit. De náutico foenore [Digesto 22, 2].

26. Lex *Periculi pretium*, ff. De náutico foenore [Digesto 22, 2, 5].

27. In relation to paragraph 2.

28. Adrian VI, *In quartum sententiarum* (Paris, 1530), De restitutione, in quaestione quae incipit occurunt.

29. Martín de Azpilcueta, *Manual de confesores y penitentes* (Salamanca, 1556), cap. 17, no. 242.

30. Lex *cum ipse*, c. De contrahenda emptione, et lex *si in emptione, si.* Ff. Eodem [Cod. 4, 38, 5; and Digesto 18, I, 34, 6].

31. Lex I, C. de Contractibus iudicum, et legibus Principalibus, c. *si certum petatur* [Cod. I, 53, I; 4, 4].

32. C. *Totum*, I, quaest. 3, Lex *Quisquis*, de legatis fideicommissis 3 [Decreto II, 3, 6; Digesto 32, 3, 5].

33. Azpilcueta, *Comentario Resolutorio de Usuras*, cap. I, 2 and 3, 14, quaest. 3 [Decreto II, 14, 3, I–3].

34. Iuxta late notata in capite *Is qui fidem*, de sponsalibus [Decretales 4, I, 30].

35. C. *Quae a iure communi*, de regulis iuris lib. 6; lex *Quod contra ratione*, ff. eodem [Digesto 50, 17, 141].

36. Molinaeus, *Tractatus commerciorum*, in libro de commerciis, nos. 7, 11, and 70.

37. In the original, "fiador."

38. Laurencio, *Tractatus de usuris*, cap. *Consuluit* [Decretales 5, 19, 10], part 3, quaest. 31.

39. In praesenti [De usuris Rubrica: Decretales 5, 19, 19], no. 46, et sensit glossa unde id hauriunt Baldus et Salicetus in libro 3 Codicis, de exercitatoria [actione Rubrica].

40. Quod testatur Cajetan, *De cambiis* (Milan, 1499), cap. I; Medina, *Codex*, fol. 145; Soto, *De iustitia et iure*, lib. 7, quaest. I, lib. 6, quaest. 8, et alii alibi.

41. Azpilcueta, *Comentario Resolutorio de Usuras*, cap. I, XIIII, quaest. 3 [Decreto II, 14, 3, I] supra cum hoc commentario excuso.

Chapter 2

1. In the original: "permutación."

2. Ut late declarat dicta lex I, ff. de contrahenda emptione [Digesto 18, I, I] et lex I, ff. de rerum permutatione [Digesto 19, 3, I].

3. Per leges praedictas, et lex *ex placito*. C. De rerum permutatione [Cod. 4, 64, 3].

4. Lex I, tit. 6, part. 5. Hostiensis in *Summa*, de rerum permutatione, versiculo *Quid antem potest permutari.*

5. See paragraphs 20 and 32.

6. Castilian silver coin that was the basis of the Spanish monetary system until the nineteenth century.

7. Gold coin, originated in Venice in the thirteenth century with a weight of 3.60 grams, from where it was imitated for different European states. Unit for counting in Castile during the sixteenth and seventeenth centuries: It was equivalent to 375 *maravedis* or 11 Castilian *reales.*

8. Generic name given to the Spanish pieces of 2 gold *escudos.*

9. Spanish version of the French *angelot* (a coin with the image of Saint Michael fighting the dragon with a spear in his two hands on the obverse and a ship on the reverse).

10. In the original: "leyes de las partidas," a medieval code especially written down under Alfonso X the Wise (1252–1284) to unify the legislation. During Alfonso's reign, the kingdom of Castile-León produced a series of lawbooks. The most important were the *Fuero real* (1252–1255) and the *Libro de las leyes* (1256–1258), which, in later redactions, was known as the *Siete partidas*. The *Fuero real* contained laws for cities, and the *Libro de las leyes* was a collection of territorial laws. It is not clear, to what extent, Alfonso X and his successors played in creating these collections. (DMA, 7, 430, s.v. Law Codes: 1000–1500)

11. Tit. 6, part. 5.

12. Antonino, *Summa*, part. 2, tit. I, cap. 7, s. 49; Angelica, *Summa Angelica de casibus conscientiae* (Nürnberg, 1498); Rosella, *Summa de casibus conscientiae* (Venice, 1516); and Silvestre, *Suma*.

13. Rodulfo, *Tractatus de usuris*, quaest. I, part. 3, c. *consuluit* [Decretales 5, 19, 10].

14. Cajetan, *De cambiis*, cap. I.

15. Medina, *Codex*, fol. 154.

16. Soto, *De iustitia et iure*, lib. 6, quaest. 8, art. 2.

17. Soto, *De iustitia et iure*, lib. 6, quaest. 8, art. 2, no. 21.

18. Soto, *De iustitia et iure*, lib. 6, quaest. 8, art. 2, no. 19.

19. Soto, *De iustitia et iure*, lib. 6, quaest. 8, art. 2, no. 21.

20. Soto, *De iustitia et iure*, lib. 6, quaest. 8, art. 2, no. 31.

21. Soto, *De iustitia et iure*, lib. 6, quaest. 8, art. 2, no. 34.

22. Soto, *De iustitia et iure*, lib. 6, quaest. 8, art. 2, no. 36.

23. Soto, *De iustitia et iure*, lib. 6, quaest. 8, art. 2, no. 41.

Chapter 3

1. In lege I, ff. de rerum permutatione [Digesto 19, 3, I].

2. Ut praedictus Paulus ait ubi supra [Digesto 19, 3 I], et ante ipsum Aristotle I politicorum, cap. 6 [*Politica* I, 3, 8 = Didot I 489].

3. Saint Thomas, *De regimine principum*, lib. 2, cap. 13 et omnes recentiores de hac re loquentes, praesertim Ioannes Calderinus hic [Decretales 5, 19, 19, de usuris cap. 11], et Laurencio in c. *Consuluit* [Decretales 5, 19, 10], pars 2, quaest. 26, aptus ad hoc textus in lege *si ita*, ff. de fideiussoribus [Digesto 46, I, 42].

4. I Político, c. 6 et 7 [*Política* I, 3, 8 ss. = Didot I 489–492].

5. Thomas, *Summa theologicae*, II-II, quaest. 77, art. I, 3, communiter receptus.

6. Thomas, *Summa theologicae*, II-II, quaest. 77, art. 1.

7. De quibus Thomas, *De regimine principum*, lib. 2, cap. 14.

8. Lex s. Finalis [*non potest*], ff. commodat [Digesto 13, 6, 3, 6].

9. Quod de auro affirmat Thomas, *Summa theologicae*, II-II, quaest. 77, art. I, ad I, 3.

10. Thomas, *Summa theologicae*, II-II, quaest. 77, art. 2, 3.

11. Quippe correlativorum eadem est disciplina, lex I, C. *de cupressis*, libro 11 [Cod. 11, 77, I], quod late explicat Felinus in prooemium, Gregory [episcopus], a col. I.

12. Cap. *Cum causa* ibi *iusto pretio*, de emptione [Decreto II, 14, 4, 5].

13. Nam quoad hoc ipse cambiens emptioris loco habetur: *lex sciendum*, s. Emptorem, ff. de aedilitio edicto [Digesto 21, I, 19, 5].

14. Per cap. I et quaeque ubi n. 1 annotavimus 14, quaest. 3 [Decreto II, 14, 3, I].

15. Toto titulo ff. Et C. Locati et de locato [Digesto 19, 2, et Cod. 4, 65].

16. Cap. Plus valere quod agitur, quam quod simulate concipitur, c. *Illo vos*, de pignoribus [Decretales 3, 21, 4]; c. *Ad nostram*, de emptione et venditione [Decretales 3, 17, 5].

Chapter 4

1. C. I [Decretales 3, 17, I] et c. *Ad nostram* [Decretales 3, 17, 5], et c. *Cum causa*, ibi *iusto pretio*, de emptione [Decretales 3, 17, 6].

2. Quia in omnibus commerciis, et contractibus iustitia commutative est servanda: 5 Ethicorum [Ethica 5, 2, 12s = Didot II 55], et tradit Augustinus, lib. 13, cap. 3, *De Trinitate* [PL 42, 1017] sentit Thomas, *Summa theologicae*, II-II, quaest. 58, art. 6 and quaest. 59, art. 2, Exprimit Scotus, *Quaestiones in quattuor libros sententiarum* (Venice, 1490), dist. 15, quaest. 2, art. 2. Et quia in hoc permutans aut cambians pro emptore vel venditore est, lex *sciendum*, s. *emptorem*, ff. de aedilitio edicto [Digesto 21, I, 19, 5] facit; c. ad quaestiones cum glossa 3, de rerum permutatione [Cod. 4, 64, 3].

3. Vellum currency worth 2 units, belonging to the duke of Brittany in the fifteenth century, so called for the shield on its reverse.

4. See paragraph 11.

5. Lex I, ff. de rerum permutatione [Digesto 19, 3, I] and paragraph 11.

6. Quod Hostiensis ait esse pessimum genus usurarum in *Summa*, de usuris [Rubrica], s. *an aliquo*, sub finem: versiculo *Quid si quis pecuniam*.

7. Azpilcueta, *Comentario Resolutorio de Usuras*, c. I, 14, quaest. 3 [Decreto II, 14, 3, I], n. 26, et probatur in c. *ad nostram*, de emptione [Decretales 3, 17, 5] et in c. *Illo vos*, de pignoribus [Decretales 3, 21, 4] cum eis annotata.

8. Soto, *De iustitia et iure*, lib. 7, quaest. 5, art. 2. Cf. lib. 6, quaest. 12.2, [fol. 597]; et ante illum Silvestre, *Suma*, verb. *usura* 4, quaest. 9, quem ipse non citat.

9. *Lex Nec emptio*, ff. de contrahenda emptione [Digesto 18, I, 8].

10. Lex *Et quae nondum*, ff. de pignoribus [Digesto 20, I, 15].

11. Lex *Interdum*, ff. de verborum obligationibus [Digesto 45, I, 73].

12. S. Ea [*quoque res*] *quae*, Institutionum, de legatis [Instit 2, 20, 7].

13. Silvestre, *Suma*, verb. *usura* 4, quaest. 9, vers. septima.

14. Quod absurdum dictum est ad dicendum: lex *Nam quod absurdum*, ff. de operas libertorum [Digesto 38, I, *Nam absurdum*], et cap. *Dudum*, de praebendis lib. 6 [In Sexto 3, 4, 14].

15. Originally from the mid fifteenth century, it was the currency of Milán called the *testoné*. It was the Castilian currency called *real de a ocho* in the seventeenth century.

16. Per late notata in lege *Si pecuniam*, ff. de condictione causa data [Digesto 12, 4, 5], et lex *Ex placito*, C. de rerum permutatione [Cod. 4, 64, 3].

Chapter 5

1. The *Mons Pietatis* was a public pawnshop, regularly financed by charitable donations and run as not for profit but for the service of the poor. It charged a small fee for its care of the pawns and for the expenses of administration, including the salaries of its employees, so that the capital would not eventually be exhausted by the costs of the business (Cajetan, *De monte pietatis*, in *Scripta philosophica*, cap. I).

2. Cajetan, *De cambiis*, cap. 2.

3. Saint Porciano Durando, *In quattuor libros sententiarum*, lib. 3, dist. 27, quaest. 2, licet non asseveret.

4. Medina, *Codex*, fol. 147 [De cambiis et lucro per eadem acquisitio, fol. 155].

5. Quod ex definitione usurae in Azpilcueta, *Comentario Resolutorio de Usuras*, c. I, 14, quaest. 2 [Decreto II, 14, 3], no. 5 posita colligas [8].

6. *Quia est dignus mercenaries mercede sua*: Lc. 10 [7], c. I, 13, q. 2 [Decreto II, 13, 2, I].

7. Scotus, *Quaestiones*, lib. 4, dist. 15, quaest. 2 [fol. 93].

8. Scotus, *Quaestiones*, lib. 4, dist. 15, quaest. 2 [fol. 94].

9. C. *Non sane*, 14, quaest. 5 [Decreto II, 14, 5, 15], ubi de iudice et teste: c. *Sicut pro certo* [Decretales 5, 3, 39], et c. *nemo*, de simonia [Decretales 5, 3, 14], ubi de aliis.

10. Azpilcueta, *Comentario Resolutorio de Usuras*, cap. I, 14, quaest. 3 [Decreto II, 14, 3, I], no. 45.

11. See paragraphs 34 and 35.

12. In the original "dos leguas": a legua is a unit of distance from about 2.4 to 4.6 statute miles.

13. Innocentius receptus in c. *Quoniam*, de simonia [Decretales 5, 3, 40].

14. Azpilcueta, *Comentario Resolutorio de Usuras*, cap. I, 14, quaest. 3 [Decreto II, 14, 3, I] a no. 64 usque ad 70.

15. Cajetan, *De cambiis*, cap. 2, quem sequitur Soto nec illo, neque ullo alio relato, libro 7, quaest. 3, art. 11, *De iustitia et iure* [lib. 6, quaest. 10, art. 2, fol. 589].

16. Et ita est petitio principii, aut ratio eadem cum dicto, contra lex I, adiuncta glossa et Paulo, ff. De exceptione [rei venditae], [Digesto 22, 2, I].

17. Soto, *De iustitia et iure*, lib 6, quaest. I, art. 2, ad. 6 [4 argumentum].

18. Soto, *De iustitia et iure*, lib 6, quaest. I, art. 2, ad. 6 [4 argumentum].

19. Scotus, *Quaestiones*, lib. 4, dist. 15, quaest. 2, art. 2, s. sequitur [fol. 95].

20. Azpilcueta, *Comentario Resolutorio de Usuras*, cap. I, 14, quaest. 3 [Decreto II, 14, 3, I], no. 66.

21. Scotus, *Quaestiones*, lib. 4, dist. 15, art. 2 [fol. 95].

22. Durando, *In quattuor libros sententiarum*, lib. 3, dist. 37, quaest. 2.

23. Medina, *Codex*, De rebus restituendis, ad fol. 147 [De cambiis et lucro per eadem acquisitio, fol. 154].

24. See paragraphs 3 and 4.

Chapter 6

1. In the original: "Cambio por menudo." The small coinage for exchanging is created to substitute the large money for amassing.

2. Laurencio de Rodulfo in C. *Consuluit*, de usuris [Decretales 5, 19, 10]; Antoninus, *Summa theologicae*, 2 parte, tit. I, cap. 7, s. 47. Quibus etiam Cajetan, Medina, et Soto accedunt.

3. Iuxta singularem theoriam Scotus, *Quaestiones*, lib. 4, dist. 15, quaest. 2 [fol. 95].

4. Pragmática, 129.

5. Gold coin from Castile coined by Henry IV since 1471 with a castle in its obverse. In 1483, it was the equivalent to 485 *maravedis*. In the sixteenth century, the gold *Castilian* belonging to the Catholic Sovereigns was in use. It was carved in Seville in 1475 and weighed 4.60 grams. On the obverse the busts of the Catholic Sovereigns faced each other and on the reverse were the arms of Castile and León.

6. Name given by the Christians to the *almohade* piece of gold, which doubled the weight of the *dinar* of 2.35 grams. The system lasted until the fall of the Granadine kingdom. In general it doubles any gold coin.

7. Originally, a gold coin from Florence. Imitated principally in Aragón. In Castile in 1454 it was the equivalent to 50 *maravedis*.

8. Preadicta pragmática, 129.

9. Pragmática 126 et 127 in libro pragmaticarum.

10. Pragmática, 125.

11. Cajetan, *De cambiis*, cap. I and 6.

12. Quidquid aliqui praedictorum dicant. Non enim officium fuit causa recipiendi illud plus, sed potuisset plus aliquid recipi propter operam, et impedimenta fuit causa instituendi officium, et quamvis uterque laboret [in] numerando, gratia tamen eius qui cambium petit, uterqua labor principaliter sumitur.

13. Soto, *De iustitia et iure*, lib. 6, quaest. 12, art. I [fol. 591].

14. Pragmática, 123.

15. In the original "carta de naturaleza."

16. Pragmática, 129.

17. Argumentum eorum qui in Azpilcueta, *Comentario Resolutorio de Usuras*, cap. I, 14, quaest. 3 [Decreto II 14, 3, I], n. 45 diximus post Thomam, *Summa theologicae*, II-II, quaest. 77, art. I.

18. Portuguese coin called *cruzado de ouro*. The Portuguese *cruzado* was worth 375 *maravedis* in Castile.

19. Medina, *Codex*, De pecunia an vendi possit, fol. 157.

20. Soto, *De iustitia et iure*, lib. 6 quaest. 12, art. I [fol. 591].

21. Glossa Bartholi, Baldi, Decii, et aliorum in lege I, C. de sententiis quae pro eo quod interest proferuntur [Cod. 7, 47, I].

22. Argumentum lex *Si in emptionem*, ff. de non numerata pecunia [Digesto 22, 77, I] et eius quod ait Thomas, *Summa theologicae*, II-II, quaest. 77, art. I.

23. Pragmática 126 et 127, et melius 129, et quia in altero plus iusto recipit, in altero dat minus.

24. Quamuis aequalitas est servanda: 5, *Ethica* [Didot II, 56], et supra no. 13.

Chapter 7

1. In cap. *de plus* petitionibus [Decretales 3, 3] no. 9 dicens eum esse iustum et iuris gentium.

2. In consilium 11, de usuris [Rubrica].

3. Quia actus agentium non operantur ultra fines eorum: lex *Non omnis*, ff. de rebus creditis [Digesto 12, I, 19] et. *Cum super*, de officio delegati [Decretales I, 19, 23].

4. Argumentum lex 2, s. *finalis*, ff. locato et conducto [Digesto 19, I, 2]; *Inst*. De locato, per totum [*Inst*. 4, 65, I–35].

5. Lex *Naturalis*, ff. de praescriptis [Digesto 19, 5, 5] adiuncta *lex si*, [Digesto 19, 5, 7] cum glossa et ei annotatis, ff. De conditione causa data [Digesto 12, 4].

6. Iuxta doctrinam Bartholi in dicta lege *Naturalis*, s. *sed si facio* [Digesto 19, 5, 5, 4] sub finem [no. 6].

7. Argumentum: lex *Periculi*, ff. de nautico foenore [Digesto 22, 2, 5], et lex *Traiectitiae*, ff. De actionibus et obligationibus [Digesto 44, 7, 23] lex *Qui Romae*, s. I, ff. De verborum obligationibus [Digesto 45, I, 122, I].

8. Iuxta notata in lege *Si pecuniam*, cum glossa verbi *Poenitere*, ff. De conditione causa data [Digesto 13, 4, 5], et lex *Ex placito*, C. De rerum permutatione [Cod. 4, 64, 3].

9. Scotus, *Quaestiones*, lib. 4, dist. 15, quaest. 2, art. 2 [fol. 95] quod probatur 5 Ethica [4, 10 ss.: Didot II, 57], et per scripta Thomae, *Summa theologicae*, II-II, quaest. 58, art. 6 et quaest. 59, art. 2.

10. Bartolome Saliceto, *Lectura super IX libris codicis* (Lyons, 1500), in authentico, Ad haec, quaest. II, De usuris [Rubrica].

11. Argumentum: c. I, de constitutionibus [Decreto I, I, I], et c. *consuetudo* [Decreto Ij, I, 5] et dicta lex I, ff. de iure deliberandi [Digesto 28, 8, I], et c. *De causis*, de officio [et potestate iudicis] delegati [Decretales I, 29, 4].

12. Azpilcueta, *Comentario Resolutorio de Usuras*, cap. I, 14 quaest. 3 [Decreto II, 14, 3, I]; and paragraphs 26 and 14 in the present work.

13. See paragraph 14.

14. Azpilcueta, *Comentario Resolutorio de Usuras*, cap. I, 14, quaest. 3 [Decreto II, 14, 3, I], no. 4 cum hoc retro excuso, et tent Thomas, *Summa theologicae*, II-II, quaest. 78, art. 2.

15. Cajetan, *De cambiis*, cap. I [fol. 163]. Quod omnium soptime resolvit Silvestre, *Suma*, verbo *usura* 4, quaest. 9, et *cambium siccum* secundum omnes.

16. Cajetan, *De cambiis*, cap. I [fol. 163].

17. See Azpilcueta's discussion in paragraph 34.

18. Annanias, *Commentaria*, no. 46 [Decretales 5, 19, 10], *De usuris [Rubrica]*.

19. Quod late deducit Laurencio in dicto capite Consuluit [Decretales 5, 19, 10], 2 parte, quaest., 135.

20. See paragraphs 14 and 24.

21. Soto, *De iustitia et iure*, lib. 7, quaest. 3, art. 2, sub finem, lib. 6, quaest. 10, art. 2 [fol. 589].

22. Soto, *De iustitia et iure*, lib. 7, quaest. 6, art. I. Cf. lib. 6, quaest. 3, art. I [fol. 60].

23. *Add. R.*: Argumentum c. *tua* [Decretales 4, I, 26] et c. *is qui* [Decretales 4, I, 30].

24. See paragraph 10.

25. In c. *consuluit* [Decretales 5, 19, 10], 3 parte, quaest. I.

26. Lex 2, ff. de constitutionibus principum [Digesto I, 4, 2], Thomas, *Summa theologicae*, I-II, quaest. 97, art. I.

27. Argumentum: Lex *Praecipimus*, C. de appellationibus [Cod. 7, 72, 32], et c. I, de constitutionibus lib. 6.

28. Canon: Est iniusta misericordia, in principio; et in fine ibi: facilitas enim veniae, incentivum tribuit delinqueni [Decreto II, 23, 4, 33].

29. C. *Factae*, 4 dist. Facit [Decreto I, 4, I]; c. *Non putes*, cum multis sequentibus, 23, quaest. 5 [Decreto 2, 23, 5, 36 ss.].

30. Contra legem *Non dubium*, C. de legibus [Cod. I, 14, 5], et c. *Certum*, de regulis iuris lib. 6.

31. *Ducado de Camara*: The papal *ducat*, gold coin that weighed and was worth what the Venetian *ducat* minted by the Apostolic Chamber was, from whence its name.

32. Weighing measure for coins. In Castile it weighed 230.0465 grams for silver. It was divided into 8 ounces; for gold into 50 *Castilians*. The *mark* from the Casa de Moneda was used to weigh officially minted coins.

33. Generic name given in the Middle and Modern Ages to diverse gold and silver coins, with a shield on one of its faces. Also *Castilian* gold coin introduced in 1535 as a consequence of the casting of coins for the Tunez army. It was equivalent to 10.68 gold *pesetas*.

34. Created by Charlemagne as a counting unit. The salary for the people from Burgos consisted of 12 vellum money notes carved in Burgos.

35. *Add. R.*: Addo nunc quarto esse necessariumj, ut locus in quo est solvenda pecunias longe distet a loco in quo dentur litterae. Alioqui enim esset cambium de tempore ad tempus, quod non licet, et non de loco ad locum, quod licet, ut ex eodem commentario num. 67 colligitur, et satis probatur praedicta extravagante.

36. *Add. R.*: Lex bona memoria Caroli V qui praescripsit pretium moderatum quo campsores suorum Regnorum cambirent.

37. See paragraph 18.

Chapter 8

1. See paragraph 41.

2. Toto titulo: de contrahenda emptione [Digesto 18, I], et de rerum permutatione [Digesto 19, 4], et lex I, cum quatuor sequentibus, ff. De praescriptis verbis [Digesto 19, 5, 1–5].

3. Soto, *De iustitia et iure*, lib. 7, quaest. 5, art. 3. Cf. lib. 6, quaest. 12, art. 3 [fol. 599].

4. Argumentum: lex I, ff. de rerum permutatione [Digesto 19, 4, I], lex I, ff. de contrahenda emptione [Digesto 18, I, I], lex 3, s. Si, ff. commodati [Digesto 13, 6, 3, I]; et eorum quae scripsit Cajetan, *De cambiis*, cap. 6, et Medina, *Codex*, ad fol. 148 [De pecunia an vendi possit, fol. 157]. Quamquam quoad aliqua quae parvi ponderis sunt, dissentire videri possunt.

5. In the original: "si ello de rayz se pesare."

6. Argumentum: lex 2, ff. Locati [Digesto 19, 2, 2] et s. *Item pretium*, institut. De emptione [*Inst.* 3, 24, I, 2].

7. Azpilcueta, *Comentario Resolutorio de Usuras*, cap. I, 14, quaest. 3 [Decreto II, 14, 3, I]. Arcediano: In early days, the first or principal of deacons; ordinary judge who practiced a jurisdiction delegated from the episcopal in a particular territory.

8. Ut Laurencio in c. Consuluit [Decretales 5, 19, 10], parte 2, quaest. 6.

9. In the original: "ley de la partida." Lex 2, tit. 6, partita 5. Hostiensis in *Summa*, de rerum permutatione, v. S. *Quid autem*.

10. See paragraph 24.

11. Eadem ratione lex *illud*, ff. ad legem aquilam [Digesto 9, 2, 32].

Chapter 9

1. Azpilcueta, *Comentario Resolutorio de Usuras*, cap. I, 14, quaest. 3 [Decreto II, 14, 3, I], no. 46 et sequenti [23 s.], una cum hoc excuso.

2. Quia eadem omnino ratio, idem omnino ius suadet lex *illud*, ff. Ad legem aquilam [Digesto 9, 2, 32] et c. *Translato*, de constitutionibus [Decretales I, 2, 3].

3. Cajetan, *De cambiis*, cap. I [fol. 163].

4. See paragraph 26.

5. Quasi non esset Deus, vel non scruptaretur corda, et renes, contra psalmun 75 [25, 2]; c. *Novit*, de indiciis [Decretales 2, I, 13] et c. *Deus Omnipotens*, 2 quaest. I [Decreto 2, 2, I, 120].

6. Soto, *De iustitia et iure*, lib. 7, quaest. 5, art. 5. Cf. lib. 6, quaest. 12, art. 5 [fol. 603].

7. Soto, *De iustitia et iure*, lib. 6, quaest. 12, art. 5 [fol. 603].

8. Calderini, *Consilia*, con. 11 [*De usuris Rubrica*].

9. In repetitione c. consuluit [Decretales 5, 19, 10], quaest. I secundae partis.

10. Antonino, *Summa*, 2 parte, tit. I, quaest. 7, s. 49.

11. In praesenti [*De usuris* Rubrica c. *Naviganti* = Decretales 5, 19, 10].

12. Silvestre, *Suma*, verb. *usura*, 4 per totum.

13. Cajetan, *De cambiis*, cap. I [fol. 163].

14. Medina, *Codex*, fol. 145 [*De cambiis*, fol. 155].

15. Azpilcueta, *Manual*, cap. 17, no. 212.

16. Azpilcueta, *Comentario Resolutorio de Usuras*, cap. I, 14, quaest. 3 [Decreto II, 14, 3, I], no. 49.

17. *Add. R.*: Quibus addo nunc Pium V per extravagantem infra transcriptam statuisse, ne a principio certum interesse praefigi possit in cambiis.

Chapter 10

1. In the original, "libranzas."

2. Lex *Argentarius*, s. I [Digesto 2, 13, 10, 10, I] and Lex *Quaesdam*, s. *Nummularios*, ff. de edendo [Digesto 2, 13, 9, 2].

3. *Dignus enim est operarius mercede sua*, Lc. 10, 7, et c. I, 13, quaest. 3 [Decreto 2, 13, I, 11].

4. Quia per pactum fieri potest id quod per legem fit: lex *Non impossibile*, ff. de pactis [Digesto 2, 14, 50], C. *Contractus*, cum glossa, de regulis iuris lib. 6 [Digesto 50, 17, 23].

5. Est enim contractus locationis ex parte campsoris, et conductionis ex parte aliorum, certa mercede constituta, lex I et 2, ff. Locati, s. r. Instit. de locatione [Digesto 19, 2, I, et 2; *Inst.* 3, 15, I].

6. Soto, *De iustitia et iure*, lib. 7, quaest. 4, art. I. Cf. lib. 6, quaest. II, art. I [fol. 590].

7. In the original: "pragmáticas."

8. Pragmática, 127.

9. Pragmática, 129.

10. Regula: *Non debet aliquis alterius odio, praegravari*, De regulis iuris, lib. 6; I quaest. 4 per totam causam [Decreto 2, I, 4]; c. *Si habes*, 24 quaest. 3 [Decreto 2, 24, 3, I].

11. Argumentum: *C. ne filius pro patre* [Cod. 4, 13], *Ne uxor pro marito* [Cod. 4, 12], per totum.

12. C. *Peccatum*, de regulis iuris, lib. 6, cum his quae diximus in manuali, c. 17, no. 63 et 64.

13. C. *Quia in omnibus*, de usuris [Decretales 5, 19, 3], c. I. Eodem titulo li. 6.

14. Per canon I, 14, quaest. 3 [Decreto II, 14, 3, I], et definitionem usuarae ac alia quae ibidem posuimus [n. 3]; immo est pessimum genus usurarum [ut dicit] Hostiensis in *Summa*, de usuris, s. *An aliquo*, sub finem.

15. Quoniam eius arbitrio sunt determinanda, quae iure reliquuntur confusa lex I, ff. De iure deliberandi [Digesto 28, 8, I].

16. Psalm 36 [16]: Melius est modicum iusto super divitias peccatorum multas.

17. Matthew 16 [26]: Quid prodest homini, si universum mundum lucretur, animae vero suae detrimentum patiatur?

18. Psalm 36 [1], Noli aemulari in malignantibus, et cetera.

Chapter 11

1. In the original: "Contrato nominado."

2. *Hanega* = *Fanega*: Capacity measurement for dry fruits, variable according to Spanish regions.

3. Lex *Iuris gentium*, cum glossa, ff. de pactis [Digesto 2, 14, 7]; lex *Ex placito*, C. De rerum permutatione cum glossa [Cod. 4, 64, 3].

4. Dicta lex *Iuris gentium*, in principio [Digesto 2, 14, 7]; lex *Naturalis*, s. *Et siquidem*, ff. De praescriptis verbis [Digesto 19, 5, 5, I].

5. Lex I et tribus sequentibus, ff. de praescriptis verbis [Digesto 19, 5, 1–4].

6. Quae sunt multa iuxta notata per Bartholum in dicta lege *Naturalis*, s. *sed si facio* [Digesto 19, 5, 5, 4], no. 6, et per omnes in principio dictae legis *Iuris gentium* [Digesto I, I, 1–5], et glossam et alios in dicta lege *Ex placito* [Cod. 4, 64, 3].

7. See paragraphs 14 and 24.

8. Cajetan, *De cambiis*, cap. 6 and 7.

9. Calderini, *Consilia*, con. 11, *de usuris* [Rubrica].

10. Laurencio, *Tractatus de usuris*, 3 parte, quaest. I, c. *Consuluit* [Decretales, 5, 19, 10].

11. Soto, *De iustitia et iure*, lib. 7, quaest. 5, art. E. Cf. lib. 6, quaest. 12, art. 2 [fol. 594].

12. Laurencio, *Tractatus de usuris*, 3 parte, quaest. I, c. *Consuluit* [Decretales, 5, 19, 10].

13. See paragraphs 21 and 22.

14. In the original: "comutar," which is commuting in the sense of trading.

15. Cajetan, *De cambiis*, cap. 7.

16. Silvestre, *Suma*, verb. *usura* 4, quaest. 9.

17. See paragraphs 14 and 24.

18. Thomas, *De regimine principum*, lib. 2, cap. 14, quem Antonius, Cajetan et omnes fere Theologi sequuntur; idem tenet Calderinus, *Consilium* II, de usuris [Rubrica], et Laurencio, in c. *consuluit* [Decretales 5, 19, 10], quaest. I, parte 3, de usuris.

19. See paragraphs 12 and 32.

20. Quod docet experientia rerum magistra: c. *Quam* sit, de electione, [In Sexto 6, 6].

21. In consilium II, de usuris [Rubrica], quem sequitur Ioannes ab Annania in praesenti [*De usuris Rubrica*: Decretales 5, 19, 19], no. 46 et sequentibus.

22. French *ducat*.

23. Conveniunt enim Antoninus, Silvestre, Cajetan, Medina et Soto, *De iustitia et iure*, lib. 6, quaest. 12, art. 2, fol. 594, et Laurencio de Rodulfo, quaest. I, 3 partis c. *Consuluit* [Decretales 5, 19, 10] de usuris [Rubrica], et Ioannes Annanias hic [*De usuris Rubrica*: Decretales 5, 19, 19], no. 52.

24. Argumentum: lex *si iactum retis*, ff. De actionibus empti [Digesto 19, I, 12], et capite praesenti cum ei annotatis.

25. See paragraph 31.

26. See paragraph 43.

27. C. *In civitate*, supra eodem [Decretales 5, 19, 6] et in hoc capite [Decretales 5, 19, 19].

28. Saint Thomas, *Summa theologicae*, II-II, quaest. 78, art. I, 2, ad 7, et probatur in c. *Ad nostram*, de emptione [Decretales 3, 17, 5].

29. In lege *Cum quid*, ff. de rebus creditis [Digesto 12, I, 3], n. 7, et *lege cum aurum*, ff. de auro et argento [Digesto 34, 2, 19], et lege *Paulus*, ss. De solutionibus [Digesto 46, 4, 101], no. 6 et 10.

30. Per Baldum, Alexandrum, et Iasonem, et fere omnes alios in dicta *lege Cum quid* [Digesto 12, I, 3].

31. S. *ultimum*, de usuris [Decretales, 5, 19, 19].

32. In consilium II, *De usuris Rubrica*.

33. In c. *Censuluit*, eodem titulo, 3 parte, quaest. I [Decretales 5, 19, 10].

34. Silvestre, *Suma*, verb. *usura* I, quaest. 14.

35. Soto, *De iustitia et iure*, lib. 6, quaest. I, art. I [fol. 514]. Cf. lib. 7, quaest. 5, art. I [lib. 6, quaest. 12, art. I, fol. 592].

36. In dicta lege *Cum quid* [Digesto 12, I, 4] in tractatu monetae, col. 3, fol. 168.

37. *Celemin*: Measure for dry goods that is equivalent in Castile to 4.625 liters approximately.

38. C. *Cum canonicus*, ubi glossa [Decretales 3, 39, 6], et notatur in c. *Olim*. [Decretales 3, 39, 30], et in c. Ex parte, de censibus [Decretales 3, 39, 18].

39. In lege *Quod te*, no. 7, ff. de rebus creditis [Digesto 12, I, 5].

40. Ait etiam Molinaeus id servatum his tribus saeculis, in libro *De commerciis*, no. 696.

41. Argumentum: lex *Si iactum retis*, ff. De actionibus empti [Digesto 19, I, 12], et huius c [Cod. 4, 33], et lex *Periculi*, ff. De nautico foenore [Digesto 22, 2, 5]. Et quae tradit Molinaeus in libro *De commerciis*, n. 718 et sequentibus.

42. In lege *Cum quid*, ff. de rebus creditis, no. 7 [Digesto 12, I, 5], et lege I et Lege *Cum Aurum*, ff. de auro et argento [Digesto 34, 2, 19], et lege *Paulus*, ff. de solutionibus, no. 6 et 10 [Digesto 46, 4, 101].

43. Per Baldum, Alexandrum, Iasonem et fere omnes alios in dicta lege *Cum quid* [Digesto 12, I, 3], Ioannem Calderinum in c. *Si*, de usuris [Cod. 4, 32, I], et Laurentium Rodulfum in c. *Consuluit* [Decretales 5, 19, 10] 3 parte, quaest. I, et Panormitanum cum communi in c. *Quanto*, de iure iurando [Decretales 2, 24, 18].

44. In dicta lege *Cum quid* [Digesto 12, I, 3], et lege *Virum*, ff. de rebus creditis [Digesto 12, I, 22].

45. In lege *Quod te*, no. 7, ff. de rebus creditis [Digesto 12, I, 5], quod Molinaeus ait servatum his tribus saeculis in libro *De commerciis*, no. 696.

46. In dicta lege *Cum quid* [Digesto 12, I, 3].

47. Baldo, *De commerciis*, quaest. 90, 92a, no. 694.

48. In authentico, *Ad haec*, quaest. 17, *De usuris*.

49. Baldo, *De commerciis*, no. 707.

Chapter 12

1. Syncopated form of *coronado*. Castilian vellum coin, thus called for showing the head of the crowned king. It was equivalent to 6 *cornados*, 1 *maravedi* in the fifteenth century.

2. Copper coin minted by Alfonso V from Portugal (1438–1481), as Lord of Ceuta [Ceita or Capta]. Copper coin belonging to Juan II of Portugal (1419–1490), equivalent to one-sixth of a *real*. It continued until D. Sebastián (1557–1578).

3. Consilium II, *De usuris* [*Rubrica*].

4. In. C. *Consuluit* [Decretales 5, 19, 10], quaest. I, 3 partis.

5. Verb. *usura* 4, quaest. 5 et 6, vers. *pro notitia.*

6. Cajetan, *De cambiis*, cap. 6 s. *De temporis*, 166.

7. Soto, *De iustitia et iure*, lib. 7, quaest. 5, art. 2 et 3; lib. 6, quaest. 12, art. 2ff.

8. Iuxta illud: vox populi, vox naturae, quae Deus est; iuxta glossam legis I, ff. de iustitia et iure, verb. *natura* [Digesto I, I, I].

9. C. Legimus, 93 dist. Ibi: omne rarum pretiorum facit, cap. Praesens [Decreto I, 93, 24, 2]: omne quod rarum est, plus appetitur. Pulegium apud Indos pipera pretiosius est, cum ei annotatis.

10. See paragraphs 12 and 20.

11. *L*: Et quod aliqui dicunt pecuniae inopiam alia inminuere nascitur.

12. Laurencio, *Tractatus de usuris*, quaest. I, 3 parte [Decretales 5, 19, 10]. Annanias, *Commentaria*, no. 52 [Decretales 5, 19, 19].

13. In Portuguese, *tostao*. Silver coins minted since the time of D. Manuel (1495–1521), which weighed 9.96 grams.

14. Quia regulariter, quod valet species in specie, id valet genus in genere, c. *Quando*, 24 dist. [Decreto I, 24, 5], ut habet glossa, et Imolensis in c. sic sacerdos, de officio iudicis ordinarii [Decretales I, 31, 2].

15. Lex 4, ff. *de eo, quod certo loco dari opotet*, a nemine in hoc citata [Digesto 13, 4, 3].

16. *R*: Cur actio arbitaria alicui detur. Actio arbitaria quae sit non satis iurisconsulti conveniunt. Alii enim sic eam definiunt. Actio arbitraria est, in sua iudicis officium exercetur mercenarium actioni inserviens, propter aliquod extrinsecum praeter naturam actionis, ut cum iudex arbiter procedit contra reum contumacem. Alii sic. Arbitariam actionem Iustinianus disputat, quia ex arbitrio et potestate iudicantis pendet, ut si semel iudex aestimaverit suo arbitrio rem restituendam, aut alio modo satisfaciendum actori, obtemperetque reus, absol-vatur, sin contra minime pareat, damnetur. Alii sic. Arbitrariae actiones sunt quaeliberam habent, ex eo quod legitimum est, electionem, quae et refertur ad arbitrium iudicis. Haec Petrus Cregor. Lib. 47, cap. 39, no. 3. Qui proprius tamen accedere videtur ad D. Navarrum in lib. 49, cap. N. scribens si tamen constiterit in contractu de loco ubi fides solvenda est, primum ubi reus facienda est conveniri debet, deinde si ibi non inveniatur, ubicumque reperietur arbitraria actione.

17. L. neque is a quo aliquid emeris, mairori pretio, sed a lege constituto acciperet.

18. Silvestre, *Suma*, verb. *usura* 4, quaest. 6, cui concordat Cajetan, *De cambiis*, cap. 5, fol. 165 et Soto, *De iustitia et iure*, lib. 6 quaest. 12, art. 2 [fol. 594 s.].

19. Cuius modi novitates parum probantur, c. *Cum consuetudinis*, de consuetudine [Decretales I, 4, 9], et c. *Quis nesciat*, dist. II [Decreto I, 12, II].

20. Iuxta mentem Innocentii, et communem in c. *Quanto*, de iureiurando [Decretales 2, 24, 16], et Thomas, *De regimine principum*, lib. 2, c. 13; tradit Gabriel Biel, *Commentarii doctissimi in IV sententiarum libros* (Brescia, 1574), dist. 15, quaest. 9; Molinaeus, *De commerciis*, no. 193.

21. Lex *si tibi*, ff. De iusoribus [Digesto 46, I, 42]: I. *si ita*, Aristotle I politicorum, 6 [*Politica* I, 3, o Didot I, 489] Saint Thomas, *De regimine principum*, lib. 2, cap. 13 et 14, et Laurencio, in c. *consuluit* [Decretales 5, 19, 10] 2 parte, quaest. 26.

22. Iuxta mentem textus Innocentii, et aliorum in c. *Quanto*, de iureiurando [Decretales 2, 24, 18].

23. Medina, *Codex*, fol. 150 [*An pecunia vendi possit*, fol. 157].

24. Copper coin, primitively made of vellum, from Castile, worth 4 *maravedis*, coined from the fifteenth to the nineteenth centuries.

25. L: quia plures res certo pretio tunc per pecuniam quam ante inveniuntur, si caetera sunt paria.

26. See paragraphs 11, 12, and 32.

27. Lex *Si tibi*, ff. De fideiiussoribus [Digesto 46, I, 42: I. *si ita*], et supra eodem no. 11 est dictum et habetur 1 politicorum [*Politica* I, 3, 135 Didot I, 490], et Thomas, *De regimine principum*, lib. 2, cap. 13 et 14.

28. See paragraphs 57 and 58.

29. Soto, *De iustitia et iure*, lib. 5, quaest. 5, art. Cf. lib. 6, quaest. 12, art. I [fol. 595].

30. See paragraph 65.

31. See paragraph 26.

32. L. Sed quatenus pecunia et pretium aliorum est.

33. E quibus est Cajetan, *De cambiis*, cap. 6.

34. Silvestre, *Suma*, verb. *usura* 4, quaest. 3.

35. Soto, *De iustitia et iure*, lib. 7, quaest. 5, art. 2. Cf. lib. 6, quaest. 12, art. 2 [fol. 594].

36. Bartholus, in lege *Paulus* I, ff. de solutionibus [Digesto 46, 3, 101], no. 7 et 10, et Panormitanus in c. *Quanto*, de iureiurando [Decretales 2, 24, 18], no. 13; Thomas, *Summa theologicae*, II-II, quaest. 78, art. 2 ad 4; Calderinus, in consilium II, de usuris [Rubrica].

37. Quae omnia praedictus Soto fatetur in dicto articulo 2 lib. 6, quaest. 12 [594].

38. Thomas, *Summa theologicae*, II-II, quaest. 77, art. I, 3.

39. Scotus, *Quaestiones*, lib. 4, dist. 15, quaest. 2.

40. In the original, "comodidad."

41. Gold *escudo* piece carved by Charles I, in 1535, at a ratio of 68 for *marco* and a value of 350 *maravedis* and a weight of 22 carats.

42. In lege *Paulus*, ff. de solutionibus [Digesto 46, 4, 101].

43. In c. *Quanto*, no. 13, de iureiurando [Decretales 2, 24, 18].

44. Argumentum: c. *Ne quis*, 22, quaest. 2 [Decreto 2, 22, 2, 14], et lex *Cum quis*, ff. De solutionibus [Digesto 46, 3, 38], et C. *Quemadmodum*, de iureiurando, cum glossis [Decretales 2, 24, 25].

45. Cajetan, *De cambiis*, cap. 7, 166, et Soto, *De iustitia et iure*, lib. 7, quaest. 5, art. 3. Cf. lib. 6, quaest. 12, art. 3 [fol. 599].

46. C. *Ex tenore*, de rescriptis [Decretales I, 3, 16,] c. *Adversus*, de immunitate ecclesiarum [Decretales 3, 49, 7].

47. Late Cajetan, *Summa*, II-II, quaest. 77, art. I.

48. Soto, *De iustitia et iure*, lib. 6, quaest. 12, art. 3 [fol. 599].

49. Argumentum: Lex I, C. *de monopoliis* [Cod. 4, 59, I].

50. Quia fraus et dolus nemini prodesse debent, c. *Ex tenore*, de rescriptis [Decretales I, 3, 16]; lex *itaque fullo*, ff. de furtis [Digesto 47, 2, 12].

51. See paragraph 30.

52. Diego de Leyva y Covarrubias, *Variarum Resolutionum Liber Primus* (Salamanca, 1578), cap. 11, no. 4.

53. See paragraph 72.

54. Et ita non probant c. *Si Papa*, de privilegiis lib. 6 [In sexto 5, 7, 10].

55. Et ita probant clementinae I, de probationibus.

56. Iuxta glossam dictae clementinae I.

57. Argumentum bonum in lege 3, s. *Nunc de officio*, ff. de eo, quod certo loco [Digesto 13, 4, 2, 8], et melius in lege 4 eiusdem tituli.

58. Argumentarum praedictarum legum [Digesto 12, 4, 2 et 4].

59. Azpilcueta, *Comentario Resolutorio de Usuras*, cap. I, 14, quaest. 2 [Decreto II, 14, 3, I] cum his quae ibi late dicebamus, no. 7, 85.

60. Soto, *De iustitia et iure*, lib. 6, quaest. 5, art. I. Cf. lib. 6, quaest. 10, art. I [fol. 592].

61. In the original "carga": A certain quantity of grain, which in some places has the capacity of 4 *fanegas* and in others, of 3.

62. Lex 3, s. *Nunc de officio*, ff. De eo quod certo loco [Digesto 13, 4, 2, 8].

63. Soto, *De iustitia et iure*, lib. 7, quaest. 3, art. I. Cf. lib. 6, quaest. 10, art. I [fol. 587].

64. A certain silver coin, minted at the time of the Emperor Charles V.

65. Azpilcueta, *Comentario Resolutorio de Usuras*, cap. I, 14 quaest. 3 [Decreto II, 14, 3, I,] no. 3 per illum textum, 7, et c. *Consuluit*, eodem titulo [Decretales 5, 19, 10] et alia multa.

66. Nam a separatis non fit illatio: lex *Papiniamus*, ff. de minoribus [Digesto 4, 4, 20], c. *Sententia*, de sentential excommunicationis, lib. 6 [Sexto 5, II, 16].

67. See paragraph 74.

Chapter 13

1. Silvestre, *Suma*, verb. *usura* 4, quaest. 4.

2. Cajetan, *De cambiis*, cap. 7.

3. Consilium II, *De usuris* [Rubrica].

4. In c. *Consuluit* [Decretales 5, 19, 10], quaest. I, partis 3.

5. Argumentum: c. *Statutum*, s. proferendo, de rescriptis lib. 6 [Sexto I, 3, II] et notata per Baldum, Panormitarum et Felinum in c. I, de testibus.

6. In the original: "obligación que llaman antidoral." Lex *Sed etsi*, s. *consuluit*, ff. de petitione haereditatis [Digesto 5, 3, 25, II] et c. *cum in officiis*, de testamentis [Decretales 3, 26, 7].

7. Non enim ea quae praeter intentionem accidunt, sed natura rei est, in his inspiciendo, argumentum: lex *Si quis nec causam*, ff. de rebus creditis [Digesto 12, I, 4], cum late ibi a Iasone traditis.

8. Lex *ea*, C. de alluvionibus [Cod. 7, 41, 3]; Panormitanus in cap. *Propter*, sub finem de locato [Decretales 3, 18, 3].

9. Medina, *Codex*, tit. De causis in quas solent campsores lucrum augere, fol. 150 [fol. 158].

10. Soto, *De iustitia et iure*, lib. 7, quaest. 6, art. 2. Cf. lib. 6, quaest. 13, art. 2 [fol. 607 s.].

11. In consilium II, *de usuris* [Rubrica].

12. C. *De occidendis*, 23, quaest. 5 [Decreto II, 23, 5, 8]; c. *Sacerdos* 50 dist. [Decreto I, 50, 50].

13. Cajetan, *De cambiis*, cap. 7.

14. See paragraph 31.

Chapter 14

1. Soto, *De iustitia et iure*, lib. 7, quaest. 5, art. 2. Cf. lib. 6, quaest. 12, art. 2 [fol. 594].

2. Thomas, *Summa theologicae*, II-II, quaest. 77, art. I, receptum ab ómnibus.

3. Scotus, *Quaestiones*, lib. 4, dist. 15, quaest. 2.

4. See paragraphs 14, 24, and 41.

5. Soto, *De iustitia et iure*, lib. 7, quaest, 5. art. 2. Cf. lib. 6, quaest. 12, art. 2 [fol. 599].

6. Thomas, *Summa theologicae*, II-II, quaest. 78, art. 2, ad. 7.

7. Scotus, *Quaestiones*, lib. 4, dist. 15, quaest. 2, art. 2 dictumque fuit supra eodem, no. 14 et 24, et in Azpilcueta, *Comentario Resolutorio de Usuras*, cap. I, 14, quaest. 3 (Decreto II, 16, 3, I), no. 26, et probatur in c. *Ad nostram*, de emptione (Decretales 5, 17, 3), et in c. *In civitate*, supra eodem (Decretales 3, 17, 5).

8. In consilium II, *de usuris* [Rubrica].

9. See paragraph 62 and following.

10. See paragraph 51.

11. See paragraph 60 and following.

12. See paragraph 63.

13. In the original, "presente," which might be a mistake.

14. See paragraphs 14 and 62.

15. Soto, *De iustitia et iure*, lib. 7, quaest. 5, art. 2. Cf. lib. 6, quaest. 12, art. 2 [fol. 594].

16. Argumentum, lex I, ff. de iure deliberandi [Digesto, 28, 8, I], et c. *De causis*, de officio [et potestate iudicis] delegati [Decretales I, 29, 4].

17. C. *Consuetudo*, I, dist. I [Decreto I, I, 5], lex *De quibus*, ff. de legibus [Digesto I, 3, 32].

18. *S. venditae*, Institutionum, De rerum divisione [*Inst*. 2, I, I, 41].

19. Lex *Nec emptio*, ff. de contrahenda emptione, cum glossa [Digesto 18, I, 8].

20. See paragraph 14.

21. Alioquin enim non esset emptio nec permutatio, argumentum: lex *Non omnis*, ff. de rebus creditis [Digesto 3, 12, 19], C. *cum super*, de officio [et potestate indicis] delegati [Decretales I, 19, 23].

22. Argumentum: Lex I, ff. de iure deliberandi [Digesto 28, 8, I], c. *De causis*, de officio [et potestate indicis] delegati [Decretales I, 29, 4].

23. See paragraph 34.

24. Usurpatio autem sine titulo iusto illicita est, c. *Poenale*, 14, quaest. 5 [Decreto II 14, 5, 13].

25. At omnis contractus, in quo no servatur aequalitas, est illicitus, ut ait Scotus, *Quaestiones*, lib. 4, dist. 15, quaest. 2, art. 2 [fol. 94], et Paulo ante no. 23 et 24 est dictum.

26. See paragraph 23.

27. Azpilcueta, *Comentario Resolutorio de Usuras*, cap. I, 14, quaest. 3, no. 26.

28. Cajetan, *De cambiis*, cap. Finales [cap. 8].

29. Cajetan, *De cambiis*, cap. 8.

30. Ac per consequutionem, *usura*, c. I, 2 et 3, 14, quaest. 3 [Decreto II, 14, 1–3], ut latius diximus in commentario dicto c. I, n. 5.

31. See paragraph 61.

32. See paragraph 21.

33. See paragraph 61.

34. See paragraph 47.

35. Antonino, *Summa*, 2 parte, tit. I, c. 7, s. 50.

36. Silvestre, *Suma*, verb. *usura* 4, quaest. 13.

37. Lex 31, quinta Partita, tit. II.

38. In the original: "Consejo de Indias."

39. In the original: "Siete Partidas." Cf. chapter 2, note 10.

40. See paragraph 64.

41. See paragraph 64.

42. Silvestre, *Suma*, verb. *usura* 4, quaest. 13.

43. In the original: "recambio."

44. Cajetan, *De cambiis*, cap. 7.

45. See paragraph 34.

PART TWO

Treatise on Money (1597)

Luis de Molina, S.J.

INTRODUCTION

Luis de Molina, S.J.: Life, Studies, and Teaching

Luis de Molina was born in Cuenca (Spain) in 1535 and died in Madrid on October 12, 1600. He entered the Society of Jesus at Alcalá at the age of eighteen and was sent to Coimbra (Portugal) to finish his novitiate. He completed his philosophical and theological courses at Coimbra and was so successful in his studies that he was named professor of philosophy at this University in 1563, where he remained until 1567. By August of 1568, Molina had been transferred to Evora (Portugal) to teach theology. He expounded with great success Saint Thomas's *Summa theologicae* for twenty years, and in 1591 he retired to his native city of Cuenca to devote himself exclusively to writing and preparing for print the results of his long studies. Two years later, however, the Society of Jesus opened the Imperial College at Madrid and Molina was called to teach moral philosophy in the newly established institution. He died while still in Cuenca, before he had held his new chair in Madrid. Luis de Molina was no less eminent as a jurist than as a speculative philosopher and theologian. A proof is his work *De iustitia et iure*, which appeared complete only after his death.

In the sixteenth and early seventeenth centuries, a fairly small group of theologians and jurists centered in Spain attempted to synthesize the Roman legal texts with Aristotelian and Thomistic moral philosophy. Molina and Juan de Lugo reorganized Roman law in its vast detail and presented it as a commentary on the Aristotelian and Thomistic virtue of justice in their separately authored treatises of the same title *On Justice and Law* (*De iustitia et iure*). The traditions of Roman law and Greek philosophy became intertwined more closely than they ever had been before or were to be again.[1]

Molina's chief contribution to the science of theology was his *Concordia*, on which he spent thirty years of the most assiduous labor. The full title of the now famous work is *Concordia liberi arbitrii cum gratiæ donis, divina præscientia, providentia, prædestinatione et reprobatione* (Lisbon, 1588). As the title indicates, the work is primarily concerned with the difficult problem of reconciling God's praescientia and human free will. In view of its purpose and principal content, the work may also be regarded by the economist as a scientific vindication of the doctrine of the permanence of human free will under perfect information, and so could be interpreted, for instance, by authors such as Oskar Morgenstern,[2] J. Robinson,[3] and John Hicks.[4] These references to the problem of predestination by such economists may be sufficient reason to think that Molina would have felt at home trying to solve problems posed in our day by the economist with the theoretical hypothesis of perfect information and human freedom.

Molina's varied interests amaze the modern reader, and Vansteenberge[5] remarks that the multitude of applications Molina makes of his principles is such that with the sole aid of his books a broad but accurate picture of the social and economic conditions of his time could be drawn. So, for example, in the *Treatise on Money*, argument 408,[6] we find the following description of different kinds of businessmen.

Economic Context

Three main classes of businessmen developed in Europe in the sixteenth and seventeenth centuries: merchants, money changers, and bankers. The merchant kept in close touch with his counterpart and had his "factors" in every corner of the world. In Seville, the merchant was an imposing figure, having in his hands "the greatest trade of Christendom," and even in Barbary. To Flanders he sent wool, olive oil, and wines in exchange for cloth, carpets, and books, and to Florence cochineal and leather against gold brocade and silks. He imported linen from Flanders and Italy and had a hand in the lucrative salve trade of Cape Verde. So great were the mixed cargoes he sent to all parts of the Indies in exchange for gold, silver, pearls, cochineal, and leather that "not Seville nor twenty Sevilles" would suffice to insure them, and he had to call upon the resources of Lyons, Burgos, Lisbon, and Flanders for the purpose.

Close upon the merchant's paces followed the money changer, who traveled from fair to fair and from place to place with his table and boxes and books.[7] In theory the money changer was a public official whose business was to deal in *cambium minutum* or the changing of gold coins into silver or other money in return for a small fee. Money changers were to keep proper books "and not leave blank sheets between the pages already used," and only persons appointed by the cities or "villas" might act as brokers. The whole business of the fair was conducted through the money changers, and cash transactions were reduced to a minimum by the cancelling out of book entries. Tomás de Mercado complains that "the money changers sweep all the money into their own houses, and when a month later the merchants are short of cash they give them back their own money at an exorbitant rate."[8] In this and other ways the money changers made big profits, and it is for them that the severest verdicts of the theologians were reserved.

The proper banker was a much more dignified personage. The bankers served their depositors free of charge and used the money deposited to finance their own operations. The bankers, writes Tomás de Mercado,

> are in substance the treasures and depositaries of the merchants. . . . In Spain a banker bestrides a whole world and embraces more than the Ocean, though sometimes he does not hold tight enough and all comes crashing to the ground.[9]

As early as 1526 the Venetian ambassador had observed that although goods were abundant at the fair of Medina del Campo the most important business was done in exchange transactions. All the evidence points to an accentuation of this tendency during the succeeding decades, and the fairs of Medina del Campo, Medina de Rio Seco, and Villalón[10] lost the last traces of their old local character, and became great national, and indeed international, clearing centers. They were by this time "mainly places for settling accounts, not for true buying and selling," though of such there was still "a good share."[11]

Financial Innovation and Excesses

A contract can be defined as a mutual agreement generating an obligation from the consent of the parties. Several contracts in the sixteenth and seventeenth centuries were financial instruments. In Molina's *Treatise on Money*, argument 398, we find a description of different kinds of economic contracts. A principal division of contracts into "named" and "unnamed" contracts is established. There are four kinds of unnamed contracts: "I give that you may give"; "I give that you may do"; "I do that you may pay"; "I do that you may do." A named contract, by contrast, is one that has a proper name by which it is distinguished from any other: purchase, sale, loan (*mutuum*), hire, association (*partnership*), accommodation (*commodatum*), pledge or mortgage, deposit, and so forth. Contracts are also divided into lucrative and onerous or burdensome. Contracts by which ownership is transferred may be listed: gift (*donation*), exchange (*permutation*), loan (*mutuum*), purchase (*emptio*), sale (*venditio*), monetary exchange (*cambium*), and so forth. The important thing to note is the variety of juridical figures as a form of reply to the different social and economic circumstances that originated with the arrival of precious metals.

A special juridical figure was *dry exchange*, a term loosely applied to any fictitious operation devised to evade the usury laws. We first meet it in Florence in the later Middle Ages, and it was, in fact, nothing but a loan camouflaged as an exchange deal. The borrower drew a bill of exchange in favor of the lender on some man of straw nominated by the latter, and this nominee protested the bill on its arrival. The borrower was then legally obliged to compensate the lender for the pretended loss sustained on both the exchange and the reexchange. Dry exchange in this narrower sense was redefined and condemned by a papal Bull of 1566 and again by a Spanish pragmatic of 1598, and was stigmatized as a "manifest cankered usury" also in England by Thomas Wilson in 1572.

The Question of *Continuity* and *Change* of Paradigm

When I first published Molina's *Theory of Just Price*, appealing to the philosophical methodology of Thomas Kuhn, I wrote that

> The Spanish doctors of the sixteenth century and, more concretely Luis de Molina, used in their moral reasoning an economic paradigm that, in so far as it was to be substituted by the classical paradigm, allows one to judge how much the just price does not coincide with the equilibrium price of classical theory. It does not seem possible to defend the identification of these prices without denying by doing so the existence of an authentic scientific revolution in the second half of the eighteenth century. It seems clear that the classical and scholastic disciplinary matrices could not harbor the same offspring.[12]

Two main philosophical reasons seem to endorse this thesis: First, there was a change in the philosophical and scientific notion of causality and, accordingly, second, a change in the anthropology and vision of the economic agent. The change in the anthropological vision of the economic agent has been mentioned before; namely, the scholastic economic agent is not the *homo economicus* of the classical economists, it is closer to the "Keynesian apple." This change of the philosophical and scientific notion of causality and natural law Alexandre Koyré describes as

> the destruction of the cosmos and the geometrization of space, that is, the substitution for the conception of the world as a finite well-ordered whole, in which the spatial structure embodied a hierarchy of perfection and value, that of an indefinite or even infinite universe no longer united by natural subordination, but unified only by the identity of its ultimate and basic components and laws; and the replacement of the Aristotelian conception of space—a differentiated set of inner worldly place—by that of Euclidean geometry—an essentially infinite and homogeneous extension from now considered as identical with the real space of the world.[13]

This change was introduced in the seventeenth century by the scientific revolution, but, of course, a change of mentality does not occur suddenly, it needs time for its accomplishment. The consequence of this change of "vision"[14] by the scientific revolution was the discarding by scientific thought of all considerations based upon value-concepts, such as perfection, harmony, meaning, and aim, and finally the utter devalorization of being, the divorce of the world of value and the world of facts.[15]

The classical economists followed the epistemology and anthropology of the scientific revolution and their interpretation of the natural law was different from the scholastic interpretation. The following points were crucial in this change of "paradigm": a new concept of causal relation substituted the scholastic causal relation, and a new vision of the person as economic agent substituted the old scholastic vision.

The Old Causality and the New Causality in Relation to a Free Market: From Moral Philosophy to Natural Science

It is John Hicks who underlined the transition in the seventeenth century from the old causality to the new causality as a consequence of the scientific revolution in the seventeenth century. The old causality belongs to a

System of thought . . . in which causes are always thought of as actions by someone; there is always an agent, either a human agent or a supernatural agent, responsible for the action. It is fascinating to observe, in the literature of the seventeenth and eighteenth centuries, how this old causality broke down.[16]

The scholastic doctors developed a system of economic thought in which the subjects were active agents that maintained responsibility for their actions. In this way, scholastic economic thought shows its reliance upon the old causality. The difference between the scholastic agent and the economic agent in a free market has to do with the distinction between an agent as "price maker" and "price taker," a distinction that is grounded in the fundamental differences between the old and the new causality. A "price maker" is responsible for the market price but a "price taker," to the contrary, is not responsible for the market price. In other words, a price that depends on the subject's behavior is not a price based on a necessary law, as it is a price based on the forces of supply and demand. With the philosophers of the Enlightenment, the new causality substituted the old causality and, in Hicks's judgment, was "a permanent acquisition."[17]

Within the scholastic vision, economic agents were considered "price makers" and, therefore, morally responsible. The transition to the new causality from the old causality, to the agent "price taker" from the agent "price maker," introduced a significant change in the vision and interpretation of "common estimation" as a criterion of justice, a change that could be labeled one of "scientific paradigm." Langholm describes the change as a process of *depersonalization* of the market idea.

Taking the common estimate as one criterion of justice, the medieval scholastics, early on, conceded that this estimate, insofar as it referred to the market, would vary to some extent with supply and demand. They would not, thereby, at first, permit economic actors to disclaim subjective, personal moral responsibility for their own use of economic power. This was something that happened gradually with the increasing *objectivization* (to use Gordon's term) or *depersonalization* of the idea of the market. More than anything else, it signals the breakdown of the medieval scholastic approach to economic ethics.[18]

What Langholm calls a process of increasing *depersonalization* is no different from what I have called a process of transition from a "price maker" to a "price taker," from the old causality to the new causality. By the second half of the eighteenth century this change had been accomplished and scientific reason became the norm to follow in human economic behavior. The *necessary reason* of science had substituted the *recta ratio* of the scholastics and, as a consequence, economics was understood as a natural science instead of a moral science. It will be necessary to wait until Keynes's *General Theory* for economics to be viewed as a moral science again. It was in this new "vision" of economics that the "Keynesian apple" substituted the utilitarian *homo economicus*.

What to Smith had been a necessary process of adjustment to the scientific rationality based on the impersonal forces of supply and demand, to the scholastics had been a contingent and fallible process of adjustment to the moral norm of justice. The *depersonalization* of the idea of the market was contrary to the scholastic vision. The scholastic *recta ratio* is not a depersonalized mathematical reason: it is a probable human reason. It is true, as Langholm writes,

> Until a few decades ago, it was not uncommon in critical studies to encounter the suggestion that the medieval scholastics simply permitted the forces of the market to run their course and accepted the resultant "common estimate of the market" as the just price. More recently, [however,] this liberalistic interpretation has been challenged by a younger generation of scholars, with whose arguments, as far as they go, I fully agree.[19]

The subject as the mean of an aggregate of individuals substituted and assumed the role of the scholastic singular individual. As a logical consequence, a change was produced in the interpretation of the natural law.[20]

Probabilism and the Knowledge of Natural Law in Scholastic Thought

The scholastic doctors traced their concept of natural law back to Aristotle and the Roman jurists, although they made of it something very different. Aristotle, for example, distinguished "natural justice" from "institutional justice," but this distinction developed in a wider sense with scholastic nominalism. There are two different epistemological approaches to natural law: one based on certainty and necessity, another based on uncertainty and probability. Luis de Molina, along with the rest of the Spanish doctors, holds a view of natural law and the decision-making process that can be described as probabilistic. The reason was clear, as Molina writes,

> . . . nature does not show us what belongs to natural law in such a way that, while deducing some conclusions starting from principles, especially when conclusions are such that they follow first principles in an indirect and unclear way, some error might not get into the conclusions. Therefore, in dealing with what belongs to natural law, some error might result.[21]

According to the Spanish scholastics, uncertainty and imperfect information are two essential features of our knowledge of natural law. It was this recognition of the importance of uncertainty and imperfect information that led the scholastic doctors to *probabilism* and *casuistry* in moral philosophy. It was a logical answer to the difficult problem of the application of general first principles to the singular *case* in a decision process. The first principle of moral life can be known with certainty, but we cannot know with certainty how conduct in a singular case is related to the first principle. In most branches of academic logic, such as the theory of the syllogism, all arguments aim at demonstrative certainty; they aim to be conclusive. In scholastic *probabilism* arguments are rational and claim some weight without pretending to be certain and conclusive. Scholastic *recta ratio* does not lead to truth but to opinion, and has nothing to recommend it but its subjective probability. As Martín de Azpilcueta, doctor Navarro, had written in his *Manual de confesores y penitentes* in 1556,

> . . . science is firm and clear knowledge; faith, not clear but dim; and opinion, neither firm nor clear knowledge; doubt, neither clear, nor firm, nor judicative; and scruples is nothing else but an argument against some of the above mentioned four. It follows, also, that the first four are opposite to each other and cannot occur in the same person.[22]

The scholastic *recta ratio* was not a scientific reason: it was a moral reason, and therefore, fallible and not necessary. Molina seems to be cautious and skeptical in his approach to knowledge of the natural law, both in trying to tease out what exactly it was, and in his grave doubts as to whether in fact it was so obvious and easy to understand. It is interesting to note that, in his *Treatise on Probability*, John Maynard Keynes mentions the Jesuit doctrine of *probabilism* as "the first contact of theories of probability with modern ethics."[23]

I am not suggesting that scholastic probability is the same as Keynes's probability, or that Keynes's interpretation of scholastic probabilism is correct. But it does not seem accidental that the scholastic doctors and Keynes both agree about economics being a moral science based on fallible "opinions" about the cases considered, that both the scholastic doctors and Keynes used the philosophical distinction between the *causa essendi* and the *causa cognoscendi* when speaking of natural law, and that both accepted some kind of nominalism. If, as Peter F. Drucker writes, "Philosophically speaking, Keynes became an extreme nominalist,"[24] Vereecke's opinion is that it seems impossible to analyze sixteenth-century moral economics without knowledge of nominalism.[25] Scholastic monetary theory cannot be understood without knowledge of nominalist philosophy, and something similar may be said of Keynes's monetary theory.

Nominalism and Scholastic Monetary Theory

If, from an anthropological point of view, scholastic probabilism and casuistry go back to the difficult problem of causality and human knowledge, its philosophical roots have to be seen in nominalist philosophy. In some areas, such as political and moral philosophy, the Spanish doctors owed a large debt to Occamist philosophy and voluntarist anthropology, even when they tried to break free from these starting points.

Nominalist philosophy stressed aspects of knowledge that were of great significance and reached far into the development of monetary thought. The nominalist claimed, for example, only those propositions that could be reduced to the principle of contradiction would be considered absolutely "real," turning the causal propositions of science into merely probable propositions. They underlined the empirical dimension of moral and scientific knowledge; the logical coherence of abstract reasoning needed to be completed by withstanding the test of specific circumstances that defined the case under study. At the same time, the empirical knowledge of the case could not be understood without a general theory that was logically congruent. This is why the decision-making process was seen as a process born of a fallible subject who took a chance on a specifiable reasonable probability, which was neither truly necessary nor mathematically conclusive.

Among the nominalists, there was skepticism about the possibility of discerning an order in the world that human reason could discover. Nominalist philosophers claimed that abstract concepts were creations of mind rather than discoveries about the world. Hence, the relationship between abstract concepts, such as a unit of account (*universals*), and individual realities, such as a standard commodity (*singulars*), was a point of contention between nominalists and realists.[26] According to nominalists, "there only exists the singular or individual" (*quidquid existit singulare est seu individuum*), universal concepts are only inventions of the mind. This principle is essential for a correct understanding of scholastic monetary theory for it applied to the unit of account in its double meaning, that is, as a pure *number* or abstract unit and as a standard or *thing* referred to as a unit of account.

In Molina's monetary theory, as with the scholastics in general, there is a significant distinction between the unit of account as an *abstract* concept and the *singular thing*, which is called the standard unit of measurement. When Molina writes: "A coin can be considered in two ways: one, as a coin; another, as a metal or as gold of greater or lesser purity, of greater or lesser weight,"[27] the term *coin* is understood in a double sense: as an *abstract concept* and as the *singular thing* denoted by such a concept. The distinction between the *name* unit of account and the *singular thing* denoted by this name was interpreted by Molina and the Spanish doctors according to nominalist philosophy and, therefore, as what the philosophy of science today terms a "coordinative definition."

Scholastic Monetary Theory

A Scientific Problem: The Standard Unit of Account as a "Coordinative Definition"[28]

We can define what we mean by a unit of account or "numéraire" only by means of other concepts, but this definition does not say anything about the real value of the singular unit that can only be established by reference to a real given good (gold, silver, or any other economic commodity). In Hicks's terminology, the "numéraire" or unit of account has to be "anchored" to a real commodity.[29] A unit of account is an abstract concept and an abstract mathematical number. For nominalism, mathematical notions were altogether *connotative*: number, extension, time, and degree are connotative concepts addressing *relations* between singulars rather than naming singular objects or absolute properties of them. Of course, such connotative notions are not without a *fundamentum in re*, but they should not be hypostatized. Money as *unit of account* or "numéraire" was just an *ens rationis*, and its *fundamentum in re*[alitate] was the standard good or commodity connoted by the concept, and to which the abstract concept is "anchored." The "coordinative definition" of the unit of account seems to be a simple legal operation of "anchorage," but the legal procedure is one thing and its economic and social meaning another.

A "coordinative definition" poses to the economist a serious epistemological problem: being a nominal concept, the relationship between the nominal unit and the real commodity has to be established by law, and it is here that the problem of metrical *congruence* begins. Two different questions were asked and answered by Molina and the Spanish doctors in the sixteenth and seventeenth centuries: *Who* must define the "coordinative definition?" What are the *logical conditions of possibility* for a *neutral* (*sterile*) definition of the standard money of account? The first one poses a sociopolitical problem; the second must be seen as an analytical problem, for it has to do with the scientific and analytical meaning of such a "coordinative definition."

A Political Problem: Who Must Define the Standard Unit of Account?

According to Luis de Molina and the Spanish doctors, it is the role of the public authority to determine the economic commodity and to coordinate the nominal unit of account. The public authority has the legal right to *determine* and *declare* the economic commodity to which the mathematical and abstract unit of account has to be "anchored," for it is the right of the state to define the metrical system of the nation. After the coinage has been minted, the standard units were supposed to be worth not only what their metal would bring in the marketplace, but also what the issuing government declared it was worth. If chartalism is the doctrine that holds money is a creation of the state as Keynes writes,[30] the scholastic doctors were chartalists and not bullionists or metalists.[31] But Keynes conceded to the state a monetary function that the scholastic doctors never recognized. According to Keynes,

> . . . if the same thing always answered to the same description, the distinction [between the *abstract unit* and the *standard thing*] would have no practical interest. But if the thing can change, whilst the description remains the same, then the distinction can be highly significant. The difference is like that between the king of England (whoever he may be) and King George. . . . It is for the State to declare when the times comes, who the king of England is.[32]

In the sixteenth and seventeenth centuries, to the contrary, it was all too evident that any standard of measurement had to be constant through time and space, and the economic standard of measurement was no exception. The scholastic doctrine was summarized by Tomás de Mercado in this way:

> It is universal and necessary for (money) to be any fixed measurement, that is sure and permanent. Everything else can, and even must change, but the measurement must be permanent, because as a fixed sign we can measure the changes of the other things.[33]

The difference between Keynes and the scholastics about the possibility of a change in the standard value of the unit of account leads us to the second problem mentioned above: the *logical conditions* of possibility of a *neutral* (*sterile*) definition of the money of account. We can refer to this as the "economic congruence" problem or the metric of economic value.

A Logical Problem: The Logic of a Definition of Monetary "Congruence"

As Alfred North Whitehead wrote, we

> . . . must understand at once that congruence is a controversial question. It is the theory of *measurement in space and time*. The question seems simple. In fact it is simple enough for a standard procedure to have been settled by act of parliament; and devotion to metaphysical subtleties is almost the only crime that has never been imputed to any English parliament. But the procedure is one thing and its meaning is another.[34]

One aspect of the question is the legal "coordinative definition" of the standard unit of account but another is its use and meaning in a process of measurement in space and time. The process of measurement presupposes, first, that the quantity to measure is given, that it is an *invariable quantity* during the process of its measurement and, second, that the standard unit of measurement employed is a *constant* value. Neither of these two suppositions is unproblematic. Devotion to metaphysical subtleties may be a crime that has never been imputed to any English parliament, but the scholastic doctors were charged with such a crime, especially in relation to the notion of equality and measurement in time and space. Let us see the logical meaning of congruence in its relation to measurement and equality.

Measurement is an operation by which we know *how many* standardized units has a determinant magnitude, length, weight, economic value, and so forth. A judgment of measurement is a metrical assertion and it is essentially a judgment of *comparison*; but a *comparison* is not necessarily a judgment of measurement. Measurement and comparison are different processes, although both are judgments of comparison. Bertrand Russell provided the following explanation of the difference:

> A judgment of magnitude is essentially a judgment of comparison: in unmeasured quantity, comparison as to the mere more or less, but in measured magnitude, comparison as to the precise *how many times*. To speak of differences of magnitudes, therefore, in a sense where comparison cannot reveal them, is logically absurd.[35]

The metrical function of money is not a "comparison as to the mere more or less," it is a "comparison as to the precise *how many times*" and, therefore, presupposes a definition of the monetary unit as congruent to itself. It is of the essence of measurement that the standard unit of measurement remains unaltered, equal to itself; for ". . . it is a universal rule and necessary for (money) to be *any fixed* measure, that is, sure and permanent."[36] *Equality* is the term the scholastics used to define justice in economic exchanges and the classical economists to define economic equilibrium. It is important, therefore, to know how the logic of relations defines the relation of equality. In monetary theory this relation is fundamental to a definition of the metrical function of money.

The Logical Meaning of an Equality Relation

According to the logic of relations, a relation of equality E holds between any two successive values a and b if it holds also between values b and a, and if it is also a "symmetrical" relation. But suppose we compare values b and c, and their relation is a "symmetrical" relation, if we want to call it a "transitive" relation it must also hold between values c and a. A relation that is both transitive and symmetrical, it must also be reflexive if it has to be a relation of equality. Any value with the relation of equality E has to be *equal in value to itself.* In the logic of relations, a relation that is both symmetrical and transitive is called an *equivalence* relation, but equality is a special equivalence, it is a symmetrical, transitive, and reflexive relation of equivalence. Equality means equivalence but equivalence does not necessarily mean equality, and the difference is due to their relation to time. In relation to equality, time is not a causal factor what, indeed, it can be in relation to equivalence. Time cannot have a causal effect on a reflexive relation of equality because the passing of time cannot change a reflexive relation of equality, and this is the origin of the scientific and scholastic principle of the uniformity of nature.

A value equal to itself can be a standard measurement of value when applied successively to measure another value because the nature of its value is uniform; it is a homogeneous value. A uniform or homogeneous value means that it can move freely in time and space, and this is the reason why Russell considered the axiom of free mobility a necessary logical condition of measurement of a quantitative magnitude. Uniformity of nature and free mobility mean the same thing, and both depend on the concept of time and its relation to nature or economic value. Now, when Dempsey asks why the scholastic doctors were so vigorous in their exclusion of time as a determining factor for change in economic value, he answers:

> The reason seems to be, not the crudity of the Schoolman's concept of time, but the perfection of it. From the earliest days of Scholastic philosophy and theology, and even in positive theology, the problem of God's eternity and timelessness had forced attention on the problem of the nature of time. With such a refined concept in mind, and facing the problem of the exchange of values to an equality, they laid their emphasis on the fact that time in and by itself alters no values. With time may come changing circumstances, especially increasing risk [due to uncertainty], by which values are altered. These circumstances may found new titles or invalidate old ones. But the Schoolman consistently and characteristically insisted that this was the question of fact that required investigation and was to be probed in each case. An indeterminate appeal to the passage of time alone was of no avail.[37]

Free mobility depends on time because without a homogeneous time there is no free mobility, neither is there uniformity of nature. These two principles are fundamental to a scientific understanding of the concept of magnitude and causality in scholastic economics.[38] Differences between one event and another, between one value and another, do not depend on the mere difference of the times or places at which they occur, for time and space are homogeneous and, therefore, causally irrelevant or neutral. We will see later how this relation between causality and time can be applied to the economic concept of money as a productive economic factor (interest), but now it is necessary to return to the process of measurement, that is, to the metric of economic value.

Fungibility, Liquidity, and Quantification of Economic Value

The scholastic concept of fungibility is a homogeneous form of time, a form of externality, as Kant would say. A fungible good is a good whose unit of value can take the place (*vices fungi*) of any other unit; because *vices fungi* of any other unit, such unit of value is congruent or equal to itself in time and space and can be a standard unit of measurement. But fungibility, as with liquidity, can be perfect or imperfect, and a good whose unit of value cannot take the place of another unit is an *imperfect* fungible value. A unit of such a good or value is not necessarily equal to itself, for the passing of time or the change of place affects the quantity of such a value. An imperfect fungible value is also an imperfect liquid value, and fungibility and liquidity are qualities of economic value, they are not quantities of a homogeneous value. To pass from *quality* to *quantity* means to pass from *imperfect* to *perfect information*.

A quantitative magnitude supposes perfect information, but the scholastic economic subject did not have perfect information, and this imperfection makes him similar to the Keynesian economic subject. Fungibility, liquidity, and "reflexibility" are *qualities* referred to a temporal value, and only when a "coordinative definition" of such value is coined by the state, its degree of liquidity can be considered perfect liquidity or fungibility based on "perfect" information. But, as Molina observed,

> . . . if the circumstances were to change with time, and the value of the metal of such coins increased considerably, it should not be assumed that the legislators would want the laws that fixed the old rates to be still in force. And even if they wanted to, it would not be just nor fair. . . .[39]

The value of money "is not so rigid that it cannot rise and fall just as the goods do whose price is not fixed by law." This similar behavior of money and other economic goods introduces imperfect information on monetary values, and such imperfect information can be expressed in mathematical terms. Suppose the value of a standard unit of value, when coined by the state, is represented by an infinitesimal arc ds; after a period of time, in any other moment of time (t) its value would be $ds.f(t)$, where the form of the function $f(t)$ must be supposed as known. How are we to determine the moment t if our information is imperfect? For this purpose we require a coordinate of time and some measurement of duration from the origin of the coordinate, and here is where the axiom of free mobility must be introduced if fungibility is to be perfect.

A temporal distance from the origin only could be measured if we assume a law to measure it, but such a law must be implicit in our function $f(t)$; therefore, until we assume $f(t)$ we have no means of determining t and the value of the standard unit of value in time and space. If we accept the axiom of free mobility, the function $f(t)$ would be zero, for the passing of time would be causally neutral to economic value. But there is no certainty about the function $f(t)$ for, as Russell observes,

... experience can neither prove nor disprove the constancy of shapes [or value] throughout motion, since, if shapes [or value] were not constant, we should have to *assume* a law of their variation before measurement became possible, and therefore measurement could not itself reveal that variation to us.[40]

Ullastres referred to the divorce between the nominal unit of account and the "real" one as the "fundamental failure of the Old Nominalism," and Pierre Vilar observed how difficult it is to submit a money-commodity to the "coordinative definition" coined by the public authority. When the divorce occurs, we find ourselves before *two* economic metrical systems, two different "coordinative definitions" of the standard unit of measurement, one legal and another "real," and a choice has to be made. Molina's option was for a real commodity standard, but the important thing to remember is this: whatever the option might be, the economic subject must know that Molina's option has moral, political, and logical dimensions. Molina's option is not the result of a mechanical decision, but of a responsible moral decision guided by fallible *recta ratio*. He provides the following example of such a moral decision.

In 1558, the ratio of gold and silver set by King Sebastian was disturbed by unexpected shipments from Ethiopia and, after narrating these facts, Molina opted for the real standard of measurement, subordinating the "constitutional" or "legal" metrical system to the one "empirically" established by the people.

> They tell me that the merchants from here in Castile brought a huge amount, and that they sold each coin of 1,000 *reais* for 33 silver *reales*, which taken to Portugal were worth 1,320 *reais*. That is why I warned King Sebastian that it would be convenient to increase the price of gold, and such is what I taught from my chair as professor. But it was useless. . . .[41]

Molina concludes his narration with the following statement:

> . . . in these exchanges, more importance is given to the amount of silver comparing it to an equal amount of silver, or to the amount of gold comparing it to an equal amount of gold of the same purity than to the amount of copper and its price in different places.[42]

According to the Spanish doctors, an economic assertion belongs to moral philosophy and not to natural science; and any moral assertion is epistemologically on par with opinion in Azpilcueta's previously mentioned schema, that is, "neither firm nor clear knowledge."[43] Therefore, an economic transition from certain to uncertain liquidity, from atemporal to temporal fungibility can only be considered a moral transition, that is, the result of a personal decision in time in a world of uncertain economic relations. This was one of the scholastic reasons to study carefully the notion of time and space, even if such a study could seem like a set of philosophical subtleties.

A Dynamic Definition of Monetary Congruence: Time and the Rate of Interest

A rate of interest expresses a relation between a present value and a future value, a relation between value at moment t and value at moment t_I, two different or successive moments in time. If this relation is considered a *continuous* relation we could say that time and economic value are *mathematically continuous*. Let us fix attention on the purely mathematical problem. The relation between the new and the old value as a continuous relation in time can be named a rate of interest. Suppose that the old unit of account or measurement, as a result of its "coordinative definition" by the state, was in a moment t "anchored" to a real value ds, so that we may write $ds = 1$, this valuation of the standard unit must be considered just a convention. Now, if, after a time, the state changes the unit of account and its new value bears a definite relation of *continuity* with the old unit, this continuous relation to time of the standard unit could be written as $ds.f(t)$. Suppose a coordinative system O_1, where the axis t represents the variable time and the axis v represents different continuous values of the standard unit of measurement, the meaning of economic congruence in scholastic monetary theory could be explained in mathematical and geometrical terms as follows:

Figure 1

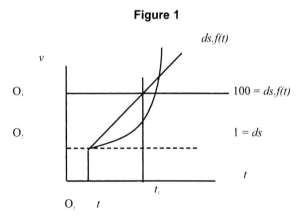

The standard unit of measurement $ds = 1$ is a congruent value in a moment of time t, the moment of its coinage or "anchorage." Suppose that in another moment t_I its value has changed to $s = O_1O_3$, this new value must be a continuous function of time, therefore, it could be expressed as $s = ds.f(t)$. It is the nature of this function $f(t)$ and its "empirical" connotation that has to do with the logical problem of the *dynamic congruence* of money as the standard unit of measurement. In scholastic monetary theory it also has to do with the productivity (or sterility) of money and the notion of "extrinsic titles" to earn interest. About the nature of the function $f(t)$ there are three possible choices:

1. $f(t)$ might be the expression of a rate of zero interest, $f(t) = 0$, and then, $ds = constant$. Therefore, $O_1O_3 = ds = s$.
2. It might express a rate of interest distinct of zero, $f(t) = 0$, but such a rate could be, (2.a) a *simple rate* of interest and, therefore, a *linear function* of time; (2.b) a *compound rate* of interest and, therefore, an *exponential function* of time.

There are three possible elections of a monetary metric regime, but the question in any of these possible elections is: *Who* must decide the kind of relation or function $f(t)$ between the present unit of measure and the future one? *How* does he know which one of these three possible functions will be the right one? The state has the right to define the standard unit in a moment of time, in the moment of its "conventional" definition and "anchorage." But this definition is a link between an abstract concept to a "real" value or economic good, and we are asking now for the relation between two "real" and successive values of the same economic good. How can the state know the "real" relation between the present and the future value of the standard unit of measurement? How does the state know if the function $f(t)$ has a zero value or is distinct of zero, if it is a linear function or an exponential function? Can it be a question of free election of a definition or it is a question of empirical recognition of the actual relation between a present and a future value? In the moment of the "anchorage" of the standard unit it was a question of social "convention" and definition, but our question now is how long such "convention" and definition must last? Can it be changed from time to time, as Keynes said, or must it be maintained permanently as a moral and legal obligation?

Although the scholastics were not acquainted with the theory of relativity, they knew the meaning of a relative relation and its temporal dimension, and this knowledge was the origin and foundation of their doctrine of the *lucrum cessans* and *damnum emergens*. Before this doctrine is presented, let us finish with the problem of the election of the dynamic congruence of the standard unit, the election of the function $ds.f(t)$. The problem will be set now in mathematical terms of first and second derivative of value in respect to time.

The Rate of Interest and the Axiom of Free Divisibility of a Continuous Time

According to the mathematical definition of interest, a *simple* rate of interest depends on the duration of the interval between t and t_1, and such an interval is *not divisible*. On the contrary, a *compound* rate of interest does not depend on the duration of the interval and, therefore, such an interval is *divisible ad infinitum*. A simple rate of interest is a magnitude with a temporal dimension, depends on time and, therefore, the passing of time is an *intrinsic* cause of a change of value. Such a time is a *discrete* magnitude, it is *not* a *continuous* magnitude, and its relation to another interval must be considered an *external* relation between different and *successive* intervals of time. On the contrary, a *compound* rate of interest does not depend on the interval of time, it has no temporal dimension, and time is a *continuous* magnitude, but such continuity must be considered an *internal* relation between successive values in an infinite period of time. Therefore, a compound rate of interest connotes an *intrinsic cause* as the origin of such a rate of interest, while a simple rate of interest connotes an *extrinsic cause* as the possible origin of the interest produced. In relation to time, there is a distinction between *internal causality* and *external causality*, *endogenous* and *exogenous* causality, and the distinction between these two kinds of causal relation is the analytical origin of the scholastic distinction between "*extrinsic*" and "*intrinsic*" titles to interest.

A simple interest is an *imperfect liquid* value, for its quantity depends on the passing of time; but this relation is unknown before an interval of time is bound. As a linear function of time, its characteristic depends on the relation between time and value, though once the characteristic is known the relation must be constant, and this constant relation means *imperfect* liquidity in any other temporal relation. Perfect liquidity is contrary to a causal relation of time and, therefore, to a simple rate of interest; perfect liquidity means causal independence with respect to time. A change on the liquidity degree can have an *internal cause*, that is, a change in the interval of time. A compound interest is a *perfect liquid* value, for its quantity does not depend on the passing of time, there is no causal relation between time and value. Therefore, any change of value must have a different origin from the passing of time—it has to have an *external causality*. This is the meaning of the scholastic phrase—"the mere passing of time does not produce interest."

The problem arises when the "coordinative definition" of the standard unit of measurement is employed in a measurement of the rate of interest. A standard unit of measurement must be independent of time but, at the same time, it must be a constant value; therefore, its dynamic cannot be the dynamic of either a simple interest or of a compound interest. Is there any other possible dynamic explanation? The dynamic of a "conventional" value, of a value defined by law and not by experience. This is the real meaning of a "coordinative definition" of the standard unit of value; it is a definition of *perfect liquidity* in as much as it is accepted and obeyed by the people. But the state can change the "coordinative definition," and this change means two different things: It is a *quantitative* change of the standard value but also a *qualitative* change of liquidity from *perfect* to *imperfect liquidity*, and it is important to note that a "coordinative definition" of perfect liquidity by the state is only a temporal definition. Keynes exposed clearly the "conventional" aspect of the definition of economic congruence when he wrote in his *Treatise on Probability* that

> We must . . . distinguish between assertions of law and assertions of fact, or, in the terminology of Von Kries, between nomologic and ontologic knowledge. It may be convenient in dealing with some questions to frame this distinction with reference to the especial circumstances. But the distinction generally applicable

is between propositions that contain no reference to *particular* moments of time, and existential propositions that cannot be stated without reference to specific points in the time series. The principle of the uniformity of nature amounts to the assertion that natural laws are all, in this sense, timeless. We may, therefore, divide our data into two portions k and l, such that k denotes our formal and no-mologic evidence, consisting of propositions whose predication does not involve a particular time reference [*numéraire*], and l denotes the existential or ontologic propositions [standard unit of value].[44]

If the state can change the assertion of law, the "coordinative definition," this change means a *quantitative* change of the standard value, but it also means a *qualitative* change of liquidity from *perfect* to *imperfect liquidity*, and these two dimensions are present and characterize the scholastic *damnum emergens* and *lucrum cessans*. A *lucrum cessans* means that a process of production stops, and this process can be a process of simple or compound interest. If it is a process of compound interest, a *lucrum cessans* must have an *external* cause, an ontologic dimension, and means that a qualitative change has been produced in the nature of the process. If it is a process of simple interest, the *lucrum cessans* can have an *internal* cause, a change in the interval of time and, therefore, a change of the assertion of law that is the "coordinative definition" of the standard unit of value. In any case, what the existence *of lucrum cessans* or *damnum emergens* means is that the principles of the uniformity of nature and free mobility in space and time are not "natural" principles but social "conventions," as the "coordinative definition" of the *numèraire* as a standard unit of measurement is also a social convention. And because free mobility in space and time is not a "natural" freedom, a congruent theory of economic value and exchange cannot be interpreted as an absolute and universal truth, but as a temporal and local theory about economic value grounded on a "conventional" definition of economic congruence.

To the Spanish doctors, the only congruent definition of any standard unit of measurement had to be an "absolute" definition, which means that it had to be founded on the axiom of the uniformity of nature,[45] and such uniformity is contrary to the lodging of a first and second derivative simultaneously in time. It is true that the axiom of the uniformity of nature, as the axiom of free mobility or any other axiom, is a nomologic proposition and not an "existential" proposition, for experience can neither prove nor disprove it. To use a scholastic distinction, it is true that the axiom of the uniformity of nature is the *causa cognoscendi* of economic values, though economic values are the *causa essendi*. But the peculiarities that define the merits of the scholastic treatises *De iustitia et iure*, to which Molina's *De cambiis* belongs, is the way in which the *causa essendi* and the *causa cognoscendi* are related to each other. The achievement of this relation was a function the scholastic doctors entrusted to *recta ratio*, and its development through the different cases (*casus*) reveals how "coordinative definitions" and empirical statements were interconnected in what today is called a *constitutional monetary regime*.

Constitutional Monetary Regimes and Personal Expectations

A monetary regime, writes Axel Leijonhufvud,

> is, first, a system of expectations governing the behavior of the public. Second,
> it is a consistent pattern of behavior on the part of the monetary authorities such
> as will sustain these expectations. The short-run response to policy actions will
> depend on the expectations of the public, which is to say, on the regime that is
> generally believed to be in effect.[46]

A simple interest supposes a monetary regime in which freedom and discretion
of the economic agents is constrained by the axiom of the indivisibility of time, for
the passing of time could produce a change of value. A compound interest is rooted
in a monetary regime in which freedom and discretion of the economic agents are
not constrained by the axiom of divisibility, for the passing of time and its free
division does not produce a change of value. The scholastic monetary system was
a constitutional regime congruent with the axiom of divisibility and, because it
was congruent with this axiom, the passing of time was considered causally neutral
with respect to the production of economic value. The scholastic metric of value,
therefore, may be called a Euclidean metric; nevertheless, the invariance of the
standard unit of value was as a matter of *definition, an assertion of law* and *not
an assertion of fact*, for there is no way of knowing whether a measuring standard
actually retains its value when it moves from time to time or changes from place
to place. The value of the standard unit had to be a fungible or homogeneous
value in space and time, and the "coordinative definition" of the standard unit of
measurement as a fungible and homogeneous value had to be a legal definition.
All these philosophical considerations must be present when analyzing scholastic
economic literature and, especially, the subject of economic contracts and the
problem of usury.

The Contract of *Mutuum*, Usury, and the Axiom of Free Divisibility

A transaction of *mutuum* is defined as a translation of ownership of some
fungible value: from the lender to the borrower and, after a certain time, from the
borrower again to the lender. A loan of *mutuum* is a "delivery" of a fungible article
(the qualities of which are fixed in number, weight, or measure) with the intent that
it immediately becomes the property of the one receiving it with the obligation to
restore after a certain time an article of like kind and quality. Your value becomes
my value (*tuum fit meum*). How do we know if the article restored to the lender is
of like kind and quality as the article received from him? How do we know if the
number, weight, or measure of the good received is or is not *equal* to the number,
weight, and measure of another good returned after a period of time? We must
distinguish the "empirical" problem from the problem of juridical and moral obligation, for without solving the empirical problem there is no reason to inquire of

the juridical and moral problem. But the empirical problem is related to the logical problem, that is, to the logical definition of congruence and its observance by the economic subjects, which, in turn, raises the moral problem.

A *mutuum* presupposes perfect fungibility or liquidity, and perfect fungibility does not change the economic value with the passing of time. But perfect fungibility is a matter of definition, as we have seen, and can be broken by a free economic agent. Therefore, the constraint to observe the definition of perfect fungibility must be a constitutional monetary constraint, for it is not a necessary physical constraint. A juridical constraint is a matter of obedience and morality and can be broken by a free economic agent but, in such a case, the nature of the legal contract should have been defined. It is a legal and moral function to determine in such cases what the actual contractual relation was between the economic agents.

The "constitutional" requirement to defend a fixed standard value in monetary transactions is a *conditio sine qua non* of perfect fungibility, and a *mutuum* is a dual transaction of perfect liquidity, from the lender to the borrower and, after an interval of time, from the borrower to the lender. The scholastic doctors were opposed in the sixteenth and seventeenth centuries to a debasement of currency because debasement was an operation contrary to a "constitutional" norm. Under a gold standard, for instance, the temporary suspension of convertibility means a temporary suspension of the "coordinative definition" of the standard, the suspension of its constitutional rule; debasement was a permanent change of the constitutional norm.

Debasement and Monetary Policy in the Sixteenth and Seventeenth Centuries

The standard value of the unit of account should not vary, but was it not evident in the sixteenth and seventeenth centuries that it varied? The experience of repeated new minting of coins had demonstrated that in difficult situations or emergencies like those that the Crown frequently experienced the public authority could change the "coordinative definition" of the standard unit of account. The question to answer is this: Should we put constraints on the exercise of discretion in monetary management? This is not the place to give an answer, but the answer given by Molina and other scholastic doctors was the following: A frequent manipulation of the currency meant an equal number of broken words, an equal number of changes in the correlation between the nominal unit of account and the real commodity chosen as the unit. The scholastic doctors reacted to these changes of the "coordinative definition" of the unit of account in the only way a moral philosopher could in the sixteenth and seventeenth centuries: condemning the public authority's failure to keep its word. Altering the value of the currency, just like altering the length of the meter or the weight of the kilogram, constituted a fraud that should be condemned. Debasement was robbery, and robbery was prohibited by moral and secular law. Juan de Mariana was explicit on this point. Asking if the king could lower the weight on a coin against the will of the people, if the king could go back on his word without the consent of society, Mariana writes:

Two things are certain here: the first, that the king can change the form or the minting of money, as long as he does not make it worse . . . the second, due to some difficulties like war or siege, he can lower its value on two conditions: one, that it be for a short period of time, or as long as the circumstances required; two, once the difficulty has abated, he must restore the losses suffered by the interested parties . . . ; because if the prince is not a lord but the administrator of the goods of the citizens, he cannot take part of their patrimony by these means or by others, as occurs each time money is devalued, since more is charged for what is worth less.[47]

The reference to the need that arises from "war or siege" allows us to inquire about a third possible need: reactivation of the economy. The answer we read in Mariana's work may be surprising formulated as it was two centuries before Smith's *Wealth of Nations*.

Mariana clearly distinguished two timeframes in which the manipulation of money by the authorities would produce its effects: the short and the long run. This manipulation "is like the drink given the sick person unduly, which first refreshes him, but later causes more serious accidents and makes the illness worse."[48] Mariana explains the "advantages" and "disadvantages" of enlarging the supply of money by minting "vellón" coins; he recognizes that money will not flow out of the kingdom and, therefore, there will be more money in circulation within the nation and the economy would be stimulated (1) by increasing domestic production, which will lead to an abundance of cheaper fruits and goods, and (2) debtors would find money cheaper.[49] In relation to foreign nations a decrease on imports will be produced, for greater domestic production would make them unnecessary and, what is more, they will be reduced to being paid with money of lower value.[50] Finally, the foreigners who still bring their goods to Spain would prefer to be paid in goods rather than in cash, which would stimulate once again domestic production. Mariana recognizes all of these short-term advantages, and that

the king would benefit greatly from it, since he would fulfill his needs, pay his debts, remove the annuities consuming him, without hurting [directly] anybody. There is then no doubt that immediate interest is great.[51]

Nevertheless, Mariana's opinion is that these immediate benefits will turn into future impediments: farming would be abandoned; commerce with foreign countries would cease and, due to this shortage, the people and the kingdom would become impoverished and prices would go up. To avoid this general increase in prices, Mariana adds,

The king will want to fix a legal price on everything, and that would make the wound fester, because the people will not want to sell at low prices.[52]

The conflict between short-term and long-term interests is thus outlined, and the scholastic doctors will solve it by offering a compromise solution. As a general rule, they rejected the manipulation of the standard value by the public authority, for debasement was considered an "infamous systematic robbery," but the Spanish doctors also recognized that socioeconomic circumstances could evolve over time in such a way that the legal definition of the standard, its "coordinative definition," no longer corresponded to the first "anchoring" of the previous definition, thus making a change necessary. Hence, the role of the public authority with respect to the standard unit of account was twofold: first, to respect the "coordinative definition" given, avoiding any practice that would involve cheating or robbing society; second, to be aware of the evolution of circumstances in time. And when these circumstances warranted, modify the previous definition, adjusting the standard measure to economic reality.

Conclusion

If the Spanish doctors agreed with Adam Smith and David Ricardo as to the invariability of the standard of measurement, they also agreed with John Maynard Keynes as to the need, according to circumstances, "to vary its declaration [of the standard] from time to time." This conclusion they learned from the experience of a persistent rise in prices, which in the first half of the sixteenth century had more than doubled. The theory developed by the Spanish doctors to explain this rise in prices is known today as the "quantity theory of money,"[53] and Pierre Vilar speaks of the "Spanish quantitativists" as authors of a "well-founded scholastic tradition."[54] Marjorie Grice-Hutchinson, like Pierre Vilar and Wilhelm Weber, is also right in insisting that the Salamancan theologians discovered the "purchasing power" theory of exchange,[55] but the meaning of a "quantity" of value must be rightly understood if we want to know why the "constitutional monetary regime" of the scholastics was contrary to usury. To understand scholastic monetary theory, a serious study of the concept of time and its role in monetary phenomena is necessary.

—Francisco Gómez Camacho, S.J.

Notes

1. J. Gordley, *The Philosophical Origins of Modern Contract Doctrine* (Oxford: Clarendon Press, 1992), 91.

2. Oskar Morgenstern, "Perfect Foresight and Economic Equilibrium," Economic Research Program, Research Memorandum no. 55 (Princeton, N.J.: Princeton University, 1963).

3. J. Robinson, *La segunda crisis del pensamiento económico* (Mexico City: Ed. Actual, 1973), 66.

4. John Hicks, *Causality in Economics* (Oxford: Basil Blackwell, 1979), 11.

5. E. Vansteenberge, "Molina," *Dictionnaire de Théologie Catholique* (1929), X, 2092 (part II).

6. The references to Luis de Molina's *Treatise on Money* throughout this introduction are to the Spanish critical edition, *Tratado sobre los cambios*, edición, introducción, y notas por Francisco Gómez Camacho, S.J. (Madrid: Instituto de Estudios Fiscales, 1990).

7. Luis Saravia de la Calle, *Instrucción de mercaderes muy provechosa* (Medina del Compe: A. de Urveña, 1544), f. xciv (verso). A. W. Crosby, *The Measure of Reality: Quantification and Western Society, 1250–1600* (Cambridge: Cambridge University Press, 1997).

8. Tomás de Mercado, *Summa de tratos y contratos de mercaderes* (Seville: H. Diaz, 1571), 87.

9. Mercado, *Summa*, IV.3–4.

10. Molina, *Treatise on Money*, arg. 409.

11. Mercado, *Summa*, IV.88–89.

12. Luis de Molina, S.J., *La teoría del justo precio*, edición preparada por Francisco Gómez Camacho, S.J. (Madrid: Editora Nacional, 1981), 98.

13. Alexandre Koyré, *From the Closed World to the Infinite Universe* (Baltimore and London: John Hopkins University Press, 1957), viii. Cf. A. Funkenstein, *Theology and the Scientific Imagination from the Middle Ages to the Seventeenth Century* (Princeton: Princeton University Press, 1986), II.B.

14. Cf. Joseph Schumpeter's notion of "vision" in *History of Economic Analysis*, ed. Elizabeth Booty Schumpeter (Oxford: Oxford University Press, 1954), Part I, chap. 4, sec. 1d.

15. Koyré, *From the Closed World*, 2.

16. Hicks, *Causality in Economics*, 6–8.

17. Hicks, *Causality in Economics*, 8. "Causation can only be asserted in terms of the new causality if we have some theory, or generalization, into which observed events can be fitted; to suppose that we have theories into which all events can be fitted, is to make a large claim indeed. It was nevertheless a claim that thinkers of the eighteenth century, dazzled by the prestige of the Newtonian mechanics, were tempted to make . . . a complete system of natural law seemed just round the corner. The laws in which 'God' expressed himself must form such a system."

18. Odd Langholm, *The Legacy of Scholasticism in Economic Thought: Antecedents of Choice and Power* (Cambridge and New York: Cambridge University Press, 1998), 99.

19. Langholm, *The Legacy of Scholasticism*, 85.

20. Cf. Francisco Gómez Camacho, S.J., "El pensamiento económico de la Escolástica española a la Ilustración escocesa," in *El pensamiento económico en la Escuela de Salamanca*,

ed. Francisco Gómez Camacho, S.J. and R. Robledo (Salamanca: Ediciones Universidad de Salamanca, 1998), 205–39; and Camacho, "Later Scholastics: Spanish Economic Thought in the XVIth and XVIIth Centuries," in *Ancient and Medieval Economic Ideas and Concepts of Social Justice,* ed. S. Todd Lowry and Barry Gordon (Leiden and New York: Brill, 1998), 503–62.

21. Luis de Molina, S.J., *De iustitia et iure* (Cuenca, 1597), I, col. 15, C.

22. Martín de Azpilcueta, *Manual de confesores y penitentes* (Salamanca, 1556), cap. 27, n. 273ff.

23. John Maynard Keynes, *The Treatise on Probability* (London: Macmillan, 1921, reprinted 1952), 340.

24. Peter F. Drucker, "Toward the Next Economics," in *The Crisis in Economic Theory,* ed. Daniel Bell and Irving Kristol (New York: Basic Books, 1981), 5.

25. L. Vereecke, *De Guillaume d'Ockham à Saint Alphonse de Liguori: études d'historie de la théologie morale moderne, 1300–1787* (Rome: Collegium St. Alfonsi de Urbe, 1986), 31.

26. It is not unfounded that new scholarship, studying Keynes's philosophy in order to get a better understanding of his economics, makes a great deal of his distinction between the medieval scholastic terms *causa essendi* and *causa cognoscendi.* The cause of an event is not the cause of our knowledge of it.

27. Molina, *Treatise on Money,* arg. 401, col. 986; arg. 410, col. 1036, B, C, D; Domingo de Soto, *De iustitia et iure, libri decem* (Salamanca, 1553), VI, q. 9; and Azpilcueta, *Manual,* cap. 17, no. 288.

28. H. Reichenbach, *The Philosophy of Space and Time* (New York: Dover, 1958), 4, 14–24.

29. John Hicks, *Critical Essays in Monetary Theory* (Oxford: Clarendon Press, 1965), 10, 13.

30. John Maynard Keynes, *A Treatise on Money* (New York: AMS Press, 1976), chap. 1.

31. Pierre Vilar pointed out how the accusation of "bullionism," which used to be levelled against the scholastic doctors, was unfounded. Pierre Vilar, *A History of Gold and Money, 1450–1920,* trans. Judith White (Atlantic Highlands, N.J.: Humanities Press, 1976), 140. Also Barry Gordon refutes Schumpeter's allegation that Aristotle was a bullionist, in *Pre-Classical Economic Thought: From the Greeks to the Scottish Enlightenment,* ed. S. Todd Lowry (Boston/Dordrecht/Lancaster: Kluwer Academic Publishers, 1987), 226–30.

32. Keynes, *A Treatise on Money,* 3–4.

33. Mercado, *Summa,* I, 220.

34. Alfred North Whitehead, *The Concept of Nature* (Cambridge: Cambridge University Press, 1964), 120. (Italics mine)

35. Bertrand Russell, *An Essay on the Foundations of Geometry* (New York: Dover, 1956), 153. (Italics mine)

36. Mercado, *Summa,* I, 220.

37. Bernard W. Dempsey, S.J., "The Historical Emergence of Quantity Theory," *The Quarterly Journal of Economics* 50, no. 1 (November 1935): 175–76.

38. Hicks, *Causality in Economics.*

39. Molina, *Treatise on Money,* arg. 401, col. 988, B.

40. Russell, *Geometry,* 153.

41. Molina, *Treatise on Money,* arg. 400, col. 979, D.

42. Molina, *Treatise on Money*, arg. 400, col. 980, C.

43. Cf. ftn. 34, 35. Molina, *De iustitia et iure*, I, col. 15, C; and Azpilcueta, *Manual*, cap. 27, no. 273ff.

44. Keynes, *Treatise on Probability*, 306–7.

45. Cf. C. B. Boyer, *The History of the Calculus and Its Conceptual Development* (New York: Dover, 1959), chap. 4.

46. Axel Leijonhufvud, *Macroeconomic Instability and Coordination: Selected Essays of Axel Leijonhufvud* (Cheltenham, U.K.: Edward Elgar Publishing Limited, 2000), 166–83.

47. Juan de Mariana, S.J., *Tratado y discurso sobre la moneda de vellón*, estudio introductario por Lucas Beltrán (Madrid: Instituto de Estudios Fiscales, 1987), 39. This Spanish translation was made by the author from his original Latin work, *De monetae mutatione* (1609). A modern critical edition of the Latin original was prepared by Josef Falzberger and published recently under the same title (Heidelberg: Manutius, 1996).

48. Mariana, *Tratado*, 48.

49. Mariana, *Tratado*, 53–55.

50. Mariana, *Tratado*, 54.

51. Mariana, *Tratado*, 54.

52. Mariana, *Tratado*, 71.

53. Molina, *Treatise on Money*, arg. 406, col. 1010, B, C, D.

54. Vilar, *A History of Gold and Money*, 140. On the scholastic tradition in the Indies, see the work of Oreste Popescu, "Orígenes Hispanoamericanos de la Teoría cuantitativa," in *Aportaciones del Pensamiento Económico Iberoamericano, siglos XVI–XX* (Madrid: Ediciones Cultura Hispánica del Instituto de Cooperación Iberoamericana, 1986), 4–33.

55. Cf. Marjorie Grice-Hutchison, *Economic Thought in Spain: Selected Essays of Marjorie Grice-Hutchinson*, ed. Laurence S. Moss and Christopher K. Ryan (Brookfield, Vt.: Edward Elgar Publishing Company, 1993), 14–16.

Treatise on Money (1597)

Luis de Molina, S.J.

Translation by Jeannine Emery

1

Argument 396[1]

Diverse Senses in Which the Terms *Barter* and *Exchange* May Be Used: To Barter in a Strict Sense

Assuming that to barter or truck[2] is similar to exchanging, and both are similar to the purchase and sale operation,[3] it is necessary to explain them. To exchange means the same as to barter, since, in a wider sense both terms mean the same.[4] However, both terms are used in a triple sense.

First, in a very broad sense, they mean any type of exchange or commutation and, in this sense, they apply to any nongratuitous contract, such as the buying, the renting, the *mutuo*,[5] and all other nongratuitous [contracts], both those that are specifically provided for by the law (nominate) as well as those that are not (innominate).[6] They are all called nongratuitous because in all of them something is done, promised, or given as payment for something received. This was the first sense in which they used the term *barter* or *exchange*, and all the other [meanings] were acquired as a result of use and have a narrower scope. This explains why they are not called contracts that are specifically provided for by the law (nominate), because in order for a contract to be judged as specifically provided for by the law it should not only keep its generic name due to custom, but it should be named as a result of its own particularities.[7] Because we are only dealing here with specific contracts, this is not the right time to take on the exchange and barter in such a broad sense.

The second meaning has a narrower scope, and refers to the innominate contract expressed in the phrase *do ut des*, that is, one thing is exchanged for a different one, both if the first is considered indeterminate as individual, but specifically or generically distinct, as if both are considered individually determinate.[8] As it happens, this contract is called one of barter or exchange because of use or custom but is different from the rest of the contracts, both the nominate and the innominate, and it applies to the two parts that constitute it: one, that by which one good that is not considered to be price is exchanged for another that is not considered to be price either, as when a horse is exchanged for an ox, wheat for oil, one horse for another, and so forth. The other [part], that by which a good that is considered price is exchanged for another that is also considered price, as when we exchange gold coins for others that are silver, or coins from one place for coins from another. Because the contract in which something that is not considered price is exchanged for another that is considered such is a contract we call a *contract of sale*, and thus, nominate.

Because of what we have said about barter and exchange as an innominate contract, in this second sense of the term all contracts that are specifically provided for by the law (nominate) are excluded, such as the buying, the renting one, and so forth. Because of what we have added to indicate that it is a contract in which a good is exchanged (not something that is done or a service) for another good, the other three innominate contracts are also excluded, that is, those that are known as *do ut facias*, *facio ut des*, and *facio ut facias*, in which at least one of the parties is exchanging something that is done or a service. Here we intend to discuss bartering in this second sense, and its parts; and it shall not be necessary to add other particular arguments about the other innominate contracts, as they do not present any special difficulty and may be sufficiently understood with what has already been expounded in argument 253 and with what we shall say on bartering and the rest of the contracts.

The third sense in which the terms *barter* and *exchange* are used is even more precise. To barter means the exchange in which none of the things being bartered is considered as price, for example, a horse for an ox. Exchange is the contract where both of the things being exchanged are considered as price and, in this sense, the exchange is different from the barter. It is in this sense that we shall study the exchange.

To barter or truck, in this third sense, is much like the buying and selling, because of which we may apply to it anything we say about this last contract, as long as the laws do not say differently.[9] For this same reason, in the barter or truck contract, and in the cases in which they could be applied to the contract of sale, there may be loss of rights, redhibitory action, and the "quantominoris."[10] Things may also be bartered when they have not come into existence yet but in hopes of when they do, because they can also be bought and sold like this, as proved in argument 340, and as long as there is nothing against it.[11] The same may be said of exchanging in a strict sense. Moreover, when buying and selling of a certain good is forbidden, then it is fair to conclude that its barter is also forbidden.

It is uncertain whether property rights are transferred in the barter and exchange as in the buying and selling operation, that is, not when the good is delivered but when the price or corresponding fee has been paid or is considered paid, as said in argument 338. Some laws[12] determine that such way of transferring property rights pertains solely to the contract of sale, because of special privilege, and that in the barter as in all other contracts in which property rights are transferred, the transference is carried out before the other party complies with the contractual obligations, which the law seems to agree with;[13] although Bartolus and the gloss judge differently,[14] that is, that in the barter and in all other contracts the property rights are not transferred by merely delivering the good, but the other party is required to meet the terms of the contract.[15] I think, however, that the first opinion is better, which seems much more in accordance with the two paragraphs from the *Institutiones* cited earlier. In addition, the fact that in the barter the property rights are transferred before the other party complies with the contract is so clear in the law,[16] that it is surprising that Bartolus does not take this law into account, nor the law that he refers to in order to prove his argument demonstrates anything at all, not even in appearance. As it only says that if the debtor goes to his creditor to ask for the security that he left as guarantee saying he wants to pay the debt, and then later the debtor spends the collateral with whom he had previously decided upon in order not to pay the debt, the creditor shall withhold his right over the security that was fraudulently taken away from him for the period of time in which it takes to pay the debt. I cannot see how Bartolus may conclude anything from this that would go to prove his argument.

On the barter or truck, in this third sense, it should be noted that the *Ordenanzas Portuguesas*,[17] in order to avoid the evils that follow, forbid the barter of wheat, wine, oil, or any other kind of good resulting from the year's crop for another good that is to be paid in the future and [it also forbids] that the person with whom the barter is carried out should buy from someone else. And those who barter in this way are imposed a penalty of *ipso facto* loss of the bartered good, which shall be given to the other person who shall not have the obligation to repay in any way, nor shall be able to waiver the privilege that the law grants him.

The benefits of bartering or trucking shall be commented upon when we discuss them.

2

Argument 397

Whether the "Alcabala"[1] Should Be Paid in Barter and Exchange Transactions?

According to Castilian law, not only should the alcabala be paid when bartering but it should be paid twice over: one for each of the goods that are bartered. As a matter of fact, each barter operation is considered to be a double sale transaction,[2] one for each of the individuals participating in the barter. For this reason, in Castile, each of the two are required to pay the alcabala according to the value of the good that they receive in exchange for [the one that was given], because each receives it as if it were its price, and, as we all know, in Castile the seller is required to pay the total amount of the alcabala according to the good's price.[3]

In Portugal the same requirement to pay the tax exists and, for the same reason already mentioned, it is paid by the two individuals who participate in the transaction. Over there it is called *sisa*, as *da sisa* appears in articles. However, each individual pays only half of the tax, because in Portugal, the seller pays half the tax and the buyer the other half, as mentioned when dealing with the buying and selling operation.[4]

There is one point of uncertainty regarding this issue. Because bartering is not considered perfect or complete before the good has been delivered by both parties, nor is it enough that only one of the parties deliver it, as pointed out in argument 253 and Lassarte acknowledges,[5] it is uncertain if the tax or taxes start to be owed only when the bartering has been completely finished, so that they should not be paid if only one of the individuals delivered the good or if, as pointed out in argument 258, once the delivery is carried out by only one of the parties, it is this [party] who should pay the tax. Finally, it is uncertain whether there is an obligation to pay the alcabala if the individuals decide to rescind the contract before carrying out the delivery.

According to common law, effective in Portugal as nothing has been legislated contradicting it, Lassarte[6] and Bartachino Firmio acknowledge that the tax is not due until the barter is concluded by both parties. According to Menchaca[7] the same happens in Castile, because even if here the right for judicial action is granted for the mere barter pact, and it is not licit to change one's mind when one of the parties has carried out the delivery, nor even if neither has carried it out;[8] however, one thing is the pact or accord to carry out and complete the barter and a different one is the action of bartering itself, that is neither considered complete nor finished before the two intervening parties carry out the delivery of their respective good. In this kingdom of Castile, the second law mentioned before does not levy the alcabala on the barter pact but on the barter itself.

Lassarte has the contrary opinion in the already cited number 25, and says that in Castile this tax is paid once the barter pact has been fulfilled, and even if the delivery is never carried out and the individuals rescind the contract by mutual agreement before the delivery is fulfilled. He holds this opinion on account of the fact that because in this kingdom a mere civil pact is enough to establish the obligation between the individuals, and an action may be brought by any one of them, and one may not withdraw against the other one's wishes either if one of the parties failed to fulfill the delivery as well as if both parties failed to do so, it follows that, in this kingdom, the barter is also perfect and complete by the mere consent of both parties, as happens with the buy-sell contract. Thus, just as in the buying and selling operation the mere consent is enough for the tax officials to have the right to collect the tax, without being able to defend oneself by bringing into play the contract's rescission by the parties' mutual consent and before carrying out the delivery, so it is with bartering, and the tax must be paid to the one who is recipient and collector of it at the time of the parties' agreement, and not to the one who may exist at the time of delivery. If the above were not true, once the contract had been executed by mutual agreement and in order to evade taxes, the contracting parties would be able to delay its fulfillment and the delivery of the goods while they allowed it, and meanwhile the door would be open to the rescission of the contract if the circumstances were favorable to it.

In my opinion, there are better grounds for the opposing argument, which many doctors defend and is based on what we all know, which is that to barter does not refer to the barter pact but to the business of bartering itself which is only considered complete and finished once the mutual delivery of the goods has been carried out, just as *mutuum*[9] is not understood as a pact or agreement to lend but as the real business of lending itself. And just as the *mutuum* belongs to the contracts specifically provided for by the law (nominate) that perfect themselves with the deed, not only with the consent or with words, as seen in argument 254, so bartering belongs to the kind of contract that perfects itself with the deed carried out, since this is what the term *bartering* means, and not the mere consent nor agreement between the parties to barter something.[10]

Therefore, as long as the tax we referred to is levied on bartering, it follows that such tax is not due nor do the tax authorities have the right to collect it before the [barter] is fulfilled. And it does not make any difference if the individuals who are performing the barter decide among themselves to delay it in order to cancel out the pact if it so suits them, as they would be exercising their full rights and in no way would be failing in their duty toward the tax authorities.

Observe that exactly as according to common law an action may not be brought against the other party if there was only an agreement to carry out a *mutuum*, it may be brought against him if said pact were coupled to another contract, precisely as was said in argument 253. Likewise, according to common law, or in the kingdom of Portugal where only this law is applied in this matter and the tax is levied on the barter, if there were an agreement to barter certain goods, or the barter agreement were associated to another contract, the right to bring an action that originates in such an agreement shall be acknowledged. However, because the barter has not been carried out thus far and there has only been an agreement, although concealed under the principle of stipulation or association to another contract, the tax shall not affect this agreement, as it only affects the barter contract, or the contract of sale. This explains why, according to the law in use in this kingdom, it becomes unacceptable that for the mere agreement to barter (the same as for any other agreement) the right to bring an action should be granted and the parties be denied the right to revoke [the agreement], stating that because of said agreement [they] owe the tax that is levied on barter contracts.

The reason why the tax is due in the contract of sale, and the tax authorities hold the right to collect it for the mere fact of the parties having reached an agreement is very different. And this reason is that, as set forth in argument 254 and explained in several others, the buying and selling operation is considered complete and perfect with the individuals' consent, and the term *buy-sell* refers to the already finished and completed contract, because of which it is sufficient in order [for a person] to owe the tax that is levied on it.

This explanation shall make it easy to understand that if in Castile or in Portugal an agreement is reached to barter some particular goods in times of a specific tax collector, but the barter is completed through the delivery of said goods in times of a different tax collector, it is this last [tax collector] to whom the tax belongs, as it was during the time [when he was tax collector] that the barter was completed. This would happen even if the initial agreement between the parties were concealed under the guise of mere stipulation and associating it to a different agreement. And this is so because the tax is not due for the barter agreement, even if the civil obligation to fulfill it is originated in this [agreement], but for the barter itself once it has been fulfilled, and it was not fulfilled in times of the first tax collector but [in times] of the second one.

Lassarte[11] believes that the tax levied on the barter is due because the civil obligation is already originated in the pact by which the parties commit themselves to barter, and calls to discuss whether the tax should be paid to the first tax collector or to the second one when the barter pact—which the common law says does not give origin to the civil obligation unless it is tied together to another contract, or were stipulated by the parties—is carried out during one tax collector's period, and the delivery [is carried out] during another tax collector's period when the civil obligation starts to be in force. He mentions Antonio Gómez's[12] opinion, whom Parladorius agrees with, and who states that it is the first tax collector who is due the tax. They believe this because, according to what they say, such obligation does not derive from the fulfillment of the pact and the delivery of the good, but from the pact itself that is followed by the delivery, this being only a condition that makes the obligation not derive from the pact alone.[13] From which follows, *sensu contrario*, that if the pact and the contract are followed by something else then there will be a right to take the legal action that is deemed convenient. And they say that since the pact that gives origin to that action was carried out during the first tax collector's period, it follows that it is to him the tax should be paid, even if the conditions that are necessary to give origin to that right take place during the second one's period.[14]

I consider Lassarte's opinion much better, that is, that the tax is due to the second tax collector and not to the first. In the first place, because the civil obligation is originated in both parts, and they are both essential to the contract and necessary for it to be considered complete and for the obligation to derive from it, as the law says.[15] And if there is anything *a sensu contrario* that the words that cite the *ex placito* law[16] prove it is merely that the obligation derives from the pact only in a particular way, which we do not deny, but they do not prove that at the same time [the obligation] does not derive from the delivery itself as part and an addition to the same contract. In the second place, because even if we say it derives only from the pact, once the condition of delivery is fulfilled, it cannot be denied that in order for the contract to be complete and fulfilled, the delivery should take place, which happens during the period of the second tax collector, and, in consequence, to him should the tax be paid. The same happens when a contract of sale is held up until the deed is written—it is not considered complete and finished and, consequently, the alcabala will be owed to the tax collector who [happens to be in office] when the deed is fulfilled.[17]

In the barter as well as in the buy-sell operation when both parties agree that in order for [the contract] to be considered complete and perfect the deed is needed, the contract shall be postponed by mutual agreement until the deed's execution.[18] In Castile, if before entering into the contract, or at the moment of entering it, somebody mentions the need of executing the deed, the contract is considered interrupted until the deed completes it. Argument 337 expounded on the same issue, regarding the contract of buying, unless from the concurrent circumstances in the case it is possible to surmise that the contracting parties had a different thing in mind, such as considering the deed only as proof and guaranty of the contract. Lassarte, however, warns us in the text cited above that, because the delivery is necessary to complete the barter, mere intent is not enough to consider the barter contract complete, even if it proceeds from both parties.

When the barter contract is interrupted until the deed is executed, common law and Castilian law allow both parties to change their mind and withdraw from the contract before the deed is executed, even if one of the parties had already delivered the good. Also, if the contract were to be executed, the tax should be paid to the tax collector in office at the moment of executing the deed, because it is then that the contract is deemed complete. Such is Lassarte's[19] opinion, which furthermore is evident.

Lassarte[20] judges correctly that no tax should be paid for contracts such as the following: I give you a certain good so that you give it to Pedro after a certain period of time, or I give you 100 units so that you give Juan 50, or I give you a certain piece of property that I own so that you pay me or someone else a certain rent. His reason is that in order to pay taxes for the contract we call *do ut des*, it is necessary for the things that are reciprocally being delivered to be different, and one be not included in the other, nor be its fruits or the rights that derive from it. But even if Lassarte may judge all these contracts to be innominate, such as the one we call *do ut des*, I would prefer saying they are different forms of donation. And we know that donations are not subject to the alcabala, as they belong to a very different kind of contract from the one of sale and of barter in their strict sense.[21]

Everyone agrees that when a good of a certain kind is handed over for another of a different kind, such as a horse for an ox, wheat for oil, and so forth, or an individual of a species for another of the same species but of a different value, as would be one horse for another, it is a barter and, as such, the double tax we all know should be paid. It is uncertain, however, if when a certain individual of a specific species is handed over in exchange for another of the same species and similar value, as would be a certain measure of wheat for another of equal amount, or a measure of wine or oil for another that is equal, it should be considered a barter or not, and if the tax should be paid. Parladorius, together with Bartolus and several others,[22] believe it should be considered a *mutuo*, because of which no tax should be paid. Lassarte seems to hold a better opinion[23] when he says that it is important to take into account if, given the circumstances, the individuals intend to carry out a *mutuo*, as may be considered from the way of entering into the contract and the circumstances in which it is carried out, and, in such case, no tax is owed. This happens, for example, when someone borrows wheat, wine, oil, even a ram, or similar things, which have to be paid later by giving back an individual of the same species and of a more or less similar value. They could also attempt a contract that is different from the bartering [contract], as would be a deposit or consignment of a dowry that is to be returned once the marriage is dissolved. And neither at that time should the tax be paid, even if the depositary has used up the good that was deposited, and has to pay up somewhere else delivering a similar good. Finally, given the circumstances and way of entering into the contract, the conclusion might be that the individuals want to execute a barter and, in that case, they should pay the tax even if they tried concealing the barter under the pretext of a *mutuo*.

There is no certain rule allowing us to know if what is being carried out is a barter that benefits the individuals, because if someone who owns wheat somewhere else requests in the very same place where he is that a friend lend him wheat for daily use, and this friend lends it so that it is rendered back when the other receives the wheat in this very same place, it should be considered a *mutuo* and not a barter. Likewise, if someone asked for a loan of wheat to pay it later with the harvest obtained from it, it should not be considered a barter, even if it is convenient to whom grants it, but a *mutuo*. However, if someone delivered wheat in the place where he is so that the same quantity is paid back in some other place where he may sell it for a higher price, it shall be considered a barter even if they try to conceal it as a *mutuo*, unless the circumstances suggest that the one who received the wheat requested and received it as a loan. So too if there were two people who lived in different places and each had wheat where the other one lived, it would be considered a barter even if they wanted to cover it up as a *mutuo*.

All these issues make it worthwhile to entrust oneself to a prudent person who, once having examined the concurrent circumstances in a case, shall judge if it is a barter or a *mutuo*.

In the event that two goods are bartered, it is the judge's responsibility or whom he designates,[24] to appraise both in order to estimate the tax amount. That is why it should not be appraised according to the value established by the parties, even if the barter contract indicates the value of the goods that are bartered. If initially a good was sold for its price and later on both parties decided by common agreement that instead of paying the price they shall pay by delivering another good, it shall not be considered a barter but a double sale; and the tax should be paid according to the price stipulated for each one of them.[25]

When a good cannot be sold because its value is considered inestimable, such as would be the right to burial and many other things that were discussed in argument 340 and in several others, the barter of this good for another that can be priced shall not be subject to a tax for either of the goods. In fact, because it is a sacred good, of inestimable value, no tax should be paid, nor does the law cited above apply.[26] Moreover, just as the sale of such goods is considered invalid because of simony, so too shall the barter for a profane good be considered invalid; and we know that for an invalid sale or barter no alcabala should be paid. For this same reason, the alcabala should not be paid in the opposite case either, that is, when a profane good is bartered for another good considered of inestimable value. On the other hand, even if spiritual goods[27] may be bartered among them and lay people barter them, as happens with the right to burial and the chapels, no tax should be paid due to the fact that they are goods of inestimable value.[28]

In this Castilian kingdom there are many things that are free of alcabala, such as books, horses supplied with bit and saddle, and many others.[29] When anyone interchanges any of these goods such as, for example, books for cinnamon,[30] the person who interchanges the books is exempt of paying the alcabala. These things are considered privileged when they take the place of merchandise, so that the alcabala is not owed for the price received for them, nor for the goods that as price are received in exchange. However, the person who barters the cinnamon for the books must pay the alcabala according to the estimated value of books, because books are not considered privileged when they take the place of the price paid for the other goods, as should be evident. This is easy to prove, as the reference to law establishes money to be free of alcabala when it takes the place of merchandise, as happens with exchanging in a strict sense; but it is not considered so when it takes the place of price since, in this case, money does not free from the alcabala the good for which that money is paid, but on the contrary, the seller pays the tax proportionate to the price.[31]

When a good is sold for an amount of money and, jointly, for another good, even if this [good] is of a much inferior value than that of the money, the Castilian law[32] orders both things to be jointly appraised by the judge, or by whom he designates, and the seller of the highest valued good should pay the alcabala for the total amount of the good plus the money he receives as payment, while the other individual must pay only for the value of the good he delivers. Thus, for example, if Pedro sells a property to Juan for 1,000 gold coins plus a mule, and the latter's value is estimated to be 100 gold coins, Pedro would have to pay an alcabala worth 1,100 gold coins. And even if the property is priced in 1,100 gold coins, Juan would only have to pay for the 100 coins the mule he delivers is worth.[33]

It is evident that the donation handed over as reward does not pay alcabala in Castile or Portugal, since it is not a barter, even if it is a reward for a good, not for a service. What happens is the donations handed over as reward are not owed out of justice as happens in bartering but originate from the individual's gratitude and generosity. And it is irrelevant that the law[34] says it should be considered a special kind of barter, since it does not confirm it is a barter but as having a certain likeness to it, that is, as reward for a benefit that was previously received.[35]

If the donation were reciprocal between the individuals, it shall be considered a barter, and the alcabala shall have to be paid. However, if when the situation is considered from a general standpoint, and not from the simple act of delivery, the reciprocal donation is seen to originate in the love and generosity that the individuals feel for each other, the conclusion may be that it is a donation as long as the circumstances persuade us that the individuals wanted to make a donation. Otherwise, we would be dealing with a barter under the guise of a donation and, in that case, the double alcabala should be paid.

Because when exchanging in a strict sense, both parties interchange money, and this is considered a privileged good regarding the payment of the alcabala, it is clear that the alcabala should not be paid for the exchange operations.

3

Argument 398

On Exchange in a Strict Sense and Its Types.
Is the Exchange Dealer's Activity Licit?

To exchange, in a strict sense, and we already pointed out in argument 396, is no less than to trade money for money, and it is not necessary for the money that is exchanged to be different from the one that is received as far as the material, shape, or engraved seal on the coins, and in spite of Juan de Medina's opinion.[1] Because, as Soto[2] believes, if the money were handed over in one place to be paid or handed back somewhere else it shall be a real exchange, even if the money to be paid back is no different from the one received as far as the material or the seal.

Even if the parties who carry out the barter in the sense described in argument 397 have the same name, and both may be equally called barterer and barteree,[3] they are not called the same in the exchange, nor do they carry out the same occupation. Because the person who is asked for the exchange may rent out the services and ability requested of him, and for this he may justly charge something more than the amount he exchanges, as shall be evident for what we shall proceed to explain. For this reason, in order to make a distinction between both parties involved in the exchange, they are given different names: the person to whom the exchange is requested, and who lends his services and resourcefulness by someone else's request is called an *exchange dealer*, especially if he holds the office in a public condition. He is also called *numulario*, *trapezita*, *collybista*, and *argentarius*, although some of these names may sometimes have a broader meaning. See Covarrubias[4] for further discussion on this issue. In Spanish he is called *vanquero*[5] [*sic*]. Conrado[6] calls the person who solicits the exchange *campsarius*; Medina and others give him the

151

same name, because just as the borrower is the one who receives a loan, the donee, the recipient of a donation, and the legatee one to whom a legacy is bequeathed, he who receives money in exchange is called a *campsario*.

Is it licit to work as an exchange dealer in order to earn a profit? It must be said that it is an activity that is dangerous in itself, more dangerous than the activity of the person who does business and looks to earn a profit by buying, bartering, or selling; an activity not suitable for some people, such as the members of the clergy, who are forbidden to engage in it. But, in spite of all this, if it is carried out as we describe below, it shall not be condemned as unjust or illicit. What is more, it may be practiced meritoriously, as said in argument 339 of those who carry out buying and selling, and bartering, seeing that both economic activities are useful to the republic, as we shall see from what we say below.

We shall not discuss the type of exchange where there is no desire to profit, as when coins of a higher value are exchanged for others of a lower value but that as a whole are equal in value both legally and in the people's common assessment. There is no uncertainty whatsoever in these types of contracts; we shall refer to the exchange that seeks a profit.

The type of exchange that seeks a profit, and where a difference is perceived in the value of what is given and what is received, may enter three categories, disregarding for now whether the exchange is licit or illicit. Because the exchange is not carried out if the coins are not different, this may be a difference in the coins themselves, such as because they are made of a different material, have a different legal seal, or have both a different material and legal seal; a difference as far as the place, because the coins are given in one place to be returned in another, for example, in Lisbon to be returned in Seville or Rome; or a difference as far as time, because they are given at a certain point in time to be returned at another. According to these three ways of specifying the difference, there are three types of exchange.

First, that in which the coins are exchanged because of the difference between the coins themselves. This type of exchange is usually called *petty exchange*, because in it coins of a greater value are usually exchanged for coins that are inferior [in value]. It is also known as *manual exchange*, as some people describe it, because it is practiced from hand to hand in one and the same place.

The second type is [the exchange] where the money is exchanged due to its different value in places that are also different. And because it is usually carried out through bills of exchange that instruct the money to be paid somewhere else, it is usually called exchange for bills of exchange (*cambium per litteras*).

The third type is that where money is exchanged because of a difference in its value over time. This type of operation may be called exchange, but it lacks precision, because, if looked upon closely, we do not find here but a loan; and if either one of the two individuals should receive anything more than the amount exchanged he would commit usury, unless the contract could be justified by reason of *lucrum cessans* (profit ceasing), *damnum emergens* (loss occurring), or any other legitimate ruling. This is the reason why I said before that I was not considering if the exchange was licit or illicit, so that this type of exchange would be included in the concept of exchange, and we will proceed to discuss it in order to admit or condemn it if such were the case.

Generally in the exchanges attention should always be paid to whether something more than the capital is received for the time difference, because whatever is received for reason of a time difference is usury and is unjustly received, as it is received for reason of the loan that formally or virtually is carried out in that deal, unless it is justified for reason of profit ceasing or any another legitimate justification.

It is worth noting that the three types of exchange mentioned above appear at times combined, because in the case of coins that are different between each other, there may be a difference due to place, and the deal for which they are exchanged is both an exchange of different coins and, also, in places that are also different. The difference due to place usually goes together with the difference of the moment in time when the money is to be returned, as they are usually places that are very distant between each other.

Soto admits a fourth type of exchange;[7] that is, one that is practiced because of the difference in value that a same kind of currency has in different places. Even if for the same coins, the *ducats*, for example, the same number of silver coins may be given in Flanders as in Spain, or in the New World, they would, however, be worth more in Flanders than in Spain, and in Spain more than in the New World, due to a lesser amount of this type of coin, and for this reason, more goods may be bought in Flanders than in Spain, and more in Spain than in the New World. I believe, however, that it is not necessary to admit this fourth type of exchange, as the difference pointed out originates from the very different circumstances that exist in places that are so distant one from the other. This problem shall be sufficiently explained, when we describe the reasons that make it licit in the exchange to receive something more than what the exchange dealer gave because of the difference of value between one place and another.

Navarrus distinguishes seven types of exchange, of which only some of them include rulings or justifications for the exchange dealer to licitly receive something more than the money given.[8] But there is no need to multiply the types of exchange; it shall be sufficient while explaining the types [of exchange] suggested here to examine the rulings that make it licit or not to receive something more than what was given. Moreover, it shall be sufficient to explain the petty exchange and the [exchange] that takes place because of the difference in places, and, at the same time, to analyze other rulings that make it licit or not to receive any increment over the capital.

The doctors also divide the exchanges into real and dry exchange, calling *real exchange* that which is true exchange and which allows drawing something more than the capital that is exchanged, and dry exchange that which is not true exchange, and thus not allowing to draw either more than the capital exchanged—that is, when in the exchange an increment is received only for the delay in time, which constitutes usury. The name *dry*, or *lacking in sap*, means it cannot produce fruit or profit. This is the sense in which these words are used in Pius V's bull on exchanges.[9] Some use dry exchange to describe the exchange that is carried out when the exchange dealer hands over some money first to get it back with an increase at a later date, even if this retrieval is in a distant place. I believe that this name also results from the same previously declared notion, that is, that such exchange was considered in itself unfruitful and usurious, because of which no profit or increase could be licitly drawn from it, as the doctors affirm and the *Ordenanzas Portuguesas*[10] set down. But we shall examine this problem further on, and we shall prove that such definition was made without grounds. Navarrus says that these doctors call it dry because in it the exchange dealer gives the money before receiving it,[11] but I prefer what I have previously argued.

Medina and Conrado also divide the exchanges into pure and impure,[12] and call the exchange that is not mixed with any other type of contract, *pure*, and *impure* that which is mixed with another contract, which may be that of a loan, rent of the exchange dealer's services, or other similar ones. Soto says, in the second article cited earlier, that it is more expressive to call the just exchange pure and the unjust one impure.

We have said all this to better understand the doctors, which in this matter usually express themselves in different ways.

4

Argument 399

Is It Licit for the Exchange Dealer to Receive in the Petty Exchange an Increment over the Price That the Law Has Appraised [the Coins] For?

It is clearly evident that petty exchange is useful to the republic, as it is often that men need coins of a lesser value in order to buy the things that they need daily, or to give alms, or for other such things in which the coinage of a higher value is of no use. On the contrary, those who wish to put away a great sum of money, or take it elsewhere, need to exchange small coins for larger ones, and likewise, those who emigrate to a place where the coins of their own land are of no value need to exchange them for others that are valuable wherever they go. For these purposes, and others of the like, the republic finds it useful to have exchange dealers who have access to diverse types of coins at the right time in order to exchange them with those who need them.

Once established this, together with the doctors' common opinion, we go on to say the following: just as with the contract of sale and all other commutative contracts in which it is necessary to abide by the equality between what is given and what is received in order for [these contracts] to be fair and there be no obligation of giving back, so in the exchange in which money is given for money should there be equality, because this is the law that rules over commutative contracts, among which is the exchange.

But money has a value that has been fixed by law, because of which, from this point of view, its value is indivisible both for the one who offers as for the one who asks for it. The question now is, mainly, what rulings or grounds allow the exchanger to justly receive something more than the equivalent of what he gives, taking into account the appraised value of the coins that are being exchanged.

We must say, together with the doctors' common opinion, that exchange dealers may licitly receive a just price for the service they carry out, either from the republic, or from those people who ask for the exchange when the republic does not pay them, and as long as that price is not unwarranted in relation to the services rendered. If the price were unwarranted, there would be obligation to give back the excess charged above the rigorous just price of the service rendered. The services rendered by the exchange dealer are: getting together and having the coins of diverse types ready for those who wish to exchange them; being present for their services, whether it is themselves or someone else, at the public place of exchanges waiting for those who want to exchange; counting the money they give and the one they receive, and other such things. All these services deserve a fair retribution.

In this kingdom of Castile, anyone can undertake the public office of exchange dealer without any charge whatsoever. However, they must be elected in the royal court by the king himself. In other places they are elected by the judges and *rulers* of the city or town in which they are to practice their duties.[1] Under the above cited law 4 in statute 18, they are allowed to receive 4 *maravedis* for the exchange of 1 *castellano*; 3 *maravedis* for the exchange of 1 *dobla* or 1 *ducat*; 2 *maravedis* for the exchange of 1 *florin*, and the same is said of the *ducat*.[2] Navarrus recalls that in Salamanca, at the time when he taught in that illustrious university, there was a public exchange dealer who used to charge 1 *maravedi* for the exchange of each *ducat*.[3]

In Portugal, they forbid that for giving or receiving gold coins that are valuable in this kingdom, coined here or elsewhere, any plus or increment should be received above the just value of these;[4] and there is a penalty depriving [the person] of the coins' value, half of which is awarded to the accuser and half to the redemption of captives, along with the penalty of a two-year exile in Africa, excepting the case where one would have been appointed by the king as public exchange dealer of a place, allocating a certain fee to him. In that case he would be able to receive the increment licitly; but if he had not been allocated any fee whatsoever, he would not be able to receive anything, and shall be subject to the same penalties as the others, in spite of the royal appointment. However, since the fee the exchange dealer receives justly is not received for the money he gives but for the service he renders, it is reasonable to believe that there are actually two contracts in the exchange, and both of them just: one, the exchange of money for money of the same value; the other, the hiring of the exchange dealers' services, for which he collects that just increment. As said in argument 304, following the opinion of Navarrus, Medina, Major, and others, in a loan, the lender may not collect anything for the loan apart from the capital, but he may, because of the very nature of the problem (*ex ipsa natura rei*), collect a moderate stipend for the job of counting the money and for other services the exchange dealer does. Likewise, he may also collect a moderate stipend for the services mentioned before.

It is uncertain whether the private exchange dealers, who have not been appointed by the republic to carry out this duty, may also receive an increment for the responsibilities they carry out in favor of those who ask for an exchange, such as counting the money and other tasks they perform. Cajetan denies this in his *opusculum* on exchange,[5] because, in the first place, he says that counting the money does not deserve a payment, as it has always been done for free; in the second place, because sometimes [the person] who seeks the exchange counts a larger amount of money than the exchanger; third, because the exchanger's action of counting is the same as the action carried out by the person who seeks the exchange. But the common opinion of the doctors declares quite the opposite, that is, that private exchange dealers, the same as the official exchanger, may also licitly collect, because of the nature of the problem (*ex natura rei*), a small increment for the action of counting or other similar services rendered, in much the same way as the official exchanger. But what they may licitly collect should be less than what the public exchange dealers collect, because the [public exchange dealers'] duty takes up many more expenses and work, as he has declared above. Thus, acknowledge Medina (although, at first glance, he seems to suggest the opposite in the preceding 1.a's issue's second to last paragraph), Soto, Navarrus, Conrado, Biel, Silvestre, and others.[6] The reason is that such service is worthy of remuneration, even if it is meager, because of which the first argument should be denied, which is the one that persuaded Cajetan. To the second [argument] we respond that even if the exchange dealer counts the money he gives as well as the money he receives, both things are carried out at the request of the person seeking the exchange, because of which both acts of counting should be paid, just as the lender should be remunerated for the service of counting, both when he gives the loan as when it is returned to him, as both actions are carried out for the borrowers' benefit and he could refuse them if he did not wish to carry out the service of lending. That is why it should be denied, in the third argument, that one job is compensated with another, as this does not happen either in the case of the loan, because in both cases all the work is carried out for the benefit of the one seeking the loan or the exchange.

All this explanation should be considered correct in accordance with the nature of the problem (*ex natura rei*), because the republic could forbid drawing for the exchanges an amount that is greater than the value of the exchanged coins, and this on account of the republic's own good, in order to prevent the increment in the price of coins, and to prevent foreigners from carrying gold or silver out of the country, offering for them a much better price, all of which would be detrimental to the republic.

Soto says in the place already referred to, in the third conclusion, that in this kingdom there has already been a law that forbids anyone from collecting an increment over the exchanges, excepting the public exchange dealers appointed by the republic. Quite the opposite, Navarrus says, in the already quoted number 19, that even if in this kingdom it is forbidden to carry out the responsibilities of a public exchanger as a result of one's own decision, it is not, however, forbidden to exchange to private persons, nor collecting for it a profit, and he quotes the laws that resolve it. He complains that Soto does not quote the law that backs his opinion. Covarrubias, in the quoted work, embraces Soto's opinion and quotes the current laws[7] in favor of it. But in these laws there is only a prohibition to carry out the duties of a public exchanger in the Court without having been appointed by the king, or by the judge or rulers in other places; but they do not forbid all the rest from carrying out exchanges in private.

Perhaps it is considered forbidden for private individuals to collect an increment for petty exchange because of the laws that today appraise gold coins (which we shall shortly discuss), which forbid collecting any increment, as Gutiérrez holds.[8] We have already said that this is the legislation in Portugal, but I believe that in neither of the two kingdoms is anything regularly collected for petty exchange.

I would like to caution that what Soto and Covarrubias declare, that is, that once the law that prohibits collecting anything for petty exchange is promulgated there is obligation to restitute if anything were received, is a complex issue, as we could be dealing here with the just price received for the service involved in the exchange. Because even if the prince might forbid in this case such increment on account of the republic's common good, and in law it is enough for a ruling to forbid something so that if it is done the contract is nullified and invalidated, however, in the present case, it would be the just compensation derived *ex natura rei* between what is received and the [good] for which something is received. Also, from what we said in argument 88, especially when confirming the first argument, the rulings that are not subject to what the law has ordered in the cited place, do not prevent the individual from receiving his just reward. That is why I believe that by violating these rulings only a sin of disobedience to the prince is committed; a disobedience that *ex genere suo* is by no means serious. And if what was received exceeded *ex natura rei* the limits of the just stipend, then the sin would certainly be *ex genere suo* serious, as a greater increment than what is just would have been received, there being obligation to restitute.

There is another resolution by which the private individuals may licitly obtain a profit, namely, when in the place where the exchange takes place they give for the exchanged money less than what it is worth, not in that place but in a different one, and then [the individuals] take the money to that other place, or they exchange it to travelers who are going there for the value it has over there, because they wish to do this favor without incurring any loss for themselves. Thus, the residents in a country usually do business by exchanging money from other kingdoms without any value in the place where the exchange is being carried out, for a low amount. In order to do this, they buy money from other countries that lack value in the place where the exchange is taking place, because of which they buy it licitly cheap since it is not worth anything there; then they take the money bought like this to a place where it has a value appraised by law, or they exchange it to travelers who are going to that place for the value it has in that country. Medina, Cajetan, and others[9] agree with this. Notice, however, that sometimes the price is so low that it does not equal the value of the coins' metal, as for example, Portuguese silver coins. In that case, it would be unjust, and there would be obligation to restitute [the amount] lacking for the lowest just price; because if the price paid for the coins were below the price of the silver sold in ingots, the contract would certainly be unjust and there would be obligation to restitute.

5

Argument 400

On Diverse Gold and Silver Coins That Have Been Coined in Castile and Portugal over Time. On Their Value at the Moment of Coinage and at the Present Time. On the Value of Gold and Silver Ingots in These Kingdoms at Different Times

In order to better understand what we need to say on exchanges, we should discuss the matters indicated in the title of this argument, as we are more familiar with the coins from Castile and Portugal than with those from other kingdoms. All things considered, what we say about those from Castile and Portugal shall make it easy to surmise what should be considered about the other coins, once we have the information about the laws that refer to them and their characteristics.

For a better understanding, take into account that a half pound (*selibra*) of gold and silver, which the Spanish call *marco*, and in other places they call *marca*, is a coin that weighs 8 ounces; and the ounce is divided into 8 eighths, which the Hebrews call *adharcon*, and the Greek and Latin call *drachmas*. The Spanish, distorting the Greco-Roman name, call it *drama*, *adarame*, or *adarme*. I suspect that, as happens with many words in our language, *adarame* is a word that the Spanish inherited from the Saracens who occupied the Spanish territories, and whose language is very similar to the Hebrew tongue. In this kingdom of Castile they call the half *ochavo*,[1] namely the sixteenth part of an ounce, a *dram* or *adarame* and so the half pound contains 64 *ochavos*, as the 8 ounces in the half pound times 8 *ochavos* make 64 *ochavos*. The gold *ochavo* has 72 grains.

Consider that in order to express the degree of purity or impurity of gold, the goldsmiths divide the half pound, or any other quantity of gold, into 24 parts, which they call *caractos*, and in Spanish, *quilates* (carats). On the other hand, each carat is divided into fourths, into eighths of a carat, and into other similar proportional parts, some bigger and some smaller. When the gold is very pure and is not mixed with any other metal, it is said that it is 24-carat, because the half pound, or any other weight of that gold, has 24 parts of gold and none of any other metal. And this is the gold they call *obryzo*, which in Greek means *sincere* and *delicate*. Others believe that the name comes from Ophir; but the etymology is uncertain. When a half pound of gold has 23 parts of gold and one part from another metal (silver, copper, or whatever it may be), it is said that it is 23-carat gold. When 22 parts of gold are mixed with 2 parts of another metal, it is said that it is 22-carat gold, and so on and so forth. Likewise, to express the purity or impurity of silver they divide the half pound (or any other mass) into 12 parts, called *denarios* (*denari*). Thus, when the half pound of silver is not mixed with any other metal but is pure silver, it is called 12 *denari* silver; and when 11 parts of silver are mixed with 1 part of another metal it is called *liga*[2] by the Spanish, it is called 11 *denari* silver, estimating it to be silver of less *denari*, the more *denari* of another metal are mixed into it. The *denari*, in turn, is divided into 24 parts, each of which is called a grain of silver. Thus, this [grain of silver] weighs much less than the grain of gold.

Also consider that in this kingdom of Castile, according to Covarrubias's account,[3] King Ferdinand and his wife, Queen Isabella,[4] ordered minting $23^3/_4$-carat gold *ducats*, hence, each of these was only short of one-fourth of a carat to be gold of the highest purity. This tiny part of metal was mixed with the gold to give it a greater consistency, as gold of the highest purity lacks solidity and bends too easily. The half pound was worked into $65^1/_3$ *ducats*, making each *ducat* contain an eighth of an ounce of gold, taking from each of the 64 *ducats* as many grains as necessary to fabricate one more *ducat* and a third of another in order to cover the mintage expenses, which made each *ducat* contain less than one-eighth of an ounce of gold, almost $1^1/_2$ grains less. These same kings ordered issuing a coin worth twice the value of a *ducat*, from that gold, which in this kingdom they call *dobla*; and another worth one-fifth [of the *ducat*], called *quintupla*, another they call *décupla* and others worth 20 and 50 *aúreos*.[5]

In this kingdom, the *ducat* is worth 11 silver *reales* and 1 *maravedi*, and the silver *real* is worth 34 *maravedis*, because of which the *ducat* contains 375 *maravedis* (11 x 34 + 1). This is the reason why they estimate that one-half pound in this type of gold ingot was worth 24,000 *maravedis*, as (64 x 375 = 24,000), allocating toward minting expenses an extra $1^1/_3$ *ducat* struck from the half pound.[6] But the *ducats* produced with a half pound were worth 24,500 *maravedis*, because the $1^1/_3$ *ducat* that was taken for expenses from the 64 eighths of an ounce used for producing the other 64 *ducats* were worth 500 *maravedis*.

From what has been said, it is easy to surmise, in the first place, [the reason] why 1 *maravedi* was added to the 11 silver *reales* of a *ducat*'s price: so that the half pound of that gold was given a value of 24,000 *maravedis* and each *ducat* had a gold *drachma*, taking away from each of the 64 *ducats* the grains that were needed in order to produce $1^1/_3$ *ducats* for minting expenses. We understand too that the Gospel's *drachmas* weighed the same as our *ducats* or silver *reales*, as we shall see from the following, as in order to prove this you only need to add to the gold and silver coins what was taken from each *drachma* for expenses. They are called *drachmas* because of the coin's weight, but they were silver and not gold. And the *didrachma* which, as also mentioned in the Gospel, was paid as tax, weighed 2 *drachmas* and was worth 2 silver *reales*. In the third place, we may surmise that at the time when those *ducats* were minted, the gold grain was worth almost $5^1/_4$ *maravedis*, because one-eighth of a gold ounce weighs 72 grains, which, at the rate of 5 *maravedis* per grain, amounts to 360 *maravedis*. And the 15 *maravedis* needed to complete 375 have 60-fourths of *maravedi*, so that in order for the gold grain to be worth in those $5^1/_4$ *maravedis*, they only needed twelve-fourths of *maravedi*.

In time, that extremely pure gold became highly coveted in other countries and was taken out of the Spanish territories. This is why, as Covarrubias[7] says, Charles V[8] ordered the mintage of 22-carat gold coins, which were called *coronas* or *escudos*. Sixty-eight *escudos* weigh the same as a half pound, and the value of each [*escudo*] is 10 *reales* and 10 *maravedis* or, the equivalent 350 *maravedis*. And if you take away an *escudo* paid as duty to the king for each half pound, plus $1^3/_4$ *tomin* for the mintage, the value of a half pound struck from a 22-carat gold ingot amounts to 23,331 *maravedis*,[9] since the *tomin* has 12 grains of gold and is worth 2 silver *reales*, so that the *tomin* and three-fourths have 21 grains and are worth $3^1/_2$ silver *reales*, that is, 119 *maravedis*. This amount, together with the *escudo*, whose value was at the 350 *maravedis*, amount to 469 *maravedis*. If these are subtracted from the 23,800 *maravedis*, the gold half pound produced out of that kind of ingot is worth 23,381 *maravedis*. The 23-carat gold half pound had 95-fourths of gold carat, and one-[fourth] of another metal. The 22-carat gold half pound only had 88-fourths of gold carat and 8-fourths of another metal, because of which 23,331 *maravedis* divided by the 88-fourths of a carat equal $265^1/_{11}$ *maravedis*. According to this calculation, this is the value of each carat. Consequently, a half pound of a $23^3/_4$-carat gold ingot, which has 7-fourths of a carat more, is worth, once the *escudos* have been minted, 25,186 *maravedis* plus 7-elevenths parts. And as the 22-carat gold half pound has 2 carats of *liga* (blend), of which two parts are silver and one part is copper, it follows that said 22-carat gold half pound has $1^3/_4$ carats of silver, as well as two-thirds carats of copper.

Therefore, as the silver half pound is worth in this kingdom 65 silver *reales*,[10] the silver carat shall have a value of $92^1/_{12}$ *maravedis*, and $1^1/_3$ carats shall be worth almost 123 *maravedis*. If you subtract this amount from the 25,186 the $23^3/_4$-carat gold half pound is worth 20,066 *maravedis*, once the *escudos* have been minted. Thus, one-eighth of an ounce of this ingot is worth $391^{39}/_{64}$ *maravedis*. If you add 500 *maravedis* to this for minting expenses, you shall see that this was the value of 1 *ducat* in those times.

In the year 1566, our king Philip II[11] raised the value of each *escudo* to 400 *maravedis*, without changing their weight nor the amount of gold or silver in the blending,[12] so that a half pound of [*escudos*] was worth 27,200 *maravedis*, which is their value today.[13] If you take away an *escudo* (worth today 400 *maravedis*) for the king's tax, plus 141 for expenses, which is what they pay today in Seville, where only 119 were paid before, the half pound of this gold ingot is worth 26,659 *maravedis*. And if they divide these between 88 highly pure gold carat quarts, which the half pound contains, as the other 8 are [part of the *liga* (blend)], one-fourth of highly pure gold carat is worth almost 303 *maravedis*, as (26,659/88 = 302,943), and the 7-fourths of pure gold carat that are also contained in the 23³/₄-carat gold half pound are worth today almost 1,222 *maravedis*. Because of which the half pound of the gold with which the *ducats* are made, without discounting anything on account of the blend, is worth today around 27,900 *maravedis*. Today almost nothing is taken away on account of the blend, because, from what I have heard in Seville, it is copper and has no silver.

The eighth of an ounce of this mass is worth around 435 *maravedis*, that is 12 silver *reales* and 27 *maravedis*, the same as what the *ducat* [of this mass] is worth if you add 541 *maravedis* for minting expenses, which are used as compensation for what is lacking in gold in each one to complete the eighth of an ounce. But law 13 cited earlier ordered [the *ducats*] to be current at 429 *maravedis*, and we must abide by it. Perhaps there is something missing to explain this price difference, or perhaps, having used external help for the calculations, as I ignore arithmetic, something was erroneously calculated, but what I have just explained sheds no little amount of light on what we shall proceed to say.

I should point out three things. The first, that the Castilian goldsmiths and their helpers at the mint apply the principles disclosed on carats not to gold half pounds but to the gold of the coins called *castellanos*, worth 16 silver *reales* or 544 *maravedis*, if they are 22-carat. This is verified in the above-cited law 13. And they say that the *castellano*'s highly pure carat is worth today 24 *maravedis* plus some particles from another *maravedi*, and because 50 of these coins weigh a half pound, they find it very easy to use this coin as a measure for counting carats. The second, that even if the silver mass is valued in this kingdom so that the half pound cannot exceed the price of 65 silver *reales*, no price is fixed for the gold mass, but only on the coins with which they are made, once they have discounted the cost of minting and the tax paid to the king. The third, that the law forbids the goldsmiths from producing gold objects that are not 24-carats minus an eighth of a carat, or 22- or 20-carats.[14] And this same law establishes penalties for those who sell gold objects with fewer carats than the ones indicated.

In this same kingdom, Ferdinand and Isabella ordered the mintage of silver made out of 11 *denari* and 4 grains in the proportion of 67 silver *reales* per half pound, because of which they had 20 grains of blend with another metal, that is, copper.[15] It was worth 34 *maravedis*, as is manifest in law 4 of the same section. The half pound of this silver in ingots was valued so that it could not be sold for more than 65 silver *reales*, as is manifest in law 5 of the same section, and since 67 *reales* were minted from it, as states the same law and also the second law already cited, it follows that each *real* only had 32 silver *maravedis*. And since 1 *real* plus 1 *maravedi* are paid for the expenses of casting the half pound, as is manifest in law 46 from the same section and according to what was said by a public officer in the Mint, it follows that the 33 extra *maravedis* are the profit of the person who gave the silver to produce the *ducats*. And this is specifically stated in law 5 of the same section.

The above has not been modified at all thus far, as is manifest in law 13 of the same section's declarations. There is only a difference in one point: that by a royal *cédula* sent to the Mints in the territories of Spain a tribute of 50 *maravedis* was established to be paid to the king for each silver half pound that was minted in them. This tribute is called *señorage*. This is the reason why a person who coins a silver half pound only receives $64\frac{1}{2}$ silver *reales*.

Almost at the same time that Ferdinand and Isabella ordered the *ducats* to be minted, similar coins were coined in Portugal with highly pure 24-carat gold, which we call here *cruzados*. The simple *cruzado*, or *ducat*, had an eighth of an ounce of gold, having taken three-fourths of a grain for expenses, as they had $71\frac{3}{4}$ grains.[16] The 10 *ducat cruzado*, called *portugués* in that kingdom, had 11-eights ounce and $64\frac{1}{2}$ grains, lacking only $7\frac{1}{2}$ grains for completing 10-eighths, as said in paragraph 3 of law 4 already cited. And since the *ducat* is worth 400 *reais* in that kingdom, it follows that the half pound of that gold ingot was estimated at the time in 25,600 *reais*. But the gold half pound, converted to those coins, was worth 25,800 *reais*, with an extra charge on account of the 48 grains that were taken for expenses from the 64 *ducats*, since at the time the gold grain was worth $5\frac{1}{2}$ *reais* plus a part of a *septil*. Seventy-two grains, at the rate of 5 *reais*, make 360 *reais*. And if each one of the 40 *reais* left to complete the 400 are divided by 2 we obtain 80 halves. And if we take from there 72 halves for the 72 grains, each grain shall be worth $5\frac{1}{2}$ *reais* plus $\frac{1}{72}$ *reais*, which make 24 *septiles*.

In the time of Charles V, João III[17] ordered minting in Portugal *ducats* called [in this country] *cruzados de cruz piquena*, encouraged by the same reasons as the emperor. Today they call them *cruzados do meio*, because they were coined during the time between [the mintage] of those first highly pure gold ones and others of an inferior purity. The gold of these was $22\frac{5}{8}$-carat, and they only had a mix of $1\frac{3}{4}$-carat of another metal. Each one weighed $71\frac{1}{4}$, just as highly pure gold *ducats*. All this is contained in paragraph 5 of the already cited law 4.

Thus, since these *ducats* maintained the price of 400 *reais*, the half pound of impure gold started being worth the same as what the half pound of that highly pure gold was worth before. Subsequently, João III ordered minting other *ducats* called *cruzados de cruz de monte calvario*, with $22\frac{1}{8}$-carat gold. They weighed $72\frac{7}{8}$ grains, because of which they only lacked one-eighth of a grain to complete the eighth of a gold ounce, as states paragraph 6 of the same law. That is why, since these *ducats* maintained the price of 400 *reais*, the half pound of this impure gold started being worth the same as the half pound of very pure gold was worth before.

Lately, King João III himself ordered minting a coin, which was the most commonly used in Portugal when I was teaching there these subjects. It was made with $22\frac{1}{8}$-carat gold. Its weight was such that 30 coins weighed a half pound, and each was worth 1,000 *reais*, hence the name *moedas de mil reais*. They had other coins that weighed half as much, so that 60 weighed one half pound and were worth 500 *reais*, and were called *moedas de quinientos reais*, as appears in paragraphs 8 and 9 of law 4 referred to earlier. Consequently, the half pound of very pure 24-carat gold was worth 25,600 *reais*, as has already been said. And when these new coins were coined, the half pound produced from the ingot of this much more impure $22^1/_8$-carat gold started being worth 30,000 *reais*. And the value of the highly pure gold coins increased in the same proportion, not only so that the price in coins of 1,000 *reais* would correspond to the same weight (at the rate of 30,000 *reais* the half pound), but so that a greater quantity of highly pure gold would correspond to a higher price in the same proportion in which the quantity of highly pure gold of the old coins exceeds the quantity contained in the 1,000 *reais* coins, subtracting something on account of the blend [of other metals] they contain, as was taken away from the coins from Castile. All of which is established in the *Extravagantes de Portugal laws*, law 4 cited above, as we shall later declare.

Law 4 fixed that price for the new gold coins, and in paragraph 11 it forbid obtaining a profit when exchanging them, and established a penalty of loss of the coins' value and two years of banishment in places in Africa. That is why the price fixed by the law was the current price. However, foreign merchants started offering for the 1,000 *reais* coins, 1,100, and for the coins of 500 *reais*, 550. And suddenly, during the time in which I instructed on these subjects, many hurried to offer for that price great quantities of them with full knowledge of the Senate and other public officers, without anyone stopping them. Even those who were in charge of the government's finances and the king's assets did this. Perhaps what I will go on to describe contributed greatly to this.

The silver of coins from Portugal has only 11 *denarios*, that is, there is a whole *denari* of another metal mixed into it.[18] As a result, in Flanders, Germany, and other nations they are not worth more than the silver they contain, taking into account, besides, their impurity. King Sebastian[19] ordered in the cited law that from the half pound of this type of silver 24 *tostoes* were minted, worth 100 *reais* each. Therefore, the half pound was worth 2,400 *reais* or the equivalent 6 *cruzados*. Since those who brought silver in order to mint it did not pay but 60 *reais* for minting expenses, as the law orders, it follows that, in those times, the half pound of that type of silver was worth in ingots 2,340 *reais*. João III's grandfather had ordered minting 26 *tostoes* from the half pound of silver of that type and, because of this, at the time of João III the half pound of these *tostoes* was worth 1,600 *reais*, that is, 6 *cruzados* and a half, as says the same law. Before João III the *tostoes* weighed more, but all the *tostoes* one remembers had a value of 100 *reais*, even if some had more silver and others, less. What is more, King Sebastian ordered in the cited section's second law that the *tostoes* that João III had ordered minting maintain the same value, and that nobody could reject them when they were handed out to pay goods or debts. During all this time, the silver *real* was worth $36^2/_7$ *reais* in Portugal, so that 11 of them were worth 400 *reais*, that is, 1 *cruzado*. And king Sebastian, in the cited section, decreed in the year 1558 that this was their price, and that nobody should receive more for them, under certain penalties.

At the time, in East India, the silver *real* was worth 60 *reais*, and in Africa it was worth 40 *maravedis*, and they were much preferred everywhere and were used to negotiate, and not the Portuguese silver coins. And from the region of Ethiopia called Mina, they bring to Portugal a great amount of gold, and they deliver there a lot of gold in exchange for silver coins. That is why in those times, without the referred to law being able to stop it, many bought silver *reales* for a price that was higher than the legal one in order to send great quantities of them to the East Indies. And even the king and his ministers did this. Everyone had a conscience problem over whether it was licit or not to buy them in Portugal for a higher price than the legal one. That being the situation while I taught these subjects and King Sebastian was getting ready to go to Africa, the price of the silver *real* suddenly rose in Portugal to 40 *reais*, making 10 of them start being worth 400 *reais*, that is, 1 *cruzado*. This was done without promulgating any law but, simply, because the king began to pay salaries and goods at that price, and the ministers of the king would force the private individuals to accept the silver *reales* at that same price. From then on, *tostoes* started being coined with a weight of $2^{1}/_{2}$ *reales*, and out of one-half pound they coin 28 *tostoes*, which are worth 100 *reais* each. But who pays for the expenditures and how much these amount to, I do not know as I live far away from there. This increase in the value of money in that kingdom contributed in no small measure to large amounts being paid for the coins of 1,500 *reais*, and to the quick spoliation of the kingdom, and to the disappearance of the great amount of them that were available in other times. They tell me that the merchants from here in Castile brought huge amounts, and that they sold each coin of 1,000 *reais* for 33 silver *reales*, which taken to Portugal were worth 1,320 *reais*. That is why I warned King Sebastian that it would be convenient to increase the price of gold, and such is what I taught from my chair as professor. But it was useless, and even today the *tostoes*, both the old as well as the new ones of little weight, are exchanged for the same price of 100 *reais*, which makes them slowly disappear, either because they are taken abroad, or because they are given to goldsmiths in order to turn them to silver ingots that are sold for a much higher price than the one they have today in Portugal. Likewise, there are many today who also exchange those gold coins, even if they are scarce today, for the price of 1,000 *reais*, or at least exchanged them up to the day when I left that kingdom.

Here I want to give one word of caution. Even if the value of gold or silver coins were to increase or diminish, the copper coin, called a *real* in Portugal, maintains the same value when it is a question of paying amounts of *aúreos* or other coins that were owed, or taxes or penalties enforced by the law, as we saw in argument 312. But they do not have the same value if it is a question of exchanging them in different places, according the merchants' usual practice, which even today is their custom. Because for 10 *reales* that are worth 400 *reais* in Portugal, 11 *reales* are not paid in Castile even if they are worth in Castile 374 *maravedis*, but only 10 *reales* are paid, exchanging them on equal terms and setting aside for the time being the increase in price due to exchange. Because in these exchanges, more importance is given to the amount of silver comparing it to an equal amount of silver, or to the amount of gold comparing it to an equal amount of gold of the same purity than to the amount of copper and its price in different places. That is why, when the Portuguese silver *real* was worth $36^2/_7$ *reais*, the Castilian *maravedi* was worth more than the Portuguese copper *real* among the merchants, at the rate in which $36^2/_7$ *reais* exceed 34 *maravedis*. And for the same reason, silver *real* and silver *real* were exchanged as equal [coins] from Portugal to Castile and vice versa, and they exchanged a *ducat* for a *ducat* also as equal coins, even if [the *ducat*] was worth 400 *reais* in Portugal and 375 *maravedis* in Castile. Therefore, because the value of the silver *real* rose in Portugal to 40 *reais*, the Portuguese copper *real* is worth today less than a *maravedi* at the rate in which 40 *reais* exceed 34 *maravedis*. Therefore, when the value of the silver *real* rose they were exchanged as equal coins from Portugal to Castile and vice versa, and the *ducats* were also exchanged as equal, even if it was worth 400 *reais* in Portugal and 375 *maravedis* in Castile. This explains why, since the value of the silver *real* rose in Portugal to 40 *reais*, the Portuguese copper *real* is worth today less than the *maravedis* at the rate in which 40 *reais* exceed 34 *maravedis*. That is why, when the value of the silver *real* rose to 40 *reais* and the weight of the Portuguese silver *tostón* diminished, the value of the Portuguese copper *real* diminished, in such a way that comparing it to the same copper coin, the value of those Portuguese coins rose among the merchants. Just as it increased when buying goods with them. And the law becomes ridiculous when it fails to increase the extra charge of these coins in comparison to a same copper coin, because one has to be a fool in order to hand over today in Portugal a coin of $27^1/_2$ silver *reales* for 25 *reales* just because in Portugal the price of the silver *real* has risen to 40 *reais*, especially since that same coin is worth much more if it is brought back to Castile or to any other nation, and since more goods are not bought today with 40 *reais* than before with 36, as prices of all goods have risen in Portugal in a continuous way with regard to that copper coin. On account of this, when the silver *real* rose to 40 *reais*, the value of the gold coins started rightfully rising in an incessant way regarding the same copper coins. So it may be understood that a $22^1/_8$-carat gold half pound is worth today in Portugal much more than 30,000 *reais*, at the rate in which 40 *reais* exceed those $36^2/_7$.

We have said all these things about the price of silver coins in Portugal in order to understand and explain all this. I hope they shed sufficient light on what we are to say about exchanges.

The mass of gold does not have a price fixed by the law in Castile and Portugal, nor does [the mass] of silver, except for the fact that in Castile the mass of 11 *denari* and 4 grains may not be sold at more than 65 *reales* for the half pound. But it is not forbidden to buy it for less, and every day they buy and sell for lower prices, each one for what he can obtain. It is easy, thus, to answer the question of whether or not the following silver purchase is just or unjust and if there is or is not an obligation to restitute.

Many people, in great need of money, sell the artistic silver objects they have, and when they offer them for sale to artisans and merchants they do not get a better price than if the silver were not carved, even if the artistic work is at times of great value. Moreover, there are times when they do not receive for the silver more than 64 *reales* for the half pound, so that, aside from the artistic value, they have to reduce even one more *real* per half pound in the silver's value. The question is whether such purchase is unfair, and if there is obligation to restitute. I believe that the answer should be this: Since no human law is broken, and the artisans and merchants invest in this material great money so that, once the silver has been purified and adapted, they can resell it for more money, the transaction may not be condemned as unjust, as long as, given all the circumstances, and in the wise men's opinion, they do not go beyond the lowest just price. Keep in mind that this is the artisans' manner of buying because of their activity, such as the booksellers buy the books they receive cheaply in order to sell them more expensively at a later date and, likewise, the merchandise offered unexpectedly is worth less. However, it may happen that the artistic value of the object is so great and so great the hope of being able to resell it in a short time for a much higher price, that the purchase may be considered unjust at times, having to restitute the difference until the lowest just price is reached, even if the half pound is paid at 65 *reales*, and regardless of the fact that in these cases the price is not undividable but allows for a wide range between the maximum and the minimum just price. And one should not condemn the practices accepted by custom, as custom is a great influence for the price in this type of purchase not to be judged unjust.

Sometimes, those who sell these kinds of objects make a deal with those who buy them wherein they do not resell them for a certain time, so that they are able to recover them within that period of time for a certain amount and a higher one than the one they now receive. Some are skeptical regarding the justness of this contract, suspecting that it conceals usury. I believe that the following should be responded. In order for that contract to be licit and just, one should abide by the following conditions: (1) the first sale should be a genuine sale, so that if during the time [when the buyer is awaiting payment] the object perishes, it perishes for the buyer; (2) the first sale should be just, according to what we have said; (3) a higher price should not be fixed for the second sale when the object is recovered, than [the price] which the first buyer, present owner of the object, could obtain from any other buyer. These conditions prevent the contract from being usurious or unjust and make it a gratuitous contribution of the first buyer to the one who first sold the object, promising not to resell it to a third party for a certain period of time. We described this in argument 376, and gave some examples to make it clear.

Finally, what we have explained in this argument shall help us to better understand the following. In olden times, in this kingdom of Castile there were *ducats* worth 375 *maravedis* and, in Portugal, those same *ducats* or *cruzados* were worth 400 *reais*, and money was taken from one place to another to carry out the contracts. In many contracts they mentioned the *ducats*, not only in these kingdoms, but in the affairs with other provinces, and even today they celebrate exchanges and other types of contracts where they order many things in terms of the *ducat* as standard. However, there has not been in these kingdoms for a long time a coin that is worth what a *ducat* [is worth], so that the value of what in other times was understood as a *ducat*, and today is still understood, is paid by compensating with an equal sum of money in other coins. Such is the evidence of everyday custom.

6

Argument 401

If a Higher Price Than the One Set by the Law May Licitly Be Received for the Coins to Which the Public Authority Assigned a Particular Value at the Moment of Coinage?

What was analyzed in the previous argument shall illustrate what we now go on to say. Pay heed to the existence of a custom, accepted in some provinces such as Flanders and Italy, by which the common price set by the law is not considered so rigid that it may not fluctuate according to the greater or lesser abundance of [coins] or the amount of people who desire them, as happens with the price of goods that are not appraised by the law. Thus, for example, they tell me that in Rome, even if the common value of the gold *escudo* is $12\frac{1}{2}$ *julios*, that value suddenly increases in copper coins, even twice a month, diminishing later. And the more or less abundance of these copper coins depends on the scarcity or demand of the *escudos*, as well as on other circumstances. Wherever this custom exists, there is no doubt that it shall be licit to receive this extra charge. The difficulty seems to present itself in those places where the price of currency is set by the public authority by law in order to keep it unalterable, such as happened in the Spanish territories and in other provinces, where they used to appraise their own coins.

However, even in that case it must be said that for reason of profit ceasing, sometimes it is licit to receive something more than the legal price for the coins, taking into account the estimation of that profit's amount. For example, if a person had set money apart to take to another place where it was worth more, or to use it to buy merchandise in a place where the coins of his place of residency could not be bought, or only by losing a part of their value, this person may, when exchanging his coins for others, collect the amount in which he estimates the profit ceasing. This is Juan de Medina's[1] opinion, among that of others.

And at the end of argument 364, in a similar case, we said that the owner of a lot of wheat the price of which is appraised by the law, could receive for reason of profit ceasing something more than that price if he was planning to take it to a place where it was worth more. However, he had to avoid creating a scandal. For the same reason, if an artisan who had prepared the coins that he was going to use to cover with gold the objects he produces were to lend them to someone who asks insistently for them, making him lose the benefit he hoped to obtain from his work as an artisan, he may receive in turn, together with the common price of the coins, the amount in which he estimates is the profit that he truly is being deprived of.

In Portugal it is forbidden to destroy silver coins, or sending to destroy them, even if they are coins from another kingdom, in order to produce artistic objects with them, or for any other reason, and there is a penalty of a ten-year banishment someplace in Africa, together with the loss of half the goods, which shall be divided between the informer and the royal tax authorities.[2] And under the same penalties it is forbidden to choose the heavier coins and sell them later according to their weight. Whoever did any of these things, if he were a minister of the king, in charge of receiving his money, would bring upon himself the death penalty and loss of all his goods. I do not know if such rigorous law is actually applied making us judge the artisan or private person who destroys a few silver coins to produce an artistic object as guilty of mortal sin, especially, after the silver *real* has risen until reaching a price of 40 *reais*, and the weight of the *tostón* has diminished, as we said in the previous argument. Because, if such law were upheld with all its force, and continued being applied because the circumstances are the same as when it was promulgated, there would be no doubt that it compels under mortal sin, because of the gravity of the offense and the harm that follows for the republic. Because, as experience proves, it is the heavier coins and of a same value that are destroyed. However, this law does not deal with the silver coins that have no value in Portugal, as the laws clearly state.[3]

In the kingdom of Castile it is also prohibited under death penalty and loss of all goods to destroy gold, silver, or copper coins, or carry them out of the kingdom.[4] But I understand that this law, promulgated by the Catholic Kings,[5] does not apply to the old coins that are today rare, and that were followed by others, when it is those that are destroyed in order to gild some objects, since this is something insignificant, and the change in times and circumstances make it licit.

Although the exchange of coins in one and the same place should be carried out for an equal value, if there were grounds to fear that over a short period of time a coin was going to be devaluated by public authority, it could be bought licitly for a lower price than the legal one, as such fear and the probability of devaluation make it lose value just as money that is at risk of a storm, or of other dangers at sea, is justly bought for a lower price than the one appraised by law. Such is Medina's opinion in the last paragraph of the place cited earlier. But meantime, while those coins are not devaluated by public authority, they may be licitly handed over at the appraised price, because in truth, they still maintain their old value, as they may be given and spent for the same uses in which they would be spent if there did not exist any fear of their devaluation.

In the already cited argument,[6] Medina ascertains that while the law that appraises a coin is still in force it is not licit to receive for said coins a price that is higher to the one appraised, even if the metal of which they are made has many other applications such as, for example, if it were gold of many carats (as usually happens with old coins) and were better for gilding objects, ornamentation, health reasons, and similar things. Medina's reason is that when a coin is appraised, they take into account the purity of the metal and the possible uses of it, and once all things are pondered, they fix the value of the metal to which a seal is applied, making it a coin. Therefore, just as with wheat it is not licit to receive a greater price than that appraised by law because the legal price is indivisible, it is not licit either in the case of coins to receive a greater price to that which is legal. And if it were received, there is obligation to restitute.

But Medina adds: If it became a custom to receive for certain coins something more than the price appraised by law, and the prince or senate knew about it and did not punish or tried to prevent it, one should consider that it is the prince's will that the law not be applied in this point, because of which such increment over the legal price may be accepted without fear. I would go on to add that, from then on, such extra charge falls within the limits of the just natural price, which is not rigid or indivisible, as would be the legal price. And this is why Medina considers that the practice that some have of receiving an extra charge for certain old gold coins is something that is free of blame and of the obligation to restitute.

According to this opinion, we shall have to decide if the first ones who started receiving that increment, before the tacit and presumed consent of the prince, did sin, and have the obligation to give back to those from whom they received it, as the law was still in force.

Soto, Navarrus, Covarrubias, Silvestre, and Cajetan acknowledge that a coin may be considered under two aspects:[7] one, as coin; the other, as metal, that is, as gold of a greater or lesser purity, greater or lesser weight. And they say that if, given all circumstances, it had a certain value as metal, it would be licit to receive a higher price than that set by the law, as the [price] set by the law refers to the coins as such, that is, as price to pay for purchases, even if when assigning that value they had taken into account the value of the material it is made of and its possible applications. Many add that no one may be forced to give for a coin a price that is above that established by the law, nor to receive it as [if it had] a lower value than the legal one, because of which it shall be licit to buy them at their legal price and sell them later for a higher price.

Regarding this issue, I shall briefly state my opinion. One word of caution before anything else is to say that when coins are minted and a price is fixed on them, the material they are made of is never worth more, even if all possible applications are taken into account, than the price fixed on them. Furthermore, it does not even reach [the price], as the minting expenses and, in this case, the tribute paid to the prince are deducted from the metal with which the coins are minted. It would be foolish for a prince who is ordered to mint a coin to fix on it an inferior price to the value of the metal it is made of. The price is fixed taking into account the abundance of a certain metal at the time, its possible applications and all other circumstances, making it improbable to find a better price for that metal. What Medina says about this is true. We should also add that for the mere fact of minting a gold coin that is inferior in carats or in weight, and fixing an equal or even higher price to that of the coins that have been on hand up to then, it should be assumed that the law that had fixed the price of the preceding coins ceases to be in force, and that everyone may increase the price of these [the preceding coins] within the limits of what is naturally just. Justice asks that, all things considered, things of an equal value have an equal price, unless the prince were to order the contrary for a reasonable cause. And it would be irrational and unjust that he order it without reasonable cause, since fixing unequal prices to goods of equal value without reasonable cause is irrational and injurious to his subjects.

The laws of Castile and Portugal are in agreement with this doctrine of ours, clear and manifest. Thus, for example, when Philip appraised the *escudos* so that from then on they would be worth 400 *maravedis*[8] and ordered that for no reason at all could anyone receive a higher price for them, he equally declared that the *ducats* that Ferdinand and Isabella had ordered minting out of finer gold had a greater value than when they had been minted, due to the greater weight and greater quantity of gold in them. And this is the reason why he ordered they be worth 429 *maravedis*, as we explained in the preceding argument. And it is undeniable that before the rise in the price of the *escudos*, nobody could justly condemn receiving a proportionate price for the *ducats*, in view of not only the greater weight but also the greater quantity of highly pure gold that they contained.

In Portugal, the law similarly explains the greater value of the grain of gold of the 24-carat *cruzados* over the value of the grain of gold of $22\frac{1}{8}$-carat coins, explaining that the grain of gold of these last coins is worth $6\frac{1}{2}$ *reais*, while the value of the grain of gold of the first coins was of 7 *reais* plus one-third of a *septil*. And in this way it goes on to explain the value of the grain in intermediate coins.

In the third place, it is important to point out that when gold coins are minted and a price is fixed on them, there is usually abundance of that kind of gold, and the price is fixed according to [this abundance], taking into account all existing circumstances. But if the circumstances were to change with time, and having carried those highly pure gold coins out of the kingdom, whether to be used for gilding or for decorating objects, the value of the metal of such coins increased considerably, it should not be assumed that the legislators would want the laws that fixed the old rates to be still in force. And even if they wanted to, it would not be just nor fair, because of which they may be sold for their natural just price not only as goods but as price with which they pay for all other things, without [there being any] sin nor obligation to restitute, because, as Medina rightly believes, the coin's purpose is always the same, under whatever form it is considered. In the case described, good public ministers do not oppose nor punish those who proceed in the way described, nor use their power to persecute their subjects harsh and unjustly but apply the interpretation[9] of the laws according to the circumstances of time, place, thing, and people and understand that such laws can no longer be applied, as the present circumstances are very different from those in which the laws were issued. Consequently, even if the laws of Ferdinand and Isabella are included in the mentioned section 21, book 5 of the *New Collection*,[10] because a great part of its content is still in force, it does not apply when it comes to the rate of the *ducat*'s value, as King Philip himself declared in law 13 cited earlier. And even before this declaration it had already ceased to be in force, as we have indicated. Nor are the words used to order obeying those rates in force. King Philip ordered that for no reason should a higher price than the one he himself appraised be received for the *escudos*, because when this law was issued there was, as even today there is, great abundance of *escudos*. But when it was time to deal with the old *ducats* he only defined the value they have today, taking into account the value that has been given to them, without adding those words that say that for no reason should it be licit to receive for them a greater price. Because, given their scarcity, the need for them and their utility for some things, it would be licit to receive for them the whole natural value that they have, presuming those circumstances exist. In brief, it is licit to receive for any coin what would licitly be received for a piece of gold of the same weight and purity at any time, as the amount of gold in the coin is not of a worse quality for being converted into coin than if it were not. On the contrary: It is of better condition and greater value, because of which one may receive for it something more than [what is received] for an equal piece of gold.

From what is declared here and was declared earlier in the preceding argument, it shall be easy to understand that the Portuguese laws that appraised the price of gold coins do not in all conscience force [anyone] today, because of which a greater price may be received for those worsened coins, even if [it should always be done] within the limits of their natural value. And the same should be said about the more impure gold coins that were appraised 1,000 or 500 *reais*, as the law that appraised the silver *real* lost its legal force for the very fact that the silver *real* increased its value up to 40 *reais*. Also, for that same reason there were no longer any scruples nor difficulties over receiving a greater price for them than the one rated by the law when they were to be carried somewhere else, as today nobody offers for them more than 40 *reais*.

Both in Castile as well as in Portugal, the laws have established today how much the price of old gold coins has risen, and how much they are worth today. Therefore, if someone wanted to pay his creditor with these coins, the [creditor] would be forced to receive them at the price fixed by the law and, in all fairness, would not be able to receive them as [if they had] a lower price, as the price fixed by the law is the lowest just price that they have today, and there is no one who hands them over for a lower price, unless they ignore their value. As regards the greater price some coins are exchanged for today, it may be taken in all fairness, even if it exceeds the legal price. This is what we said about the Portuguese coins worth 1,500 *reais*. But a creditor may not be forced to take them for that higher price, since the extra charge that is given for them does not affect the legal price but the natural one, and there are many who hand over those coins for the price fixed on them by the law in other times. And as long as nothing else is ordered or declared, one should judge that that price does not go beyond the limits of the lowest just price. It is the debtor who may choose to find someone who gives him a higher price for them, and then make the payment in other currencies.

7

Argument 402

If an Employee Who Was Taking Money in Gold Coins to Pay Some Debts, or to Make Some Purchases, Took Advantage on the Way of an Opportunity Offered to Exchange Those Coins for a Better Price, Could That Employee Appropriate for Himself the Extra Charge Obtained in This Manner?

The matter we are discussing in this argument happened frequently in Portugal when I was teaching these subjects. At the time there was an abundance of coins (1,500 *reais*) and debts were paid with them, or they were handed over to an envoy to be used to buy merchandise for their owners. According to what we have said, it was possible to exchange the coins with an additional benefit over the price they had been appraised for when minted, without breaking the law for it. The issue in question is whether the envoy under discussion, when knowing beforehand who was willing to give that extra charge, or looking for [that person] himself, might carry out that exchange and get for himself the extra charge using the rest of the money to pay the debt or buy the merchandise as they had ordered him to do. May he keep the extra charge or should he restitute it? And who does he owe the restitution to?

The same uncertainty exists regarding the officers of the king who are in charge of collecting the royal revenue, and other ministers who carry out similar duties for other members of the aristocracy and, in general, the depositaries to whom many debts are paid in currency that they have no obligation of assessing for a higher price, and then, by order of the king, or of whomever they are ministers of, pay salaries, debts, and other expenses. During the time between the collection and the payment, these people have the opportunity to exchange the collected coins for other [coins], thus obtaining an increment, and it is uncertain whether they may keep that extra charge or should restitute it.

I believe the doubts regarding this issue shall be explained with the following conclusions: First, in all of the above cases, if after exchanging the gold coins with an extra charge, the officer or depositary buys other gold coins that are similar to those initially received and with them carries out the commission for the one who ordered him [to do so], he may certainly keep the extra charge as the fruits of his ingenuity, even if for obtaining it he may have taken someone else's money as an instrument to do so. It is clear because by doing so he did no harm, either [by hurting] the person in whose name he negotiated or the person to whom he had to hand over the money, due to the fact that, as we are to assume, he gave this person in due time coins of the same type and the same value as those that had been handed over to him, which make it evident that he carried out the commission he received, allowing him to keep the profit that the extra charge stands for. This is substantiated by what shall be said in the third conclusion.

If the owner's usual wish were that the debt be paid in the same currency as that which he handed over, because he favored the payee's own good to that of the envoy's, and the payee wanted to employ it in lesser expenses with an equal or greater benefit in the exchange, the envoy shall be forced to restitute the payee of all the profit he was deprived of, unless he delivers coins of the same quality as those received. It is clear because against the will of both the payer and the payee, the [payee] is denied the just benefit that he was going to collect with the coin exchange, because of which there is offence and he should receive restitution.

It could happen that the payee did not intend to obtain any special benefit from the coins, because for example, he was thinking of spending them, handing them over for their usual lowest price, and that the owner of the coins regularly favored the envoy's own good to that of the payee's, or did not even bother about it. In that case, I believe that the envoy would be able to keep that profit, and it would not be an impediment that the sender wanted that profit for himself rather than for the employee.

To prove this conclusion it is necessary to go over what was said in argument 327, which is that what the usurer, thief, or payee gain when they negotiate with something that is not theirs, is consumable by use, and is acquired through usury, theft, or received as deposit, is acquired for themselves and they are not forced to restitute except those things they received that belonged to someone else, or other equivalent things, as well as the profit ceasing the owners could have endured because of the delay in restitution. From this we can establish the following argument to prove the first part of the conclusion: in the case set forth, the profit does not belong to the sender nor to the payee more than what it would had the envoy stolen the money or extorted money from them through usury. Therefore, just as neither the thief nor the usurer have the obligation to hand over the profit obtained, and they only have to pay up what they took (as we clearly proved in the above cited argument), neither shall the envoy in our case be forced to restitute that profit, except only to give back what he took. In truth, this is what he does when he gives the payee the money for what it would be worth in his hands. We may also use the following argument: if the envoy had not obtained any profit with the money but had lost it gambling or had spent it buying goods for their lowest price as was sometimes done, and if the payee was going to spend the money with a better exchange, it is certain that no confessor would force to restitute but the part that would have been spent in that better way. In our case, the envoy should not be forced either to further restitution.

The following objection may be raised: Such profit obtained by the thief, usurer, or envoy proceeds from something that belongs to someone else, and only from the value it has when the thief, usurer, or envoy take hold of it. Consequently it does not belong to these, but to the owner of the money or to his payee as the fruit of something that belongs to them, and not of the ingenuity of the one who carried out the exchange, even if neither the sender nor the payee had the intention of collecting that gain. So we see that the fruits from a farm or from a horse belong to the owner of the farm or horse even if the owner had not collected them.

To this argument I respond allowing the antecedent but refuting the consequence. Because even if such profit comes from the thing itself and its value, it is not, however, the fruit of it but of the ingenuity of the person who negotiates with it, and of the person who buys with it to his own advantage or disadvantage: and if by giving it such use it should perish, it does not because of this perish for its owner, who has to receive full payment. And the one who negotiates with [the profit] without owning it, shall have to account for it in case there is a judicial complaint. The fruits of the thing, for example, of the horse or the farm, are not the thing itself and its value, but the fruit of them or of the use that has been made of them, or they are the price received for those fruits, which is a subsequent fruit to the thing received, for example, for the use of the horse or for the apples produced by the farm. Now then, what is earned by negotiating with a good at the risk of only the person who negotiates [with it] is fruit of his ingenuity and, thus, the profit we refer to belongs to the envoy who at his own risk and for his own benefit exchanged the coins.

I shall go on to prove the second part of the conclusion, that is, that in case the sender is usually satisfied that the profit from the exchange is greater for the envoy than for the payee (or simply, did not bother about it), the envoy could licitly keep said profit, even in the case in which the payee could have obtained a greater profit in the transaction. Because the money sent, either as donation, or as payment for a debt, or in exchange for something else, does not belong to the payee until he accepts it. Until said moment of acceptance it belongs to the sender, who may revoke the donation or the order (as said countless times in argument 263 and others). Consequently, everything the sender or the envoy does with the money, before the acceptance happens on the payee's part and according to the owner's presumed decision that at least it is not something he finds objectionable, is not injurious to the payee and, so, does not require compensation for the fact of depriving him of the profit that through the coin exchange he wished to obtain. However, if the one transporting the money is a servant of the payee, or someone who accepted the money following his orders and received it in his name, then, because the payee acquired the property by accepting the money, according to what was said in the above mentioned argument and in several others, by depriving him now from the profit obtained for the exchange, the envoy is wronging him and must compensate for everything he is being deprived of collecting, even if the envoy had obtained with his transactions a smaller profit or even none at all.

The third part of the conclusion said that it made no difference that the sender's disposition was such that he preferred the profit for himself rather than for the envoy. It is clear, because if the envoy had stolen the money under discussion from the sender, the subsequent profit would not belong to the owner of the money, notwithstanding his desire such profit would go to him instead of to the thief, who would not be compelled to compensate but for the losses, including the profit ceasing. Consequently, in our case, the profit does not belong to the owner of the money either but to the employee, notwithstanding the master's contrary disposition to it.

It should be pointed out that, sometimes, the property of a deposit does not belong to the depositor but to the depositary, who receives it at his own risk, without being compelled to return the same [deposit] in numeric terms. Such is the case of the public money depositaries and recipients, whom they call *almojarifes* or *treasurers* of the king, and others of the like. Consequently, what we said is even truer, as even if they receive gold coins at the current price, they fulfill their obligations by giving back its value in any other currency, and by paying the king in any currency, or whomever are his ministers, or anyone else by his command. And if they make any profit by exchanging the coins, theirs shall be the profit, as this is one of the advantages they obtain in the form of salary for their occupation.

8

Argument 403

On the Usefulness of Exchanging Money from One Place to Another; on the [Type of] Exchange in Which the Banker Receives the Money in Advance

We have explained up to here what petty exchange is. Let us now discuss the exchange from one place to another, that is, by means of bills of exchange. This type of exchange is useful and even necessary for many reasons. Because often there is someone who needs in one place money that he has in another [place], whether to bring merchandise from there to where he needs it, or to live there or for any other expense. However, he cannot take that money there whether because it is forbidden to carry it out of the kingdom or because it may not be carried by sea without great danger and with due speed, because of thieves or other similar causes, and without incurring in great expense, effort, and inconveniences. And even if none of these circumstances were true, the money under discussion may not be worth anything in the place where he needs it, or may not be worth as much as in the place in which he has it. For these and other reasons, men find it useful many times to exchange money in one place for money [they have] available in another, for their own good or the common good. We would like to examine now if bankers may licitly charge an increase and obtain a profit for this exchange of money taking it from one place to another.

Money may have in different places a different value for several causes, and it is necessary to ponder how much the exchange should increase or decrease because of the difference in value in order to make the contract licit and just. Therefore, we must first of all examine if in the case when the money has the same value in both places the banker may collect an increase because of the formal or virtual transportation he carries out for the sake of the person seeking the exchange. This type of exchange may be carried out in two ways: the first one, when the banker receives the money first to hand it back later in a different place personally or through his correspondent—and in this case, it does not seem to be a loan nor, for this reason, usury on the banker's part. An example may be someone who is considering going to Rome and gives the banker 100 here so that when he gets to Rome, [the banker] or his correspondent in the city give him 90. The other way would be if the banker first gives the money to receive it himself or through a correspondent in another place with an increase, and here it does appear there is a combination of a loan on the banker's part. The doctors' opinion of each of these cases is different, because of which we shall discuss the first case in this argument, leaving the second for the following one.

All doctors agree that it is licit to charge an increase for the exchange carried out in the first case, as long as, in the prudent people's opinion, it does not exceed the value of the formal or virtual transportation of the money from one place to another, taking into account the distance, dangers, and the rest of the circumstances.[1] King Sebastian did not forbid these types of exchanges in the law he promulgated in 1570. What is more, he ratified them, as is clear to whomever reads said law. Pius V is of the same opinion in the bull he published on exchanges.

The reason for accepting it is the following: the transportation of the money for the sake of whom solicits the exchange warrants a price, since the muleteer and navigator licitly charge payment for transporting money from one place to another. And they charge more the greater the distance, the greater the dangers on the road, the greater the amount of money, and so on regarding other circumstances, which may increase the value of transportation. So, too, the banker licitly receives the stipend that corresponds to the transportation he is carrying out. And it is beside the point that, in general, the banker is not the one carrying out a formal or real transportation because in far away places he has employees or correspondents who carry out the payment of the money, because, as the doctors are right in pointing out, the person who solicits the exchange for a certain place is rendered the same service as if they [the bankers] were truly transporting the coins there. And the fact that they can do this easier than others and with minimum expense and no danger and almost no effort, is due to their cleverness and organization, and is not an impediment for them to be able to charge a proportionate stipend for the services rendered. Notice, however, that the means they have in many places to bring or take sums of money at the service of not one but many [people], and the possibility of dedicating themselves at the same time to other lucrative businesses, decreases the value of the transportation under discussion, and the banker may not in justice charge each one as if he actually took the coins of one and not of many. The just price of this exchange, if not appraised by the law—and it usually is not—cannot be established with absolute precision but fluctuates within certain limits that a prudent person should establish, in much the same way we said in argument 348 the limits of the natural just price should be set. In order to judge if a price is right in these matters, it helps to know what is regularly charged, as long as more than what the circumstances call for is not charged through the tyranny of a monopoly or for the insatiable thirst of increasing the price of things. It is evident that the amount of those soliciting the exchange and the scarcity of bankers increase the price of this exchange, as, on the contrary, the amount of bankers and scarcity of those who solicit the exchange decrease it. It is the same as with everything: The multitude of buyers and scarcity of sellers make prices rise and, on the contrary, the multitude of sellers and scarcity of buyers makes them fall. Medina, Navarrus, and Major have already observed this in the already referred to places, regarding the price of exchanges, even if Medina appears not to have understood the reason regarding virtual transportation.

In the type of exchange discussed in this and the following argument there is a combination of two contracts: one, the exchange of one coin for another, which should be carried out respecting the equality; the other, the rental of services and the necessary activity to transport the money from one place to another, at least virtually. Because of this last [endeavor], a stipend may be received. Both in the money exchange, as well as in the payment of the increase for the service rendered or which shall be rendered, there is a transfer of property.

In the exchange we are referring to in the present argument there may be injustice on the banker's part, and there shall be obligation to restitute if he were to charge a greater increase than what was warranted for the services rendered. But there cannot be usury, as the banker does not formally or virtually grant a loan. But whoever signs with him an exchange contract does virtually grant the banker a loan, as he first gives him the money in one place so that it is returned somewhere else. The person who grants it may commit usury, because of which he would be forced to restitute. For example, if he realizes that the banker needs the money here and he gives it to him so that [the banker] gives him back the same amount in a distant place, because, in that case, he would be asking in addition to the capital for the effort of transporting the money to a distant place, which deserves payment. Thus, he commits usury and has to restitute the amount in which the transportation is estimated. So say Navarrus and others in the places before cited. He would have the obligation of a much greater restitution if he stipulates that [the banker] give him an equal sum of money in a place which, for the reason we shall shortly explain, the money shall be worth more. Because, in such case, he would virtually receive a much greater increment for the money he gave in advance. But if the money had the same value in one and the other place, and the distance between them were not great, it could be presumed that the banker turns it [the increment] down out of generosity, or as a reward for other favors, due to the fact that the stipend for transportation would be small. But if the stipend were important, there would need to be sufficient reasons to persuade oneself in good conscience that the banker absolves him from his payment. And if two people needed to transport money, for example, one from Lisbon to Toledo and the other from Toledo to Lisbon, even if one of them is a banker and the other is not, it would be licit to hand over the money in one place in order for the other person to hand back the same amount in the other place. Because, as we shall see in the two following arguments, either one of them can licitly sell the virtual transportation of the money that the other needs, and there would even be more sense in licitly compensating each other for the respective transportations.

9

Argument 404

On Whether It Is Licit for the Banker to Charge a Certain Increment for the Exchange He Gives When He Anticipates the Money in One Place to Recover It in a Different Place?

Some experts considered this type of exchange to be illicit and usurious, and forced the person to restitute the increment thus received. They justified their opinion saying that it does not seem that the banker transports any money, which would be the reason why he could licitly receive said increment due to the services he rendered [by transporting it]; and there does not seem to be any other reason for that increment other than waiting for future payment, making it a formal or virtual loan, and therefore usurious, [as] the increment thus received [is considered such]. This opinion is defended in the *Ordenanzas Portuguesas*,[1] when they condemn this contract as usurious and consider the banker who acts in this way liable to the penalties established against the usurers.

However, the contrary opinion seems more usual among the doctors, that is, that said contract of exchange shall not be usurious as long as the increment is not received for reason of the delay in payment but for the service and virtual transportation of the money. So say Conrado, Cajetan, Soto, Navarrus, Juan de Medina, and others.[2] King Sebastian's law promulgated November 5, 1577, agrees with this opinion, [in which law] Portugal was conceded four fairs or markets that were never celebrated. That law authorizes, not only in fairs, but at other times receiving money in exchange in Seville to pay it back with a certain increment in Portugal. In his bull on exchanges, Pius V not only does not reject this opinion but explicitly approves it.

This opinion may be proved by observing that the money that is given in a far away place is not worth so much that its delivery there may be compensated with the same goods that would be delivered here for [that money] if it had any value here. Because as far away money it is coupled to the transportation that with effort and expense shall carry out the person who must make the payment, there being a just price for this transportation. Thus, when the banker anticipates the money in one place and accepts receiving the payment in another place, if the person who receives [the money] is released from the effort and expense involved in transporting the money he has elsewhere, in order to compensate with [that money] the amount he receives here, the exchange dealer may receive as just price for the transportation he provides the same amount that another exchange dealer would receive from this same person in order for the money [the exchange dealer] gave him in the place where [the person] is to be paid in the far away place referred to in the contract with the first exchange dealer. And it is beside the point if this exchange dealer has a representative in the place where the money is, allowing him to carry out the money transference without any effort or expense, as this is something that happens *per accidens*, due to his fortunate situation. This service may be assessed in monetary terms.

This is the reason Cajetan identifies in the place already cited, and Navarrus considers more extensively in the cited *Comentario*, numbers 62 and 63, and it is of no consequence if the banker hands over the money before receiving compensation for [the money] and for releasing the client of the effort of transporting extra money to carry out the payment (as both things should be paid). Because the fact that he shall expect payment for both the money he hands over as for releasing the client from the effort of transporting it is a favor he does for him, as long as he does not receive anything for waiting to get paid, unless it is because of profit ceasing. This point is proved in the fact that the banker who receives here the money to hand over [the money] that is needed in Rome, for example, to dispatch some bulls, does not need any more cleverness nor incurs more expenses than the banker who with the same end in mind gives the money in Rome that will be returned to him later on. More so, the service he gives is greater as he gives before receiving. Therefore, what the banker could licitly receive in the first case he may also receive in the second, as he does not receive anything on account of the payment.

Regarding the arguments of [those] whose opinion is contrary [to this one] we should say that the banker under discussion transfers the money, at least virtually or as if it were real, since he releases the person who receives the exchange from the effort of transferring it, as we have already explained, and has been demonstrated with a just argument allowing for the increment. Regarding the *Ordenanzas Portuguesas*, it should be said that even if the *Ordenanzas* considers that the contract we are dealing with here is illicit *ex natura rei*, and makes the banker liable to the established penalties against usurers, this is not so, as we have already proved, because of which the legislators were wrong and such law is not even in force in a court of law. We should add that King Sebastian approved such contract in the law he later promulgated.

From what has been said, we understand that someone who buys a thing in a far away place may pay a lower price [for it] than what it is worth over there when the seller cannot sell it there by retail, if he can bring it without great expense. And this is so even in the case in which the buyer can use it in the place where it is without expense, or can easily sell it by retail in the market for a just price. The reason is that, given the circumstances, the thing is really worth less for the seller who is released from much effort and expense in selling it. All this is extensively explained by Cajetan and Navarrus in the already cited places.[3]

From here I conclude that what the Genovese did in the kingdom of Castile was not something by nature unjust. Many Castilians who lived far away from Seville had annual revenues there that the king owed them for the money he had taken as tribute. When the fleet from the New World arrived in Seville, the Genovese handed over to these people lower annual revenues in the places where they lived, in exchange for the revenue they had in Seville. I do not condemn this exchange of one income for another if the difference that results from the lower payment is moderate, taking into account the burden they released the owners of such tributes from and, also, the great effort it was sometimes to recover from the ministers of the king the sums handed over.

From what has been said I also conclude that there is nothing illicit in doing something that I have been often asked about in Lisbon. Many ladies of the Lisbon nobility have annual revenues in Castile, which are given to them ordinarily by the ministers of the king at certain dates. One part of that income is given to a merchant as payment for getting the ministers of the king to pay them the whole amount, receive it, transfer it to Lisbon, and give it to them. What is more, some of them [the ladies] allow a present to be offered to the minister of the king, leaving him a share of the owed quantity, so that when the merchant shows up to collect [the money] the payment is not deferred. In this matter, the king should set clear standards on how the ministers are to proceed, and prevent them from unjustly receiving these gifts and turn these mercenary payments into legitimate settlements. Of course, he should punish them and make them restitute the gifts received. The confessors, in turn, should question these ministers regarding these practices and force them to restitute the gifts that were offered in a not wholly voluntary way to avoid inconveniences to the creditors. On this issue some God-fearing tradesmen were questioned and told me that they went to these same places, and there received the money they needed for their commercial dealings, giving it back later in Lisbon from the money they had there. I have told them that the fact that it is useful to them and may do it with scarcely any work is no impediment for them to licitly receive the amount of what is worth for these ladies to carry out their commercial dealings in such a far away place and the virtual transportation of the money. This shall be easier to understand when we explain the following argument.

The stipend they usually receive is the following: They give each lady the entire amount of the gold coins that is theirs (the value of the *ducat* in Portugal is 400 *reais*, while in Castile it is worth 374 *maravedis*), but for each *aúreo* they receive in Castile 11 silver *reales* and, in Portugal, only 10, so that for each *aúreo* or *ducat* they earn 1 silver *real*, which certainly does not seem excessive for collecting the revenues in Castile and taking them back to Portugal, although it is the prudent people who should judge this, and it is always wise to act with moderation in such stipends and profits, especially, since these commercial dealings demand little work, scarce effort, and no risk.

Regarding the exchange we are referring to in this argument, in general we should know that nothing is collected for the delay in payment, and because of this, anything that is collected over the rigorous just price that is owed for the other rulings, may not be drawn for the delay in collecting, and is usurious and liable of restitution. Because of which it is not more licit to receive it when the payment shall be granted later somewhere else than if the payment is to be granted instantly, or if the money had been previously handed over somewhere else in order to be handed back here later. This was established by Pius V in his bull on exchanges. This, however, should be accepted as long as there is not a real profit ceasing for the delay in payment, as Navarrus[4] says.

Even if Pius V forbids in his bull that the banker fix from the beginning, or whenever, a standard interest rate, even in the case of absence of payment, as Navarrus says when he declared these same words in the number cited, this is based on the hypothesis that it is collected for veiled usury and not for profit ceasing [that is a consequence of] the delay in payment. Because if it were received for a profit that really is ceasing, in the person's conscience it would be licit and just to receive it, and would not be subject to restitution. Because the law that is founded on a hypothesis does not apply to the person's conscience when it is evident that the opposite of what is assumed happens to be true.

To prevent any usury from taking place on account of late payments, in the same bull on exchanges Pius V prohibits exchanges made to any but the next fair, if the bills of exchange were signed for a place where these were being celebrated. And if the [bills of exchange] were signed for a place where a fair was not being celebrated, bills of exchange should not be given but for the nearest fair, according to the custom of allowing changes for that place. Of course, if the next fair were so close in time that it would not be possible for the bills of exchange to arrive on time in order to carry out the payment, then the "next fair" would be considered the following one, as what they are talking about is the next fair in which the payment can be carried out.

Navarrus, in the number 301 cited, says when explaining these words that it is not forbidden to arrange the payment for the second, third, or fourth fair, as long as for extending the deadline the exchange is not increased more than if it were arranged for the nearest fair. Because it is considered a service and an act of charity to grant a greater time to pay without an increment, something the pope has no intention of prohibiting.

A God-fearing merchant from Lisbon did not concede exchanges but for the next fair, according to what Pius V's bull ordered, and asked me about this. You should know, he said, that the instrument we merchants negotiate and obtain profit with is money. And the longer you have to wait at one place for the next fair, the greater the number of merchants who take exchanges for that date, and the less time there is for the fair the fewer the merchants who want exchanges for that place, and with lower increments. That is why, if the fair of Medina (for example) is celebrated in four months, the exchange market for that fair would be regularly more expensive than after one month went by and, [after] only one month went by more expensive than two months gone by, so that, ordinarily, the less time there is until the fair, the lower the increment that is given or taken for the exchanges. The reason for this is that the longer payment for the exchange is deferred, the greater the increment that is given and taken because of the greater profit for the merchants; and the less it is deferred, so much less is given, because of the lower profit for the merchants.

My question, asked the merchant, is the following: When there is a longer period of time until the next fair may I licitly receive all the increment that is currently offered in the exchange market, or should I refrain myself from such great increment for considering I have received it for the greater delay in payment, and for this reason, in an usurious way? If I have to refrain myself, he added, no one will want to grant the exchange in those conditions, as we merchants negotiate and make a profit with money. And if the God-fearing among us refuse to grant those exchanges, only the greedy shall take advantage of them, and consequently since those who grant the exchanges shall be fewer and many more those who solicit it, such increment shall increase, a thing not only detrimental to the God-fearing but also harmful to the public affairs and to those who solicit exchanges.

I answered that there is no reason why one should refrain from carrying out those exchanges at the current market price, as the abundance of solicitors shall make the price increase, if not for reason of the transfer of money then for other rulings that we will shortly discuss. And the fact that this is the current price in the public market greatly contributes to consider it just. We should add that the scarceness of merchants who give and take money to exchange, and the profit obtained when dealing with money are circumstances that make the price of exchange rise, even for those who take the exchange not for negotiating and earning money but with other ends in mind.

The doctors agree that everything received in excess of the capital when money was given to someone else to be given back with an increment in another place where, however, he does not have money nor anyone to pay for him, but it is presumed that it shall be paid with the increment in the same place where the exchange was carried out, is usurious and subject to restitution. This is the kind of exchange that the nobles receive in the Spanish territories to pay, for example, in Flanders or in France with the usual increment for the exchanges for those places, where they neither have money nor anyone to pay for them.

In view of the fact that in this type of exchange money is not transferred, whether formally or virtually and, in point of fact, no one who has money in a place is released of the effort of taking it to the place where he took the exchange, as there is not even an exchange of money in one place for money in another, but of money here for money also here, it is evident that to receive an increment should be considered usurious or "dry exchange," as something would be charged for reason of delay or deferment of payment.

There is even greater injustice in allowing such individuals, in the case of not being able to pay in the place and time established beforehand, to reexchange the bills of exchange from that place to this one with a new increment. In such a contract there are two unjust exchanges with obligation to restitute both increments. And the banker may not excuse himself by writing to the place for which he gave the first exchange saying it is the people who took the exchange and did not pay it there who are to blame for the absence of payment, because he was willing to receive the money there. So say, among others, Cajetan and Silvestre. Today Pius V thus defines it at the beginning of the bull on exchanges.

In Portugal, King Sebastian established in law in 1570 that whoever carries out an exchange in such way is subject to the penalty of losing *ipso facto* the totality of what he hands over. And the person who takes the exchange may not waive the right this law grants him, and even if he were to pay, he or his heirs could claim what was thus handed over. It also established severe penalties for the person who received an exchange under these conditions and gave back something to the banker in money or an equivalent. And the law he later promulgated regarding these exchanges, in 1577, does not modify this opinion in anything.

Navarrus and Silvestre say that in order for the exchange not to be usurious and dry it is sufficient that, even if the person who receives it for a certain place does not have at the moment of receiving the exchange neither money nor someone to answer for him there, it is probable that he shall have it by the time that has been set for payment, which will allow him to pay it, whether because he hopes to obtain the money through a loan or because he shall take it with interest for another place, or in any other way. I believe, however, that this should be understood when he is hoping to obtain the money from a third party and not from the person whom he has to pay or from his representative.

What happens if the banker gave money in exchange for a certain place to someone he thought could pay him there, but then it happens that said person has no money or representative there but will pay in the same place where he received the exchange? May the banker justly accept in this case the increment on the exchange in the same place where he delivered the money? Whatever others may say, I believe that the banker may receive in this case, not only compensation for damages and losses that he has suffered for giving him the money—because if he had not given it to him he could have given it to someone else in exchange or he could have used the money in some other respectable business, but also, even if they are small losses he may also receive an amount as compensation for the opportunity he has missed for using the money that he should have received together with the increment in the preestablished place, and he may obligate the person who took the exchange to put that money with the increment at his own expense in the preestablished place, if that were possible. I believe this because the contract was licit in itself, entered into in good faith on the banker's part, who furthermore has fulfilled it. And because it is not an innominate contract, it may force the other contracting party to fulfill his part, if he is able to fulfill it, or if he is not able to, to pay in the place where they are the total amount of what the banker would have paid for the contract to be fulfilled in that other place, according to the legal dispositions. This was said in argument 253 and, especially, in 255. And this is valid not only in conscience but also in a court of law.

Although if there are any signs that the banker knew or should have known that the person with whom he was dealing with did not have any money nor representative in that other place, the contract shall be condemned as usurious in a court of law, and the banker shall be liable to the usurers' penalties. What has been said may be confirmed. Because frauds and tricks should not benefit their instigators. And also, as said in arguments 327 and 380, the sale of something belonging to someone else on the thief's part is a valid contract, not in the sense that the buyer acquires the property of the thing, but in the sense that the thief, in case of eviction, is responsible as long as it is convenient to the buyer that [the thief] be considered owner of the thing. What we said in argument 352, regarding someone who in good faith brought some oxen to a supposed owner who was renting them, is in accordance with the above.

10

Argument 405

Answers to Some Questions Regarding What Has Been Said in the Two Preceding Arguments. What Can Be Said About Those Who for a Salary Bring with Them the Horses They Needed to Rent for the Trip? Is It Licit to Receive an Increase for the Exchange Carried Out from One Place to Another Within the Same Kingdom?

First question. There is uncertainty as to whether the two types of exchange we have explained in the two preceding arguments, in which an increment over the principal was collected, are licit not only for public bankers whose job it is to practice exchanges but also for the regular citizens. The answer is affirmative, because the service rendered in favor of whom asks for the exchange is worth that increment, whoever the person is rendering the service, and there is no law prohibiting the exercise of such type of exchange to regular citizens.

Second question. Let us suppose that someone had money, let us say, in Lisbon, and had to transfer it to Flanders to buy some goods, pay some debts, or with some other end in mind, and let us suppose that this person had thought of giving it to a merchant so that he returned it in Flanders with some kind of discount. Finally, let us suppose that some other person came along who needed in Lisbon the money that he had in Flanders and asked the first person to exchange the money he had in Lisbon for the one the other had in Flanders, for which he would pay an increment. May the person who has his money in Lisbon licitly accept the increment they are offering him, given that he is very interested in transferring the money from Lisbon to Flanders, just as the other is in bringing his from Flanders to Lisbon? The answer has to be affirmative, as the service he carries out for the other person is really worth that increment, and if that happens to be to his advantage, it is something that occurs *per accidens*. In contracts what matters to see if they are just or not is if what one person does is equivalent to what he receives from the other in compensation, and this is what happens in our situation, as affirm Soto and Medina.[1]

Something similar happens when someone takes to a particular place a horse that he rented and that he had to give back to the owner, incurring certain expenses. If he found a third person who was willing to rent the horse to travel to the place of origin, he may licitly rent it for a just price, without there being an impediment that in so doing he saves money for the expenses he would incur in order to return the horse. And since there is equality between the use of the horse, which is what is granted, and the price that is paid for it, the contract thus entered shall be just, even if on the other hand, and *per accidens*, he obtains an economic advantage.

Similarly, I believe the following: Let us suppose that someone decided to rent a horse to travel to a certain place, and he found someone else who, without knowing of this trip, wished to hire him to take a horse to that same place. It must be said that he may licitly rent out his services and receive a just stipend for the job of taking the horse, without it being an impediment for doing so that he is taking the horse to the same place he was thinking of traveling, saving money on what he would have spent to rent the horse himself. The reason is the same as above: that the service he renders the other person deserves remuneration, even if *per accidens* it brings to him a greater advantage. I also say that if one were looking for someone to take a horse to a certain place and found out that another person has a need of a horse in that same place, both could agree to mutually render themselves the service, reciprocally absolving themselves from the total or partial price, as what is agreed between them shall be considered just. The reason is that neither one is obliged to enter into the agreement in order to benefit the other, nor needs to mix the contract in which they agree to render a service with another different contract. But if for reason of the personal need that is simultaneously satisfied one of them wanted to give a discount or reduction, it is something he may do. The same must be said about two merchants who know of the mutual need of transferring money from one place to another.

What was said above is consistent with strict justice and theoretical strictness, as moral and fraternal charity reasons may request loosening up that strictness. However, one may not condemn as guilty the person who does not wish to loosen up his position; or at least, he may not be accused of mortal sin.

In the cited issue, Juan de Medina affirms that if someone needing 1,000 *ducats* in Flanders gives them to a merchant in the Spanish territories so that he looks for someone who wants to receive them in exchange and give them back in Flanders with an increment, he would commit usury, because in doing so he would put his money in Flanders with a profit for himself. I do not see how this may be judged as usurious as, in truth, the owner of the money uses the right he has to give it for an exchange, this being an operation in which anyone else who did not need money in Flanders could make a profit on it. And the fact that *per accidens* his money is transferred to Flanders as he expected, does not make that contract illicit, as we have already explained and Medina himself concedes. The fact that there is an invitation to directly or indirectly practice a money exchange—which in all other respects is just—does not make it illicit either.

As for the last part of the argument, namely, whether it is licit to receive an increment or benefit for the exchange carried out from one place to another in the same kingdom, as would be from Seville to Medina, even if Soto denies it, doctor Navarrus affirms it in the earlier cited *Comentario*,[2] and argues that it is by nature licit as long as the increment is moderate and proportional to the distance. I fully agree with his opinion, and it may be proved correct in the following way: If the activity of carrying money from one place to another outside the kingdom deserves remuneration, the same goes for carrying it within the kingdom itself, although it should be less significant if the distance is lesser and fewer the dangers of transportation, especially since there is no prohibition to transport the money within the kingdom itself as there usually is to take it out of it. And so we see that the students' errand boys justly charge their price for the formal transportation of money, and they may charge it even if they do not transport the money materially but only in a virtual way, receiving it in one place and later handing it over at the students' residence place. I do not believe Soto had any intention of denying this, but only that that transportation did not deserve such high prices as the merchants usually charged the nobles for picking up the money they gave them in the King's Court to take it to the place where the nobles have their income and residence. This is the way merchants usually conceal usuries.

Even if this is so by nature, both the citizens as well as the foreigners in this kingdom are forbidden from giving money in exchange in order to take it from one place to another in the kingdom with an increment or interest, or to take it to a fair carried out in the same kingdom.[3] The penalty established is the loss of all the money for the person who received it in exchange, and all the penalties established against the usurers for the person who gave it.

In Portugal, instead, even if King Sebastian prohibited these same [actions] in the law he promulgated in 1570, he later allowed them in those cases in which the money was received in one of the four fairs he established in Portugal (and which were never carried out) in order to reimburse it in one of those other fairs, or when the money was received someplace else than where the fairs took place in order to pay it in the following fair. Apart from this, the same king Sebastian, in one of his resolutions prior to the 1577 law (of which I have a copy), revoked that first law from 1570 in what regards the exchanges considered licit according to Pius V's bull, the Portuguese law, and the natural law. The result of which is that in Portugal today it is not illicit to exchange from one place to another in the kingdom, charging an increment, as long as this is moderate.

In the places cited earlier, Navarrus says that these laws that prohibit the exchange of money between places in the same kingdom should apply only to the cases in which the banker hands over the money first and later receives it with an increment somewhere else, as there may be concealed usury, such as for example, if the increment were received for reason of the loan being made, or the delay in payment, but that [the laws] should not apply when the banker first receives the money that he shall give back later somewhere else as, in this case, there is no danger of committing usury nor of concealing it. However, the prohibition in these cases could be an impediment for transferring the money from one place to another, thus being detrimental to the regular citizens and to the common good. I believe that the law of Castile cited earlier does not apply to these cases due to the fact that in them money is not given for an interest, the activity such law expects to correct.

It is worth asking oneself if in the case that someone—against what these laws regulate—received for the exchange carried out from one place to another a retribution that would be considered licit and just if it were not for such laws, he would be forced to restitute such amount *ipso facto*, that is, even before the judicial decision was issued. My opinion is that the answer is negative, because, in truth, the service rendered is worth what has been received for it. Even if the contract were null for reason of such laws (which does not seem to be the sense of the cited law of Castile, which only prohibits doing it under severe penalties), the person receiving the money would not be forced to give it back before a judicial sentence was issued forcing him to, and not without taking before a just compensation for the service rendered gratuitously. What happens in this case is the same as in those contracts where some goods are exchanged for others: If the contract is annulled, the one who carried it out does not have to give back what he received if he in turn does not get back what he gave, or is compensated for it. And even if the law enforced it, in this matter it should be considered as mere penal law, which would lack power in the conscience's realm before the judicial sentence was issued.

11

Argument 406

On How the Same Amount of Money May Have Twice As Much Value in Different Places

In the three preceding arguments we have examined one of the rulings or reasons for which the exchange carried out from one place to another charging an increment over the principal may be licit. Before examining two other reasons for which this type of exchange may be licitly practiced we must explain the issue before us.

A same amount of money may have more value in one place than in another in two ways: first, because according to the law or accepted custom it has, in comparison to other coins, a different value in places that are also different. Thus, for example, a *ducat* is worth 400 *reais* in Portugal and 375 *maravedis* in Castile; and a silver *real* is worth 34 *maravedis* in Castile and today it is worth 40 in Portugal. And in the kingdom of Valencia the *real* is worth fewer *dines* than in Cataluña. The *dines* are the smallest common copper coins in those kingdoms. In other places, the *real* has different values. Consequently, 11 silver *reales* are worth 374 *maravedis* in Castile, and in Portugal they are worth today 440 *reais*, disregarding other places for the time being. The gold *escudo*, which in the past was worth in Castile 10 silver *reales* and 10 *maravedis*, that is, 350 *maravedis*, was worth in Rome $11^1/_2$ *julios* (the *julio* is equivalent to the silver *real*), and in France and in other places it had different values. Today, in Castile, its value has increased to 400 *maravedis*.

There is another way that money may have more value in one place than in another: namely, when it is more abundant. In equal circumstances, the more abundant money is in one place so much less is its value to buy things with, or to acquire things that are not money. Just as the abundance of merchandise reduces their price when the amount of money and quantity of merchants remains invariable, so too the abundance of money makes prices rise when the amount of merchandise and number of merchants remain invariable, to the point where the same money loses purchasing power. So we see that, in the present day, money is worth in the Spanish territories much less than what it was worth eighty years ago, due to the abundance of it. What was bought before for two today is bought for five, or for six, or maybe for more. In the same proportion has the price of salaries risen, as well as dowries and the value of real estate, revenues, benefices, and all other things. That is exactly why we see that money is worth much less in the New World, especially in Peru, than in the Spanish territories, due to the abundance there is of it. And wherever money is less abundant than in the Spanish territories, it is worth more. Neither is it worth the same in all parts because of this reason, yet it varies according to its abundance and all other circumstances. And this value does not remain unaltered as if it were indivisible, yet fluctuates within the limits defined by the people's estimation, the same as happens with merchandise not appraised by law. This money's value is not the same in all parts of the Spanish territories, but different, as ordinarily it is worth less in Seville—where the ships from the New World arrive, and where for that reason there is usually abundance of it—than what it is worth in other places of the same Spanish territories.

In addition to this, the greater need of money there is in one place, for example, to buy merchandise, war expenses, the Royal Court's expenditures, or for any other reason, makes money there be worth more than in other places. What is more, these same reasons make money worth more at some times than in others in one and the same place. Money that in one place is exchanged for money in another place functions as merchandise not appraised by law, whose value rises at some times and falls at others, depending on whether there is more or less need of it. That is why, the abundance of one type of merchandise, the greater or lesser need of it and the greater or lesser number of merchants who want it, make its value rise or fall in a particular place. This is exactly what happens with money: its greater or lesser abundance in one place, the need there is of it, the greater or lesser number of those who want to exchange it for diverse places and of those who can and want to accept those exchanges, are the reasons for which money at a certain time is worth more in one place than in another, or at different times. And even in the same fair and in one and the same place, it shall be worth more or less according to whether at the beginning, middle, or end of the fair there are more or less people who need money and want to take it in exchange for other places, and more or fewer people who want to hand it over.

When in the kingdoms and republics the value of larger coins is appraised in relation to the smaller ones, such rate only applies to the exchange of some coins for others in a same place, and in the purchase of goods in that place. The kingdoms and republics have never wanted to appraise the coins as far as the value we are referring to now, that is, to exchange them for coins in other places, as this value is not constant, even if the other [type of value] is appraised by law. And because it is a just value even after the legal appraisal, appraising them [the coins in order to exchange them for coins from other places] would be to the disadvantage of kingdoms and republics, whose merchandise would start going scarce due to this [appraisal]. That is why the custom has always rightfully and notwithstanding the appraised price respected the fact that coins had this other variable value when exchanging them for coins in other places. And in his bull Pius V approved this type of exchange with an increment.

I explained that the money from one place that is exchanged for money in another, et cetera, functions as a merchandise not appraised by law, et cetera, because concerning the place where it is it always retains the value appraised by law or accepted by custom. Because even if in Medina or in any other place where exchanges are usually taken, the value of money varies because the exchange is given more expensively for one place than for another, and even in one and the same place the exchange is given more expensively to some people than to others due to the fact that it is not indivisible and during the same fair it may vary according to the circumstances, however, in comparison to Medina itself and to the merchandise that is bought there at different times, or to pay debts, it always maintains the price appraised by law, and according to that price merchandise is bought and debts are paid, even if that other value of the coin increases or diminishes. What is more, in all the places where the exchange has to be compensated, the amount of money to be paid according to the contract entered into is always estimated according to the value appraised by the law for the money in that place.

12

Argument 407

If Coins That by Law or Generally Accepted Custom Had a Different Value in Relation to Other Copper Coins of a Lesser Value, in Places Also Different, Can They Be Justly Exchanged Between Those Places Keeping to the Equality?

The issue is of great utility, and worth knowing seeing that the practice of the merchants and the doctrine of many doctors do not agree with each other. Some look for weakly ploys and try to make them prevail in order not to condemn the practice in some places, this being so that if their main assertion were true, such practice would be usurious, especially if the banker gives the money first so that it is later returned to him in another place. Consider that in this argument we are not discussing the increment the banker may licitly charge for reason of the exchange, nor the rulings that allow him to licitly charge it. We are discussing the commutation itself (putting aside such rulings and such increment), and want to know if there is an equality when money that in comparison to the small copper coins is worth less is exchanged for the same money to be delivered in a place where in comparison to the copper coins it is worth more, or if, on the contrary, there is no equality in such practice, and such excess or difference must be compensated in order for there to be equality in the contract, and, thus, if the one changing the money in the place where it is worth less should reduce the exchange of the similar coins that he has to give back in another place. And vice versa, if the one who carries out the exchange where they are worth more may and should increase in the exchange the respective increment.

Some examples. When the *ducat* began to be minted, it was worth in Castile 375 *maravedis*, in Portugal 400 *reais* and, in Flanders, its value in what they call *gruesos* in that province was equivalent to 400 *reais* or *maravedis*, according to the estimation of the merchants and to the consensus in exchanges and in all negotiations. But since today there is no coin that has precisely that value—as said in argument 400—the *ducat*'s value in these three regions is still the same to the present day, whatever the coin used to pay. What is more, if in the exchanges, or in any other business or contract, the *ducat* is suddenly mentioned for any reason, its value is understood to be in Castile 375 *maravedis*, [and] in Portugal and in Flanders 400 *reais* or *maravedis*. The question, therefore, is: when those gold coins had that value in former times, and when today, that they no longer exist, they speak of *ducats* in the exchanges making reference to the explained value, do they observe the equality when exchanging a *ducat* in Castile for a *ducat* in Portugal or in Flanders? And vice versa, when a *ducat* in Portugal or in Flanders is exchanged for a *ducat* in Castile, do they observe that equality?

Another example is that of the silver *reales* that in Castile are worth 34 *maravedis*, in Portugal 40, and in the kingdom of Valencia are worth a lower amount of *dines* than in Cataluña (the so called *dines* are each worth $1^1/_2$ *maravedi*). The question is: Is due equality observed if 100 *reales* in Castile are commuted or exchanged for the same number in Portugal, or, the other way around, 100 in Portugal for the same amount in Castile? Or, in a similar way, 100 *reales* in Valencia for the same amount in Barcelona, and the other way around? The result of this is a much greater increment for the *ducat*, as 375 *maravedis* make in Castile 11 silver *reales* with 1 *maravedi*, and in Portugal 400 *reais* make only 10 silver *reales*. The question is: Is due equality observed in the commutation or exchange of 100 *ducats* in Castile for the same amount in Portugal, and the other way around, of 100 in Portugal for the same amount in Castile? Because if the value of a coin in comparison to the small copper coins is in one place greater than in another, but they are considered equal in the exchange from one place to another, we have here a new ruling for which an increment may be taken through the exchange from the place where it is worth more to the place where it is worth less, and for reason of which the exchange shall have to be reduced, in order to make it on both parts equitable and just when it is carried out from the place where it is worth less to the place where it is worth more.

Navarrus believes that if someone gives 100 *ducats* in Castile to get the same amount back in Portugal, or if he gives 100 silver *reales* in Castile to get back the same amount in Portugal, it is not a commutation on equal terms but an unjust and usurious loan.[1] Because, he says, the *ducat* and the silver *real* are worth more in Portugal than in Castile; and he refers to the time when the silver *real* was worth a little over 36 *reais* in Portugal, and when the *ducat* was worth 11 silver *reales*, which amount to 400 *reais*. And the same would say Navarrus in the other examples we have included. Others who wrote after him were of the same opinion.

Even if Soto is of the same opinion when the same coin is worth more in one place than in another,[2] and gives the example of a *ducat* worth more silver *reales* in Italy than in the Spanish territories, when the *reales* have all the same value, or the *ducat* is worth more *gruesos* in one place than in another, I do not know, however, if he would say the same in the examples we have included.

Navarrus's argumentation: Navarrus's argument is that the copper coin that is called *real* in Portugal has the same value as the Castilian *maravedi*. Because in the same way that said copper coin is worth in Portugal 6 *ceptis*, and half of it is worth 3, in Castile too, in the time where they had *cornados* and *meajas*, 6 of these were worth 1 *maravedi*, and 3 were worth half, which in Castile they call *blanca*. Today, in the kingdom of Galicia, 6 *cornados* are worth 1 *maravedi*. Therefore, since the value of the *maravedi* and that of the Portuguese copper *real* are the same, it is unjust to receive in Portugal 1 silver real with a value of 36 *maravedis* for 1 silver *real* received in Castile with a value of 34 *maravedis*. And it shall also be unjust to receive in Portugal 1 *ducat* of 400 *reais* for a *ducat* worth 374 *maravedis* received in Castile.

This may be proved as follows: If one and the same measure of wheat is worth more in Portugal than in Castile, as usually happens, it is certainly unjust to commute one measure of wheat in Castile for an equal one in Portugal, even if the wheat from Castile is better than that of Portugal. And it would be usury to be loaned one measure of wheat in Castile for an equal one in Portugal, since the value of the one received in Portugal is greater than the [loan] of wheat that was given in Castile. For this same reason there shall be injustice and usury, with obligation to restitute, if a loan of 100 silver *reales* or 100 *ducats* is received in Castile for a same amount to be given back in Portugal, since more would be given back in Portugal than what was received in Castile.

Contrary to this, and always has been, is the practice of merchants who are more familiar with the estimation of goods than the scholastic doctors, and whose judgment we should abide by in these matters, especially when applied to the dealings they carry out with one another in which none of them complain or object. In the issue set forth concerning commuting money from one place to another, the merchants refer to the silver or gold coins which, taken from one place, maintain their value in all parts, more than to the copper ones, because these, as coins, ordinarily have a different value in the different kingdoms and regions, and the [coin] that is valuable in one place has no value in another, and for reason of the copper they possess they are worth almost nothing, because of which the expense of taking them from one place to another exceeds the value of the copper they are made of. That is why the merchants, for their exchanges and dealings from one place to another, do not take the small copper coins as standard to measure the value of those made of gold and silver, but on the contrary, they make gold and silver the measure of value of the copper coins in that place. That is why, in many places, they carry out the exchanges for diverse places using as unity the silver *marcas* (which we call *marcos* and the Latin *selibras*). And when they carry out the exchanges in *ducats* or *escudos*, as they were usually carried out for the Spanish territories or from the Spanish territories, given that the silver *real* was readily accepted in all places and the majority of the exchanges were paid off with it, they decided that when dealing from one place to another, the silver *real* would have the same value in all places. That is why, since that *real* has a different value in different places due to appraisal or custom, they decided that the small copper coins that in different places have been made the measure of the silver *real* (and, consequently, of the *ducat* and the *escudo*) should not have the same value to buy merchandise in that region, nor to pay debts or carry out exchanges of small coins for other bigger ones. The value of small copper coins is different in the proportion in which the number of copper coins that are given for a silver *real* in one region exceeds the amount of coins that are given for it in another region. And so, among merchants, it was decided that the *maravedi* from Castile should be worth more than the Portuguese *real*. And today, in comparison to the same Portuguese coin, it has a much greater value than before, because the Portuguese silver *real* has increased its value to 40 *reais* from the 36 *reais* it was worth before.

The merchants are of the same opinion regarding the *maravedis* in Castile in comparison to the *gruesos* in Flanders, and the same should be said about the copper *denarios* from the kingdom of Valencia in comparison to the copper *denarios* from Cataluña. In agreement with this opinion is the law Charles V promulgated on exchanges, according to what Navarrus[3] says when he states that 375 *maravedis* from Castile are worth in Portugal 400 *reais*, when he is talking about the time before the silver *real* was worth in Portugal 40 *reais*. And even if Navarrus, in the cited number 60, says that one should not abide by such law, the truth is quite the contrary, as it is reasonable and such law is supported by the general opinion and the merchants' practice, which has so much weight to determine the just price of things. Another substantial argument is the one saying that the more copper coins that, according to the law, should be given for a silver *real* and for other silver and gold coins, the lower the price of the small copper coins. Experience showed in Portugal that as soon as the silver *real* increased to 40 *reais*, there was an immediate increase of the price of things expressed in those small copper coins.

If Navarrus's opinion were true, today usury would be carried out by the person who gave a loan of 1,100 silver *reales* in Castile in order to get back only 1,000 in Portugal, or what is the same, the person who gave a loan of 100 *ducats* and 11 silver *reales* in exchange for only 110 *reales* to be received in Portugal. This would be usury, and the person who gave the money in Castile would be forced to restitute 26 *maravedis* for each *ducat*, because 11 *reales* of each *ducat* he loans are worth in Castile 374 *maravedis*, whereas for the 10 *reales* he receives in Portugal he would receive 400 *reais*. And if these have the same value as the Castilian *maravedi*, our man would receive in Portugal 26 extra *maravedis* for each *ducat* given in Castile. Who is the fool who would be willing to give in Castile 11 silver *reales* and 26 *maravedis* in exchange for only 10 silver *reales* he would receive in Portugal? Or who would accept in Portugal only 10 *reales* in exchange for 11 and 26 *maravedis* he would have to give back in Castile? Is there anyone who can be persuaded that such contract is equitable and just? I do not think so.

But one should take into account that such increase in the value of the gold and silver coins in relation to those of copper in the province itself where the increment is decided upon, has a certain importance, since from then on those coins shall be used to pay greater debts than before, and it shall be possible to buy more goods than before. As that is the reason why more silver and gold coins of that type arrive from other regions: that something is gained from bringing them to this province. Because of which such increase slightly reduces the price of bartering and exchanging said coins from the place where they are worth more.

Regarding this there cannot be a better rule than to pay attention to the current price in the exchange market, and to the exchanges the merchants carry out among themselves from one place to another, and to accept that price as just and accepted by the merchants' common estimation. It should be noted that after the value of the silver *real* increased to 400 *reais*, and 10 *reales* amount to 1 *ducat* of 400 *reais*, if changes are made from Portugal to Castile or from Castile to Portugal taking the *ducat* as unity (as was usually done before), one should note that the exchange from Portugal to Castile has lost almost the eleventh part of its old value in the same way that the *ducat* has diminished in an eleventh fraction. On the contrary, the exchange from Castile to Portugal increased almost in an eleventh part of what the Castilian *ducat* exceeds the Portuguese [*ducat*].

There are, however, today some Portuguese who grant exchanges from Lisbon to Medina for an equal amount of *ducats*, and wait to be paid a whole year, which is manifest usury and explains why a certain God-fearing merchant from Medina warned us, when I was in Lisbon, to be against this type of usury and ruin to one's own conscience. Because if such is the way 100 *ducats* are given in exchange in Lisbon, it turns out that for 1,000 silver *reales* that are given in Lisbon they want to be paid 1,100 in Medina after a year's time, deceiving other learned men by saying that they have granted exchanges on an equal basis, that is, a *ducat* for a *ducat*, but without telling them that the Castilian *ducat* exceeds the Portuguese *ducat* in the eleventh part of its value. And the confessors pay no heed to this.

To Navarrus's argument we answer by denying that the Portuguese copper *real* has the same value as the Castilian *maravedi* when the exchanges are from one place to another. Because even if in the past 1 was worth 6 copper coins, called *ceptis* in Portugal, and *cornados* and *meajas* in Castile, when the silver *real* increased its value in Portugal in comparison to those copper coins, the value of these—called *reais* and *ceptis*—diminished in the same proportion in comparison to the *maravedis* that in the past were called *cornados* and *meajas* in Castile, as has already been explained. We admit the antecedent and deny the consequence for the argument of confirmation, as we have already explained that the *ducat* was never more valuable in Portugal than in Castile, and today it is worth much less.

13

Argument 408

On the People Who Travel from One Place
to Another to Carry Out Exchanges

Before embarking upon the last reason for which in the exchange of money from one place to another the price may licitly be increased and sometimes it is better to reduce it, we must explain a few practical issues on exchanges, which shall put an end to all this subject. And before anything else, who is involved in the business of exchanging.

Three types of people, who depend on each other, are involved in the exchanges. One type are the merchants, who on their own or through their own delegated employees (whom they call *factores*), or through correspondents, practice trading in different places, such as Lisbon, Seville, Medina, Flanders, Genoa, Florence, Venetia, and the Green Promontory, The Isle of Santo Tomé, several places in the New World, the East Indies, and other similar places, taking from one place the things that are worth more in others, and sending to the first ones those that are more valuable there. The following examples shall make it clearer. From Portugal they send to Flanders oil, salt, wine, pepper, and other things that arrive in Portugal from the East Indies, Brazil, and other lands in the Portuguese trading area. From Flanders they bring to Portugal all the things that are necessary in Portugal itself, and in the East Indies, Brazil, and all the other regions that trade with Portugal. There is a similar commerce between the kingdom of Portugal and the several provinces and cities of the Spanish territories, France, Italy, and so forth. From there they bring paper, books, silk, scarlet fabrics (they call *rajas*), and the rest of merchandise that is necessary in the kingdom of Portugal, and in the provinces of its commercial area. And, in turn, from Portugal they send to those places those things that from Portugal and its commercial area are offered with an advantage. To Seville they bring from many provinces and cities in Europe those things that are typical of these places, and from diverse places in the New World and the Islands of the Ocean, subject to the crown of Castile. From Seville, in turn, they send to several provinces the things that there is abundance of in Seville, namely, in addition to money and great quantities of gold and silver that arrive there from the commerce with the New World, other innumerable merchandise, characteristic of the Betica,[1] or, particularly, brought from various places across the sea. Other similar examples may be found in other provinces and cities. Consequently, the most important merchants of each province do business in several places, so that at times they are owed money for the merchandise they have sent and at others it is they who owe money for the merchandise they have bought and carried away. At times they are in need of money, and at others they have an abundance thereof. That is why, in all those places they need employees and correspondents, and what they call credit, that is, people who accept their bills of exchange in that place and pay the amounts they order, and who receive the amounts that other similar bills of exchange order be given to them, managing their business in that place.

From all this multiple and varied negotiation they carry out in diverse places it comes to pass that, often, merchants need for their dealings and profits the money they have in other places in abundance, which gave origin to the practice that whoever needed money in one place demanded of those who had it there in abundance to exchange it for the money that they had somewhere else, or for a place where they could pay more easily. Thus, the merchants helped each other in the exchanges to facilitate their dealings and profits. This was the beginning of the exchanges between merchants, the only ones who practiced them among themselves. On the other hand, the exchange usually resulted in a profit in the place where it was remunerated, whether because the exchange itself deserved that the person carrying it out would benefit from it, as was proved before, or because ordinarily those to whom the money was given in exchange by doing business and buying merchandise to take to other places where it was worth more obtained a much greater profit than those who had given them the money. Consequently, anyone who had money, attracted by the chance of profit they saw in the exchange and by the safety of the business and the little effort, started to help merchants in the main business centers, and give them money in exchange, in different places in their own name or in the name of their employees and correspondents. And this business was so profitable that, exercised with ability, it brought about a great amount of money to the places where, for its very conditions, they expected it would be worth more. They even took money in exchange with a small interest for those places from which they could later give it in exchange for other places with a greater interest. And so it happened that many people ceased trading to dedicate themselves entirely to the business of exchange. And this is the second type of people involved in the practice of exchanges. They happen to be only, or mainly, exchange dealers by profession, who help the merchants in one way or another and depend on them in their business.

These people need to have their correspondents in the places where they practice trading and grant the exchanges, no less than the merchants. They also need to have credit there, for which they need people in those places to whom they can send bills of exchange to be cashed in that place, and who in their name [the exchange dealers'] give the money they have there for exchanges, whether for the place where the main banker lives, or for another where the increment is greater or is expected to be in the future. All according to the orders received, or to whatever they deem more convenient according to the circumstances.

Also the main exchange dealers often need to exchange money in the place where they are in order to take it to other places where they can make a greater profit with it in new exchanges drawn to other places, or to transfer it through successive exchanges to the place where they shall need it and expect it shall be worth more, or for other reasons of usefulness or convenience. Frequently, it is also true that they find it useful and necessary to take money in exchange in other places, whether because they need the money to pay for the exchanges they bought for that place, or to send it through successive exchanges to the places where they shall need it, because they think it shall be worth more there. For these and other reasons, the main exchange dealer, no less than the merchants themselves, need correspondents and credit in several places.

This negotiating with exchanges is frequently carried out with credit, obtaining great profit, more so than using one's own money in cash, even though having a lot of money in different places greatly contributes to success. Because even if an exchange dealer does not have much money, if he has credit and correspondents in several places and, also, is skillful, he can give orders so that in his name his correspondents take money in exchange at those times when it is worth less to take to those other places where it is worth more, and where he will be able to pay for them more easily, and then, he can order again to give a certain amount of money in exchange with a greater increment at a time when it is worth more, or for those places where it shall be worth more, or is expected it shall be. And so, taking in exchange money from some and giving it to others, they can make a great profit with the money that initially was taken in exchange.

In a similar way, an exchange dealer has a special ability to speculate on the time and place in which money shall be worth much more for its scarcity and for the need merchants and many others shall have of it: for example, when the prince in that place is preparing for a war and collects all the money of the region, whence it is likely believed that the merchants of the fairs in that region will have great need of that money as not rarely happened in Flanders when Charles V dwelt there. If our exchange dealer in addition to foresight had the ability to transport through successive exchanges a great amount of money to have it ready at the correct time and place, he shall be able to obtain great profits by giving money in exchange with large increments for the places from where he took it out of, and on the fourth month, or later, he shall recover the money in a much greater quantity in the same places.

The third type of men who dedicate themselves to the business of exchanges are those called bankers. Their job, in those places where commerce and exchanging are the main activities, consists of receiving the money that the merchants and exchange dealers deposit in their bank, and be trustees of that money, pay the amount of money ordered by the depositors, keep a written account of all the amounts received and given under their orders, have the tally with their dealings with other clients always ready. Before they assume their responsibilities, these men have to bring in guarantors and post a legal bond in those republics where they are to practice their occupation as guarantee that they will practice their occupation with integrity and pay the whole amount of what they receive in deposit.

These bankers, says Mercado, are somewhat different in Seville and in the places where they celebrate fairs, such as Medina and other similar places. Because in Seville, there are so many advantages to such deposits that they do not receive any other retribution, and they still consider it no small benefice that merchants and exchange dealers want to deposit their money in the bank, and utilize their services in that region. Navarrus says this is also what happens in Rome and in some places of the Gaul and the Spanish territories.[2] Because the bankers, with the money that has been deposited, make a profit sometimes of 2,000 or 3,000 *ducats* in three or four months, giving it for exchanges or negotiating with it during the time in which the owners do not need it, or sending merchandise to the New World and other parts, from where they obtain no small profit. Sometimes it happens, though, that when the winds of fortune change they collapse into extreme poverty, being in danger and subject to harm by those they brought in as guarantors. When they are reduced to such poverty that they cannot pay the deposits and other debts, they say the bank has gone bankrupt. But as long as fortune is not so unfavorable to them, since they have deposited the money of many merchants and exchange dealers (from Lisbon, Genoa, Florence, Medina, Toledo, etc.), and from many of these they have many thousands of *ducats*, it never happens that all the depositors need their money so that they do not leave many thousands of *ducats* in deposit, which the bankers can do business with for their benefit or loss. Because these bankers, as everybody else, are the true owners of the money that is deposited in their banks, which makes them very different from other depositaries, as we shall explain later when discussing deposits. Consequently, if the money perishes, it perishes for them and not for the depositors, as they receive the money not in custody and to give back the same numerical amount, but to be ready to give back an equal amount whenever the depositor solicits it. Therefore, they receive it as a loan, under temporary use and enjoyment, and, consequently, at their own risk, so that they return it all at once or in installments when it is required of them and in such way as is required of them.

There are other bankers, especially in the places where fairs are celebrated, who receive the money from those who want to deposit it in their bank. These pay the letters of payment that the depositors send them, give or take money according to their instructions, keep an account of everything given and received and, finally, keep the clients' accounts. For this reason, at the end of the fair they receive from each one of these the price for their work, greater or lesser according to the volume of business carried out. Mercado says that, ordinarily, these commissions furnish each banker with 1,500 or 2,000 *ducats* in each fair.

Regarding the bankers, especially those of the first type, they should be cautioned that they mortally sin if the money they have in trust is engaged in their businesses to such a great degree that they are later unable to give back in due time the amount that the depositors request or send to disburse with a charge from the money they have deposited. Also, they are compelled to restitute the damages, including the profit ceasing, of not having complied with the order they had received to pay. Because the money was received in trust with the obligation of returning it when ordered to do so, and, thus, when the time comes and they do not pay, they sin against justice and against the pact they have with the depositors, because of which they shall be compelled to restitute the damages that followed, including the profit ceasing. Also, they mortally sin if they dedicate themselves to the type of transactions where they run the risk of getting involved in a situation where they will be unable to pay for the deposits. For example, if they send such a great amount of merchandise across sea that in case of shipwrecking, or the ship being caught by pirates, it is not possible for them to pay for the deposits, not even by selling their assets. And they not only mortally sin when the business ends badly, but also even if it were to end favorably. And this for reason of the danger they exposed themselves to, causing damage to the depositors and guarantors that they had brought in themselves for the deposits.

Regarding those who deposit their money with those bankers who do not charge anything, either for the deposit or for the rest of services we mentioned before, it is uncertain if the depositors should pay them an adequate stipend (regardless of the fact that the bankers are able to obtain advantages when doing transactions with the money that has been deposited), or, if they do not, commit usury in not paying it. Navarrus responds affirmatively.[3] The following argument apparently proves this opinion: Such deposit is really a loan, as has been said, and the property of the money deposited is transferred to the banker, because of which in case it perishes, it perishes for the banker. Therefore, regardless of the profit the banker manages for himself by dealing skillfully with the money deposited, even if it were a great one, the depositors may not demand nor receive from the banker any money, nor anything that is worth [that money], for that deposit and loan. Otherwise, they would commit usury and would have to restitute what they received.

This argument proves it is about, not so much a deposit in favor of the depositor, but a loan in favor of the banker, even if *per accidens* the money that the clients enter their bank accounts happens to remain in his power, the same as the money of a loan remains in power of the borrower. That is why the argument is not as sound as it would appear on the surface. Because as we said in argument 405, when two people have a simultaneous need, one of returning a horse to a certain place and the other of renting a horse to go to that same place, either one of them may refuse to sign any other contract that is not one that cedes his service in favor of the other, for which he may receive the adequate price even if such contract brings about a great advantage for himself. Likewise, in the issue above, the banker may decide not to receive in his bank the money of others if they do not pay for the rights of custody and pay for the rest of the services he renders, and it shall be no impediment that such deposit shall provide him benefices, namely, that with such money he may carry out transactions and gain a profit. For all of this, the banker may licitly enter an agreement for an adequate stipend for such services, and may receive it regardless of obtaining a greater profit.

But on the other hand, it should be said, on the contrary, that the merchants and exchange dealers, in view of the profit the banker obtains when dealing with that money and of the need he has of it for making a profit, may not want to enter with him but a loan contract in terms that are favorable to the banker and, thus, doing him a favor by choosing him to others who would also like to [enter the contract]. It shall be no impediment to [carry this out] that with such a loan they manage to protect their money, and they get it back all at once or in installments whenever they want. Therefore, if they only had the intention of entering a loan contract, as they are capable of doing and we presume is their wish, they shall certainly not owe anything to the banker for protecting the money, [something] that is linked to the contract *per accidens*, and even if *per accidens* it happens that, as with the rest of the borrowers, they do not owe anything for such protection.

They shall not owe him anything either for the effort or for the service of counting the money, either when he receives it or when he pays it, and whether it is to the depositors themselves or to others by their orders (just as nothing is owed to other borrowers for these services, as the contract is favorable to them). Neither will they owe [the bankers] anything for reason of what is given and received, even if it is necessary to write down some documents for this, as the lender does not owe anything to the borrower for the documents that for the debts' security are signed at the time of making or paying the loan, for the borrower's own security. Because as the loan is carried out for the benefit of the borrower, it is he who has to pay for all the expenses, and not the one granting the benefice of lending.

And if the banker rendered other services to the depositor, apart from the inherent advantage to this type of loan that brings about so many benefices to him, he shall only be owed the corresponding stipend for them, unless, as is reasonable, he shall want to fulfill them gratuitously as compensation for the benefice of what it means to be chosen among all [other bankers] to carry out the deposit with him and give him access to so many advantages. Or unless he renders these services as gifts in order to attract merchants and exchange dealers to enter the money in his bank and not in others. That is why in this matter I would not worry the merchants and exchange dealers. Especially, since if a banker were ungrateful and wanted stipends on top of the great advantages and profits gained from the deposits, he would deserve the withdrawal of these. And since the merchants and exchange dealers rightly believe that these are gratuitous, if one of them did not want to carry it out [gratuitously], there shall be many others willing to readily carry it out. That is why, the merchants and exchange dealers who find out *a posteriori* that the services that they thought free of charge were not, are not forced to pay them, as they did not intend to buy them, but to receive them as compensation for the greater benefices that they were conceding with their choice, and they would have easily found someone to give them free of charge. Because of which, if the banker intends to charge for the services, he shall have to say it beforehand so that the merchants and exchange dealers are bound to pay them. We shall later explain this more carefully, when we deal with business management.

As for the second type of bankers, all the doctors agree that they can licitly receive a stipend from each one of the merchants who does business with their bank. Because receiving, counting, and safekeeping the money, counting again when returning it, carrying a record of the transactions with third parties, giving them a copy, all with the risk of making mistakes in counting, examining, settling accounts, in accepting bills of exchange from those who at that particular time do not have the money in the bank, and being responsible for their debts, all this has a price, so much the greater because in order to render these services a person of a certain category, with some talent, ability, and qualifications is required, and [so much greater] the greater the profits they earn. The stipend is not appraised by law but is left to the parties' discretion. That is why [the merchants] in whose benefit the banker renders these services usually pay the banker at the end of the fairs what is proportionate to the managed business according to the prudent man's judgment, as said earlier.

It should be noted that although in some places they have the three types of persons we have talked about in the present argument, in others, however, it is the merchants themselves who do the work of exchange dealers and call themselves bankers. What is more, in the same places where there are people who have posted a bond before the authorities in order to be depositaries and carry out the profession of bankers, there are, in addition to them, merchants who give money in exchange. And there are public bankers who practice trading with their own money, and who by their own authority grant exchanges with their own money to their own advantage or disadvantage.

14

Argument 409

On Some of the Ways in Which Money Is Paid for in the Exchanges. On Bills of Exchange. May the Bankers Licitly Receive Any Other Stipend?

In order to understand the practice of exchanging and examine if the bankers may licitly receive any other stipend, there are a few things worth examining. There are many who say that the exchanges are received in many places, but Mercado states that neither in Rome nor in Seville do they commonly receive them.[1]

There are two ways in which bankers receive the money: one, in cash, by giving currency to them; the other, by bills of exchange, or any other letter of payment given to them, by virtue of which the person who has to pay the bill starts owing the bank the amount stipulated there to be paid into the account of the person who enters the bill in the bank.

And just as there are two ways of paying the money to the banker, there are also two ways in which he can pay: one, in cash; the other, without utilizing currency and by doing one of the following: by transferring the amount to the bank account of one of the bank's debtors, from where it shall be charged; by furnishing a bill of exchange for a place where the creditor prefers; by setting up the bank as debtor for that sum in relation to the creditor who wishes the money to be paid into the account he has in the bank, or in relation to others to whom the creditor transfers the credit and they prefer to enter the amount into their bank account, or pay with it a debt that they have with the bank.

This is the reason why in the fair of Medina or in any other where many go to buy merchandise, even if there are many transactions carried out in cash, the majority are through documents that prove that the bank owes them or that it accepts paying by entering the money into the bank. This is how deals are closed, by compensating some debts with others and through the signature of bills of exchange issued to different places.

Also note that the bills of exchange are drafted utilizing several phrases and so, in some of them it says: "As soon as you receive or read the present [document]," or some such sentence. These payments are usually called "in full view," because the money has to be paid the moment the bill is shown and read. Other times it says: "On such day or in so many days, months, or whatever it is, after receiving the present [document]." In that case, the money must be paid on the appointed day. In some bills it says: "In such fair," for example, Medina or Amberes, you shall pay a certain amount. In that case, one should abide by custom, and if [custom] were that such bills had to be paid at the beginning of the fairs, then they should be paid at that time. However, I believe that usually, the custom is to pay at the end of the fairs, when there is a fixed time to pay off those debts, formalizing through signed documents the majority of the transactions that are previously carried out; since money is not so abundant that it allows buying in cash the enormous amount of merchandise that is taken there to be sold if the payment is to be carried out in cash, nor that it allows carrying out so many transactions. The merchants call this period in which accounts are closed and money is given to those who are creditors "setting up the tables"[2] for the payments in the fair, and "opening the exchanges."[3]

What Soto says[4] on fairs and the practices of exchanges is in keeping with what has been said. His sources of information are the accounts of merchants. He says that in the kingdom of Castile there are four main fairs, spread out according to the four seasons of the year, and they correspond to another four fairs in Flanders and in other places. In these fairs they accept exchanges for other fairs held in different places, and for places where they do not have fairs. In a similar way, in other places and other fairs they accept exchanges for these ones.

The first of these four fairs takes place in Medina del Campo in the month of May, and in them they set up the tables and open the exchanges on the fifteenth day of July, and the payments last until August 10. This fair corresponds to another one in Flanders in the month of September, where they set up the tables and open the exchanges on November 10, and the settlements last all month.

The second fair takes place in the other Medina, the one they call Rio Seco. There the exchanges open on September 15 and last until October 10. This fair corresponds to another in Flanders, which takes place at Christmas time. There they open the exchanges on February 10 and the settlements last until the end of the month.

The third fair takes place in Medina del Campo in October, and in it the exchanges open in December, and the settlements last until the end of the month. This fair corresponds to the fair of Resurrection in Flanders, where the exchanges open on May 10 and last all month.

The fourth fair takes places in the region of Villalón. Its exchanges open in the middle of Lent and last until Resurrection. It corresponds to the fair in Flanders in June, where the exchanges open in August and last until the end of the month.

However, sometimes the four fairs that take place in Spain, especially that of Medina del Campo, continue by order of the king until the arrival of the fleet from the New World, or for other reasons, according to Soto. The purpose of this practice of carrying out the exchanges between the Castilian fairs and those of Flanders is allowing only three months for the payment, which is the period of time until the next Flemish fair, and is considered sufficient to send the bills of exchange from Castile. Inversely, the same amount of time is granted between the fairs of Flanders and those of Castile. Because if in the fair that in May takes place in Medina an exchange dealer draws up the balance at the end of July or beginning of August for the fair of Flanders, the money should be paid in Flanders in the next fair, that is, the one in September, when the exchanges are opened there. According to Soto, the same happens regarding the other fairs that are related to each other.

The above should not be interpreted as if money in cash could not be taken for the exchanges at the beginning of the fair and during the year even if there were a need to do it; or as if the bills of exchange that have been sent in which a payment is ordered on a certain day, or as soon as they are handed over, cannot be paid at that moment and had to wait until the exchanges are open and the tables set up. Note that it is not considered that someone is buying on credit if the price is debited from his own bank account, even if the payment is not in cash for the time being, because the banker shall pay in cash whatever is the balance due, in any case at the end of the fair. In the fairs it is considered that someone is buying on credit when he buys to pay at some other time. Finally, you should know that the bills of exchange are not usually addressed to the banker, but to one of his representatives who will assume responsibility for the amounts indicated in the bills of exchange. The representative enters the money in his bank account so that the bank pays the money on the day specified in the bill of exchange—if its specifications were to pay an amount to whoever presents it—or receives the money on behalf of the one sending the bills of exchange if it is ordered in it that such amount of money be paid to its sender or representative in that place.

Once explained this, Mercado, Soto, and Navarrus[5] report than in many places the custom is that the banker, when he pays the bills of exchange in cash, charges a 5 or 6 per 1,000 over the amount paid, a commission he does not receive if the payment is not in cash but using bank accounts in any of the ways described above. Thus, when someone charges the bank what is owed to him, he receives the total amount of what the bill indicates, because when the banker enters the amount into the account he enters the total amount that he shall pay in cash when the time comes, unless there is a compensation that shall prevent him from paying in cash. However, and after all, both if he pays the total in cash as if he pays part of the amount entered, he charges a 5 or 6 per 1,000 from the amount he pays in cash. That is why the sellers of merchandise sell them more expensively to anyone paying through the bank. In addition to this, the seller shall have to wait until the end of the fair to collect. This explains why when selling in fairs, the merchants ask what the method of payment shall be before fixing a price.

In order to better understand when the things we are talking about take place, and in order to expose some abuses, we point out that when one deposits money in cash in the bank to withdraw it later, the banker does not charge this 5 or 6 per 1,000 but gives a free service. For the same reason, if the depositor sends bills of exchange, or other similar ones, so that from his money something is given to another person, the banker does not receive anything for carrying out this delivery in cash, since he does not have just motive to do so, nor do I think it is the custom. What is more, they tell me that in some places, the banker usually gives the depositor an interest of 4 or 5 per 1,000 as compensation for the profit earned from using the money deposited, and that in other places, the custom is that if the depositor has deposited, for example, 10,000 *ducats*, he obtains credit with the banker for another 5,000, so that if the depositor authorizes the bank to make payments of up to 15,000 *ducats*, the bank takes charge of them, and compels himself to pay them without getting any stipend for that greater credit and the obligations he takes on himself.

Although it seems Soto accepts this at the end of the last article,[6] both practices are usurious by nature if the banker carries them out by virtue of a pact and not out of generosity or gratitude, as it would mean a profit originated in a loan since, as we have proved before, this type of deposit is equivalent to a loan. Navarrus[7] and Mercado agree with us in the place cite above.

But if the banker were to do it out of generosity and gratitude, as a reward for the benefit received and with the intention of encouraging the depositor with this favor to continue his deposit, it shall not be usury nor sin, as long as scandal is avoided.

In the cited chapter,[8] Mercado says that this is so only when whoever sends the bill of exchange does not have any deposit in the bank where the payment is to be authorized; because, in that case, in order for the bank to feel compelled to pay that money at the end of the fair, it is an accepted custom in some places to charge a 5 or 6 per 1,000, to be paid in cash, in addition to the stipend that is usually charged for managing the business of its usual clients. He considers that this is a good enough reason, because the guarantor may licitly charge an adequate price for the obligation he assumes in lending, as we saw in argument 319. So the same may be said of the banker who assumes the obligation of paying that money at the end of the fair in the name of whoever sends the bill of exchange: He may justly receive a reward. Aside from this, Mercado points out that the bills of exchange are sent to the representative in the following way: In such a fair you shall pay 1,000 and shall consign this bill in the bank with a 6 per 1,000 commission for paying it. The point of this, he says, is that 1,006 are deposited in the bank so that whoever presents the bill can charge the total amount to the person who sold him the merchandise, and the bank pays him in this way at the end of the fair. When the banker pays in cash a part of the money at the end of the fair to the person who presented the bill, or to whoever he ordered it be paid to, the banker shall receive the 6 per 1,000 of what he paid in [cash]. The result of which is, all things considered, that those 6 per 1,000 are paid by the person who sent the bill and in it he cedes those 6 per 1,000 to whoever accepted it as means of payment. The 6 per 1,000 shall go to the banker if he pays the bill in cash. And whoever draws the bill is acting in his own interest when he concedes those 6 per 1,000, because since he does not have money in the bank, he would have to take it in exchange in his own name, and exchanges are very expensive during the fair, as there are many who want them to be able to carry out their dealings. But once the fair is over they are not as expensive. Therefore, instead of taking money in exchange they prefer to draw a bill with a 6 per 1,000 commission so that the banker takes responsibility for paying the 1,000 when the fair is over.

Soto[9] seems of this opinion, although he does not explain it as clearly, and suggests that in the kingdom of Castile the law says that those 6 per 1,000 should be paid to the banker when the payment is settled in cash. But Navarrus is right when he rejects this opinion, because if a law existed before approved by Ferdinand and Isabella, they themselves revoked it.[10] Navarrus absolutely condemns the custom of charging a 5 or 6 per 1,000 to the person to whom a payment is made by order of whomever deposited the money in the bank,[11] and says that the banker has the obligation of restituting that 6 per 1,000 to the person it was charged to. The only exception is the case where the person that should receive the restitution has already sold the merchandise at a higher price for reason of such charge, or when he simply wants to exonerate him. But in this matter mere presumption is not enough, and the reason for this is that everything the banker does he does as a service for the person who gives the order to pay that sum of money, and in whose name he acts. Therefore, it is to him he should ask for the stipend, and not to the person [the banker] pays.

Navarrus supposes that the custom is that, when the payment is in cash, they do not consign in the bank 1,000 and then 6 that the banker shall receive in the end, but only the 1,000 owed to the person for whom the money is consigned. He even says that it happened to him to go to the bank to collect some money they had sent him in a bill of exchange from another place and the banker refused to pay him without charging the 6 per 1,000, and since all his arguments were useless to convince him, he was not able to rightly receive the money. I shall give my opinion on this matter in a few conclusions.

First conclusion: In the case where the banker takes responsibility for paying an amount of money at the end of the fair on behalf of someone who does not have money deposited in the bank, it does not seem that the banker should be condemned for collecting a 6 per 1,000 of what he pays, especially if it is the custom there. This because he has just reason to charge it, namely, accepting the obligation, as Soto and Mercado rightly say.

Second conclusion: That interest should be formally or virtually paid by the person in whose name the money was entered into the bank in the first place, and not by those who are to be paid. This may be proved with Navarrus's argument: that the obligation the banker assumes, in truth, is assumed by himself and not by the person in whose name the money was first deposited, and in whose favor he pledges to carry out the payments. Therefore, that is the person who should pay the stipend, and not those to whom the payments are made. If, as Mercado says happens, someone who owes another person 1,000 *ducats* consigns 1,006 in the bank because of the stipend that the banker shall receive at the end, it is he who shall formally pay such stipend. However, if he were only to consign 1,000 because that is the value of what he bought from the other person, and this person knew about or should know about the operation, the banker would be able to retain from those 1,000 the amount corresponding to his payment and, in such case, the person in whose favor the money was consigned in the bank shall pay the stipend.

Third conclusion: When 1,000 *ducats* are consigned in the bank and that is the amount that has to be paid in cash to the person in whose name they were consigned, without [this person] having any reason to think differently, the banker may charge for himself the stipend taking it from the 1,000 *ducats* he pays in cash, as one should deem that he wanted to obligate himself with the requirement of receiving the usual stipend. It is evident that the person to whom the 1,000 were owed in their entirety has a right to request from the person who consigned the money to pay the 1,000 *ducats*.

Fourth conclusion: When there has not been a previous commitment on the banker's part to pay in cash in someone else's name, the banker may not deduct any amount from what he pays in cash, but must make do with the stipend that in any case he should collect from the person whose business he manages. This may be proved because the counting and paying of that money, if he gives it so that it is returned to him in the same place, has the characteristics of a loan, because of which he may not licitly receive more than what was loaned.

Here, I must refer to another abuse bankers usually put into practice. When there is an amount of money consigned in their bank to pay at the end of the fair, if the person for whom it was consigned in the first place in order to pay creditors from whom he has bought merchandise demands that the money be paid before the end of the fair, the bankers usually give it to him but charging the interest, which is usually charged on money given in exchange to other places or any other interest. Therefore, whatever is received in this way is usurious and must be restituted, as the anticipated payment is virtually a loan, because of which anything that is received for it shall be usury, unless it is received for reason of the profit ceasing the banker incurs when he anticipates the payment, which rarely happens. So much more shall it be considered sinful, when the time of payment comes and in order to prevent the payment from being delayed, to receive something from the creditor. So, too, do these have obligation to restitute, because everything that is received in this way is only halfway voluntary, and is received unjustly when it is not a sign of the generous spirit of the giver.

15

Argument 410

On Exchanges and the Different Value of Money in Different Places, Not in Comparison to Small Coins Any Longer but Because of Concurrent Circumstances. Thus, We End Our Study on Money.

In argument 406 we introduced a distinction in the value of money, considering it according to a double aspect. In the second of these, money, not this or that from a certain region, but all of money is worth more in one place than in another comparing equal amounts in one and the other, even if in one and the other place they are equal coins as far as material, weight, metal alloy, and the seal itself, and to which the law has assigned the same value in comparison to the other coins in the place. We were saying that this value does not originate in the currency itself, but in the circumstances, and is a very inconstant value, which is not fixed in an indivisible point but moves within certain limits. It is like the value of the other merchandise, which as long as it is not appraised by the law is not fixed in one exact point. What we are trying to find out now is if for reason of the difference in this type of value it is licit to increase the price of exchanges from one place to another or if it is more convenient to reduce it sometimes according to the greater or lesser value that money has in that place.

Soto, Navarrus, and others respond affirmatively,[1] and their opinion may be proven because the commutation of two things that are equal in value is in itself licit. Therefore, if at one point 360 *maravedis* in Flanders are worth the same as 400 in Medina (for the scarcity of coin in Flanders and the abundance in Medina, and for other concurrent reasons), it shall be licit—if all other circumstances are equal—to exchange 360 *maravedis* given in Flanders for 400 to be delivered in Medina. And, quite the contrary, it shall be licit to exchange 400 given in Medina for 360 to be delivered in Flanders, the same as it is licit to exchange 100 units of wine or oil given in the Spanish territories for 80 that are given in Flanders. And, on the contrary, 80 that are given in Flanders shall be exchanged for 100 to be given in the Spanish territories, as 80 units of wine or oil are worth in Flanders the same as 100 in the Spanish territories, reason for which wine and oil are taken to Flanders.

For this motive, it is frequently licit to exchange a greater amount of currency, which is handed over in the place where the currency is worth less, for a lesser quantity that shall be handed over where as currency it is worth more. And, quite the opposite, it is also licit to exchange a lesser amount of currency where as such currency it is worth more for a greater quantity to hand over where as currency it is worth less. According to Soto, in the cited place, and Mercado,[2] the exchange dealers take into account today this greater or lesser value of money for their exchanges from one place to another. And this is the way they justify the exchanges they carry out.

Against this argument—most important reason for the exchanges from one place to another such as they are practiced today—someone could argue: If in the place where there is less money and more need of it, it is licit to exchange a lesser amount in order to give back a greater amount where there is a greater abundance and lesser need [of it]—and this because due to circumstances, money is worth less in one place than in another—it follows that it is licit in one and the same place to exchange a smaller amount of money at the time when in that place it is scarce and there is a greater need of it, for another greater amount to give back at a time of greater abundance of money and lesser need. Now then, no one shall admit the consequent and, in consequence, neither the antecedent.

Soto, in the cited article 2, denies that one thing follows the other, and gives no other reason but that when money is given back in the same place and at a different time, it will be a loan, and for reason of the loan, nothing may be collected. But when the money is given back somewhere else there is an exchange of two things of equal value, although unequal in amount, which is licit.

However, this solution is not acceptable, because also in the loan, if what is given back is equal—at the time in which it is given back—to the value of what was loaned—at the time in which it was loaned—the contract shall be licit, without there being any problem in giving back a greater amount than what was received. For example, it shall be licit to loan 2 units of wheat at the time when each one is worth 2 *ducats* in order to get back 4 units at the time of harvest when it is estimated that each unit shall be worth 1 *ducat*, since here is seen the equality between what is given and what is received, even if there is inequality in the amount or number of units. What is more, it would be usury to lend 4 units of wheat in times in which each one is worth a *ducat* to be given back as many units when it is estimated that each shall be worth 2 *ducats*. Thus was said in its place in the ruling *Naviganti de usuries*,[3] and Soto himself approves of this. Because of which, if a lesser amount of money is now worth because of its scarcity and need the same as a greater amount shall be worth later in that same place for the abundance they expect, there is no reason to deny that one thing follows the other.

The true reason for which this inference should be denied appeared at the end of argument 406. Money, both if there is scarcity and need as if there is abundance thereof, should never be considered merchandise in relation to the place where it is, but always retains the price or value appraised by law or accepted by custom (I am talking about the countries in which the prices of coins are fixed and do not depend on the will or pact between the private persons), and, because of this, in relation to that place it is not worth more at one time than another. Its value only varies when exchanging for coins from another country, as was explained there. One should take into account, however, that for reason of profit ceasing, because money was lent at a time in which there was less abundance of it in order to get it back when there was a greater one, one may receive an increase that is equivalent to the estimated profit ceasing. For example, at a time when money is scarce and therefore the price of things drops, if the person who has money had been thinking about buying things to make a profit or to support his family and had to do without this opportunity in order to lend money to someone else, when giving the loan he may agree an increment on the loaned capital that is equivalent to the estimated profit ceasing. Likewise, the one who when lending foresees that later he will have to buy at a higher price whatever he needs for his family, may agree to an increment that is equivalent to that loss occurring. In a similar way, if he was thinking to give money in exchange for another place with a good profit, which he has to do without when accepting that the money be given back in the same place, he may agree to an increment that is equivalent to the profit he is being deprived of.

To sum up all this matter of exchanges practiced from one place to another, and bring the rest of the argument to an end, we must consider simultaneously three rulings to judge if the exchange is just or not, and to judge what increment it is just to collect in each case, and when—in order for the exchange to be just—not to collect any increment to begin with, or even to receive a sum that is inferior to the one handed out. And we are not referring here to dry exchange, which we said enough of in argument 404 but to the rest of exchanges carried out from one place to another. We shall proceed with those three rulings but not in the same order in which they were presented.

The first ruling is the different value a coin may have in comparison to the petty coins. Thus if the exchange is carried out reckoning in larger coins, such as *ducats*, *escudos*, or silver *reales* (which is the custom), and if the value of these coins is different in the place where the exchange is being carried out and in the place for which it is given, it has already been proven in argument 407 (against what some doctors think) that although one should consider somewhat this greater or lesser value, this should have a very small influence in the increase of the type of exchange, if it is to be considered just.

On the contrary, if the exchange is carried out expressing the amounts in petty coins (which is not frequently done), for example in *maravedis* to be given back in *reais* in Portugal, and vice versa, then, as the *maravedis* are worth in Castile more than the *reais* in Portugal, as was proven in that argument, one should take into consideration such difference of value. Because, abstaining from other arguments that allow the type of exchange to rise or fall, if for 374 *reais* given in Portugal an equal amount of *maravedis* were received in Castile, it would not be an exchange of equal for equal and, thus, it would be unjust and there would be obligation to restitute. Because in Portugal, for those *reais* they would give us a little over 9 silver *reales* and, in Castile, for the *maravedis*, they would give us 11 whole silver *reales*.

The second ruling is that of the formal or virtual transport of money from the place where the exchange dealer gives the money to the place where he receives it. By this ruling the exchange dealer may increase the exchange as much as the value of said transport is estimated according to the prudent people's judgment, taking into account the distance between both places, the difficulty of transport and all other circumstances, as we explained in argument 403 and the two following ones.

The third ruling is the different value of money in diverse places due to the abundance or scarcity of it, the need there is of it and other circumstances, as we have explained in the present argument and in argument 406. But although by virtue of this ruling—and the same goes for the virtual transport—it is licit to frequently increase the exchange, it happens sometimes that by reason of this ruling it shall be necessary to reduce it so that the exchange is equitable and just. For example, when the value of the money in the place in which it is given is lower in comparison to its value in the place in which it has to be received, as has already been said. And if the value of the money in the place in which it is given is inferior in an equivalent amount to the cost of transport, then, in order for the contract to be equitable and just, the exchange should be carried out for equal sums of money, compensating the cost of transport with the inferior value of money in the place where it is given. If the cost of transport were to exceed that difference, the excess may be reflected in an increment in the amount to be received for the exchange. On the contrary, if the difference exceeds [the cost of transport] then and only then shall it be necessary to increase the amount of money given in comparison to the one received in order for the contract to be just.

However, neither the cost of transport nor the excess of value that money has for this third ruling can be fixed with all precision but shall be just within certain limits. That is why it is sufficient that the contracting parties do not break away from the limits of what is just. Consequently, the bounds specifying what is just in the exchanges, taking into account all the rulings for which the type of exchange may be increased or decreased, may not be fixed with all precision, and there shall be a greater laxness the more rulings there are according to which the justice of the exchange from one place to another is to be judged.

Soto says that when this third ruling may be applied, namely, charging an increment because money is worth more where the exchange dealer hands it over than where he receives it, it is not licit to charge on top of this another increment for reason of the virtual transport of the money, unless perhaps a very small quantity.[4] This may be confirmed because when you transport for me an amount of money from a place where it is worth less to another where it is worth more, the increase in value should be in my favor, as I pay for the transport. Therefore, if the exchange dealer charges a price for the formal or virtual transport, he may not besides licitly charge more because of the greater value money has there, and, if he charges for reason of the greater value of money in that place, he may not charge for the transport, as he is not transporting anything for the person who takes the money in exchange.

Despite this argument, I believe it more plausible to state that it is licit to charge something for the virtual transport or, rather, for the discharge it means for the one asking for the exchange of not having to transport the money. This is evident because when giving the equivalent value to him in the place where he needs the money he is really discharged of the job of transporting and taking it there, and that is something that deserves remuneration and may be sold. Therefore, in order to accomplish this in his favor I may receive a just stipend, notwithstanding the fact that I may *per accidens* get the job done easily and without expense through a correspondent I have there, as was explained in argument 403. This is so because to the prudent merchants' judgment, 370 in Flanders are worth the same as 400 in Medina, for example, and apart from that, the virtual transport of money from Flanders to Medina (or rather being discharged of the need of taking care of the transport) is worth another 10. Therefore, the exchange is licit when the exchange dealer gives 400 in Medina for 370 that shall be given back in Flanders, so that 360 are given as equal value to the money he received in Medina, and the other 10 for saving the transport from Flanders to Medina. For the same reason, if the exchange dealer gives 360 in Flanders he may receive in Medina something more than 400, so that 400 are the payment for the equal value of money given in Flanders, and the excess is given for having discharged from the need of transporting the money.

The conclusion is obvious, as in neither of the two cases is there a formal transport of the money but simply an avoiding the annoyance of transporting it and, in both cases, leaving aside the amount that is received for this, there is an equality between what is given and what is received if one takes into account the difference in value of the money in one place and the other. Soto would not deny the antecedent as in such exchange nothing is received for reason of the greater value of the money in the place in which the exchange dealer gives it, as the money is worth less in Medina, where he gives it, than in Flanders, and that is why in Flanders less money is received than what is given in Medina. And Soto himself states that when an increment is not received for reason of the greater value that money has in that place, it may be received for reason of virtual transport. And notice that the exchange dealer, apart from what he receives for reason of the virtual transport, does not receive an increment either in the amount of money or in its value there where money is worth more, but there where it is worth less he receives an increment, not in the value but in the amount of money in order to compensate the greater value that his money has in the other place.

To the argument we have presented in favor of the contrary opinion we must say: in the first place, that it implies something that is false, namely, that the exchange dealer receives the money in the place where the money is worth more. Let us add that the antecedent is true when the money is really carried, but not when the equivalent is given in a place for the equivalent in another and the one who receives it saves himself the job of transporting it, because then what each one gives is valuable for him in the place where he gives it and not in any other place. Also, the person who is requested by another to discharge him through that commutation of the annoyance of transporting the money, may receive a just stipend for his involvement.

From what we have just said it is evident that one should not condemn the fact that an exchange dealer who gives 360 in Flanders receive in Medina more than what he himself gives in Medina for the 360 that they give him back in Flanders, because Soto says that when there was no difference in the value of money in two places, it was a practice in his time that an exchange dealer gave in Medina 410 in exchange for receiving 360 in Flanders, and, on the contrary, when he gave exchange in Flanders for Medina, for the 360 he gave in Flanders he received 430 in Medina. However, Soto condemns this last [case], as he says that if the first exchange was equitable, the second was not so.

In spite of this, it may be responded that both exchanges are just for the following reason: because 360 in Flanders may be worth because of the state of affairs the same as 420 in Medina, and so, if an exchange is solicited in Medina for Flanders, the exchange dealer acts justly when subtracting 10 from the 420 for the job of discharging the person who asks for the exchange. And if an exchange is solicited from Flanders to Medina, he justly adds 10 to the 420, which they are to give him back in Medina for his work in discharging the person who asks for the exchange.

As said above, the just value of money in the different places and in a certain moment in time cannot be determined with all precision but fluctuates between certain limits the same as the rest of merchandise that is not appraised by law and, since the just price of the virtual transport of money from one place to another cannot be determined with all precision either, it follows that the just price of the exchanges, not only in different places but in one and the same place and at one and the same moment in time, is situated within a range of a certain amplitude. Moreover, the circumstances that make the value of money and its transport increase or decrease change easily, all of which makes it logical for the just price of exchanges to change and be different, not only regarding exchanges between different places, but also regarding exchanges in one and the same place at different times, mainly, because when the amount of money increases or decreases, the just prices of the rest of things vary, as vary too the just profits that are pursued with the exchanges.

Because men do not want to employ their money to give exchanges unless these bring about greater benefits, otherwise, they prefer using it in other endeavors.

I would like to caution here that we do not mean that the examples presented here dealing with exchanges carried out between one place and another, and which may be found in the doctors' writings, reflect real life, as if the practice of exchanges should adjust itself to them, seeing that with the passing of time circumstances vary and we find very different practices.

Because the natural just price of all things depends on the common estimation in one place (as said in argument 348 and frequently in others), we should not consider the commonly accepted price for exchanges from one place to another unjust, but rather just and a standard to judge whether the [exchanges] that greatly move away from it because of excess or insufficiency, exceed what is just. This must be understood as long as the actual price has not been manipulated by means of monopoly or other frauds. Because if those who have the money agree that neither one of them shall give in exchange except with an agreed upon increment, and that increment exceeds the price that would be current if it were not for the monopoly, those who provoked that excessive and unjust price, certainly, do not only mortally sin but are forced to restitute that increment to those who paid it.

Likewise, if before the fair takes place, or at the very beginning of it, some take all the money there is in that place to exchange in different places in order to give it later during the fair with a much greater increment and at their own discretion to those who would need it, since they are the only ones who have money, they certainly also mortally sin, and are forced to restitute if they give it for a price that exceeds the strictly just one that would be current if it were not for them, and is the equitable [price].

Because if neither these nor the others exceeded the strictly just price, I would not force them to restitute, according to what we said on this matter in argument 345, and was later proven. There may be, certainly, a sin against charity against one's own brother and against the country, a sin that deserves being prohibited and punished, as was said before. But if any, foreseeing that the money shall be very expensive in one fair, took before [this fair] exchanges for diverse places for the amount of all the money that there is in that place, in order to give exchanges later at the maximum just price that is equitable given the circumstances, he should not be condemned of mortal sin, because in acting as he did he has used his right and has harmed no one. His actions are born of his ability and experience in doing business. This principle must be accepted as long as that usual price does not obey any ruling for which something may be obtained unjustly, as would be if for an extension in time a greater price were usually given for the money offered for exchange: that would be a sin with obligation to restitute the excessive increment, even if it is a usually accepted practice. As Navarrus well notes,[5] the abundance of buyers, when the thing is sold unjustly, does not make the price of the thing increase. Therefore, the just price of the thing is not reflected in the common use.

Finally, we must observe two things: the first, that in the exchanges sometimes by the name of *ducat* one and the same value is understood in the place where the exchange is given and in the place where it is later paid. So the increases or deductions are expressed adding or taking away *ducats* from the sum to be paid in the place for which the exchange is given. For example, in a certain place 110 or 115 *ducats* are received for which bills of exchange are given so that in another place 100 *ducats* are paid. This means that an increment of 10 or 15 *ducats* are received. I understand this to be so even when the *ducats* have a different value appraised by law or accepted by custom in the different provinces. It happens in Portugal, where the *ducat* is worth 400 *reais*, but only 10 silver *reales*, while in Castile it is worth 375 *maravedis* or also 11 silver *reales* and 1 *maravedi*. That is why, when exchanges are carried out from Castile to Portugal, expressing the sums of money in terms of *ducats*, we may apply what we have described above. As the Castilian *ducat* is worth 1 silver *real* more than the one in Portugal, if the exchange is given from Castile to Portugal with an increase of 3 or 4 percent, 100 *ducats* are received, for example, in Castile and letters of payment are given in Portugal for 113 or 114 *ducats*. Since 100 *ducats* in Castile and 110 in Portugal are equal quantities (as both quantities are worth 1,100 silver *reales*), the person who gives said exchange from Castile to Portugal receives an increment of 3 or 4 Portuguese *ducats*. And if with the same increment an exchange were given from Portugal to Castile, 100 *ducats* would be received in Portugal and bills of exchange would be given for Castile for a value of a little over $93\frac{1}{2}$ or $94\frac{1}{2}$.

Because in Flanders there were frequent variations in the value of coins, in 1527 the merchants adopted by common agreement a fixed value for those coins, which had to be maintained among them forever, even if their value changed in one region or another. And so, in the bills of exchange that were given in Flanders, they often said: You shall pay so many *ducats*, the third part, for example, in gold, and the rest in silver according to the valuation of coins in 1527.

Sometimes, however, the merchants do not use in their contracts the term *ducat* with the valuation this [coin] has in the place from which or for which the exchange is given, but with a conventional valuation that they themselves establish when the contract of exchange is drafted, namely, increasing or reducing the value of the *ducat* in the place in which the exchange is to be paid, according to the circumstances. This is the way that 100 *ducats* [worth] 360 *maravedis* were usually received in Flanders in exchange for another 100 [worth] 400 *maravedis* to be paid in Medina. And in Medina bills of exchange were given in the following way: You shall pay 100 *ducats* worth 400 *maravedis* each. And since neither then nor now did they have in Medina *ducats* with such value, the merchants gave them an imaginary reality for their exchanges and businesses. In a similar way do they "create" today *ducats* and *escudos* for different places with different values, according to what the merchants agree among themselves. Navarrus[6] was strongly against these imaginary *ducats* but then changed his mind[7] and believed they should be admitted.

The second thing that must be observed is that what has been said on this matter of exchanges should be interpreted with benevolence. Because we have stretched the doctrine to the limit of what is just in order that it may be used as a guideline to confessors and others who must respond to questions on the subject, so that they do not force the exchangers to restitute when they do not have obligation to do so, and do not condemn what does not deserve to be condemned. But that does not mean that very frequently one should not advise men to abstain themselves from such exchanges because of the abuses that in them they frequently commit and for the danger of losing the eternal salvation to which the not-too-God-fearing who devote themselves to this business expose themselves.

As far as if the intermediaries employed by the exchange dealers and all the others who help in illicit exchanges sin and are forced to restitute, what was said in argument 331 about those who cooperate with usury can also be applied to them.

NOTES

Argument 396

1. Luis de Molina's *Treatise on Money* (arguments 396–410) was originally published as part of a collection of consecutively arranged arguments on contracts in volume 2 of his multivolume work, *De iustitia et iure* (Cuenca, 1597). The full collection of these arguments on contracts, including the ones preceding 396 and following 410, can be found in Ludovico Molina, S.J., *De iustitia et iure, tomus secundus de contractibus* (Mainz, 1602). Molina makes numerous references to earlier and later arguments in the pages to follow, readers who are interested in reviewing those arguments should not hesitate to consult volume 2 of *De iustitia et iure*. The present translation of arguments 396–410 was based on the Spanish critical edition, *Tratado sobre los cambios*, edición, introducción, y notas por Francisco Gómez Camacho, S.J., in the series *Clásicos del Pensamiento Económico Español* (Madrid: Instituto de Estudios Fiscales, 1990).

2. In the original: "permuta o trueque."

3. Leg. 2. ff. de rerum permuta.

4. Diego de Covarrubias y Leyva, *De collatione veterum nummismatum* (Venice, 1581), c. 7, no. 5. Cf. Covarrubias, *Opera omnia* (Venice, 1581), t. 1.

5. *Mutuo*: Actual contract in which money, oil, grain, or any other fungible thing is given, so that the other party takes it as one's own, with the obligation to restore the same quantity and the same kind on a designated date.

6. Innominate contracts are those that lack any special nomination or classification in the law.

7. See argument 253.

8. See argument 253, where Ignacio de Lassarte quotes Padilla, Pinel, and others with whom he agrees. Ignacio de Lassarte, *De decima venditionis et permutationis* (Madrid, 1599), c. 17, no. 7.

9. Leg. 2. ff. de rerum permut.; leg. 2, C. eod. tit. (Cod. 4, 64, 2); argument 253.

10. *Quanti minoris* is the action of reducing the price for defects in an article sold.

11. Martín de Azpilcueta, *Manual de confesores y penitentes* (Salamanca, 1556), cap. 17, no. 287. Contra Domingo de Soto, *De iustitia et iure, libri decem* (Salamanca, 1553) and Silvestre de Prierias, *Sylvestrina suma, qua summa summarum merito nuncupatur* (Lyons, 1555).

12. Gloss.leg.2. C. de rerum permut. (Cod. 4, 64, 2); leg. 1. ff. eod. tit.; leg. traditionibus C. de pactis. (Cod. 2, 3, 20).

13. *Inst.* 2, 1, 1, 41.

14. Leg. 2. C. de rerum permut. (Cod. 4, 64, 2); leg. si servus, § locavi. Ff. de furt.

15. Leg. 3. ff. de pignorat actione.

16. Leg. cum precibus. C. de rerum permut. (Cod. 4, 64, 4).

17. *Ordenanzas Portuguesas*, lib. 2, tit. últ.

Argument 397

1. *Alcabala*: A tribute of a certain percentage of the price paid to the tax authorities by the seller in the contract of sale and by both contracting parties in the contract of barter.

2. Leg. sciendum, ff. de aedil. edicto.

3. *Novae Collect.*, law 2, tit. 17, lib. 9 (N. R., 9, 17, 2). N. R. is an abbreviation for *Nueva Recopilación* (i.e., *Recopilación de leyes de estos Reynos*), the principal Spanish law code of 1569. Prior to 1569 the Catholic Kings Ferdinand and Isabella assigned the title *Ordinamentum* to the collected *novellae*, that is, authoritative determinations (such as laws, edicts, judgments, and so forth) that had been compiled into various legal digests. (DMA, 7, 429–30, s.v. Law Codes: 1000–1500; and DMA, 7, 522–23, s.v. Law, Spanish).

4. See Lassarte, *De decima venditionis et permutationis*, in schollis ad leg. 2. cit., ante c. 1 and 17, no. 1.

5. Lassarte, *De decima venditionis et permutationis*, c. 17, no. 3; leg. 1, ff. de rerum permut.

6. Lassarte, *De decima venditionis et permutationis*, no. 25; Barachino Firmio, *Tractatus de gabellis* (Lyons, 1533), pt. 3, part. 8, no. 48.

7. F. Vázquez de Menchaca, *Controversiarum usu frequentium libri tres* (Barcelona, 1563), lib. 1, c. 11, no. 11; Lassarte, *De decima venditionis et permutationis*, c. 17, no. 35.

8. See arguments 257 and 258.

9. *Mutuum*: A type of loan agreement by which a lender lends money or things upon agreement that the borrower will return an equal number, type, and quality of such things at the end of the contract, with or without interest.

10. Leg. 1. ff. de rerum permut.

11. Lassarte, *De decima venditionis et permutationis*, c. 17, no. 43.

12. Antonio Gómez, *Opus praeclarum et utilissimum super legibus Tauri* (Salamanca, 1567), c. 8, no. 2; Parladorius, *De rerum quotidianarum libri duo* (Salamanca, 1595), c. 3 § 3, no. 35.

13. Leg. ex placito, C. de rerum permut. (Cod. 4, 64, 3).

14. The gloss of the *leg. Placito* (Cod. 4, 64, 3), and the *Inst.* de actionib. verb. ex permutatione seem to agree with this opinion.

15. Leg. 1. ff. de rerum permut.

16. Leg. ex placito (Cod. 4, 64, 3).

17. Gómez, *Opus*, t. 2, c. 2, no. 17.

18. Leg. contractus. C. de fide instrumentorum (Cod. 4, 21, 17). Such affirms Lassarte, *De decima venditionis et permutationis*, c. 17, no. 47, and the doctors usually.

19. Lassarte, *De decima venditionis et permutationis*, c. 17, no. 47.

20. Lassarte, *De decima venditionis et permutationis*, c. 17, no. 7.

21. Argument 382, on the sale of real property, which is subject to payment of annual payments secured by a census on the property (*censo reservativo*), and on the alcabala.

22. Parladorius, *De rerum quotidianarum*, no. 33.

23. Lassarte, *De decima venditionis et permutationis*, c. 17, no. 9; leg. 2, tit. 17, lib. 9, *Novae Collect.* (N. R., 9, 17, 2).

24. *Novae Collect.*, law 2, tit. 17, lib. 9 (N. R., 9, 17, 2).

25. Arias Pinel, *Ad rubricam et legem secundam C. de rescindenda venditione commentarii* (Salamanca, 1568), part. 2, c. 1, no. 16; Lassarte, *De decima venditionis et permutationis*, c. 17, no. 17.

26. *Novae Collect.*, law 2, tit. 17, lib. 9 (N. R., 9, 17, 2).

27. C. ad quaestiones, together with the gloss. (Cod. 4, 64, 3).

28. Lassarte, *De decima venditionis et permutationis*, c. 17, no. 18.

29. *Novae Collect.*, law 2, tit. 17, lib. 9 (N. R., 9, 17, 2).

30. In the original, "cinamomo," which may refer to the tree or to cinnamon, the aromatic substance.

31. Lassarte, *De decima venditionis et permutationis*, c. 17, no. 19.

32. *Novae Collect.*, law 2, tit. 17, no. 9 (N. R., 9, 17, 2).

33. Lassarte, *De decima venditionis et permutationis*, c. 17, no. 20.

34. Leg. Si et si. § consuluit. ff. de petit hereditatis.

35. Lassarte, *De decima venditionis et permutationis*, c. 17, no. 53.

Argument 398

1. Juan de Medina, *De cambiis* (Salamanca, 1550), q. 1.

2. Soto, *De iustitia et iure*, lib. 6, q. 8, a. 1.

3. In the original: "permutador o permutante."

4. Covarrubias, *De collatione veterum nummismatum*, c. 7, in princ. ad finem no. 4.

5. *Vanquero* becomes *banquero* or banker.

6. Conrado de Summenhart, *Opus septipartitum de contractibus* (Hannover, 1500), q. 99; Medina, *De cambiis*, q. 1.

7. Soto, *De iustitia et iure*, lib. 6, q. 8, a. 2.

8. Azpilcueta, *Manual*, cap. 17, no. 286; Martín de Azpilcueta, *Comentario Resolutorio de Usuras* (Salamanca, 1556), no. 10.

9. A bull is an occasional letter issued by the Roman Pontiffs of their most important utterances. The quasi-official collection of bulls and briefs is known as the *Bullarium Romanum* and includes encyclicals, motu proprios, and other similar constitutions that possess just the same force, as sources of the canon law, as the decretals one would expect to find there. After the thirteenth century, due largely to the great codifying and systematizing work of Innocent III, bulls are commonly classified as either *tituli* or *mandamenta*. The *tituli* were for the most part acts of grace (*indulgentiae*), concessions of privileges, confirmations, decisions on points of doctrine or law, and so forth. Whereas the *mandamenta* represented the ordinary correspondence of the Holy See. They were orders of the Pope, commissions to conduct an inquiry or to reform abuses, letters written to communicate some important

knowledge, or to invite the cooperation of temporal sovereigns, or to prescribe a line of conduct for clergy or laity. It is important to note that the decretals, upon which the structure of canon law was built, almost always took the form of lesser bulls, that is, simple letters or *mandamenta*. The first known *Bulla in Coena Domini*, containing the "Reserved Cases" of the Holy See, issued by Urban V in 1364, was a *mandamentum*. The range and scope of issues that this particular bull addressed grew over time and included such items as how to handle tyrannical princes, usury, and matters pertaining to coinage. (ERE, II, 891–97, s.v. Bulls and Briefs) By the time of Pius V's pontificate (1566–1572), the *Bulla in Coena Domini* was used effectively to address a wide range of issues pertaining to commercial ethics and to assert the supremacy of the Holy See over the civil power.

10. *Ordenanzas Portuguesas*, lib. 4, tit. 14, § antepenúlt.

11. Azpilcueta, *Manual*, cap. 17, no. 286; Azpilcueta, *Comentario*, no. 10.

12. Medina, *De cambiis*, q. 2; Conrado, *Opus septipartitum de contractibus*, q. 99, suppositione 5.

Argument 399

1. N. R., 5, 18, 1.

2. N. R., 5, 21, 62.

3. Azpilcueta, *Comentario*, cap. final.

4. *Ordenanzas Portuguesas*, part. 4, tit. II, law 4, § 9.

5. Tomás de Vio Cajetan, *De cambiis* (Milan, 1499), tract. 7, caps. 1, 6.

6. Medina, *De cambiis*, q. 2 and q. 1, § penúlt; Soto, *De iustita et iure*, lib. 6, q. 9; Azpilcueta, *Manual*, cap. 17, no. 288; Azpilcueta, *Comentario*, no. 19; Conrado, *Opus septipartitum de contractibus*, q. 99, concl. 5; Gabriel Biel, *Commentarii doctissimi in IV sententiarum libros* (Brescia, 1574), dist. 15, q. 11, a. 3, dub. 12; John Major, *In quartum sententiarum quaestiones utilissimae* (Paris, 1521), q. 37; Covarrubias, *De collatione veterum nummismatum*, cap. 7, no. 4, in prin.; Silvestre, *Suma*, verb. usura, t. 4, q. 7, pronunc. 3.

7. N. R., 5, 18, 1.

8. Gutiérrez, *Practicarum Quaestionum circa Leges Regias Hispaniae* (Salamanca, 1589), lib. II, q. 178.

9. Medina, *De cambiis*, q. 9 § últ.; Cajetan, *De cambiis*, cap. 6.

Argument 400

1. *Ochavo*: Means both one-eighth and the Spanish copper coin weighing an eighth of an ounce and worth 2 *maravedis*.

2. *Liga*: Mix, blend.

3. Covarrubias, *De collatione veterum nummismatum*, cap. 3, no. 2, in pr; no. 2 § 1; N. R., 5, 21, 1.

4. This is a reference to the monetary policy promulgated by King Ferdinand II of Aragón (1452–1516) and Queen Isabella (1451–1504) in Medina del Campo in 1497.

5. *Aúreo*: Gold coin.

6. N. R., 5, 21, 4.

7. Covarrubias, *De collatione veterum nummismatum*, cap. 3, no. 2, in princ; no. 4, § 1; N. R., 5, 21, 10.

8. Charles I of Hapsburg (1500–1558), later became Emperor Charles V of the Holy Roman Empire. As the son of Philip the Handsome, Duke of Burgundy, and Joanna, third child of Ferdinand of Aragón and Isabella of Castile, he was heir presumptive to an empire vaster than Charlemagne's, and over which the "sun never set." The empire included the Netherlands and claims to the Burgundian circle; it included Castile, Aragón, the conquered kingdoms of Navarre and Granada, Naples, Sicily, Sardinia, the conquests of the New World, and possessions in North Africa, all of which after the death of Ferdinand he ruled jointly with his mad mother; and it included the Hapsburg duchies of Austria with rights over Hungary and Bohemia, inherited from his paternal grandfather, Emperor Maximilian I. The main objective of his reign was not new conquest but the protection and consolidation of his inheritance, which he sought to accomplish through strategic matrimonial alliances. But, as it turns out, his reign would be plagued with international conflict that would eventually overcome him. The conflicts were exacerbated by the Lutheran Reformation in Germany. Shortly before his death, Charles' proposal of the succession of his son Philip to the imperial title was rejected at the Diet of Augsburg and that event, in conjunction with several other blows, led him to abdicate his office. He gave the governments of the Netherlands, Spain, and Sicily to Philip. To Ferdinand he handed over the Hapsburg Empire, but not the title of Emperor, which he retained until 1558. (NCE, III, 503–06, s.v. Charles V, Holy Roman Emperor)

9. N. R., 5, 21, 46.

10. N. R., 5.

11. Philip II (1527–1598), son of Charles I of Spain (the Emperor Charles V) and Isabella of Portugal, began his reign in 1543 as regent in Spain during his father's absence in Germany. In 1556 Philip succeeded to the throne, which included the crown of Castile with Navarre and the Indies, the crown of Aragón-Catalonia with Sardinia, and the crown of Sicily: a veritable world empire. But financial difficulties forced him to settle in Spain, impose his authority, and withdraw from the widespread commitments of his father. He distrusted subordinates and governed as an absolute monarch, but he always respected the autonomous status of the constituent kingdoms. (NCE, XI, 272–73, s.v. Philip II, King of Spain) Philip II's monetary policy originated in the parliamentary assembly of Madrid in 1566.

12. In the original, "ley."

13. N. R., 5, 21, 13.

14. N. R., 5, 24, 4. (N. N. R., 9, 10, 19).

15. N. R., 5, 21, 2.

16. *Ordenanzas Portuguesas*, part. 4, law 4, § 4.

17. The double marriage between the king of Portugal, João III (1521–1557) and Dona Catarina, sister of the Holy Roman Emperor Charles V, in 1525, and between João's sister Isabella and the Holy Roman Emperor in 1526, "constituted a stunningly prestigious diplomatic victory for Portugal and a testimony to its wealth. In the 1540s, a similar double marriage, between the crown princes of Portugal and Spain and their respective sisters, prepared the ground for the eventual union of Portugal and Hapsburg Spain in 1580." (EtR, 5, 135, s.v. Portugal)

18. *Ordenanzas Portuguesas*, part. 5, tit. 8, law 1.

19. Sebastian of Portugal (1554–1578) succeeded to the throne in 1557 following the death of Dom João III. Sebastian, a young child and grandson to Dom João III, now embodied all the hopes of the Avis dynasty. But Sebastian was chronically ill, both physically and mentally. Though he lived into adulthood, his weakness and unwillingness to leave an heir left considerable doubts about the dynasty's future. These doubts were realized in 1578

when Sebastian was killed in the battle of Alcacer Kebir (Qsar al-kabir), in an ill-conceived attempt to rekindle the Portuguese conquest in Morocco. His elderly great-uncle, Cardinal Dom Henrique, a caretaker king, proved unable to manage a smooth dynastic transition. A brief war of succession ensued in 1580, but Philip II of Spain met little resistance in laying claim to the throne of Portugal, which temporarily united Spain and Portugal. (EtR, 5, 135, s.v. Portugal)

Argument 401

1. Medina, *De cambiis*, q. 3, § antepenúlt.
2. *Ordenanzas Portuguesas*, lib. 5, tit. 6, § últ.
3. *Extravagantes*, pt. 4, tit. 11, law 3.
4. N. R., 5, 21, 67 (N. N. R., 12, 8, 3); N. R., 8, 17, 6 (N. N. R., 18, 8, 2).
5. The title "Catholic King" or "Catholic Kings" refers in the singular either to Ferdinand II of Aragón (1452–1516), son of John II of Aragón and Johanna Enríquez or, in the plural, to Ferdinand II of Aragón and Isabella (1451–1504), daughter of John II of Castile and Isabella of Portugal.
6. Medina, *De cambiis*, q. 3, § antepenúlt.
7. Soto, *De iustitia et iure*, lib. 6, q. 9; Azpilcueta, *Manual*, cap. 17, no. 288; Azpilcueta, *Comentario*, cap. últ., no. 20; Covarrubias, *De collatione veterum nummismatum*, cap. 7, no. 3, in Princ.; Silvestre, *Suma*, verb. usura, 4, q. 3; Cajetan, *De cambiis*, cap. 6.
8. N. R., 5, 21, 13.
9. In the original, "epiqueya."
10. That is, the *Nueva Recopilación* mentioned earlier in note 3, argument 397.

Argument 403

1. Conrado, *Opus septipartitum de contractibus*, q. 99, concl. 4 and 11, reg. 3; concl. 12, corol. 3, 5, and others, especially 12; Medina, *De cambiis*, q. 4; Soto, *De iustitia et iure*, lib. 6, q. 10, art. 1; Cajetan, *De cambiis*, caps. 1 and 6; Azpilcueta, *Manual*, cap. 17, no. 289; Azpilcueta, *Comentario*, cap. final, no. 21; Biel, *Commentarii*, dist. 15, q. 11, art. 3, dub. 12; Major, *In quartum sententiarum quaestiones utilissimae*, q. 37; *Ordenanzas Portuguesas*, lib. 4, tit. 14, § 5.

Argument 404

1. *Ordenanzas Portuguesas*, lib. 4, tit. 14, § 6.
2. Conrado, *Opus septipartitum de contractibus*, q. 99; Cajetan, *De cambiis*, cap. 6; Soto, *De iustitia et iure*, lib. 6, q. 10, art. 1; Azpilcueta, *Manual*, cap. 17, nos. 289, 290, 294; Azpilcueta, *Comentario*, cap. final, no. 25; Medina, *De cambiis*, qq. 4 and 5.
3. Cajetan, *De cambiis*, cap. 6; Azpilcueta, *Comentario*, cap. final, nos. 62, 63.
4. Azpilcueta, *Manual*, cap. 17, no. 301.

Argument 405

1. Soto, *De iustitia et iure*, lib. 6, q. 10, art. 1; Medina, *De cambiis*, q. 5.
2. Soto, *De iustitia et iure*, lib. 6, q. 10, art. 1; Azpilcueta, *Manual*, cap. 17, no. 290; Azpilcueta, *Comentario*, cap. final, no. 28.
3. N. R., 5, 18, 8 (N. N. R., 9, 3, 3).

Argument 407

1. Azpilcueta, *Manual*, cap. 17, no. 295; Azpilcueta, *Comentario*, cap. últ, nos. 60 and 61.
2. Soto, *De iustitia et iure*, lib. 6, q. 12, art. 1.
3. Azpilcueta, *Comentario*, cap. últ., no. 30.

Argument 408

1. *Bética*: Relative to that old Roman province, today Andalucía.
2. Azpilcueta, *Manual*, cap. 17, no. 293.
3. Azpilcueta, *Comentario*, cap. últ., no. 40; Azpilcueta, *Manual*, cap. 17, no. 295.

Argument 409

1. Tomás de Mercado, *Summa de tratos y contratos de mercaderes* (Seville, 1571), cap. 13.
2. In the original: "montar las mesas."
3. In the original: "abrir los cambios."
4. Soto, *De iustitia et iure*, lib. 6, q. 12, art. 2.
5. Mercado, *Summa*, cap. 13; Soto, *De iustitia et iure*, lib. 6, q. 11; Azpilcueta, *Comentario*, cap. últ., no. 37; Azpilcueta, *Manual*, cap. 17, no. 293.
6. Soto, *De iustitia et iure*, lib. 6, q. 11, art. últ., ad finem.
7. Azpilcueta, *Comentario*, cap. últ., no. 4; Azpilcueta, *Manual*, no. 293; Mercado, *Summa*, cap. 13.
8. Mercado, *Summa*, cap. 13.
9. Soto, *De iustitia et iure*, lib. 6, q. 11, art. 1.
10. N. R., 5, 18, 5.
11. Azpilcueta, *Comentario*, no. 37; Azpilcueta, *Manual*, cap. 17, no. 293.

Argument 410

1. Soto, *De iustitia et iure*, lib. 6, q. 12, art. 2; Azpilcueta, *Comentario*, cap. últ., nos. 51, 59, 65; Azpilcueta, *Manual*, cap. 17, no. 294.
2. Soto, *De iustitia et iure*, lib. 6, q. 12, art. 2; Mercado, *Summa*, lib. *De los cambios*, caps. 5ff.
3. Gregory IX (1170–1241) was elected to the papacy in 1227. In addition to a strained relationship with Emperor Frederick II, Gregory's pontificate was marked by a continuous battle against heresy as indicated by the constitutions inserted into the *Corpus iuris canonici*, among which was included the ruling *Naviganti de usuries*. This famous ruling condemned all known forms of usury and became the starting point for subsequent learned discussion of the intricacies pertaining to usury doctrine throughout the medieval and early modern eras. (NCE, VI, 775–77, s.v. Gregory IX, Pope) Azpilcueta quotes from the *Naviganti* ruling in the preface to his *Commentary on the Resolution of Money* and makes several references to it subsequently.
4. Soto, *De iustitia et iure*, lib. 6, q. 12, art. 2.
5. Azpilcueta, *Comentario*, cap. últ., no. 59.
6. Azpilcueta, *Comentario*, cap. últ., no. 53.

PART THREE

A Treatise on the Alteration of Money (1609)

Juan de Mariana, S.J.

INTRODUCTION

Lord Acton stated that "the greater part of the political ideas of Milton, Locke, and Rousseau may be found in the ponderous Latin of Jesuits."[1] The late-scholastic period (approximately 1300–1600) generated some of the most detailed moral analyses of social issues ever produced by Christian writers. In particular, the moral theologians working from, and around, the University of Salamanca in Spain offered penetrating insights into economics, politics, and other social concerns. Prominent among the Latin Jesuits was Father Juan de Mariana.

Juan de Mariana, S.J. (1536–1624) was one of the most extraordinary persons of his time.[2] He achieved acclaim for his works *On Monarchy* (*De rege et regis institutione*)[3] and *History of Spain*.[4] John Neville Figgis wrote concerning one chapter of Mariana's book on the monarchy: "The course of the argument is singularly instructive, and much of it might have been written by Locke."[5] Mariana's treatise on money, presented here for the first time in English, also should have earned him a reputation as one of the most profound economic thinkers of his period.

While pursuing my economic education, I had the privilege of studying and living in the area where Mariana spent most of his life—Toledo, in the heart of Castile. Walking the same cobblestone streets, trekking across the countryside where luxurious villas still dot the landscape as they did in Mariana's day, one cannot but notice the confluence of Jewish, Muslim, and Christian cultures. When one reads Mariana's *History of Spain*, one enters the heart of this rich cultural mix. Reading *On Monarchy*, one gets inside the palaces, court disputes, and the dilemmas of authority that characterized the day.

When Mariana was twenty-three years old, just before his ordination, he was asked to teach philosophy and theology at the prestigious Roman College. It was there that he had Saint Robert Cardinal Bellarmine, S.J.,[6] as a student. Bellarmine spent eleven years teaching at the Roman College (starting in 1576). Bellarmine, who was later made a cardinal and canonized, had political beliefs similar to those of Mariana. Their ideas have been regarded by many as having influenced some of the intellectual movements behind the founding of the American Republic. More generally, the Jesuits were seen as influencing the turn in the seventeenth and eighteenth centuries away from the theory and practice of despotism by divine right and toward the rehabilitation of medieval notions of natural rights and duties, constitutionalism, and popular sovereignty.[7]

When he was thirty-three, Mariana was asked to teach at the University of Paris, the most renowned institution of higher learning at the time. Health problems, however, forced him to return to Spain only four years later. It was there that he wrote his *History of Spain* (1592) and his treatise *On Monarchy* (1599). The work, requested by Philip II and dedicated to Philip III, gained notoriety upon the assassination of Henry IV of France in 1610. Mariana's argument that kingly power derives from the people, some believed, had provided justification for tyrannicide. In some circles, though, Mariana became an unpopular figure, especially in France. Unsurprisingly, Henry's IV's assassin had never heard of him. J. Balmés questions: "Is it not, therefore, remarkable, that the famous book [*De rege*] ... which was burned at Paris by the hand of the public executioner, had been published in Spain eleven years before, without the least obstacle to its publication, either on the part of the ecclesiastical or civil authority?"[8]

Mariana further immersed himself in controversy with the publication of his attack on monetary debasement and accusation of fraud against Spanish fiscal officials.[9] The last decade of his life was more peaceful, as he confined himself to a scholarly treatment of Scripture. Mariana died in Toledo in 1624. Talavera, his place of birth, honored him with a monument in 1888.

The translation of *De monetae mutatione*, Mariana's treatise on currency debasement, gives the reader a glimpse of Mariana's knowledge of history and political science, tackling the topic with an economic profundity that I have not been able to find in any other previous work on political economy.

Given contemporary specialization in the academy, many readers might at first be puzzled as to why a moral theologian would write a treatise on money. The scholastic thinkers were, however, men of wide and deep knowledge. For most of them, moral analysis was their primary concern. Yet, as good moral theologians, they understood that performing proper moral analysis requires a practical understanding of the matter at hand. If one wants to understand just prices and fairness in market exchanges, one first has to understand price theory and how a market operates. In Mariana's case, the issue before him was monetary policy and its effects on the common good of the kingdom. He wrote this treatise to offer his insights to the king, advising him on how to protect the economic well-being of the land. As such, it is not only a moral examination of monetary policy but also a brilliant economic treatise.

Mariana is still best known for his historical contributions. John Laures, S.J., wrote that Mariana's *History of Spain* "is still considered a masterpiece of classical

Spanish style."[10] Nor did his historical work pass unnoticed by the Founding Fathers of America. In fact, Thomas Jefferson recommended and sent Mariana's *History of Spain* to James Madison.[11] Yet, Edwin R. A. Seligman states in the introduction to Laures's study on Mariana's monetary theories: "Mariana's fame or, rather, his notoriety as a defender of monarchy, has caused the modern world entirely to overlook his substantial achievement in the field of economics."[12]

Still, Mariana's attributes as an economist were rightly noted by Oscar Jàszi and John D. Lewis, who, in their work of political science, *Against the Tyrant*, stated that Mariana was an "acute political economist."[13] Mariana's major topic as an economist—monetary theory—was a controversial one in the context of sixteenth- and seventeenth-century monarchical absolutism. George Albert Moore, in his outstanding introduction to Mariana's *De rege et regis institutione*, explains the hazards of the subject matter:

> The *De monetae mutatione* likewise was a dangerous subject, for, as Bodin points out in his Response to Malestroit's *Paradoxes*, this matter of depreciating the currency was the peculiar graft of the kings and princes. This tract caused him to be imprisoned from four months to a year, the loss of his papers, which it seems were never returned to him, a threat of dire action by the dread Inquisition, and all this in his advanced age.[14]

Henry Hallam, the great historian of the Middle Ages, labeled the usual practice of monetary debasement as an "extensive plan of rapine" and "as mingled fraud and robbery."[15] Castelot, writing about Mariana in the *Palgrave's Dictionary of Political Economy*, also mentions that this writing caused him to be "confined for a year in the convent in Madrid."[16] In spite of opposition, Mariana fearlessly maintained (in the *Monetae*) that the "king, having no right to tax his subjects without their consent, had no right to lower the weight or quality of the coinage without their acquiescence." In an era in which monarchs regularly abused monetary power at the expense of their nation's citizens, Mariana defended those citizens and demanded responsible use of the government mints.

In this treatise, we find an insightful analysis concerning how monetary debasement and inflation increase prices, which proceeds to illustrate how such increases do not affect everyone equally—in effect, causing a revolution in fortunes. In a parallel argument, Mariana explains how government, if given control of other forms of private property, would also debase the values of those forms and use them according to its own interests.

Mariana understood that currency debasement threatened the entire economic order of the kingdom. Property rights, the ability to trade goods and services, and fair wages—all of these things require stable currency. To cite Mariana:

> But if a prince is not empowered to levy taxes on unwilling subjects, and cannot set up monopolies for merchandise, he is not empowered to make fresh profit from debased money. These strategies aim at the same thing: cleaning out the

pockets of the people and piling up money in the provincial treasury. Do not be taken in by the smoke and mirrors by which metal is given a greater value than it has by nature and in common estimation. Of course, this does not happen without common injury. When blood is let by whatever device or strategy, the body will certainly be debilitated and wasted. In the same way, a prince cannot profit without the suffering and groans of his subjects.

A short-sighted optimism caused by a reduction in monetary debasement during the last decade of the twentieth century might lessen the impact of this first English edition of Mariana's treatise on currency debasement. Yet, governments throughout the world still regard the control of money as an essential tool and sometimes use it to debauch their citizens rather than to protect them. Reading this text, one is struck by the urgency of Mariana's entreaties as he bluntly challenges his reader to show him where his analysis is wrong.

But why, one may ask, does Mariana's text have such an urgency, so much so that he is prepared to use awkward phrasing or avoid detailed explanation of certain events and matters because Mariana is, as he himself states, "hurrying to end this discussion?" For one thing, the perils emanating from currency debasement that Spain and its empire faced at the time of this treatise's composition were great. Calamities had befallen the kingdoms of the Iberian peninsula in the past as a result of debasement. Hence, we discover Mariana stating: "What has happened will happen. Previous events are very influential: They convince us that what sets out on the same path will reach the same conclusion."

However, also blended into this treatise are constant references to the manner in which the act of currency debasement defies "right reason." This is not coincidental. Like others from the School of Salamanca, Mariana belonged to the natural-law tradition, of which the Roman Catholic Church has been the staunchest defender for almost two thousand years. In short, the evil of currency debasement is derived from deeper sources than its immediate economic consequences. To Mariana's mind, the very act of currency debasement is *in itself* evil. In Mariana's treatise, we do not find a trace of the consequentialist mentality that has proved so destructive of sound moral thinking since the nineteenth century.[17] The act of defrauding people is, in each and every instance, *wrong* and consequently threatens the salvation of persons engaging in such activity. This sobering thought is perhaps Mariana's most important warning to those contemplating equivalent monetary manipulations today.

—Alejandro A. Chafuen

Notes

1. John Emerich Edward Dalberg Acton, *The History of Freedom and Other Essays* (New York: Classics of Liberty Library, 1993), 82.

2. For an excellent biography, see G. Kasten Tallmadge, "Juan de Mariana," in *Jesuit Thinkers of the Renaissance*, ed. Gerard Smith, S.J. (Milwaukee: Marquette University Press, 1939), 157–92.

3. Juan de Mariana, S.J., *The King and the Education of the King*, trans. G. A. Moore (Chevy Chase, Md.: Country Dollar Press, 1948). Moore's introduction is a superb analysis of Mariana's life.

4. Juan de Mariana, S.J., *History of Spain*, trans. Captain John Stevens (London: Richard Sare, Francis Saunders, and Thomas Bennett, 1699).

5. Figgis wrote further: "It is notable that, although deciding in chapter 2 that monarchy is the best form of government, Mariana would yet surround his king with all sorts of limitations, so that he really leaves the sovereignty with the people." John Neville Figgis, *The Divine Right of Kings*, 2d ed. (Cambridge: Cambridge University Press, 1922), 219–20.

6. Lord Acton described Bellarmine as "the most famous controversialist of the sixteenth century" and "one of the masters of revolutionary Catholicism, and a forerunner of Algernon Sidney." Acton, *Lectures on Modern History* (London: Macmillan, 1929), 169.

7. See, for instance, Moorhouse F. X. Millar, S.J., "Scholasticism and American Political Philosophy," in *Present-Day Thinkers and the New Scholasticism*, ed. John S. Zybura (St. Louis: Herder, 1927), 301–41.

8. J. Balmés, *European Civilization: Protestantism and Catholicity* [*sic*] *Compared*, 3d ed. (London: Burns and Lambert, 1861), 296.

9. *New Catholic Encyclopedia*, s.v. "Mariana, Juan de."

10. John Laures, S.J., *The Political Economy of Juan de Mariana* (New York: Fordham University Press, 1928), 3.

11. Thomas Jefferson, *Jefferson: Autobiography, Notes on the State of Virginia, Public and Private Papers, Addresses, Letters* (New York: Library of America, 1984), 820–25.

12. Laures, *Political Economy*, v.

13. Oscar Jàszi and John D. Lewis, *Against the Tyrant* (Glencoe, Ill.: Free Press, 1957), 68.

14. Mariana, *The King and the Education of the King*, 79–80.

15. Henry Hallam, *View of the State of Europe during the Middle Ages*, 4th ed. (London: Alex Murray and Son, 1868), 110–11.

16. André Castelot, "Juan de Mariana, S.J.," in *Palgrave's Dictionary of Political Economy* (London: Macmillan, 1926), 2:692.

17. For a devastating critique of consequentialism, see John Finnis, *Natural Law and Natural Rights* (Oxford: Oxford University Press, 1993), 112–19, 131–32.

A Treatise on the Alteration of Money (1609)

Juan de Mariana, S.J.

Translation by Patrick T. Brannan, S.J.

ARGUMENT

At the time that there was a great shortage of money in Spain and the treasury was completely exhausted by long and drawn-out wars in many places and by many other problems, many ways to make up for this shortage were thought out and tried. Among others, consideration was given to the debasing of money, and that in two ways: First, by doubling the value of existing money, the king gained a good deal: half of the entire sum, which was huge—a great profit in the situation! Second, new money was minted from pure copper with no addition of silver, as was customary. Rather, their weight was diminished by half. In this way, the king profited by more than two-thirds. Men's plans are not provident. Seduced by present abundance, they gave no consideration to the plan's inherent evils into which they were rushing. There were, however, those who were more cautious because of their knowledge of history and past evils, and they criticized this approach within their own circles and even in writing. Very soon, events proved that they were not foolish prophets. Things got worse. Some convenient reason was being sought for destroying or recalling that money. Some consultants recommended the debasement of silver money to make up, with that profit, for the loss that they saw was necessarily coming because of the old copper money. The cure was more deadly than the disease. It has been rejected until the present. Rather, there was a recent decree recalling a large part of the new money, and for compensating the owners from the royal revenues. Such was the occasion for a new effort to publish this treatise, which we began earlier. It aims at letting other generations learn from our misfortunes that money is hardly ever debased without calamity to the state: Profit for the moment is intimately connected with manifold ruin along with rather great disadvantages.[1]

PREFACE

May the immortal God and all his saints grant that my labors may benefit the public, as I have always prayed. The only reward that I seek and wish is that our king, his advisers, and other royal ministers entrusted with the administration of affairs, may carefully read this pamphlet. Here I have clearly, if not elegantly, attempted to illustrate certain excesses and abuses, which, I think, must be strenuously avoided. The point at issue is that copper money, as minted in the province today, is of inferior quality to earlier coins.

Indeed, this practice inspired me to begin and complete this slight, but not insignificant, endeavor without consideration of men's judgment. Doubtless, some will indict me for boldness and others for rash confidence. But, reckless of danger, I do not hesitate to condemn and revile things that men of greater prudence and experience considered a cure for ills. Nonetheless, my sincere desire to help will deliver me in part from such accusations and faults, and the fact of the matter is that nothing expressed in this controversy is original with me. When the entire nation, old and young, rich and poor, educated and uneducated, is shouting and groaning under this burden, it should not seem remarkable that from this multitude someone dares to put in writing something that is censured with some emotion in public and in secret gatherings, and in squares and the streets. If nothing else, I shall fulfill the rightful duty that a well-read man should exercise in the state, since he is not unaware of what has happened in the history of the world.

The famous city of Corinth, as Lucian[1] tells us, knew from reports and rumors that Philip of Macedon[2] was hastening against it in arms. The citizens, in fear, acted swiftly: Some prepared arms; others fortified the walls; others prepared provisions and instruments of war. Diogenes the Cynic[3] was living in that city, and when he saw that he was not invited to have any part in the work and preparation and was considered useless by everyone, he came out of the barrel in which he used to live, and began to roll it quite eagerly up and down. The citizens, indignant inasmuch as he seemed to make fun of the common calamity, asked him what he was doing. He answered: "It is not right for me alone to be at leisure when everyone else is busy." At Athens again, as Plutarch[4] tells us, when there was civil unrest and all parties were bent on revolution, Solon,[5] no longer able to help the fatherland because of his age, took his stand in arms before the doors of his house, to show that he wished to help despite his lack of physical strength. Ezekiel[6] says that even the trumpeter does his duty if, at the appointed times, he blows into his instrument and his blast sounds—now attack, now retreat—at the leader's command, even though the soldiers may not follow the commands.

At a time when some are restrained by fear, others held, as it were, in bondage by ambition, and a few are losing their tongues and stopping their mouths because of gold and gifts, this pamphlet will achieve at least one goal: All will understand that there is someone among the people who defends the truth in his retirement, and points out the public threat of dangers and evils if they are not confronted with dispatch. Finally, like Diogenes, I will appear in public, I will rattle my barrel; I will openly assert what I think—whatever the final outcome. Perhaps my earnest activity will be of some use, since everyone desires the truth and is eager to help. May my readers be open to this instruction. It was undertaken with a sincere heart. To this end, I pray to our Heavenly Majesty and to our earthly majesty who is his vicar, and to all the citizens of heaven as well. And I earnestly entreat men, of every condition and dignity, not to condemn my undertaking, or pass negative judgment on it, before they have read this pamphlet carefully and assiduously examined the question at issue. In my opinion, it is the most serious of issues to arise in Spain in many years.

1

Does the King Own His Subjects' Goods?

Many enhance kingly power beyond reasonable and just limits—some to gain the prince's favor and to amass private wealth. These most pestilent of men are not concerned with honesty and are commonly found in the courts of princes. Others reason to the conviction that an increase in royal majesty enhances the protection of public welfare. But they are mistaken. As in the case of other virtues, power has definite limits, and when it goes beyond limits, power does not become stronger but rather becomes completely debilitated and breaks down. For, as the experts say, power is not like money. The more gold that one amasses, the richer and happier one is. Power, rather, is like nourishment; the stomach groans equally if it lacks food or is burdened with too much food. It is bothered in either case.

But royal power increased beyond its limits is proven to degenerate into tyranny, a form of government that is not only base but weak and short-lived. No power and no arms can withstand the fury of its offended subjects and enemies. Surely, the very nature of royal power—if it is legitimate and just, arises from the state—makes clear that the king is not the owner of his subjects' private possessions. He has not been given the power to fall upon their houses and lands, and to seize and set aside what he will. According to Aristotle, the first thing that brought kings to eminence was their protection of citizens from the impending enemy storms when their people were mustered around their standards.[1] Thereafter, in time of peace, they were given in time the power to punish the guilty, and the authority to settle all litigation among their people. To protect this authority in a dignified manner, the people established fixed revenue by which the kings could support their original lifestyle and they also decided how this money was to be paid. This process establishes the king's right of ownership over those revenues that the state conferred, as well as of those possessions that he acquired as a private citizen, or that he received from the people after becoming king. But he does not exercise dominion over those things that the citizens have kept either publicly or privately to themselves, for neither the power conferred upon the leader in time of war nor the authority to govern subjects, grants the authorization to take possession of the goods of individuals. And so, in the chapter of the *Novellas* constitutiones, beginning "Regalia," which treats of all aspects of the royal office, such dominion is not found.[2]

Indeed, if the possessions of all subjects were under the king's will, the actions of Jezebel, as she appropriated Naboth's vineyard, would not have been censured so severely.[3] If she had been just pursuing her own rights, or those of her husband who was certainly king, she would have been claiming what was her own. Had this been true, Naboth would have been accused of contumacy for unjustly refusing to pay his debt. Therefore, it is the common opinion of legal experts (as they explain in the last law of the chapter, "Si contra ius vel utilitatem publicam"[4] and, as Panormitanus[5] presents it, in chapter 4, *De iureiurando*) that kings cannot ratify any law that would harm their subjects without the consent of their people. Specifically, it is criminal for kings to strip their people of their goods, or part of their goods, and to claim these goods as their own. Indeed, it would not be legal to initiate a suit against the prince and to set a day for trial, if everything were under his power and law. The response would be automatic: If he has stripped anyone of anything, he did not do it unjustly but of his own right. He would not purchase private homes or land when he needed them but would seize them as his own. It is useless to develop this obvious point further: Lies cannot destroy it; no flattery can present darkness as full day. On the one hand, it is the essence of a tyrant to set no limits to his power, to consider that he is master of all. A king, on the other hand, puts a limit to his authority, reins in his desires, makes decisions justly and equitably, and does not transgress. A king maintains that the goods of others are entrusted to him and under his protection, and that he does not strip his people of their possessions except, perhaps, according to the prescripts and formalities of law.

2

Can the King Demand Tribute from His Subjects Without Their Consent?

Some people deem it a serious matter and not in keeping with majesty, to make the prince's treasury depend upon the will of the people, so that he cannot demand new tribute from them without their consent. That is to say, it is a serious matter when the people, and not the king, become the judge and moderator of affairs. They go on to maintain that if the king summons a parliament in the kingdom when new taxes are imposed, this fact should be attributed to his modesty. He is able to levy taxes of his own volition, without even consulting his subjects, as affairs and fiscal necessity might demand. These pleasant words are dear to kingly ears, and they have sometimes led neighboring kings into error—witness the French kings.

As Philippus Comineus[1] reports at the end of his life of Louis XI, King of France, the king's father, Charles VII,[2] was the first to follow this approach. Financial problems were especially pressing in the large part of the country occupied by the English. He placated the nobles with annual pensions, but he chose to oppress the rest of the people with new taxes. Since then, as the saying goes, the French kings came into their own but stopped protecting their people. After many years, the veritable wound that they received by offending the people has not healed; it is bloody even to this day. I might add that the recent French civil wars, waged so violently for so many years, arose from no other source.[3] For this, oppressed people—most without home or fortune, with possessions lost—agreed to take up arms. They are destined either to destroy or be destroyed, choosing to end their misery by death, or, as conquerors, to plunder riches and power. To help achieve this goal, they cloaked their obstinacy with a veil of religion, and their perversity with rectitude. Countless evils have ensued.

There is certainly little benefit in summoning procurators of the states to parliaments in Castile. Most of them are poorly equipped to manage affairs. They are men who are led by chance—insignificant men of venal disposition who keep nothing in view but their desire to gain the prince's favor and to benefit from public disaster. The temptations and threats of the courtiers, mixed with prayers and promises, would uproot and fell the cedars of Lebanon. It is beyond doubt and, as things now stand, sufficiently obvious that these men will never oppose the prince's wish that he should be in total command. It would be better if these parliaments were never held. They are an excuse for useless expenditures and widespread corruption. Be that as it may, here we are not discussing what is happening but rather what right reason demands. New taxes should not be imposed on subjects without their free consent—not by force, curses, or threats.

As Comineus also advises, the people should show themselves amenable and not resist the prince's wishes. Rather, as need arises, they should manfully come to the aid of the depleted treasury; but the prince should also afford a patient ear, listen to the people, and diligently consider whether their substance and means are up to bearing the new burden, or whether there may not be other solutions to the problem. The prince may have to be exhorted to moderate and responsible spending. This, I understand, was occasionally attempted at earlier parliaments within the kingdom. The established principle, therefore, is that the prince is never permitted to oppress his subjects with new burdens without the consent of those concerned, at least of the leaders of the people and state.

What I said above confirms this point: The private goods of citizens are not at the disposal of the king. Thus, he must not take all or part of them without the approval of those who have the right to them. This is the pronouncement of legal experts: The king does not have the power to make a decision that results in loss of private goods unless the owners agree, nor may he seize any part of their property by planning and imposing a new tax. Why? Because the office of leader or director does not give him this power. Rather, because the king has the power from the state to receive specific income to maintain his original lifestyle, if he wishes these taxes to be increased, he would fulfill his duties by approaching those who originally decide on that specific income. It is their job to grant or deny what he seeks, as seems good to them, under the circumstances. Other countries may do things in different ways. In our country, this method is forbidden by the 1329 law that Alfonso XI,[4] King of Castile, granted to the people in the parliament of Madrid in response to petition 68: "Let no tax be imposed on the nation against the will of the people." Here is the law: "In addition, because the petitioners have requested that no extraordinary tax be imposed, either publicly or privately, unless the people have been previously summoned into parliament and the tax has been approved by all of the procurators of the states. We reply to this request: We are pleased with it. We decree that it is to be done."

In the previously cited place, Philippus Comineus repeats these words in French—twice: "Therefore, to pursue my point, no king or prince on earth can demand, except by way of violence and tyranny, even one *maravedi* from his nation, if those designated to pay it are unwilling." A little later, in addition to the claim of tyranny, Comineus adds that a prince who would act contrary to this law would incur the penalty of excommunication. His source may be the sixth chapter of the *Bulla in Coena Domini*[5] that excommunicates anyone who imposes new taxes in his realm. At this point, some documents read: "Unless authorization has been granted for this purpose." Others read: "Except where it has been granted by right and law." Let others judge whether kings who do otherwise are exempt from this excommunication. How can they be? Neither do they have the power to tax, nor has the additional right been given to them. Yet, since Comineus was a literary man, and not in sacred orders, what he affirmed in such a statement depended upon the authority of the theologians of that time who were agreed on this point.

I personally add that not only any prince who acts this way in regard to taxes, is guilty of this crime and punishment but also any prince who would fraudulently establish a monopoly without the consent of the people, for it is equally fraudulent under another name, and stealing the possessions of one's subjects, to sell things for a higher price than is fair, without authorization. In fact, for some years the prince has established some monopolies on lotteries, corrosive sublimate, and salt. I do not call these monopolies into question. Rather, I consider them prudently established and concerning the uprightness and the fidelity of the prince, one must believe that he has done nothing that goes beyond right reason and the laws. But the point is, that as monopolies do not differ from taxes, caution in establishing them legally and in demanding popular consent should be no less. An example will make the point clearer. In Castile, there has frequently been talk of publicly imposing a tax on flour. Until now, the people have resisted it with difficulty, but if it were permissible for the king to buy up all the grain in the land, to monopolize it, and to sell it at a higher price, then it would be superfluous and meaningless to have the imposition of taxes depend upon the will of the people. In such a case, the king has the freedom to gain whatever he wishes through a monopoly that yields the same or even greater advantages than taxes. From what has been said, the point is firmly established that, if a king is not permitted to demand new taxes, he cannot even set up monopolies for merchandise without the consultation and approval of the people concerned.

3

Can the King Debase Money by Changing Its Weight or Quality Without Consulting the People?

Two things are clear. First, the king may change at will the form and engraving of money—provided that he does not diminish its value. That is the way I interpret the legal experts who grant the king the power to change money. The king owns the mints and administers them, and under the heading of "Regalia," in the *Novellas* constitutiones, money is listed among the other royal prerogatives. And so, without any loss to his subjects, he determines the method for minting money as he pleases. Second, we grant the king the authority to debase money without the people's consent, in the pressing circumstances of war or siege—provided that the debasement is not extended beyond the time of need and, that when peace has been restored, he faithfully makes satisfaction to those who suffered loss.

In a very harsh winter, Frederick Augustus II[1] was holding Faenza under siege. Those under siege were powerless. The siege was protracted, and money was lacking for salaries. He ordered money struck from leather, with his image on one side and the imperial eagle on the other, and each coin had the value of a gold coin. He did this on his own, without consultation with the people of the empire. The salvific plan brought about the conclusion of the affair. With his forces reassured by this device, he took over the city. When the war was over, he replaced the leather money with just as many golden coins. Collenucius[2] relates this occurrence in the fourth book of his *History of Naples*. In France, as well, money was struck on occasion from leather and decorated with a small silver key. Budelius,[3] in the first book of his *On Money* (chap. 1, no. 34), recalls that money was made from paper when Leyden in Holland was under siege in 1574. These facts are undisputed.

But the question is this: Can a prince in every case solve his fiscal problems on his own authority and debase his kingdom's money by diminishing its weight or its quality? Certainly the common opinion of legal experts agrees with that of Hostiensius,[4] expressed in his *De censibus* in the paragraph *Ex quibus*. Among these experts are Innocent[5] and Panormitanus who, in the fourth chapter of *De iureiurando*, maintains that a prince may not do this without the consent of his subjects.

One concludes, therefore, that if the king is the director—not the master—of the private possessions of his subjects, he will not be able to take away arbitrarily any part of their possessions for this or any other reason or any ploy. Such seizure occurs whenever money is debased: For what is declared to be more is worth less. But if a prince is not empowered to levy taxes on unwilling subjects and cannot set up monopolies for merchandise, he is not empowered to make fresh profit from debased money. These strategies aim at the same thing: cleaning out the pockets of the people and piling up money in the provincial treasury. Do not be taken in by the smoke and mirrors by which metal is given a greater value than it has by nature and in common estimation. Of course, this does not happen without common injury. When blood is let by whatever device or strategy, the body will certainly be debilitated and wasted. In the same way, a prince cannot profit without the suffering and groans of his subjects. As Plato maintained, one man's profit is another's loss.[6] No one can abrogate by any means these fundamental laws of nature. In chapter 5 of *De iureiurando*, I find that Innocent III judges to be invalid the oath by which James the Conqueror,[7] King of Aragón, bound himself for a considerable time to preserve the debased money that his father, Peter II,[8] had minted. Among other reasons for this opinion is the fact that the consent of the people was lacking. Both Innocent and Panormitanus support this view. They confirm that a prince cannot establish anything that would cause injury to the people. We call it an injury when anything is taken from a person's fortune.

Indeed, I do not know how those who do these things can avoid the excommunication and censure pronounced for all ages by the *Bulla in Coena Domini*, because it applies to monopolies. All such schemes, under any pretense, aim at the same thing: to weigh the people down with new burdens and to amass money. This is not permissible. For if anyone maintains that our kings were granted this power long ago by the people's carelessness and indulgence, I find no trace of this custom or permission. Rather, I find that the laws concerning money of both the Catholic King[9] and Philip,[10] his great-grandson, were always passed in the nation's parliaments.

4

The Twofold Value of Money

Money has a twofold value. One is intrinsic and natural and comes from its type of metal and its weight, to which may be added the cost for labor and equipment in minting. The other is called the legal value and is extrinsic, inasmuch as it is established by the law of the prince, who has the right to prescribe the worth of money as well as of other goods. In a well-constituted republic, it should be the care of those who are in control of such matters to see that these two values are equal and do not differ, for just as in the case of other goods, it would be unjust for something to be appraised at ten when it is worth five in itself and in common estimation, so the same thing holds for money if the legal value goes astray. This point is treated by Budelius in the first book of his *On Money* (chap. 1, no. 7), among other scholars, and they commonly consider anyone who thinks otherwise, ridiculous and childish. If it is permissible to separate these values, let them mint money from leather, from paper, from lead, as we know was done in strained circumstances. The reckoning would be the same, and the cost for manufacturing less than if money were made of bronze.

I do not think that a king should produce money at his own expense, but I think it fair that some value be added to the worth of the metal in consideration of the labor of minting and of the overall monetary ministry. It would not be out of place if some small profit accrued to a prince from this function as a sign of his sovereignty and his prerogative. This opinion was ratified in the law, promulgated in Madrid in 1566,[1] concerning the making of silver coins (*cuartillos*). In the fifth chapter of his *De iureiurando*, Innocent III implies this practice even if he does not mention it explicitly. I, however, maintain that these two values must be diligently and accurately kept equal. This same conviction may be gathered from Aristotle's *Politics* (bk. 1, chap. 6[2]) where he says that it was originally taken for granted that men would exchange one thing for another. By common opinion, it seemed best to exchange merchandise for iron and silver, to avoid expense, and to ease the aggravation of transporting long distances wares that were heavy and cumbersome for both parties. Thus, a sheep was exchanged for so many pounds of brass, a horse for so many pounds of gold. It was difficult to weigh metal consistently. Public authority undertook to see to it that parts of the metal were marked with their weight to expedite commerce. This was the first and legitimate use of money, though time and evil produced other devices and deceptions that are certainly at odds with ancient and wholesome usage.

As our own laws tell us, our countrymen clearly decided that the two values be kept equal. Indeed, gold and silver are clear instances of this equality. Sixty-seven silver coins are made from 8 ounces of silver, called a *mark*, while the same weight of natural silver is exchanged for 65 silver coins, both in accordance with the prescripts of law. Thus, only 2 silver coins are added for the work involved in minting. Each silver coin is equivalent to 34 *maravedis*, while the same weight of natural silver is valued at about 33 *maravedis*. What about gold? Sixty-eight gold coins, called *coronas*, are struck from 8 ounces of gold. Natural gold is worth about the same amount. Copper money is valued in the same way, but in this case it seems more difficult to reconcile the legal value with the natural value.

According to the law promulgated in Medina del Campo in 1497, the Catholic Kings ordained that 8 ounces of copper, mixed with 7 grains of silver (about the weight of $1^1/_2$ silver coins), would make 96 *maravedis*. The silver was worth more than 51 *maravedis*. The 8 ounces of copper and the cost of labor approximate the other 44 *maravedis* in value. In this way, the legal value is easily reconciled with the value of the metal and the labor.

Then in 1566, Philip II, King of Spain, abrogated the previous law and established that 4 grains of silver—the weight of 1 silver coin—were to be mixed with 8 ounces of copper. From this mixture, 110 *maravedis* were to be minted. In so doing, he took away more than half of the silver from the quality of the metal, and added 14 *maravedis* to the old value. He was, I think, considering the expense of minting, which, doubtless had doubled with time, as well as made a profit from his supervision. Led on by this modest and slender hope, many men—after they had been authorized by the king to produce this money—made an immense profit. Consequently, as in past years, this business was considered especially lucrative. Yet, the two values of money were not unreconciled in this approach, because the value of silver was mixed in with the 8 ounces of copper, and one must include both the price of copper and of production, both of which were estimated by at least two other silver coins. Moreover, debased money, which we call *blancas*, valued at half a *maravedi*, was being frequently minted and was a source of much greater vexation and nuisance.

At this time, no silver was mixed with copper in copper money, and 8 ounces of copper yielded 280 *maravedis*. The entire cost for stamping did not exceed a silver coin. Copper was selling at 46 *maravedis*. The cost of stamping and value of the metal thus came to 80 *maravedis*. The profit was therefore 200 *maravedis* on each *mark*, because the legal value of this money exceeded the intrinsic and natural value of the metal. The great danger that this fact presents to the state needs explanation. First, as indicated above, it is inconsistent with the nature and original concept of money. How, then, can anyone be stopped from debasing money in like circumstances, when enticed by the hope of gigantic profit? Finally, these values will adjust in business, as people are reluctant to give and take money that is worth more than its natural value. Fictions and frauds, once discovered, quickly collapse, and a prince who opposes the people will accomplish nothing. Would he be able to insist that rough sackcloth be sold for the cost of silken velvet, or that woolen clothing be sold for cloth of gold? Clearly, he could not. Try as he might, he could not justly make such a practice legal.

The French kings frequently devalued the *solidus*, and our silver coins were immediately valued higher than before. What was previously worth 4 *solidi*, when we were dwelling in France, became worth 7 or 8 *solidi*. If the legal value of debased money does not decrease, surely all merchandise will sell at a higher price, in proportion to the debasement of the quality or the weight of the money. The process is inevitable. As a result, the price of goods adjusts and money is less valuable than it previously and properly was.

5

The Foundations of Commerce:
Money, Weights, and Measures

Weights, measures, and money are, of course, the foundations of commerce upon which rests the entire structure of trade. Most things are sold by weight and measure—but everything is sold by money. Everyone wants the foundations of buildings to remain firm and secure, and the same holds true for weights, measures, and money. They cannot be changed without danger and harm to commerce.

The ancients understood this. One of their major concerns was to preserve a specimen of all these things in their holy temples so that no one might rashly falsify them. Fannius[1] bears witness to this fact in his *De ponderibus et mensuris*, and a law of Justinian Augustus[2] concerning this tradition is extant (*Authent. De collatoribus* coll. 9). In Leviticus (27:25) we read: "Every valuation shall be according to the *shekel* of the sanctuary." Some conclude that the Jews were accustomed to keep a *shekel* weighing 4 *drachmas* of silver in the sanctuary to ensure easy recourse to a legitimate *shekel*, so that no one would dare to falsify it by tampering with its quality and weight. It was so important to maintain standards that no amount of care was considered superfluous. Even Thomas Aquinas warns (*De regim. Principum*, bk. 2, chap. 14[3]) that money should not be altered rashly or at the whim of a prince. The recent change in the liquid measure in Castile, by which new tribute was exacted on wine and oil—not without protest—is reprehensible. In addition to other inconveniences, there is a problem adjusting the old measure to the new, and further confusion in our dealings with others. Those who are in power seem less-educated than the people because they pay no attention to the disturbances and evils frequently caused by their decisions, both in our nation and beyond. Obviously, debasing money will profit the king, and we have proof that the ancients were frequently lead into fraud by that hope, and that these same men soon became aware of the disadvantages of their decisions. To remedy these ills, new and greater ills were needed: The situation is like giving a drink at the wrong time to a sick man. At first, it refreshes him but later aggravates the causes of his illness and increases his fever. The clear fact is that great care was once taken that these foundations of human existence be not disturbed. In my *De ponderibus et mensuris*[4] (chap. 8), I explained that the Roman ounce remained unchanged for many centuries and that it is the same as ours. The same should be true of the other weights. Our weights should not differ from those of the ancients.

6

Money Has Frequently Been Altered

A widespread opinion among the Jews was that the money, measures, and weights of the sanctuary were twice as great as the common ones: the *bathum*, *gomor*, *shekel*, and all the rest. They thought this way because their special effort to preserve the weights and measures in the sanctuary could not prevent the people from diminishing the common ones and, under some conditions, making them less than half. Thus, different passages in ancient writers, that vary in specifics or are at odds with sacred letters, may be reconciled.

We know—and Pliny[1] (bk. 33, chap. 3) testifies to this fact—that in ancient Rome, the *as*, (a copper coin with the value of 4 of our current *maravedis*) under the pressure of the First Punic War,[2] was debased to 2 ounces, which they called a sextantarian *as*,[3] which weighed about $\frac{1}{6}$ of a pound—then 12 ounces, like the Italian and French *pound* today. Thereafter, under pressure during the war with Hannibal,[4] the Romans reduced the *as* to an ounce, $\frac{1}{12}$ of the previous *asses*, and finally the reduction in weight reached half an ounce. The *denarius*, with a value of 40 *maravedis*, was initially minted from pure silver. Then under Drusus, the Tribune of the Plebs,[5] it was mixed with an eighth part of copper, and its previous purity was changed, as Pliny indicates in the same passage. In subsequent years, more copper was added. Actually, not a few *denarii* are being unearthed in our time that contain much less silver and are of less purity because of the greater weight of copper added—more than a third. Likewise, gold money of outstanding purity and weighing 2 *drachmas* was minted during the reigns of the first emperors. At

267

that time they were minted from 6 ounces of gold and were called *solidi*. They weighed about the same as our *castellano*. A law of Emperor Justinian concerning *solidi* can be found under the heading *De susceptoribus, praepositis et arcariis*, and begins with "Quotiescumque."[6] Commenting on the freedom to innovate in one of his prologues, the ancient poet, Plautus,[7] seems to suggest the Roman view of debasing money when he says:

> Those who use old wine I consider wise.
> For the new comedies produced these days
> are much worse than the new coins.

Money still in existence today indicates how frequently the Romans changed the value of their money. The same thing has taken place in all countries within recent memory. Princes, with or without their subjects' consent, have frequently debased coins in quality or by subtracting from their weight. The search for examples in other countries is superfluous when domestic ones are at hand in abundance.

The history of Alfonso XI, the King of Castile (chap. 14) affirmed that money was altered by King Ferdinand the Holy[8] and by his son Alfonso the Wise,[9] as well as by Sancho the Brave,[10] and by his son Ferdinand,[11] and his grandson Alfonso XI. Therefore, during the reign of these five kings, which was sufficiently long, money enjoyed no stability; it was constantly changed and debased. Remarkably, Peter,[12] the king of Castile and the son of the last Alfonso does not seem to have debased the currency. I suspect that, rather inhibited by the inconveniences caused by the adulteration of money when his father was in power, he did not follow Alfonso's example and was careful to mint proper money. This is attested by the money minted under his name. His brother Henry II,[13] ridden by debt that he owed to his companions and assistants in exchange for winning the kingdom, and burdened with larger illegal debts for the future, had recourse to the same remedy. He minted two types of money: *reales* (silver coins) worth 3 *maravedis*; and *cruzados* worth 1 *maravedi*, as the chronicles (chap. 10) for the fourth year of his reign testify.

Serious inconveniences arose from this contrivance, but his successors were not afraid to follow his example. To pay Alencastre,[14] the duke of a rival kingdom, the money agreed upon in a peace treaty, John I[15] devised a new coin by the name of *blanca*, worth 1 *maravedi*, and shortly thereafter he decreed that the *blanca*, almost halved in value, be evaluated at only 6 *dineros*, called *novenes*. This took place in the parliaments of Burgos in 1387. The right to devalue money by diminishing quality and increasing value continued into the reign of Henry IV.[16] These were the most unsettled of times and, although the historians of the period do not say so, this fact is patently clear from the fluctuations in the value of silver; for when Alfonso XI was king of Castile, 8 ounces of silver were worth 125 *maravedis*. During the reign of Henry II, a silver *real* was worth 3 *maravedis* and, consequently, a *mark*[17] was worth 400 *maravedis*. Under John I, Henry's son, it went up to 250 *maravedis*; a silver coin was worth 4 *maravedis*, a gold coin, 50 *maravedis* or 12 silver coins. Such is found in the 1388 parliament of Burgos (Law 1). Under Henry III,[18] his successor, the value reached 480 or even 500 *maravedis*. Indeed, at the end of his reign and the beginning of John II's,[19] the value increased to 1000 *maravedis*. Finally, in the reign of Henry IV, it was valued at 2,000 and at 2,500 *maravedis*. All of these variations and increases in value did not come from variation in the metal; it was always composed of 8 ounces of silver with a small addition of copper, but the frequent debasement of *maravedis* and of other coins caused the value of silver money of the same weight to seem to be greater by comparison. Indeed, all the variations in the value of silver are taken, for the most part, from Antonio Nebrissensi's *Repetitionibus*.[20] In fact, the extant coins of these kings are all rough and indications of the tendency to debase money during these years.

But the Catholic rulers, Ferdinand and Isabella, stabilized this volatility by a law that set the price for 8 ounces of natural silver at 2,210 *maravedis*, but when minted at 2,278. This is the price, even today. Philip II diminished the quality and weight of the *maravedi*, but since it was by a slight amount, there was no change in the value of silver in relation to the *maravedis*. I think that the recent change in copper money will alter its value and make 8 ounces of silver the equivalent of more than 4,000 *maravedis*, as presently minted. Am I wrong?

7

Advantages Derived from Alteration
of Copper Money

A careful examination and investigation of the advantages and disadvantages that result from altering copper money are in order so that the wise and prudent reader may consider calmly and without prejudice which issues are of greater weight and importance. This is the way to the truth that we seek.

First, when such a change is made, we are freed from an expenditure of silver. Lessening the quality of silver provides this advantage. For years, a great weight and many talents of silver used to be mixed with copper to no profit. Because the money weighs less, it is easier for the merchants to transport and use in trade (the cost of transport used to be high). The increased money supply expands commerce in the nation, while the desire of eager outsiders to get their greedy hands on gold and silver money is curtailed. Those who have it will share it willingly with others; thus, debts will be liquidated, farms will be cultivated in the hope of greater profit, and workshops (frequently idle for lack of money) will be busy. In short, there will be a greater abundance of flocks, fruit, and merchandise, of linen, wool, silk cloth, and of other commercial items. No doubt, abundance will produce affordable prices (whereas in the past only a few could find those who would lend them money for such goods—and then at great interest). In these circumstances, we will be content with our lot and plenty and have less need for outside merchandise. Importing goods diminishes our silver and gold and infects our people with foreign customs. Men born for war and arms are physically weakened by the softness of merchandise, and their warlike vigor of spirits is extinguished. Also, foreigners will not come to us as often as they used to, both because of our abundance of native merchandise and because of our money, which they will refuse to take back to their native land at no profit after it has been exchanged for their goods. In general, with the money received for their merchandise, they will purchase other items in our country, as convenient, and will transport them to their native land.

It is not insignificant that a good deal of money will flow into the king's treasury, for payment of his creditors to whom he has mortgaged his tax revenues—a major disaster—and this can be accomplished without injury to, or complaint from anyone, just by changing the value of money. The king will certainly profit greatly.

Thus, Pliny, in the passage cited above, confirms that the Romans by diminishing the weight of the *as* escaped from extreme straits, and paid debts that weighed them down. The history of Alfonso XI, King of Castile (chap. 98), report the same phenomenon, and those of Henry II for the fifth year (chap. 10)[1] report that he was relieved, after ridding himself by this means of most oppressive war debts. A great deal of money had been promised to others, but especially to Bertrando Klaquino,[2] and to foreigners by whose aid he had stripped his brother of the kingdom.

The ancient Romans, and other nations in our time, used copper money exclusively with no admixture of silver or other precious metal. Indeed, this usage seems to have once been more usual and common with other monies because the Romans commonly called their money "copper." Perhaps this custom has influenced us to explain by *maravedis* the size of someone's property or yearly taxable income. The Spaniards once used gold *maravedis*, but, at a time when they had to make great changes, they removed all gold from the *maravedis*. Thus, we should not be astonished if silver is now removed from our money. It is of no use and never was of any advantage to anyone.

These advantages are important and should be considered. We will pass over the disadvantages that a diligent observer may claim to result from the recent intervention. Nothing in this life is entirely simple and free from all harm and blame. Therefore, it is the wise man's job to choose what affords the greater and less-blameworthy advantages, especially since human nature is perverse in such circumstances and is used to criticize changes and new ways. We hold firmly to traditions, as if nothing could be corrected in, or added to the practices of the ancients.

8

Different *Maravedis* of Varying Values in Castile

Before I explain the disadvantages necessarily involved in the new plan for devaluing copper money, it is worth explaining the different kinds of *maravedis* and
their values as used in Castile at various times. The understanding of these coins
is involved and complicated but is worth having, if we are to reach the truth that
has been shrouded in darkness.

The gold coins in frequent use at the time of the Goths have first place. Indeed,
the Romans in the later Empire struck coins of less weight than the old ones: They
used to mint 6 coins from an ounce of gold, 48 from 8 ounces or a *mark*. These
coins were a little bigger than our *castellano*. They called these gold coins *solidi*,
and the value of each was 12 *denarii*. But if the value of a Roman *denarius* was 40
quadrantes or *maravedis*, the value of a *solidus* came to 480—a little more than
our *castellano*. And so, in subsequent time, the *solidus*, although struck from silver
and finally made for the greater part from copper, still always kept the value of 12
denarii—even when the latter were no longer made from gold but from copper.
Certainly in France and among the people of Aragón, where the name *solidus* is still
found, each *solidus* is worth 12 *denarii*. When the Goths invaded with the sword,
the Roman Empire was still flourishing in Spain, as was Roman money, laws, and
customs.[1] When government in Rome changed, the victors introduced some of
their own customs and adopted some customs from the conquered. In particular,
the Goths began to use Roman money. Then, when the new government was established, they devised and struck new coins that they called *maravedis*. There is
no need to go into the meaning of the word, but each *maravedi* was valued at 10

273

denarii, or 400 *quadrantes*, as much as our current gold coin,[2] that is, 400 *maravedis* or *quadrantes*. It was established that the *maravedis*, although first made of silver and then of copper, would still be valued at 10 *denarii*.

The norm for the *maravedi* was that it would contain 2 *blancas*, 6 *coronados*, 10 *denarii*, 60 *meajas*. This was their relationship to the *maravedi*, although they completely disappeared because they were worthless. The Roman *solidus* and the Gothic gold *maravedi* differed little in value. Consequently, for the number of *solidi* imposed as punishment by the courts under Roman law, the Goths substituted a like number of gold *maravedis*. Many coins of the Goths are now being unearthed in Spain that are not made from good gold. We have evidence that their worth is debased by half: They are half-*maravedis*, coins called *semises* or rather, *tremisses*, weighing one-third of the Goths' *maravedi*.[3] We will consider this matter later.

Tumultuous times followed. Everything, money included, was in a state of frightful confusion. After Spain was defeated by the weapons of the Moors,[4] a new race of kings sprang up, given by God for the salvation of a nation that was oppressed by every evil. We will not talk about the money of the Moors,[5] but there were three kinds of *maravedis* under the government of the kings of León and Castile.[6] There were the gold ones, which were also called *good, old, standard,* and *usual*. We must first speak about these *usual* ones and explain their value and quality, because our understanding of the other types depends upon an explanation of the *usual* ones.

The value of the *usual* ones was not constant but changed with the times. It is difficult to define this variation: The only legitimate source for a guess is by reference to the value of a silver *mark*. These *maravedis* must be compared to our *maravedis* in the exact proportion as the *mark* of that age is compared to the value of the *mark* of our age. At this time, a bullion *mark* is worth 2,210 *maravedis*, but, once minted and made into coins—2,278 *maravedis*. Moreover, the quality of the silver does not enter into consideration: It has always been more or less of the same purity as today, as the chalices, and other sacred vessels and instruments, preserved in our Church treasuries, bear witness. Then the silver *mark*, in relation to the varying value of the *maravedi*, was always worth 5 gold coins (popularly called *doblas*)[7] or a little more, and equal to 12 silver coins—not 14, as some say. Likewise the *mark* used to be worth 60 or 65 silver coins, as we can see from the laws of King John I of Castile, but debate rushes in from another source.

The oldest known value of the *mark* is 125 *maravedis*. This was certainly the value of the *mark* in the age of King Alfonso XI, as witnessed in the history of his accomplishments (chap. 98). Thus, a silver coin was just 2 *maravedis*; now it is 34: So a *maravedi* at that time was worth as much as 17 and a bit more of ours, and there was no doubt about the quality of the silver that its value declared. In the reign of Henry II, a silver coin was worth 3 *maravedis*, as the history of his fourth year (chap. 2) declares. And so, the *mark*, at this time, increased to 200 *maravedis*, each one equal to 11 of ours. Henry was succeeded by his son John I, and the *mark* increased under him to 250 *maravedis* or *quadrantes*, when a silver coin was valued at 4 *maravedis*, and a gold one at 50 (see the first law he enacted in the parliament of the kingdom of Burgos in 1388). Thus, the *maravedi* of that time was equal in value to 9 or 10 of ours. Even more clear is a previous law promulgated in Burgos that punishes abuse of parents by a fine of 600 *maravedis*. During the reign of Ferdinand and Isabella, that law was introduced into the *Ordinamentum*[8] (bk. 8, title 9). It stated that the 600 *maravedis* mentioned in that law are good money and equal 6,000 *maravedis* in that time, which is also our own; for, since that time, there has been no change in the value of the *mark* or *maravedi*.

Let us look at the reigns of other kings. According to old documents, under Henry III the *mark* reached to 480 and even 500 *maravedis*. Therefore a silver coin was worth about 8 *maravedis*, and the *maravedi* was equal to about 4 or 5 of ours. Under John II, Henry's son, the *mark* was worth 1,000 *maravedis*, especially at the end of his life. Thus his *maravedi* was worth $2^1/_2$ of ours—a remarkable variation in value! But this fluctuation was not confined to his reign. Among many other serious ills, under Henry IV, the silver *mark* reached 2,000 *maravedis*, and then 2,500, according to Antonio Nebrissensi's *Repetitionibus*. His *maravedi* was worth what ours is, and there has not been great change in the value of the *maravedi* since that time. This stability must be attributed to the care of Ferdinand and Isabella and their successors. With these facts established from laws and chronicles, let us evaluate the other *maravedis*.

The gold *maravedi* was equal to 6 of the *maravedis* current in the time of Alfonso the Wise. Law 114[9] of the *Lex stili*[10] states that, after this king looked into the matter, he found that a gold *maravedi* was equal to 6 of the *maravedis* of his day. This is not, as some claim, that the *maravedis* of King Alfonso were made of gold. Rather, the value was discovered by weighing *maravedis* of both kinds, and from establishing their proportions of gold to silver—12 to 1. Moreover, the law of Alfonso XI in the parliament of León of 1387[11] stated that 100 *maravedis* of good money, namely, of gold, were worth 600 of those of that age. Two important things may be gathered from these facts. First, that from the time of King Alfonso the Wise (also known as the Tenth) up until Alfonso XI, his great-grandson, there was absolutely no change in the value of the *mark* and *maravedi*, inasmuch as under both kings the gold *maravedi* equaled 6 *usual* ones. Second, inasmuch as the *maravedis* then in use equaled 17 of ours (or even a little more, as mentioned above), those who said that the gold *maravedi* was equal to 36 or 60 of ours are necessarily mistaken. Rather, they were worth as much as 300 silver ones or more. This is my opinion, and it is founded on firm arguments. I am also of the opinion that the gold *maravedis* were the *tremisses* of the Goths. The first kings of Castile used them. They did not mint new ones. Their value agrees with the known one of a little more than 3 silver coins. These coins of the Goths turn up here and there, but no gold coins struck with the crest and name of the kings of Castile have been found at all. It would be incredible if all of them have disappeared without a trace. So much for the gold *maravedi*!

Most people say that each of the old *maravedis* was worth $1^1/_2$ of ours. The pronouncements of those who have a greater understanding of our law, will carry more weight on this issue. Perhaps there was agreement among the legal experts that, whenever the old *maravedi* occurs in our law, $1^1/_2$ of ours may be substituted, just as the gold *maravedi* found in those laws is popularly evaluated at 36 or 60 of the *usual*.

But, strictly speaking, the old *maravedis* did not have one value but varying and complex values. For whenever the quality of money was diminished, as frequently happened to avoid abolishing the old money, the kings decreed that it should coexist with the new one, and be called "old." Thus, it will be easy for some of the usual *maravedis* and those of the older kind to be compared with one another and with ours. If, for example, the *maravedi* of Alfonso XI is compared with the *maravedis* minted by his son, Henry II, it will be worth $1^1/_2$ of the latter and, if compared with ours, it will be worth 17. Thus, the old *maravedis* were sometimes the usual *maravedis*. Therefore, from the value of the usual *maravedis*, as we have explained, one ought to establish the value of the old ones, and from those that are called "new," one ought to establish their value when compared with ours. These are subtle and thorny considerations, but we are hurrying to end this discussion. We add that, under our law, the *maravedis*, which are current today and were current in the time of the Catholic King Ferdinand, are commonly called "new." At this time, the laws of earlier kings were gathered together in a few volumes.[12] The *maravedis* of the earlier kings were called "old" *maravedis*.

And so from the value of the *maravedi* in use under the individual kings, a decision may be made about the old *maravedi*. The *maravedi* of Alfonso XI was worth 17 of ours; that of Henry II, 11; that of John I, 10; that of Henry III, 5; that of John II, $2^1/_2$. Careful consideration must be given to the times, and determinations must be made accordingly concerning the value of an old *maravedi* in any law, and the value of a new one, both among themselves and in comparison with our own *maravedis*. It should not be overlooked that the old *maravedi* was sometimes called "good," as in the above-mentioned law (*Ordinamentum*, bk. 8, title 9) by which John I prescribed the punishment of 600 *maravedis* for the abuse of parents. The experts who incorporated this law in that book added on their own that the *maravedis* were good coins, equal to 6,000 of the *usual* ones. This means that the law was not referring to gold *maravedis* but to old ones that were in use under that king, and that each was worth as much as 10 of ours. Remember that from the time of Ferdinand the Catholic, the value of the *maravedi* remained unchanged.

Moreover, by a law passed by John II in Caraccas[13] in 1409 (the first law in *Ordinamentum*, bk. 8, title 5), something is forbidden under punishment of excommunication of thirty days and a fine of 100 good *maravedis*, which make 600 of the old ones. But if the obstinacy continues for six months, the fine increases to 1,000 good *maravedis*, which equal 6,000 of the old ones. In this citation, the good *maravedis* are gold, the old ones are those that were current under the Kings Alfonso the Wise and Alfonso XI. For only at that time, as stated above, did each gold *maravedi* equal 6 current ones. But if the punishment seems very harsh—it is equivalent to 3,000 of our silver ones, since each gold *maravedi* equals as much as 3 silver ones—even more serious punishments are inflicted today. When someone is suspected of heresy, he will not escape the bond of excommunication for a full year.

Finally, in the history of King John II[14] (the twenty-ninth year, chap. 144) a mandate was introduced in the parliament of Burgos for the minting of half-*mara-vedis*, which we call *blancas* because of their whiteness, in accordance with the quality and weight of the coinage of his father, Henry III. That money, however, was discovered to be inferior. When the affair was investigated and the defect and fault recognized, the procurators of the kingdom decreed that the previous *maravedi*, namely that of King Henry III, should be valued at $1^1/_2$ of the new *maravedis*. This is related in this king's history (the forty-second year, chap. 36). By universal decree, from this time on, the procurators seem to have taken the opportunity to declare that an old *maravedi* was worth $1^1/_2$ of ours, whereas they should have rather said that the *maravedi* minted by Henry III, was worth $1^1/_2$ of those minted by John II. Indeed, if we consider the value of the *mark* under both kings, the defect was not adequately remedied, and the previous *maravedi* was worth fully 2 of the later ones. If a comparison is made with our *maravedi*, the *maravedi* of John II was worth $2^1/_2$ of ours; the *maravedi* of Henry III was worth fully 4 or 5 of ours.

9

Disadvantages Derived from
This Alteration of Copper Money

In serious issues, it is not fair to advance subtle and speculative arguments from our own heads and thoughts. They are frequently deceptive. It is better to do battle with data from our own time and from our ancestors. This is the safest approach, and the assured way to the truth, because the present is certainly similar to the past. What has happened will happen. Previous events are very influential: They convince us that what sets out on the same path will reach the same conclusion.

Some disadvantages appear to be great but, in reality, are not. We could put up with them to avoid the greater disadvantages that derive from the alteration of money. First, some critics claim that this practice has never been used in our country and that, because of its novelty, every innovation triggers fear and is risky. But this argument is proved untrue by what has already been said. Obviously this process has frequently been tried in our country. With what success is not yet the issue! They also argue that there has been less cultivation of the land and farms, and that citizens are discouraged from working when wages are paid in debased money. This is true. Among other advantages of alteration and multiplication of copper coins, however, is the fact that with this money on hand and available to everyone, the fruits of the earth and the products of handicraft will be more easily produced. In the past, they were frequently neglected for lack of money. And so this argument proves inconclusive, and because it can be used by either side, it is not convincing for either.

These critics then assert that commerce will be hindered, especially with those who come from outside Spain with the sole hope of exchanging their goods

for our silver. Facts speak for themselves, they say, and debased coinage will create great havoc with commerce with the Indies because most things sent to that
region, are imported into Spain from outside nations. The answer to this objection
is not difficult either. One may argue that it is no disadvantage for Spain to obey
its own laws, as it is strictly forbidden to export silver to other nations. Moreover,
how is it advantageous to despoil the country of its silver? Rather, it would seem
beneficial if the copper money of commerce deterred outsiders from coming into
Spain. Certainly, they will exchange their goods for our goods when the hope of
carrying off our wealth has been removed. This is and should be the common desire
of a nation. Further, there is no danger of harming trade with the Indies, because it
involves goods that are native to us: wine, oil, wool, and silk cloth. But if there is
need for commerce with outsiders, silver will arrive from the Indies now and then
and allow our merchants to buy such things as linen cloth, paper, books, trifles, and
the like. Nor does copper money prevent us from minting this foreign silver, as we
have done before. There is a ready response to the next objection that denies that
the king has the authority to borrow money from outsiders to meet the necessary
expenses of the fleet and the salaries of the soldiers. We might rather say that there
would be a greater supply of money for the king if his debts to his countrymen were
paid in copper money. He could pay his foreign debts in the silver that is offered to
him every year. Nor is copper money so wicked or barren that silver will completely
disappear, as if chased away by a wicked and magical incantation.

It is true, we must admit, that when there is a great supply of copper, silver
disappears among the citizens. This fact should be numbered among the principal
disadvantages of copper money. Silver flows into the royal treasury because the
king orders that taxes are to be paid in that money. It does not return to circulation,
because he pays whatever he owes his subjects with copper money. Thus, there
will be a superabundance of copper money, while he exports the silver. Moreover,
the silver that remains in our citizens' hands disappears, since all first spend the
copper money and hide the silver, unless forced to produce it.

Some argue that the great supply of debased money would bring about this
disadvantage, but the reasons for their position are not satisfactory. They advance
two reasons for their position: The first is that royal money cannot be distinguished
from counterfeit money once the silver, which used to be mixed with the copper,
has been completely removed; the second is that the hope of profit will tempt many.
This profit is three times larger than before because, while the actual value of the
money has changed little, the legal value has changed much. I will not dispute these
arguments. How could I? The latter one, based on the hope of profit is quite valid,
as 200 gold coins become 700 because of debased money. This fact will certainly
tempt many to expose themselves and their possessions to any risk for profit. Who
would bridle his inflamed desire suddenly to escape indigence in this way? But the
previous argument is not based on facts. It rests on the belief that silver was mixed
with copper to prevent adulteration of copper money. In fact, the silver remains

from the early quality of the *maravedi*, which was once solid silver but was later defiled with many additions. Nonetheless, some silver was always found in it. The first Catholic kings did not ordain this, but they determined by law how much silver was to be mixed with copper, lest the debasing of that money proceed further by an ever greater amount of copper. It would not be bad if no silver were mixed into copper money. As a matter of fact, the expense of silver would be avoided.

If my argument is in any way valid, I would like the stamp on coins to be more refined, as it is on coins from the mints in Segovia. Moreover, the silver *real* would be exchanged for more copper coins, as happens in France. There, 12 *dineros* are given for a silver *solidus*, which is almost a *cuartillo*,[1] and each *dinero* is worth 3 *liardi*. At Naples, a *carlino*, less than our silver coin, worth not more than 28 *maravedis*, is exchanged for 60 *caballi*, each with the weight and mass of 2 earlier *maravedis*, before they were constantly adulterated. All these facts confirm that the value of a silver coin is equal to the metal and the cost of minting, and this means accommodating the legal value to the natural value. Few people would undertake to debase that money because of less profit; nor would it be easy for ordinary people—and such, for the most part, are those who make counterfeit money—to maintain mints to coin similar money. If anyone does mold coins from melted copper, they will be readily distinguishable from struck money.

As a matter of fact, silver is minted in these mills at a great loss; coins of equal weight cannot be produced because of the variations in the silver ingots placed on the press. This disadvantage does not exist with copper because it is a base metal. I pass over the other proposed disadvantages—they are more apparent than true—to address greater disadvantages, which arise not from empty speculation but are proven by the experience of former times and the memory of antiquity. Critics add that with the multiplication of copper money and its currency, no fortunes would be piled up by the rich for use in pious works. But surely, so many people spend piles of money in harmful and ludicrous things that it would not seem to be a great loss if fortunes were not amassed. Copper money does not stand in the way of quantities of silver yearly arriving from the Indies. Who will prevent the owners from hoarding as much of the silver as they want? Others find fault with the cost of transportation: They do not wish the merchants to have to transport purchased goods from afar at that cost. But those same merchants, after reckoning the cost of shipping to the end of the country (from Toledo to Murcia), claim that the expense is only 1 percent. Then, some say, it is very laborious to count this copper money, and keeping it is particularly bothersome.

But others say that these troubles are sufficiently compensated for by the advantages that this money entails. Critics also find fault with the expense of copper, because of the great amount minted, and they cite the difficulty of forging it at home. As a result, outsiders, who have a great deal of this metal, will grow rich at our expense. A few years ago, a hundred-weight of copper sold for 18 *francs* in France. And so, 8 ounces (what we call the weight of a *mark*) was fixed at 13 *maravedis*; in Germany, it was even cheaper. Currently, the same weight is fixed, nonetheless, at 46 *maravedis* in Castile. And the price of minting copper money endlessly increases out of necessity or, rather, out of cupidity. This is a real, not fictitious disadvantage, but there are other much greater ones in comparison with which, this one—whatever damage it causes—could seem ridiculous and relatively unimportant.

10

The Major Disadvantages Derived from
This Alteration of Money

First of all, the current large supply of copper money is against our Spanish laws. There is no limitation on gold and silver money in the 1497 decree of the Catholic kings.[1] An individual was allowed to mint as much of these metals as he had. They decreed, however, in the third law, that no more than ten million *maravedis* were to be struck, with the responsibility for this minting divided, according to a determined ratio, among seven mints. Then Philip II, king of Spain, decreed in a 1566 law that it was not advantageous to manufacture more copper money than would be enough for common use and commerce. He therefore commanded that such money was not to be minted without royal authorization.

Moreover, copper money should be commonly employed only in small purchases, and gold or silver was to be used in greater monetary exchanges. Anything beyond these limits would involve public damage and upheaval, for money was invented to facilitate trade, and that money is more acceptable, which better and more opportunely accomplishes its end, as Aristotle remarks in his *Politics* (bk. 1, chap. 6[2]). But abundance of copper money brings about the opposite. Counting it is a great burden: A man can hardly count a thousand gold pieces in copper coins in a day. As for transporting coins, it is laborious and expensive to carry them to distant places to buy goods. For these reasons, an inundation of this money is opposed by our laws. Of course, I would not approve of minting just silver money as, for example, in England under the recently deceased Queen Elizabeth[3] and in some German states. I realize that it can be divided into tiny parts. It is said that

Renato,[4] the Duke of Anjou, made a thousand coins out of an ounce of silver (I would prefer a pound). With these coins, however, one could not buy tiny and cheap trinkets and give alms to the needy. Much greater harms result if the abuse is in the other direction—if the land is inundated with copper money like rivers flooded with winter storms. So much for the first disadvantage.

A second disadvantage is not only that it is against the laws of the land—that could be overlooked—but it is against right reason and the natural law itself—it is a sin to change them. To prove my point, one must remember what was established above: The king is not free to seize his subjects' goods and thus strip them from their lawful owners. May a prince break into granaries and take half of the grain stored there, and then compensate for the damage by authorizing the owners to sell the remainder at the same price as the original whole? No one would be so perverse as to condone such an act, but such was the case with the old copper coin. The king unjustly appropriated one-half of all the money, merely by doubling the value of each coin, so that what was worth 2 *maravedis* was thereafter worth 4. Would it be right for a king to triple by law the price for woolen and silk cloth at its present supply, while the proprietor keeps one-third for himself, and turns over the rest only to the king? Who would approve of that? But the same thing is happening with the copper money that has recently been minted. Less than a third of it is given to the owner. The king uses the rest for his own advantage.

Such things, of course, do not take place in other forms of commerce. They do, however, happen in the arena of money because the king has more power over money than over other things. He appoints all the ministers of the mint and changes them at will; he controls the dies and types of money, has complete authority to change them and to substitute debased coins for purer ones, and vice versa. Whether this is done rightly or wrongly is a controversial point. But Menochius[5] (*Consilium*, no. 48) deems it a new kind of crime to repay, with debased money, debts, incurred at a time when money was sound. He proves with many arguments that what was paid out in sound money is not rightly repaid in debased money.

We come to the third disadvantage: The cost of trade will be in proportion to the debasing of money. This is not simply a private judgment. Rather, such were the evils our ancestors experienced when our money was debased. In the history of the reign of Alfonso the Wise (chap. 1), reference is made to alteration of money at the beginning of his reign: Less sound *burgaleses* were substituted for the usual sound money, *pepiones* (gold coins). Ninety copper *burgaleses* were equal in value to a *maravedi*. This money change resulted in a general inflation. To remedy this situation, as chapter 5 recalls, the king taxed all sales. His remedy, however, caused the ailment to break out again. The merchants refused to sell things at that price. Necessarily, things came to a halt lest he arouse the hatred of the nation, or especially (as we believe) the arms of his nobles, who, after he was driven out, transferred affairs to his younger son, Sancho. Not content with his previous fraudulent mistake, he substituted the recalled *burgaleses* with bad money with the value of 15 *maravedis* in the sixth year of his reign. Thus, he remained obstinate in evil—a man deceitful by nature with a shattered genius that was ultimately evil.

The history of King Alfonso XI of Castile (chap. 98) informs us that he minted *novenes* and *coronados* of the same quality and stamp as his father, King Ferdinand. To avoid inflation with the change of money—doubtless, it was not sound—great care was taken to keep the price of silver from rising. Eight ounces of silver were valued at 125 *maravedis*—no more than before. This concern was feckless. There ensued scarcity of goods, and the price of silver increased. Here we should consider the fact that inflation is not the immediate and necessary consequence of changing money. As a matter of fact, a silver coin is now worth 34 of these debased *maravedis*—its previous worth—and 8 ounces of silver (which we call a *mark*) sells for 65 silver coins as it actually did before. Our account has made it clear that this condition cannot continue longer without disturbance. John I, in order to pay his rival, the Duke of Alencastre, a great sum of money, which had been agreed upon, minted unsound money, which he called "good." Shortly thereafter to avoid a scarcity of goods, he approved its payment at almost less than half, as he testified in the 1387 parliament of Burgos.

Then, there is Henry II, the father of John. As head of the kingdom, he had almost exhausted his treasury in wars against his brother Peter. Finally, reduced to dire financial straits, he minted two kinds of money: *regales*, worth 3 *maravedis*, and *cruzados*, worth 1 *maravedi*. As a result, prices and other things increased. The gold coin, known as the *dobla*, rose to 300 *maravedis*; a *caballo* was selling at 60,000 *maravedis*. This fact is found in his chronicles (the fourth year, chap. 10). Indeed in the sixth year, chapter 8, the *caballo* rose to 80,000 *maravedis*. Inflation soared. Under this pressure, this prince decreed devaluation of each coin by two-thirds. Indeed the gold coin was previously worth 30 *maravedis*, as Antonio Nebrissensis states in his *Repetitionibus* and as may be deduced from the value of silver, of which, 8 ounces, or a *mark*, were valued at 125 *maravedis* or certainly a little less (see chapter 8 of this treatise for an explanation of gold and silver's increase in value at that time). As a result of the alteration in coinage, the value of gold suddenly increased almost more than tenfold. I am convinced that there is never an alteration in coinage without subsequent inflation. To illustrate, let us suppose that the value of silver is doubled: What was worth 34 *maravedis* is now worth 68.

Some believe and maintain that if the value of silver were increased, the state would benefit to a greater or lesser degree. If this is true, one must ask, If someone wishes to buy 8 ounces of debased silver for 65 silver coins as its value is set by law, would the seller comply? Of course not! He will not sell it for less than 130 new silver coins, which is almost the weight of the silver itself. But if the value of silver is doubled because the value of coins is doubled, or should the coins increase to sixfold or fourfold, the same thing will happen with the value of natural silver. We see the same thing happen with the current copper coins; they are changed in some places into silver coins at the rate of 100 percent interest; in other places at 50 percent. Doubtless, what we have shown to occur in the case of silver will happen to other commodities as well: Their price will increase to the degree that the coins have been debased or the value of the coins increased, for that is exactly the way it is.

There is no doubt that it leads to new money. Each of these developments will contribute to commercial inflation. Abundance of money makes it worth less. As in other commercial enterprises, supply leads to low prices. Next, the baseness of coins will cause those who have this money to want to get rid of it immediately. Merchants will not wish to exchange their goods for that money, except with a great increase in price. All this leads to the fourth disadvantage: There will be trade difficulties, and trade is the foundation for public and private wealth. This problem always arises with debasement of money. Taxation of goods and sales to increase prices is a rather deadly solution to the problem. This approach is burdensome for merchants, and they will refuse to sell at that price. Once trade is destroyed and commercial inflation is in place, all the people will be reduced to want, and that will lead to disturbances. Thus, as experience has frequently taught us, the new money is either completely recalled or is certainly devalued, for example, by half or two-thirds. Then, suddenly and as in a dream, someone who had 300 gold pieces in this money, now has 100 or 150, and the same proportion applies to everything else.

King Henry II, according to his chronicles (sixth year, chap. 8), faced this situation and of necessity devalued the *real* from its previous worth of 3 *maravedis* to 1, and reduced the *cruzado* to 2 *coronados*, a third of its previous value. Henry's son, John I, devalued his good money to 6 *dineros*, almost half of its previous value. The resulting inflation continued, as the king admits in the 1388 parliament at Burgos. There is no need to recount how much trouble occurred in the regions. The facts speak for themselves. At the end of chapter 8, we noted occurrences of this type under John II. Eduardius Nunnius[6] recalls in his *Chronicles of Portugal* that, under King Ferdinand,[7] a great inflation resulted in Portugal because of the devaluing of money, and that a large amount of this counterfeit money was brought in by foreigners. He also says that the younger people, of necessity, viewed this money with a singular severity because many people were reduced to helplessness. Nonetheless, he says that, in our time, the same error was imprudently committed. During the reign of Sebastian[8] they minted copper money, called *batacones*, with the same evil results and the need to institute the same remedies.

Let us pass over the old examples, although what happened in Portugal is not that old. Sanderus[9] in his first book, *De schismate Anglicano*, affirms that, as he left the Church, Henry VIII[10] rushed into evils, and one of them was the fact that there was such a great devaluation of money. Consequently, whereas previously only a one-eleventh part of copper was mixed with silver coins, he gradually caused the coins to have no more one-sixth part silver to five parts copper. Then he ordered the old coins gathered into the treasury, and exchanged with an equal number of the new coins. A great injustice! After his death, the citizens approached his son

Edward[11] for a cure for these evils. The only solution was to devalue the new money by half. Elizabeth, Edward's sister, succeeded him, and devalued the new money by another half. Thus, someone who had 400 coins in that money quickly found them reduced to no more than 100. And the cheating continued. When the problems connected with this money did not slacken, a new decree had all that money remitted to the mints in the hope of compensation. Such compensation was never made. An infamous highway robbery! A most disgraceful peculation!

A prudent reader should notice whether we are getting on the same road; whether that historical moment is a portrait of the tragedy certainly threatening us. The fifth disadvantage, the king's subsequent poverty, may not be greater than the ones already mentioned, but it is certainly inevitable. A king receives no income from his ruined subjects and cannot prosper when the country is sick. Both these reasons are closely connected. If the citizens are crushed with penury, if trade is in turmoil, who will pay the king his customary revenue? The tax collectors will collect much less royal tribute. Are these statements dreams? Are they not verified by much history?

When Alfonso XI, king of Castile, was a still a minor, his guardians were forced to render an account for all the royal revenues. It was discovered that all together they did not exceed 1,600,000 *maravedis*, as found in his history (chap. 14). Those *maravedis* were, of course, worth more than ours: Each one was worth 17 of our current ones. Nevertheless, it was a remarkably paltry income and seemed incredible. The historian ascribes two reasons for so great a disaster: the first, the greediness of the nobles who possessed many towns and strongholds of the kingdom; the other that, from the time of Ferdinand, five kings had altered money either by debasing it or increasing its value. In this way, with trade hampered and the nation reduced to penury, the nation's common disadvantage reached the king.

We conclude with the final disadvantage, the greatest of them all: The general hatred that will be stirred up for the prince. As a certain historian says, everyone takes responsibility for prosperity, the head is responsible for adversity.[12] How was the victory lost? Obviously, the supreme commander was imprudent in organizing his battle lines, or he did not pay the soldiers the salary owed them. About 1300 A.D. Philip[13] the Fair, king of France, was the first-known French king to debase money. As a result, Dante,[14] a celebrated poet of the time, called him "a forger of money." Robertus Gaguinus[15] reports in his life of the king that Philip, at his death, repented his deed and told his son, Louis Hutin,[16] that he had to put up with his people's hatred because he had debased the coinage, and that Louis Hutin, therefore, was to correct his father's mistakes and hearken back to old reckonings. This concern proved useless. Before the people's hatred was defused, the one responsible for the monetary disaster, Enguerrano Marinio,[17] was publicly freed at the command of King Hutin, with the encouragement of some nobles, and the approval of the whole land. This was a clear-cut crime, but it did not prevent the future kings from following in the same footsteps. French history makes clear that Charles the Fair,[18] the brother of Hutin, caused a lot of trouble for his people. There is a law extant against him, the *De crimine falsi* of John XXII,[19] the Supreme Pontiff, and of Philip of Valois,[20] cousin and successor to both of these kings. Because of well-remembered misfortunes, the people of Aragón, in their dedication to, and interest in holding onto their freedom, demand from the king at his coronation an oath that he will never alter money. Petrus Belluga[21] mentions this point when he presents the two privileges granted to the people of Valencia by their kings in 1265 and 1336 (*Speculo Principum*, rubric 36, no. 5).[22] This is, doubtless, a healthy and prudent precaution. Greed causes blindness; financial straits create pressure; we forget the past. In this way, the cycle of evils returns. Personally, I wonder if those in charge of affairs are ignorant of these things. If they do know them, I wonder why they so rashly, despite their prudent knowledge, wish to rush headlong into these perils.

11

Should Silver Money Be Altered?

All the disadvantages that we have explained as coming from adulteration of copper money are found more forcefully in the case of silver money because of its quality and abundance. Gold money is always less used, and if the government is prudently administered, there will not be a great supply of copper money. Actually, silver is the backbone of commerce because it is conveniently exchanged for all other goods and used to liquidate contracted debts. Some, however, are not affected by the disadvantages derived from the debasing of copper coinage. They maintain that debasing silver coins would greatly benefit the state. I have therefore decided to explain now whether such a move would correct the damage experienced or cause all affairs of state to be subverted, everything going topsy-turvy. I personally believe that the latter will happen. Would that I were a false prophet!

This approach, they say, is the way to safety and peace. Outsiders will not be enticed by its quality to lay their greedy hands on our silver and seek profit by diverting it to other nations. Meanwhile, our legal provisions are rendered powerless through fraud and ambition. It is a fact that Spanish silver money is better than that of its neighbors by at least a one-eighth part. Although they do not go into it, silver would be a greater means of curing the king's financial needs, for, if from the exchange of base copper money of little value they bring into the treasury over 600,000 gold pieces, can we imagine what would happen if silver were debased? It is in great supply in Spain, and each year—incredibly—a greater amount is imported from the Indies. There is the further advantage—that we have no need to get this metal from outsiders, as we do, at great expense, with copper. When they

289

exchange their copper for our silver and gold, they gain a greater benefit—one is reminded of Glaucus and Diomedes.[1]

Certainly, we could make a huge profit if the silver were debased by a third or a fourth. Consider, for example, that silver could be devalued in three different ways. First, its value can be increased while the coin remains intact. Then, a silver coin, now worth 34 *maravedis*, would by law increase to 40, 50, or 60. Second, the weight could be diminished. We currently strike 67 silver pieces from 8 ounces of silver. In this situation, we would strike 80 or even 100, and each coin would continue to have its earlier value of 34 *maravedis*. On examination, this approach differs little from the previous one, because in either case the weight of silver is lessened, and the value increased.

The third way involves change by adding more copper, and this is the direction that the tricksters are going. Today 20 grains of copper are mixed with 8 ounces of silver; then they go further: Another 20 or 30 grains are mixed in. In this way, a profit of as much as 6 silver pieces on 8 ounces of silver is made, because each grain equals in value about 8 *maravedis*. Now if the yearly shipments from the Indies bring in 1,000,000 silver *marks*, at least 500,000 gold coins would be added to the treasury annually by means of this debasing. And this income, if sold at 20 percent interest, would annually collect revenue in gold, and the profit from this sale would increase to 10,000,000 gold pieces, or, according to the Romans, 4,000 *sesterces*. Once this type of fraud is introduced, if more copper is added—as seems likely—profit will increase in direct proportion to the corruption of the metal.

We must recall that silver in Spain for some time has been stamped with the standard of purity of 11 carats (minters call them *dineros*, a standard of silver with 24 grains) and 4 grains, namely, with the admixture of no more that 20 grains of copper. This is established by law for the minters of the kingdom. Silversmiths follow the same rule in regard to bullion and unworked silver. This is the same silver that they work with in their shops and make into different vessels. The same has been true for many centuries for the old silver in our churches. There is also a law of John II, king of Castile, as promulgated in the 1435 parliament of Madrid (petition 31)—the first law in *novae recopilationis* (bk. 5, title 22). Under these circumstances, I wish to ask these men who want to debase silver: Would their decree apply only to mints, or would it extend also to the workshops of the silver-smiths? If they answer, "both places," confusion will certainly reign. The silver already worked will not remain at its previous price. It will also vary in relation to the time when it was made.

Moreover, experts in this field say that silver, debased with more copper, will not be fit for elegant craftsmanship because of its crudity. Should people wish to resist corruption in money and not extend it to silversmiths, they should always bear in mind that silver, both as bullion and as minted, must be of the same qual-ity. Furthermore, silver, as bullion, will always necessarily be worth more than debased money, to the degree that the money has been debased. The complicated process has been going on for a great many years and only the destruction of the robbers and of the entire land will bring it to an end, as Tacitus maintains in a similar instance (*Annals*, bk. 20).[2]

What, then, is to be done about silver already minted? Is it to be worth the same as new debased money? That would be unjust, because the old is better and will contain more silver. Everyone will prefer it to the new, given the choice. But will it be worth more? That would be fair but also confusing: With the same weight and stamp, some silver coins would be worth more and others, worth less. But if we wish to go back to an earlier state, and to exchange them for just as many new ones, as we indicated was formerly done in England, that transaction will be just as profitable for the king, as it was in the case of copper money. One must consider, however, if this is a new speculation: to exchange good money for bad. It is not profitable to try people's patience. Patience can become exasperated and wear out and can destroy everything else, as well as be self-destructive.

Now, what will become of gold money? That must be considered, too. And this issue will certainly confound the highest with the lowest, and turn upside down things better left undisturbed. Once again, the same problems will arise. But if gold is not debased, it certainly follows that a gold piece (which we call a *corona*) will not be valued at 12 silver coins but, rather, at 14 or 15, in proportion to the debasing of silver. As silver is debased, commodities always become more expensive. Then foreigners and natives as well, conscious of the situation, will say: "Twelve new silver pieces contain no more silver than 10 of the previous ones; I will subtract the same proportion from the goods I used to give as well." We explained above what will happen if controls are imposed. Furthermore, not all prices can be controlled. Commerce, when interfered with, is like milk that is so delicate that it is spoiled by the most gentle breeze. As a matter of fact, money—especially silver money, because of its quality—is the ultimate foundation of commerce. When it is altered, everything else resting upon it will necessarily collapse. The stability of silver explains why the disadvantages from the alteration of copper money are not completely obvious. It acts as a restraint on copper money, because, as before, a silver piece is still exchanged for 34 *maravedis* of this new and debased coinage. Without this restraint, commerce would all but fail; everything would cost much more than before.

Moreover, suppose that our only money is copper and that silver is not being transported from the Indies. All the evils described in the previous chapter would suddenly come upon us in one fell swoop. Silver wards off these evils, because it is honorable and there is a good supply of it in the country. If this last reason seems weak, then a new and valid argument appears. All monetary income will be diminished to the degree that silver is changed. Someone who has an annuity of 1,000 gold pieces will suddenly receive only 800 or fewer, depending on the degree of debasing of silver. Certainly, when payment is necessarily made in new money, 1,000 gold pieces of new money will not have more silver and will not be more useful for living than 800 previous ones. And so, people, scarcely coping with previous taxes, will be oppressed by a new and very heavy one. Among those affected will be churches, monasteries, hospitals, gentlemen, and orphans—no one will be spared. Earlier, the point was clearly made that a new tax cannot be imposed without the people's consent. We still have to respond to the arguments advanced for the other side. The king gains nothing by profiting at the expense of his subjects, nor may he seize the citizens' possessions by either sheer force, cunning, or deceit. One man's loss is another man's gain. There is no way around that fact.

However, the previous argument asserted that silver was exported because of its excellence. I deny this statement outright, and point out that, although French gold pieces are somewhat better than ours and more valuable, ours are nonetheless found in that country in abundance. Two particular reasons explain this. First, Spaniards import the foreign goods they need, and since they cannot exchange an equal amount of their own goods for the imports, they have to pay money for the excess. Linen cloth, paper, books, metals, leather goods, trifles, different objects and, sometimes, grain are imported. Foreigners are under no obligation to give these goods free of charge, but they do so for other goods they need, and exchange them for money. Second, the king's yearly expenses and payments to foreigners reach 3,000 *sesterces*, seven million a year.[3] Unless this sum were paid out to bankers with the authority to postpone payment, when the king needs it, it would not be at hand. Someone, however, may tenaciously insist that the excellence of silver serves the same purpose. I do not disagree, provided that my adversary understands that there is no way to keep foreigners from constantly making their money inferior to ours. In this way, they get their hands on our silver, which they certainly need more than life.

Is there, then, a way to correct the disadvantages that arise from the debasement of, and abundance of copper money? I have never believed that a concrete disadvantage may be corrected by a greater disadvantage, or a sin by a sin. Some cures are worse than the sickness. Furthermore, I am not aware of any cure for this illness, except the one that our ancestors constantly used in similar straits, namely: The value of the new money is reduced by half or by two-thirds.[4] If that approach is not enough to heal the wound, the bad money is to be completely recalled and good money put in its place. It is, of course, only just that either solution makes the one who profited from the general disaster pay. But since I see this approach is not common—indeed never employed—it is preferable for those who are in possession of the money to suffer a loss. Otherwise, by continuing longer in error, we aggravate the causes of a stubborn illness. On the other hand, we can have recourse to devaluing money. This would involve general disaster for all. It is clear that the pivots on which this entire issue turns are those two values of money that were explained in chapter 4. They must be mutually adjusted if we want things to be sound. That means that money should be legal, but if the values are separated (which, it seems, will happen if silver is debased) every possible evil will come upon the state.

We end with this point: In 1368, when a great part of France was under the English kings,[5] the Prince of Wales,[6] who was running affairs in France for his father, the king, levied a new tax on his vassals. He did this because his treasury was exhausted by the wars he was waging on behalf of Peter,[7] the king of Castile. Very many refused to accept this new burden; others like those in Poitiers, Limoges, and La Rochelle agreed, on condition that the prince would not alter money for the next seven years. Jean Froissart,[8] the French historian, relates this in his *Annals* (vol. 1). This account makes it clear that princes have debased money, but that the citizenry have always disapproved of and rejected it as they could. It would be beneficial if our people would learn from this example and agree to financial subsidies when the king requests them, on condition that the prince promises that money would be stable for as long as they could demand.

12

Concerning Gold Money

Gold money varies greatly. I am not talking about the still extant money of the first Roman Emperors—gold coins minted from the most pure gold with their names inscribed on them. On the other hand, when the Goths were in control in Spain, impure and base gold was coined—gold of 12 or 13 carats—because of many additions. Nonetheless, some of their kings' coins of better gold have been discovered. We have, moreover, seen one coin that was 22 carats. We need not go into the monetary arrangements of the kings of León and Castile when Spain was coming into power: We do not happen to see gold from that period, and it would be very laborious to delay on it.

I will deal only with those changes that were made in gold from the time of King Ferdinand and Queen Isabella. At the beginning of their reign, these rulers minted coins from very pure gold of $23^{3}/_{4}$ carats, which they called *castellanos*: 50 from 8 ounces of gold, with each coin worth 485 *maravedis*. Thus, the 8 ounces, once minted, were worth 24,250 *maravedis*. But as bullion of the same quality, the *mark* was worth only 250 *maravedis* less. This difference, after the gold was minted, used to be divided equally among the officers of the mint and the owner of the gold. At the same time, 8 ounces of 22 carat gold bullion was worth 22,000 *maravedis*, and the bullion weight of a *castellano* was worth 440 *maravedis*, because gold of that sort was not being minted at that time. Only goldsmiths employed it in their craft. Neighboring nations used gold minted in accordance with our quality and price. This fact created no difficulties.

Then, a little while later, to the glory and prosperity of our nation, the western passage to the Indies was opened and a large amount of gold was imported every year. In their desire for our gold, some of our neighbors debased the quality of their own, and others increased the price of ours. Conscious of these ploys, our people did not debase the quality of their gold at that time; they just increased its price. Therefore, in the 1497 parliament of Medina, the same rulers[1] decreed by law that no more *castellanos* were to be minted but, in their place, *ducats*[2] were to be minted, which they called "excellent." From the previous 8 ounces of gold of the same purity, 65$\frac{1}{3}$ such coins were to be minted, each valued at 375 *maravedis*. And so, minted gold advanced to 24,500 *maravedis*; gold bullion or jewelry of the same weight was worth 24,250 *maravedis*. At the same time, 8 ounces or a *mark* of 22 carat gold was worth 22,500 *maravedis*, and the value of a *castellano* was 450 *maravedis*. This rate continued for several years until it was noticed that the neighbors were further debasing gold.

Thus, in the 1537 parliament of Valladolid, Charles Augustus[3] changed things completely and decreed by law that gold of precisely 22 carats was to be minted. Sixty-eight coins were to be minted from 8 ounces, and, called *coronas*, each was worth 350 *maravedis*. As a result, 8 ounces of this money were worth 22,800 *maravedis*. There was no legislation concerning gold bullion or gold, either coined or as jewelry. It was bought and sold by agreement like merchandise. The *novae recopilationis* (bk. 5, pt. 1, law 4, title 24) decrees that goldsmiths were to work no other gold but the purest, or 22 carat, or at least 20 carat. Therefore, unlike silver, gold bullion did not always parallel minted gold and was not governed by the law for minted gold. Nonetheless, for the most part, 22 carat gold was minted and was common with goldsmiths. Because of its lower price in Castile, foreigners kept exporting gold, which had been exchanged for crafts and goods. This fact compelled Philip II, king of Spain, to increase the price of gold in each *corona* by 50 *maravedis* in the parliament of Madrid. Consequently, what used to be valued at 350 *maravedis* went up to 400 *maravedis*. With this law, 8 ounces of minted gold reached 27,200 *maravedis*. The *castellano* was worth 16 silver coins or *reales*.

At this point, we may consider the possibility of debasing gold coins. Just as the quality of copper coins was diminished, and just as they are thinking about doing the same with silver coins—as rumor has it—would the state benefit if the same thing were done with gold coins? They would have less quality and be increased in value. The issue is the same. I personally believe that every alteration in money is very dangerous. It is never expedient to mint unlawful money and thus increase by law the cost of something that is commonly considered to be worth less. Nor can our neighbors be prevented from further debasing their money because of our example. We have learned by experience from the four changes made in gold since the time of the rulers, Ferdinand and Isabella, that it is impossible to prevent the gold from being carried off.

But if gold coins are greatly debased, perhaps foreigners would scorn it. Certainly, it would lose much of its value. I doubt that such a situation would befit the majesty of Spain. In my opinion, however, it would not cause serious harm if gold were altered by taking away part of its quality and increasing its price. This is especially true because such a change in the past, when repeated frequently within a few years, did not bring serious disadvantages. The supply of gold is always small in comparison to silver, and its use as money is less common and usual. And so, I have not been accustomed to believe that it would be very disadvantageous if an alteration were to occur. In any event, I have always been convinced that I would wish things to hold to their course and not be concerned with money. Nor does the opposite approach benefit in any way, except to provide income for the prince. And income should not always be our goal, especially by this means, that is, debasing money. As a matter of fact, provided that the original quality and reckoning of copper and silver money remain intact, I would not be too concerned about what happens to gold in either way. Two things are important: One, that it be done with the consent of the subjects concerned; the other, that the money always be legitimate or legal, and not otherwise. To achieve this end for copper money, both values must be equal: The value of the metal, whether mixed with silver or not, must be computed, as well as the cost of minting. Thus, if 8 ounces, or a *mark*, of copper along with the expenses of minting cost only 80 *maravedis*, it is unreasonable to permit its value to be increased by law to 280 *maravedis*, as is now done. It is unlawful to do so to the degree that legal value deviates from real value. To preserve parity in the case of gold and silver, their proportional relationship must be considered. If they are of equal purity, gold is compared to silver by a ratio of 12 to 1, as Budaeus[4] says in *De asse* (bk. 3). I say of each, "purity or quality," because just as the purity of gold is commonly divided into 24 grades, which the goldsmiths call "carats," so the purity of silver is divided into 12 *dineros*.[5] Thus, silver of 11 *dineros* ably corresponds to 22 carat gold. And this proportion generally holds between these two metals. Of course, the ratio would change because of the scarcity or plenitude of one or the other metal. They are like other goods: An ample supply lowers the price, and scarcity raises it. As a result, we should not be surprised that the ancient authors do not agree on how gold and silver were related to one another in value. Therefore, gold and silver money of the same purity and weight should be carefully exchanged at the rate of 12 silver coins for 1 gold coin, as now happens. For that is lawful. If that value is exceeded or lessened, the whole transaction smacks of fraud. For example, if a gold *corona* is exchanged for 16 or 18 silver ones (*reales*), this transaction is a clear-cut violation of monetary justice, unless, of course, the purity of the gold is increased or the purity of the silver lessened. When such is the case, what seemed to be unjust is lawful and in keeping with equity. Finally, it is of the utmost importance that princes do not profit from debased money. Were that permitted, it would be impossible to curb the greed of foreigners and countrymen who, in the hope of great profit, would force upon us counterfeit and adulterated money of the same kind.

13

Is There Some Way to Assist the Prince in His Need?

The popular proverb is quite true: "Necessity knows no law." But another one says: "The stomach has no ears," which is to say that it is a harsh demander: It does not give way to arguments. But that problem is easily handled: The stomach settles down after eating. Certainly, such needs and wants arise in the state that it is not surprising that those in charge of administration dream up some uncommon and inept remedies. One such remedy is clearly the recently adopted debasement of money. We have explained this point in the arguments of this disputation, but if this remedy is not satisfactory, we will have to find another more suitable way to fill up the treasury.

I do not intend to treat so great an issue. My purpose has been to condemn the alteration of money as a base crime that is full of great disadvantages. It would be pleasant to address some other ways and means—perhaps more suitable and ultimately more fruitful—of enriching the prince. One might add that there are ways and means that involve no injury to, or groaning of the nation; they will, rather, meet with the greatest approval. First of all, somehow, court expenditures could be lessened, for reasonable and prudent moderation is more splendid and manifests more majesty than unnecessary and unseasonable consumption.

In an account of royal taxes and expenses, receipts, and outlays of John II, king of Castile, for the year 1429, we find that the annual expenses of the court, including the ministers' salaries, gifts, and the royal table, amounted to hardly 30,000 gold pieces. Someone might say that these accounts are very old; everything has changed; prices are much more expensive; kings are more powerful, and, therefore, greater pomp and majesty are found at court. I do not deny these facts, but, really, all of these do not adequately explain the difference between the 30,000 of those days and the 120,000 that are spent at this time for the support of the court. Moreover, a more recent account of royal taxes, with the expenses for 1564 for the court of Philip II, king of Spain, for the support of prince Charles, his son,[1] and John of Austria,[2] reports that annually they amounted to no more than 40,000 gold pieces.

How, you ask, can court expenses be curtailed? I do not know. Prudent men who are involved in the court should make that determination. Common opinion has it that whatever the purveyor hands over to the stewards is stored in the pantry and paid for automatically. Second, royal gifts would perhaps be smaller if a large tax were added to them. I do not believe that a king should have a reputation for being cheap, or not be sufficiently generous in response to his people's good works and services. I believe that two things have to be taken into consideration. There is, of course, no nation in the world with more and greater public rewards available: commissions, offices, pensions, benefices, military towns, and gifts. Were these distributed reasonably and deliberately, one could dispense with extraordinary gifts from the royal treasury and other income. Too, we should remember that excessive gifts do not make men more disposed for service, or even well-disposed to the giver. It is human to be led on more by the hope of a future reward than by the memory of a favor received. So true is this, that those who have prospered much at court constantly think of retirement and the peaceful life.

No king of Castile lived more magnificently than did Henry IV, and in no other time was the unrest as great. As a result, after Henry's abdication, the nobles made his brother, Alfonso,[3] king. After his death, they offered the kingdom to Isabella, who was the sister of both of them. Tacitus makes a telling comment at the end of book 19[4]: "Vitellius,[5] inasmuch as he wished to have friends because of the greatness of his gifts rather than because of the constancy of his morals, bought more friends than he had." Robert of Sorbonne,[6] his confessor and Archdeacon of Tornai, tells us in his life of Saint Louis,[7] king of France, that when he wanted to establish a college in Paris that still bears his name, the Sorbonne—no other college in the world may be compared with it for learning—he asked the king for a contribution. The king answered that he would willingly comply with his request if only chosen theologians, after examining public expenses and income, would determine how he might lawfully contribute to this work. He was a great king and a real saint. If he did not lavish money on this holy work without discernment and examination, would he squander it on fattening up the courtiers, on the vain pleasures of gardens and unnecessary buildings? The reality is that a king has income from the nation to support public works. When he has taken care of them, he may direct it to other things—but not before. If I were to send a commissioner to Rome to foster my affairs, would he be permitted to divert the money that I gave him for necessary expenses to other uses?

A king is not permitted to apply money given to him by his subjects as freely as he may apply income from lands held as a private citizen. Furthermore, he should exempt himself from unnecessary expenditures and from wars. Parts that cannot be cured should be timely cut off from the rest of the body. Philip II, king of Spain, wisely separated the Belgians from the rest of his empire.[8] Mapheius[9] indicates in *Indicarum historiarum* (bk. 6) that the Chinese nation—an empire once much bigger than it is now—as if in a blood-letting and correction of excess, gave up many lands that it could not conveniently govern. Emperor Hadrian[10] did the same thing when he destroyed the bridge that Trajan had built over the Danube. He wished the Danube on the north and the Euphrates in the East to be the limits of the Roman empire, which was already struggling under its own weight.

The fourth rule should be that, first of all, court ministers must be accountable, and after them, the magistrates of the provinces and all others who play any role in the state. We are in a dangerous situation where hardly anyone is safe. The way that people think is really pitiful. They believe that merit now has nothing to do with gaining anything in our land: office, commission, benefice, even a bishopric. Everything is for sale, and nothing is conferred without its price. Although it may not be true and is exaggerated, it is pernicious to have such a thing stated. In general, royal ministers, penniless nobodies, enter upon public commissions, and almost instantly become blessed and reckon their annuities in thousands of gold pieces. All these things come from the blood of the poor, from the very marrow of litigants and office-seekers. Moreover, such transformations have led me to think that the state would benefit if it adopted the ways of the Church. Before they assume office, bishops must present a witnessed account of all their possessions. Then, at death, they may leave these things, and nothing else, to those whom they wish. The chosen ministers of court, or magistrates, or other commissioners should have to do what bishops do. Through periodic investigations, they will be forced to render an account of their newly acquired wealth, and will be stripped of that wealth whose definite sources and causes they fail to identify. The treasury would greatly profit from money recovered should this inquiry and investigation be instituted.

Public opinion often condemns those in charge of royal taxes because, by agreement with tax collectors, they usurp a sizable part of the gain and money that the collectors gather. Worse yet, in every city, leaders make money by selling the local or royal laws every year to those who refuse to obey them. They openly grant public privileges to those from whom they secretly receive money. We cannot ignore the different forms of corruption and ways of cheating the provincials. When King Philip II recently decreed that the value of *coronados* rise by an eighth, a favorite of the king, with knowledge of this decision, was proven to have scraped together all the gold brought across the Atlantic each year, and to have made a huge profit.

A certain Jewish chief treasurer asked one of the earlier kings of Castile—John II or his father, Henry,[11] I believe—why he did not play dice with his courtiers to pass the time. The king answered: "How can I do that since I do not own a hundred gold pieces?" The treasurer let that pass at the time. Later, at an opportune moment, he said, "O King, your statement to me the other day sorely disturbed me. So much so, that I thought I was being indirectly rebuked. If you agree, I will make you wealthy and happy instead of poor." The king went with his proposal. Then, the treasurer said: "I want control of three secluded castles." There he intended to keep money and the prisoners proved guilty of crimes in the use of royal money. Then, questioning minor treasurers, he kept finding the royal name on forged documents and other bequests of the prince, paid with a third or a fourth subtracted for those who handled the royal promissory notes. Then he asked those who had been defrauded, if they would be content with half of what they had lost, and if they would give the rest to the king. They agreed, considering the offer a gain, since until then they had no hope of future compensation. When these arrangements had been made, he put the treasurer and his bailsmen into chains, where they remained until payment of all the money. In this way, he enriched the treasury.

It would be nice if such could occur at the present time. It would save a large amount of money. Nowadays, this new corruption is an indication of the perverted government—treasurers purchase their positions at a large price—and have to sell the office and profit from the misery of others. They invest the royal money in commerce and do not meet royal debts for a year or two. And most conveniently, after four or eight months, they pay the debt, even with some expense deducted, namely, an ounce or two ounces from the entire sum, as they agreed with the creditor. Such corruption could be eradicated if individuals were investigated as we mentioned above. But, truly or falsely, the claim is commonly made that every one of these treasurers has supporters in the court among the magistrates. Part of the explanation for this is, of course, the hope for peculation. And this misfortune is no less-deadly than the earlier ones. Above all, the royal taxes and income should be taken care of diligently and faithfully. Under current practice, scarcely half of the taxes and income is turned to royal use. Money, transferred through many ministers, is like a liquid. It always leaves a residue in the container. Our *Annals*[12] (bk. 19, chap. 14) testify that the king of Castile, Henry III, by exercising such care, escaped the shameless poverty once found in his court. He used to have to buy ram's meat for dinner and finally wound up very wealthy. He left his son, John II, huge treasures without any complaints from the provincials. His only warning to him and to his brother, Ferdinand,[13] was not to let the ministers get their greedy hands on public money.

Finally, strange and luxurious merchandise—which softens people and which we can do without and suffer no harm—should be sold at a high tariff, for such an approach will discourage their import, something very desirable. Or, if they are imported, the treasury will be bolstered by the tariff levied upon delicacies of foreign people: gold brocade, tapestries, all sorts of perfumes, sugar, and delicacies. Alexander Severus[14] did this once in Rome and was endlessly praised. We have discussed this point rather fully in our *De rege et regis institutione*[15] (bk. 3, chap.

7), and so, there is no need to dwell on it here. I add only this point: The ways to provide for the royal needs discussed here, indeed any one of them, would provide more than the 200,000 gold pieces annually, which is the same amount the first authors promised the king in their paper on debasing copper money. Moreover, this will happen without any censure from the people. Rather, the poor will enthusiastically support the measure.

There might be an objection that we should not be surprised to find a means—that is, debasing coinage, being employed that different kings used in the past. We readily reply. Times have changed much since the past: The king's income was much less then; there was no sales tax; there was no gold from the Indies; there was no tax on wine and oil; there were no monopolies, no Church tithes, no crusade subsidies, and kings were not grand masters of military orders. Every year, all of these provide abundant income. The problems were greater at that time: The Moors were at the gates; there were wars with neighboring kings; the nobles were frequently in revolt, and internal rebellion resulted. Now, on the other hand, by the grace of God, there is internal peace throughout all of Spain. I will say absolutely nothing about foreign affairs. In 1540, Francis I,[16] king of France, debased the *solidus*—the nation's common coin—and his son, Henry,[17] mixed in even more copper. Charles IX,[18] following the example of his grandfather and his father, reduced its quality and weight even further. Great difficulties were certainly impending, but the monetary troubles were so great that there was no need to lament the other evils. The afflicted people were in tumult: Ancient religious convictions were changed at random, and very many, driven by want, changed their countries and lived at the mercy of others.

The account in our *Annals* (bk. 29, chap. 12) deserves mention here. Because of Philip of Austria's death and the weakness of his bereaved wife, Maximilian Augustus[19] and Ferdinand the Catholic were long at odds over the administration of Castile and were considering some means of reaching peace. Among other things, Augustus was demanding the payment of 100,000 gold pieces from the income of Castile. The Catholic king was not able to grant the request and pleaded, as an excuse, that the public debt had increased to 500,000 gold pieces. Clearly, this is a remarkable response. Taxes were much less than they are now; wars were more serious than ever; and corresponding hopes were aroused. Portugal was conquered and driven out of our territory; Atlantic trade was open; the kingdom of Granada was subjugated; the coasts of Africa, the Basques, and Neapolitans were defeated; moreover, there was peace in the kingdom, and the Italian wars, in which the kingdom always played a major role, were abating. Nevertheless, the kingdom was oppressed by a burden that was indeed light if compared with the debts of our day. It makes sense. A prince of outstanding prudence kept account of income and outlays and did not wish to be pressed further. And that is great wisdom. It is not reasonable to blame the times. That incident took place in 1509, when a good deal of gold was being brought into the treasury every year. I do not believe that times have changed since then, but men, abilities, morals, and pleasures have changed. The weight of these evils will dash this empire to the ground if God does not support it with his favor and saving hand.

Such are my thoughts on the subjects discussed in this disputation, and particularly on the subject of altering and debasing copper money. If such is done, without consulting the people, it is unjust; if done with their consent, it is in many ways fatal. If my arguments have been true and reasonable, I thank God. If, however, I have been mistaken, I certainly deserve to be pardoned because of my sincere desire to help. My knowledge of past evils makes me afraid that we will fall into misfortunes from which it will be difficult to extricate ourselves, but if my statements in this disputation have irritated anyone, he should recall that salubrious remedies are frequently bitter and stinging. Moreover, when a subject is a common concern, everyone is free to express his opinion on it, whether he speaks the truth or is mistaken. Finally, I beg God to shed his light upon the eyes and minds of those who are responsible for these things, so that they may peacefully agree to embrace and put into action wholesome advice, once it is known.

NOTES

Preface

1. Lucian of Samosata (ca. 120–180 A.D.), a Greek satirist who traveled widely as a rhetorician until approximately 165, when he left rhetoric to study philosophy and write in Athens. He composed 80 prose pieces in various forms, essays, speeches, letters, dialogues, and stories, in which he satirically portrayed the manners, morals, and beliefs of Athenians. His writing was influenced by Aristophanes, Theophrastus, and Menippus, and his amusing burlesques of myths, poets, and historians; of bluff, cheating, and necromancy made him a favorite of Renaissance humanists. (NCE, VIII, 1058, s.v. Lucian of Samosata) A fuller account of Corinth's attack can be found in Thucydides' *Peloponnesian War* (II.91–95), which Lucian's report is likely based upon.

2. Philip II of Macedon (382–336 B.C.), father of Alexander the Great and conqueror of Greece, Illyria, and Thrace, ruled Macedonia from 359–336. After the Battle of Chariots described in Thucydides' *Peloponnesian War* Corinth became a Macedonian garrison.

3. Diogenes the Cynic (ca. 400–325 B.C.), after his arrival in Athens, seems to have been attracted by the austere character and way of life of Antisthenes, which perhaps influenced him in his fanatical espousal of the "natural" life, the subject of many anecdotes. While in Athens he was reputed to have lived in a tub (of earthenware) belonging to Metroon (temple of the Mother of the gods). Later, while on a voyage, he was captured by pirates and sold as a slave to a Corinthian. This is how he ended up in Corinth, which is where he is said to have met Alexander the Great. For him, happiness consists in satisfying only the most elementary needs of food and shelter, living on one's own natural endowments, and renouncing all possessions and relationships. Physical and mental self-discipline is the key to achieving the kind of self-sufficiency Diogenes sought. (OCD, 473–74, s.v. Diogenes the Cynic)

4. Plutarch (ca. 46-ca. 120 A.D.), Greek biographer, historian, and moral philosopher, studied philosophy at Athens under the Platonist Ammonius. He is the author of a series of fifty biographies known as *Parallel Lives* in which he relates the life of some eminent Greek (statesmen or soldier) followed by the life of some similar Roman offering some points of resemblance, and then a short comparison of the two. He includes biographies of such people

as Solon, Themistocles, Aristeides, Pericles, Alcibiades, Demosthenes, Alexander, Pyrrhus, Pompey, Mark Antony, Brutus, Julius Caesar, Cicero, and others. Plutarch's object in the *Lives* is to bring out a subject's moral character, rather than to recount the political events of the time. However, besides interesting anecdotes, the *Lives* contain memorable historical passages related to specific events in the Peloponnesian War such as the one Mariana recounts of Solon. (OCD, 1200–01, s.v. Plutarch)

5. Solon (ca. 640-after 561 B.C.), Athenian statesman and poet, wrote elegiac and iambic poetry to publicize and justify his political policies. He was elected archon in 594/3 at a time when Athens was on the brink of revolution, largely because of an agrarian system in which landowners grew rich and the poor were reduced to slavery. Solon's moderate and humane reforms helped to produce the constitutional framework that made the eventual transition to democratic rule easier. In a famous reply to the poet Mimnermus, who had said that he wanted to die when he reached 60, Solon declared that the poet should rather say 80. This remark should probably be taken in conjunction with another famous line by Solon to the effect that even as he grows old he still continues to learn. (OCD, 1421–22, s.v. Solon)

6. Old Testament prophet who was among the Jews exiled to Babylon by King Nebuchadnezzar in 597 B.C. Ezekiel was a man of broad knowledge, not only of his own nation's history but also of international affairs and history. Mariana's reference is likely to Ezekiel 33:1–7.

Chapter 1

1. Aristotle (384–322 B.C.) was a student of Plato and later founded his own peripatetic school of philosophy. Moreover, he was also Alexander the Great's private tutor. Aristotle developed a comprehensive philosophy that encompassed such domains as logic, physics (natural science and metaphysics), ethics, and politics. Mariana is likely referring to V.x.1–10 in Aristotle's *Politics*.

2. *Novellae* are authoritative determinations (such as laws, edicts, judgments, etc.) that actually provide legal supplements and have been compiled into the form of a digest. The exact date of composition of these short treatises and the binding force associated with the legal compilations was the so-called *Nueva Recopilación* (i.e. *Recopilación de leyes de estos Reynos*) of 1569. Prior to 1569 the Catholic Kings Ferdinand and Isabella assigned the title *Ordinamentum* to the collected *novellae*. (DMA, 7, 429–30, s.v. Law Codes: 1000–1500; and DMA, 7, 522–23, s.v. Law, Spanish)

3. The story of Naboth's vineyard can be found in 1 Kings 21.

4. Over time numerous commentaries and handbooks (with varying degrees of authority) were written and appended to the *Nueva Recopilación*. In his Spanish translation of the work in question Mariana assigned the title *De iuresdictione*.

5. Nicolò de' Tudeschi (1386–1445), also known as "abbas modernus" or "recentior," "abbas Panormitanus" or "Siculus," was a Benedictine canonist. In 1400 he entered the Order of Saint Benedict; he was sent to the University of Bologna to study under Zabarella; in 1411 he became a doctor of canon law, and taught successively at Parma (1412–18), Siena (1419–30), and Bologna (1431–32). Meanwhile in 1425, he was made abbot of the monastery of Maniacio, near Massina, whence his title "abbas." In 1434 he placed himself at the service of Alfonso of Castile, King of Sicily, obtaining the See of Palermo in 1435, whence his name "Panormitanus." During the troubles that plagued the pontificate of Eugene IV, Nicolò at first followed the party of the pontiff but subsequently allied himself with the

papal contender Felix V who, in 1440, named him cardinal. In his *Tractatus de concilio Basileensi* he upheld the doctrine of the superiority of a general council to the pope. It was his canonical works, especially his commentary on the decretals of Pope Gregory IX that won him the title of *lucerna juris* ("lamp of the law") and insured him great authority; he also wrote *Consilia, Quaestiones, Repetitiones, Disputationes, disceptationes et allegationes*, and *Flores utriusque juris*. (CE, XI, 69, s.v. Nicolò de' Tudeschi)

Chapter 2

1. Philippe de Comines (1447–1511) wrote the biography of Louis XI, King of France, which was originally titled: *Les mémoires de Messire Philippe de Commines, Chevalier, Seigneur d'Argenton sur les principaux faicts et gestes de Louis onzième et de Charles huictième, son fils, Roys de France*. Louis XI (1423–1483), the son of Charles VII and Mary of Anjou, took the throne in 1461. Louis, due to a quarrel with his father in 1447, was living in exile in Burgundy when he succeeded to the throne in July 1461. Afterward Louis set out to persecute his father's principal ministers, but Louis' Burgundian friends began to take advantage of his weaknesses. He then attempted to thwart the Burgundians through several costly efforts. After buying off Edward IV's invasion of France in 1475, he subsidized Swiss attacks on his father's loyal associates. To augment his revenue he encouraged French trade and industry and suppressed several independent fiefs when the direct lines died out. He abolished the Pragmatic Sanction, but retained control of the Church, as his father had. Louis was disliked for several reasons, not the least of which concerned his financial exactions, tyrannical manner, and diplomatic duplicity. (NCE, VIII, 1012, s.v. Louis XI, King of France)

2. Charles VII (1403–1461) succeeded to the throne in 1422 as the fifth of the Valois dynasty. Charles VII, son of the insane Charles VI, inherited a divided France whose northern half was ruled by an Anglo-Burgundian coalition. Charles was largely unsuccessful in his attempt to overthrow the northern coalition until Joan of Arc appeared and raised the siege of Orléans. After Joan's capture (May 13, 1430) inactivity followed, but in 1435 Philip the Fair, Duke of Burgundy, switched sides, an event that made French victory inevitable. Soon Paris was taken, then Normandy, and shortly thereafter Guienne. Though frail, Charles is credited with helping to create French absolutism by centralizing administration, including permanent and arbitrary taxation, and creating a standing army. Charles was also the victor in the Hundred Years' War. (NCE, III, 501, s.v. Charles VII, King of France)

3. The civil wars in France during Mariana's lifetime (1536–1624) were the front line in the religious wars between Roman Catholics and Protestants. The unrest in France was also fomented by Francis I's creation of the *trésorier de l'épargne*, which was designed to facilitate the collection of taxes and provide needed revenue for warfare and a lavish court. Although the *trésorier de l'épargne* attempted to centralize all monetary activity, its purpose was never quite accomplished, and Francis continually searched for new sources of revenue. (NCE, VI, 27, s.v. Francis I, King of France)

4. Alfonso XI (1311–1350) of Castile and León, son of Ferdinand IV and Constance of Portugal, succeeded to the throne in 1312 and began his reign in 1325. During the reign of Alfonso XI, "Significant legislative work and judicial streamlining were carried out at the Cortes of Burgos in 1328 and at the Cortes of Segovia in 1347. In 1348, the Cortes meeting at Alcalá de Henares produced the very important *Ordenamiento de Alcalá de Henares*, which confirmed previous laws; set up new rules on matters of procedure, wills, contracts,

and royal dealings with the nobility; and above all, established the order of precedence of the law then in force in Castile and León." (DMA, 7, 523, s.v. Law, Spanish)

5. A bull is an occasional letter issued by the Roman Pontiffs of their most important utterances. The quasi-official collection of bulls and briefs is known as the *Bullarium Romanum* and includes encyclicals, motu proprios, and other similar constitutions that possess just the same force, as sources of the canon law, as the decretals one would expect to find there. After the thirteenth century, due largely to the great codifying and systematizing work of Innocent III, bulls are commonly classified as either *tituli* or *mandamenta*. The *tituli* were for the most part acts of grace (*indulgentiae*), concessions of privileges, confirmations, decisions on points of doctrine or law, and so forth. Whereas the *mandamenta* represented the ordinary correspondence of the Holy See. They were orders of the Pope, commissions to conduct an inquiry or to reform abuses, letters written to communicate some important knowledge, or to invite the cooperation of temporal sovereigns, or to prescribe a line of conduct for clergy or laity. It is important to note that the decretals, upon which the structure of canon law was built, almost always took the form of lesser bulls, that is, simple letters or *mandamenta*. The first known *Bulla in Coena Domini*, containing the "Reserved Cases" of the Holy See, issued by Urban V in 1364, was a *mandamentum*. The range and scope of issues that this particular bull addressed grew over time and included such items as how to handle tyrannical princes, usury, and matters pertaining to coinage. (ERE, II, 891–97, s.v. Bulls and Briefs)

Chapter 3

1. Frederick Augustus II (1194–1250), son of Emperor Henry VI and Constance, daughter of Roger VI of Sicily, succeeded to throne in 1220. Frederick's reign united the Hohenstaufen claims to the imperial throne and his mother's claim to rule the Kingdom of Sicily. In 1220 Frederick descended into Italy to claim his mother's territory. At this time, Honorius III placed the imperial crown upon his head, while Frederick pledged anew to take up the cross. But unrest in the Kingdom of Sicily increased the difficulty in establishing his rule there, which took five years to resolve. Mariana's reference to the events surrounding Frederick's siege of the northern Italian city of Faenza took place early in the Italian invasion. Of all the heirs of Charlemagne, it is said that Frederick II came closest to sharing his vision. With Frederick's death, the Holy Roman Empire lost most of its spirit and vitality. (NCE, VI, 86–87, s.v. Frederick II, Roman Emperor)

2. Pandolfo Collenuccio (1444–1504), historian, poet, scientist, and statesman, studied law at Padua, and then entered the service of the Sforza at Pesaro. He was an accomplished diplomat and carried out numerous missions for his patrons, until he was expelled from Pesaro by his lord, Giovanni Sforza. Collenuccio's great reputation as a lawyer, man of letters, and skillful diplomat brought him into contact with Lorenzo the Magnificent, Ercole I d'Este, the Emperor Maximilian, and Pope Alexander VI. Collenuccio wrote a history of Naples (*Compendio della historie del regno di Napoli*), Latin and Italian poems, and made the translation *Anfitrione* of the comedy of Plautus. (NCIRE, 257, s.v. Collenuccio, Pandolfo)

3. René Budel was born in Ruremonde in 1530, his death date is unknown. He was a lawyer and worked as a diplomat in the service of the Electors of Cologne and the Dukes of Bayern, who appointed him as the mint-master in the Duchy of Westfalen. His work, *De Monetis et Re nummaria libri duos: his accesserunt tractatus varii atque utiles tam veterum quam neotericorum authorum*, which Mariana cites, appeared in Cologne in 1591. The first

book treats the art of money stamping, while the second evaluates legal questions, which earlier scholars had divided into strict compartments, tied up with a monetary system. (Nbg, VII-VIII, 726, s.v. Budel or Budelius, René)

4. Hostiensius (1200–1271), also known as Henry of Segusio or Enrico Bartolomei, was a cardinal and canonist whose writings exerted great influence on canon law in the thirteenth century and beyond. He was not only one of the most famous decretalists, he was also a competent diplomat. Innocent IV appointed him archbishop of Embrun. His important work, the *Lectura in quinque libros decretalium*, is a commentary upon all of Gregory IX's decretals. The *Lectura*, along with his *Summa 'Copiosa'*, both written early in his career when he taught in Paris, synthesized Roman and canon law and thus accomplished a summary of the *utrumque ius*. These treatises became the stock-in-trade of canonists until well into the seventeenth century. (NCE, VII, 170–71, s.v. Hostiensis [Henry of Segusio])

5. Pope Innocent III (1160/61–1216), whose papacy began in 1198, embodies better than any other medieval papal representative the belief that the pope was the true Vicar of Christ on earth. He brought into clear relief the exclusively legal function of the pope as the successor of Peter, at the same time making precise the definition of Petrine powers as vicarious powers of Christ himself. In one of his consecration sermons Innocent declared that he was less than God, but greater than man, standing as it were in the middle. The exercise of the papal plenitude of power was the hallmark of his papacy. His pontificate was characterized by a large legislative output; more than 6,000 letters are extant of which many were decretals. This enormous corpus stimulated canonistic scholarship at Bologna and led to a number of canonical collections in his pontificate. As the administrator of the Roman Curia, Innocent created a sound, orderly financial administration: His pontificate was one of only a few that did not experience financial difficulties. (NCE, VII, 521–24, s.v. Innocent III, Pope)

6. Plato (428/7–349/8 B.C.), student and devoted follower of Socrates, founded his own philosophical school in Athens, called the Academy, after Socrates' death in 399. Through the Academy, Plato intended not only to promote philosophy and science but also to affect politics from a distance. He is credited with composing 28 dialogues, of which modern scholars generally agree that only 24 are probably authentic. Mariana is likely referring here to Plato's discussion of plutocracy in the *Republic* (VIII.550c–555b).

7. James I (1208–1276), also known as James the Conqueror, succeeded to the throne in 1213. During his youth he was a ward of Pope Innocent III. James used the political resources of Aragón-Catalonia to conquer the Moslem kingdom of Valencia and the Balearics. By encouraging the communes, the newly developing mendicant orders, and the universities, James was instrumental in transforming a feudally organized society into a proto-kingdom. Though he endowed numerous churches and introduced religious orders on a large scale, he witheld a disportionate share of the tithes, repudiated his wife despite papal exhortations to the contrary, and persisted in a life of public adultery. (NCE, VII, 806, s.v. James I, King of Aragón)

8. Peter II (1174–1213), son of Alfonso II, succeeded to the throne of Aragón-Catalonia in 1196 and reigned until his death on the battlefield of Muret in 1213. In 1204 he married Mary, lady of Montpellier, and a few months later had himself crowned at Rome by Pope Innocent III, to whom he agreed to pay an annual tribute. This event increased his prestige among the Christian monarchs, and led quite naturally to his ambitious role in the united crusading army that defeated the Almohuds at Las Navas de Tolosa in 1212. Like his father, Peter's opulent and extravagant lifestyle led him to turn compensations for the maintenance

of monetary stability and peace into territorial subsidies, but in the process there was a terrible abuse of precedents and customs. As a result, in 1205 the Catalonian barons tried unsuccessfully to impose a charter on Peter, who countered desperately by imposing a money-tax (ostensibly a compensation for maintaining stable coinage) not only on Catalonia (for the second time in his reign) but also, for the first time ever, on Aragón. (DMA, I, 408–21, s.v. Aragón, Crown of [1137–1479])

9. The title "Catholic King" or "Catholic Kings" refers either in the singular, as in this instance, to Ferdinand II of Aragón (1452–1516), son of John II of Aragón and Johanna Enríquez or, in the plural, to Ferdinand II of Aragón and Isabella (1451–1504), daughter of John II of Castile and Isabella of Portugal.

10. Philip II (1527–1598), son of Charles I of Spain (the Emperor Charles V) and Isabella of Portugal, began his reign in 1543 as regent in Spain during his father's absence in Germany. In 1556 Philip succeeded to the throne, which included the crown of Castile with Navarre and the Indies, the crown of Aragón-Catalonia with Sardinia, and the crown of Sicily: a veritable world empire. But financial difficulties forced him to settle in Spain, impose his authority, and withdraw from the widespread commitments of his father. He distrusted subordinates and governed as an absolute monarch, but he always respected the autonomous status of the constituent kingdoms. (NCE, XI, 272–73, s.v. Philip II, King of Spain)

Chapter 4

1. The monetary policy of Philip II originated in the parliamentary assembly of Madrid in 1566. The laws of 1497 and 1566 concern nearly all of the various monetary species.

2. Mariana's reference to chapter 6 of book 1 is inaccurate. Aristotle addresses the art of acquisition (or exchange) in book 1, chapter 9 of the *Politics*.

Chapter 5

1. It is not entirely clear who Mariana has in mind with the reference to Fannius. Fannius was a common Plebeian nomen, attested historically from the beginning of the second century B.C. Perhaps, Mariana is referring to Fannius, the Plebian aedile and mint master in 86 B.C., who went on to become a judge and later (in 80) the praetor and chairman of the court for murder cases. (BNP, 5, 350–52, s.v. Fannius)

2. The Roman Emperor Justinian (527–565 A.D.), born *c.* 482 of Thracian-Illyrian origins as the son of a farmer, with the Latin name Petrus Sabatius in Bederiana by Tauresium. Justinian owed his rise to Iustinus I, his mother's brother. When his uncle came to power in 518, he adopted Justinian and crowned him co-emperor in 527, after which Justinian's name became Justinian Augustus. Justinian's most important achievement, which stood the test of time, was the compilation of the *Corpus iuris civilis*. In 528 Justinian charged a commission with collecting all imperial laws. The commission completed its task in 534. In 533 the *Institutiones*, an elementary legal treatise, became law, and that same year, the *Digest*, the codification of classical jurisprudence, was promulgated. The laws made after 534, the *Novellae*, were not officially sanctioned as Justinian had intended; they were passed down in private compilations. (BNP, 6, 1136–39, s.v. Iustinianus; and DMA, 7, 418–25, s.v. Law, Civil—*CORPUS IURIS*, Revival and Spread)

3. Even though Thomas Aquinas (1225–1274) left behind no systematic treatment of politics, his treatise *De regimine principum*, which was compiled for the education of a

prince and followed the pattern of similar handbooks in the Middle Ages, was widely read in its day and considered to be a valuable source of his political theory. The commentaries on Aristotle's *Ethics* and *Politics* were also valuable sources of information for Thomas's understanding of politics. By far, however, the most important material is to be found in his philosophical and theological works, from the commentary on Peter Lombard's *Sentences* to the great *Summae*. "But," as A. P. D'Entrèves cautions, Thomas's treatment of politics "is scattered and fragmentary, and the greatest care must be taken in severing such fragments from the general frame in which they fit and from which they derive their significance" (p. viii). *Aquinas: Selected Political Writings*, ed. A. P. D'Entrèves, trans. J. G. Dawson (Oxford: Basil Blackwell, 1974), vii–xxxiii.

    4. Juan de Mariana, S.J., *De ponderibus et mensuris* (Toledo: apud T. Gusmanium, 1599).

Chapter 6

    1. Pliny the Elder (4–79 A.D.), Gaius Plinius Secundus, prominent Roman equestrian, commander of the fleet at Misenum, and uncle of Pliny the Younger, best known as the author of the 37-book *Naturalis Historia*, an encyclopedia of all contemporary knowledge—animal, vegetable, mineral, and human. Pliny's summation of universal knowledge in the *Naturalis Historia* became a model for later writers such as Iulius Solinus and Isidorus, and attained a position of enormous cultural and intellectual influence in the medieval west. (OCD, 1197–98, s.v. Pliny the Elder)

    2. The First Punic War lasted from 264 to 241 B.C. This war was one of three in which Rome successfully fought Carthage for dominance in the western Mediterranean. The scene of the first campaigns was Sicily. In 263 the Romans won a victory that resulted in Hieron II, tyrant of Syracuse, entering into alliance with Rome. In 262 the Romans won Segesta and Agrigentum, but realized that to drive the Carthaginians out of Sicily they needed to overcome the latters' naval superiority. They were successful in 260 but the situation in Sicily remained indecisive. So the Romans sent a force to Africa in 256 at which they were ultimately successful. The Carthaginians evacuated Sicily, which became the first Roman province, and had to pay an indemnity of 3,200 talents. Thus, at the end of the First Punic War, Carthage was in dire financial straits and turned to Spain to recoup wealth and manpower. (OCD, 1277–78, s.v. Punic Wars)

    3. *Sextantarius*, or containing a sextans, is a sixth part of a measure.

    4. Hannibal's (247–182 B.C.) attack on Rome's Spanish ally Saguntum in 219 precipitated the Second Punic War (218–202 B.C.). Hannibal intercepted Roman dispatches sent to Spain and Africa and then invaded northern Italy. He reached Italy in 218 and ultimately engaged the Roman army head on at Cannae in 216. Rome suffered a bloody defeat there but later managed to cut off Hannibal's reinforcements from Spain. After the capture of Syracuse in 211 the tide began to turn for Rome. The war ended in 202 with the final defeat of Carthage who had to pay an annual indemnity of 10,000 talents. Needless to say, the war seriously taxed Roman financial resources. (OCD, 665–66, s.v. Hannibal)

    5. Tribunes, were the officers of the people (plebs), first created in 500–450 B.C. These officers were magistrates who were themselves plebian and of free birth. The original number of the tribunes was two; by 449 it had risen to ten. The tribunes were charged with the defense of the persons and property of the plebians. Their power derived not from statute initially but from the oath sworn by the plebians to guarantee the tribunes' inviolability (*sacrosanctitas*).

Elected by the plebian assembly and exercising their power within the precincts of the city, the tribunes could summon the people to assembly and elicit resolutions. They asserted a right of enforcing the decrees of the people and their own rights; in subsequent years they possessed a right of veto against any act performed by a magistrate. In time, however, the tribunes became indistinguishable from magistrates of the state; and beyond that, became active in the pursuit of the people's interest, popular sovereignty, and public accountability. Mariana's reference to Drusus may be to Marcus Livius Drusus, tribune of the plebs in 122 B.C., a supporter of the aristocracy against C. Gracchus. (BNP, 4, 726–27, s.v. Drusus; and OCD, 1549–50, s.v. Tribuni Plebis [or Plebi])

6. This subject is treated in a law found in the *Codex repetitae praelectionis* (12 books, ca. 534 A.D.), a smaller collection of laws contained within the *Codex Iustinianus*. The law itself dates from the year 367 and is located within the *Corpus iuris civilis* (Book III; *Codex repetitae praelectionis* X 72, 5). (DNP, 8, 1023–27, s.v. Novellae)

7. Titus Maccius Plautus (250–184 B.C.) is the first Roman comic playwright. He is the author of *fabulae palliate* between c. 205 and 184 B.C. and his plays are the earliest Latin works to have survived complete. While some ancient authorities credit him with having written 130 plays, Varro drew up a list of 21 plays that were generally agreed to be by Plautus, and there is little doubt that these are the 21 carried over into modern editions. Nearly all of Plautus' plays are thought to be adaptations of Greek New Comedy with plots portraying love affairs, confusion of identities, and misunderstandings. But, it should also be noted, "he adapted his models with considerable freedom and wrote plays that are in several respects quite different from anything we know of New Comedy. There is a large increase in the musical element. The roles of stock characters such as the parasite appear to have been considerably expanded. Consistency of characterization and plot development are cheerfully sacrificed for the sake of an immediate effect. The humour resides less in the irony of the situation than in jokes and puns. There are 'metatheatrical' references to the audience and to the progress of the play, or explicit reminders that the play is set in Greece. Above all, there is a constant display of verbal fireworks, with alliteration, wordplays, unexpected personifications, and riddling expressions." Plautus was well-known in Renaissance Italy, particularly after the rediscovery of twelve plays in a manuscript found in Germany in 1429, and his plays were performed and imitated all over Europe until the seventeenth century, but more sporadically thereafter. The lines that Mariana quotes came from the prologue to *Casina*, verses 5, 9, and 10. (OCD, 1194–96, s.v. Plautus [Titus Maccius Plautus])

8. Ferdinand III of Castile (1198–1252) succeeded to the throne in 1217, and is remembered for uniting Castile and León and reducing Muslim power in Andalusia to the kingdom of Granada. Ferdinand was born of the ill-fated union of Alfonso IX of León and Berengaria, daughter of Alfonso VIII of Castile. He succeeded to the Castilian crown after his mother, inheriting it upon the premature death of her brother Henry I, had abdicated. His father opposed his son's accession to the throne but was unsuccessful in blocking it. Tolerant toward the Jews and Muslims who came under his authority, Ferdinand strove to re-Christianize the conquered peoples through the new mendicant orders. He advanced legal studies through his promotion of the University of Salamanca. And by centralizing the administration of his two kingdoms, he initiated the compilation of a uniform code of laws, a project completed by his successor, Alfonso the Wise. (NCE, V, 886–87, s.v. Ferdinand III, King of Castile, St.)

9. Alfonso X of Castile (1221–1284) was the son of Ferdinand III and Beatrice of Suabia, and was king of Castile and León (1252–84). He faced almost insurmountable social,

economic, and political crises. Some of these problems were of his own making, and others he inherited from his father. Alfonso's reign was, with the exception of his patronage of letters and his legal program, which was not accepted until a century later, a failure. During his reign Spanish culture and literature reached one of its high-water marks. He established schools in Seville, Murcia, and Toledo, in which Christians, Muslims, and Jews cultivated the arts and sciences. He also actively continued and contributed to the famous school of translators founded at Toledo in the twelfth century by Archbishop Raimundo (1130–50). (NCE, I, 311, s.v. Alfonso X, King of Castile)

10. Sancho IV of Castile and León (1258–1295) succeeded to the throne in 1284 against his father's strong protestations to the contrary. His marriage to his cousin, María de Molina, was within the forbidden degrees of consanguinity. The pope's reluctance to accept their union, therefore, cast a shadow over the legitimacy of his line. Moreover, during the early years of his reign, Sancho IV came under the influence and control of Lope Díaz de Haro, lord of Vizcaya, who controlled the military and financial life of Castile. When the Castilian nobility revolted as a result of the spoils of the kingdom being monopolized by the Haro family, Sancho followed the sage advice of the king of Portugal to assassinate Lope Díaz. However, in the wake of this event, several conspiracies and revolts followed one after another. With the exception of some minor victories over the Muslims, Sancho had little to show but a realm divided by internal conflict and the nobility of Castile often allied to Granada against their own king. (DMA, 3, 134, s.v. Castile)

11. Ferdinand IV of Castile and León (1285–1312) was still a minor when his father died in 1295. Once again, Castile sank into anarchy. The prominent families fought each other for the regency. Several claimants sought the throne. Armies from Aragón and Portugal entered Castilian territory with the intention of setting the son of Ferdinand de la Cerda over a dismembered kingdom. It was only because of the energy and determination of the queen mother, María de Molina, who rallied the urban centers and their militias to the cause of her son, that the realm survived. The leagues of towns became the protectors of the boy king. Even so, Ferdinand IV could claim his throne in 1301 only after major concessions to his enemies. His troubled reign came to an end in 1312, leaving yet another child who was just over a year old, Alfonso XI, to assume the throne in time. (DMA, 3, 134, s.v. Castile)

12. Peter I of Castile and León (1334–1369) succeeded to the throne in 1350 following his father's death at Gibraltar. Peter began his rule with Castile devastated by the plague and by a severe economic and social crisis. He made an effort to solve some of these problems at a meeting of the cortes in Valladolid in 1351. His economic and political objective—to destroy the power of the high nobility, to make the king supreme in Castile, to make Castile supreme in Spain—was carried out with the support of the newly university-trained elite and the Jews. During the latter half of his reign, a protracted civil war broke out between Castile and Aragón. Peter's opposition sought an alliance with and the support of Charles V of France, in addition Bertrand du Guesclin and his mercenary companies were hired to kill Peter. In response, Peter enlisted English support and Edward of Wales entered Spain and, joining forces with Peter, defeated their enemies in 1367. However, when Peter could not fulfill his promises to the English, he was left alone, an easy target for the angry nobility and the French. Eventually, Peter was murdered in a plot by Du Guesclin and Henry II of Castile and León in 1369. (DMA, 3, 136–37, s.v. Castile; BU, 12, 172–76, s.v. DUGUESCLIN [Bertrand])

13. Henry II of Castile and León (1333–1379) succeeded to the throne in 1369. Henry began his reign under attack by Peter's supporters and by a coalition of Portugal, Navarre,

Aragón, and Granada. In addition, to a large extent he owed the throne to the aid received from the nobility, and now the time had come to pay his debt. His huge grants to the aristocracy weakened the financial foundations of the realm and led to the formation of a powerful and extremely wealthy oligarchy. (DMA, 3, 137, s.v. Castile)

14. The duke of Lancaster (John of Gaunt, second son of Edward III of England) laid claim to the throne through his marriage with Constance, the daughter of Peter I of Castile.

15. John I of Castile and León (1358–1390) succeeded to the throne in 1379. He made every effort to check the excesses of the nobility and to centralize royal authority. His reforms of the financial and administrative bodies—the Royal Council, audiencia, and leagues of towns—and the prominence of the cortes were worthy accomplishments but were ultimately overshadowed by his failure in Portugal. John's monetary reforms should be placed within the broader context of the 1387 monetary reform in the parliament of Burgos and the economic effect of the Hundred Years' War on Europe generally. When Ferdinand I of Portugal died in 1383, John I claimed the throne through his wife, Beatriz of Portugal, but his ambitions were thwarted by the resistance of the Portuguese and their election of a new king, John of Avis. (DMA, 3, 137, s.v. Castile)

16. Henry IV of Castile and León (1425–1474) succeeded to the throne in 1454. Henry, a complex and tragic figure, was vilified by the supporters of his half sister Isabella, and dominated from early youth by a succession of favorites, especially the greedy John Pacheco, marquess of Villena. The first half of his reign evidences a desire for reform, indicated by judicious policies carried out either by the king or his advisors. However, his war policies against Granada, a war of attrition rather than the frontal attack called for by the aristocracy, and Henry's dependence on obscure nobles, precipitated a revolt of the nobility in 1464 and, for all practical purposes, the decline of royal influence. (DMA, 3, 138, s.v. Castile)

17. That is, 8 ounces of silver.

18. Henry III of Castile and León (1379–1406) succeeded to the throne in 1390. He reached his majority in 1393. Although set back by ill health, he achieved some important gains. During Henry's reign Castile began its expansion in the Atlantic with the conquest of the Canary Islands early in the fifteenth century, and the high nobility stayed relatively quiet and content during this time. When Henry died in 1406, his programs were still in their infancy and had not yet been consolidated. (DMA, 3, 137–38, s.v. Castile)

19. John II of Castile and León (1405–1454) succeeded to the throne in 1407. In the long reign of John II power was always held by people other than the king. The dual regency of Catherine of Lancaster and Ferdinand, duke of Peñafiel and brother of the late king, kept peace throughout the realm. Ferdinand, a forceful and capable statesman, prevented the nobility from making any gains. He also won important victories against the kingdom of Granada, the most important being that of Antequera (1410), from which he took the name Ferdinand of Antequera. After 1419 John II fell under the influence of Álvaro de Luna, a grandnephew of Pope Benedict XIII and a mysterious figure, who freed the king from his bondage to the aristocratic oligarchy. Álvaro kept the king under his control. Exiled twice, he returned to the court, always with greater power, until a coalition of the high nobility and John's second queen, Isabel of Portugal, led to his execution in 1453. The king died the following year.

The political and financial developments of Castile from the time of King Ferdinand the Holy to John II (ca. 1198-ca. 1454) can be summarized as follows: "Despite the political upheaval and dynastic wars, the foundations for a stable, strong, and centralized monarchy were laid down in this period. For instance, a comprehensive system of taxation was established. Most important among the taxes collected were the *servicio*, an extraordinary tax voted by the cortes during times of need that, by the fifteenth century, had become quite regular, and the *montazgo*, or *servicio y montazgo*, a tax on the transhumance. The *mesta*, in fact, became the main source of royal income after 1350. In addition, the *alcabala*, a sales tax, was turned into a permanent and generalized tax under Henry II and John I" (p. 138). (DMA, 3, 138, s.v. Castile)

20. Antonio de Nebrija (1441–1522), Spanish humanist, was born to an hidalgo family at Lebrija, near Seville. Nebrija received his primary education at Lebrija, then went to the University of Salamanca in 1455. Five years later he obtained a position at the Spanish College at the University of Bologna, where he spent ten years studying theology and acquainting himself with Italian humanist scholarship. Like many other humanists, Nebrija wrote poetry, commented on classical literary works, and promoted the study of classical languages and literature. For a short time (1513–1515) he participated in the editing of the Complutensian Polyglot Bible at the invitation of Cardinal Francisco Jiménez de Cisneros, the archbishop of Toledo and primate of Spain. He is remembered primarily for introducing the critical philological scholarship of Italian humanism into Renaissance Spain. The title, *De Repetitionibus*, was commonly used for practical handbooks of jurisprudence (canon and civil law) at the time. (EtR, 4, 288–89, s.v. Nebrija, Antonio de)

Chapter 7

1. The history of Henry II's reign was written by the Castilian Chancellor, Pedro López de Ayala (1332–1407), and is available in a modern critical edition under the title, *Crónica del rey don Pedro y del rey don Enrique, su hermano, hijos del rey don Alfonso onceno*, 2 vols., ed. Germán Orduna, intro. Germán Orduna and José Luis Moure (Buenos Aires: SECRIT: Ediciones INCIPIT, 1994–1997).

2. Bertrand Du Guesclin (1314–1380), or Beltran Claquin, was the constable and protector of France, celebrated fourteenth-century mercenary, and the liberator of Spain. His colorful and intriguing life touched several notable figures in the period of mid to late fourteenth-century France. He had dealings with such prominent individuals as the duke of Lancaster, Charles de Blois, Charles V of France, Peter I of Castile and León, and Henry II of Castile and León, to mention only a few. See chapter 6, note 12, for more on his role in the assassination of Peter I. The *Bibliothèque historique de France* lists no less than nine manuscripts treating the life of Du Guesclin. (BU, 12, 169–80, s.v. DUGUESCLIN [Bertrand])

Chapter 8

1. The Roman influence in law was an especially strong and enduring legacy. "The seventh-century Visigothic Code (*Leges Visigothorum*) contains a number of elements derived from Roman law. Roman law teaching was revived in non-Arabic Spain by the early thirteenth century, and by the middle of the century the various redactions of the *Fuero real* (between 1252 and 1255) and the *Libro de las leyes* (a later redaction of which is known as *Las siete partidas*) show a native legal system imbued with Roman ideas" (p. 422). (DMA, 7, 418–25, s.v. Law, Civil—*CORPUS IURIS*, Revival and Spread)

More specifically, the Roman legal influence, which can be traced to the seventh century "work of four Visigothic kings, with the active participation of the church, through the famous councils of Toledo (the Eighth and Twelfth), led to the compilation of a highly romanized code, the *Liber iudiciorum* or *Lex barbara visigothorum* (not to be confused with the earlier *Lex romana visigothorum*, or Breviary of Alaric). Began probably under Chindaswinth (642–652), with the work continuing under his son Receswinth (653–672), the *Liber iudiciorum* became the sole guide for the administration of justice in Visigothic Spain. All previous legislation ceased to have binding force in the king's court. The sources for the *Liber* were Leovigild's Code, Justinian's law codification . . . , other assorted Roman legal texts, and St. Isidore's *Etymologies*. . . . The *Liber* consisted of twelve books. It included discussions of the law and the legislator, judicial organization and procedure, civil and criminal law, and a variety of other topics such as treatment of heretics, Jews, and the sick. . . . The *Liber iudiciorum* was undoubtedly the greatest legacy of Visigothic Spain. It far outlived the barbarian kings, influencing later Spanish legal systems and the law of the Spanish colonies around the world" (p. 520). (DMA, 7, 518–24, s.v. Law, Spanish)

2. The current gold coin during Mariana's time had the name *escudo*.

3. Independent confirmation of Mariana's account of currency devaluation after the fall of Rome can be found in an essay by numismatic historian Mark Blackburn. According to Blackburn, "During the first two centuries following the collapse of the western empire, the currencies of the new barbarian kingdoms were based largely on locally produced gold coins. Only in Italy under Ostrogothic and later Byzantine control was a range of silver and bronze coins also issued in substantial quantity. The Franks, Burgundians, Suevi, Visigoths, Lombards, and Anglo-Saxons all had essentially mono-metallic currency systems based on the gold solidus and increasingly the tremissis (one-third solidus). However, apparent shortages of gold for currency in western Europe resulted in progressive reductions in fineness, seen first in the late sixth-century coinage of Visigothic Spain and during the early seventh century in that of the Franks. By the third quarter of the seventh century the fineness of the Frankish and Anglo-Saxon coins had fallen to as little as 25% gold or less alloyed with silver, and during the 670s these base gold tremisses were replaced by new coins of virtually pure silver. The old tremisses were quickly driven out of circulation leaving once again a mono-metallic currency in Francia and England" (p. 539).

"Elsewhere in Europe, in Italy and briefly in Spain, the use of gold coinages lingered on. The Visigothic tremisses of the late seventh century were heavily debased, but their issue continued until the Arab conquest of Spain in 711–15" (p. 540). See Mark Blackburn, "Money and Coinage," in *The New Cambridge Medieval History*, vol. II, *c. 700–c. 900*, ed. Rosamond McKitterick (Cambridge: Cambridge University Press, 1995), 538–59.

4. The Arab conquest of Spain took place from 711–715.

5. According to Blackburn, "The Umayyad governors replaced the Germanic system of coinage with an Arabic one, consisting initially of gold dinars and their fractions similar to those of North Africa but of inferior and very variable fineness. These coins belong to a transitional phase in which pseudo-Byzantine types were still giving way to purely Islamic ones in the western provinces of the caliphate. Between 711/12 and 720/1 (AH 93–102) three successive types of gold coinage were issued in Spain: Arab-Byzantine types with Latin inscriptions, Arab-Byzantine types with bilingual inscriptions, and Arabic types with entirely Kufic inscriptions. These Kufic dinars, of restored (*c.* 98%) fineness, were struck in small numbers down to 744/5 (AH 127), after which no further gold was issued in Spain for some

two hundred years, until the Spanish Umayyads conquered North Africa, gaining access to Sudanese gold. The currency became one based essentially on silver dirhems weighing *c.* 2.9 g, more than twice as heavy as the Frankish denier, supplemented with some low-value copper coins." Blackburn, "Money and Coinage," 540.

6. The united government of León and the primitive earldom of Castile, which had been ruled in common since 1035 under Ferdinand I, came to an abrupt end in 1230 with the reign of Ferdinand III (also known as Ferdinand the Holy).

7. Also known as *doubloons.*

8. The development of parliamentary institutions was a common phenomenon throughout western Europe from the thirteenth century on. In Castile, León, Burgos, Aragón, Catalonia, and other provinces, the king traditionally consulted with the nobles and bishops of his curia on matters of significance. As towns became more important as centers of administration, trade, and industry, and as sources of military forces, their representatives were summoned to counsel the king. With that the *curia regis* was transformed into the *cortes,* which is the plural of *corte,* the Spanish vernacular term for the king's court. The cortes came to be viewed as an assembly of estates—prelates, nobles, and townsmen—who, together with the king, formed the body politic. The Castilian cortes submitted petitions to the crown that, on being drawn up as ordinances and approved by the king, had the full force of law. Alfonso XI in 1348 promulgated the *Ordenamiento de Alcalá,* an extensive law code prepared by his jurists, in the cortes. The principle that the laws enacted in the cortes could be abrogated only by the cortes was stated in 1305, 1313, 1379, and 1387. Of course, it goes without saying that new laws could always be added to the *Ordinamentum* as was the case with the law promulgated in Burgos concerning the abuse of parents. (DMA, 3, 610–12, s.v. Cortes)

9. The Spanish text says, Law 144. Cf. Juan de Mariana, S.J., *Tratado y discurso sobre la moneda de vellón,* estudio introductorio por Lucas Beltrán (Madrid: Instituto de Estudios Fiscales, 1987).

10. The 252 *Leyes del estilo* are laws pertaining to custom, the forms and arts of convention, for all types of formal proceedings. They date from the first half of the fourteenth century.

11. The text on this point is inaccurate. According to the record of the cortes, the parliament of León under Alfonso XI had enacted this policy already in the years 1342, 1345, and 1349.

12. The new legal collection was given the title *Ordinamentum* (*Ordenanzas Reales de Montalvo*).

13. That is, the parliament of Guadalajara in 1409.

14. The history of John II's reign was originally thought to have been written by Álvar García de Santa María (1349–1460), but is now generally considered a compilation from the works of several authors, including the prominent Fernán Pérez de Guzmán (?1376–?1460). A modern critical edition of the *Crónica del serenissimo rey don Iuan,* ed. Angus Mackay and Dorothy Sherman Severin (Exeter: University of Exeter Press, 1981), is available with an English introduction and commentary that accompany the complete Spanish text.

Chapter 9

1. That is, a quarter of a *real.*

Chapter 10

1. This is a reference to the monetary policy promulgated by King Ferdinand and Isabella in Medina del Campo in 1497.

2. Mariana's reference to chapter 6 of book 1 is inaccurate. Aristotle addresses the creation of currencies to facilitate exchange over vast distances (the portability of money idea) and to serve as a measure in exchanges in book 1, chapter 9 of the *Politics*.

3. Elizabeth I (1533–1603), reigned as Queen of England's golden age from 1558 to her death, and was the architect of England's final break with the papacy. She was the daughter of Henry VIII and Anne Boleyn, whom Henry accused of adultery and executed. Even with this frightful beginning, Elizabeth enjoyed a peaceful childhood and was educated in the new learning by such brilliant English humanists as Roger Ascham. The long reign of Elizabeth I was one of the most remarkable in English history, and the Queen was a legend in her own lifetime. During these 45 years English Protestantism and English nationalism achieved success, and England experienced new maritime supremacy, a strengthened economy, and a brilliant literary vitality. (NCE, V, 281–82, s.v. Elizabeth I, Queen of England)

4. René I (1409–1480), duke of Anjou, count of Provence and of Piedmont, king of Naples, Sicily, and Jerusalem was the second son of Louis II, king of Sicily, duke of Anjou, count of Provence, and of Yolande of Aragón. Louis II died in 1417, and his sons, together with their brother-in-law, afterwards Charles VII of France, were raised under the guardianship of their mother. The elder, Louis III, succeeded to the crown of Sicily and to the duchy of Anjou, René being known as the count of Guise. When his brother Louis III and Jeanne [Giovanna] II de Duras, queen of Naples, died, René succeeded to the kingdom of Naples. Louis had been adopted by Jeanne II in 1431, and she left her inheritance to René. The marriage of Marie de Bourbon, niece of Philip of Burgundy, with John, duke of Calabria, René's eldest son, cemented peace between the warring Burgundian princes of Philip the Good and Antoine de Vaudemont. In 1438 René set sail for Naples, which had been held for him by the Duchess Isabel. His prior captivity and ransome enabled Alfonso V of Aragón, who had been first adopted and then repudiated by Jeanne II, to make some headway in the kingdom of Naples as he was already in possession of the island of Sicily. In 1441 Alfonso laid siege to Naples, which he sacked after six months. René returned to France the same year, and though he retained the title of king of Naples he never recovered his rule. (EB, 23, 97–98, s.v. René I)

5. Giacomo Menochio (1532–1607), famous legal scholar, and professor of law at Pavia (1556–1560, 1588–1607), Mondovi (1561–1566), and Padova (1566–1588). Mariana cites his main work, *Consiliorum sive responsorum liber quartus* (Venice: apud Franciscum Zilettum, 1584).

6. Duarte Nunez do Lião (1528–1608) was the resident scholar at the court of Sebastian of Portugal (1554–1578). His intellectual pursuits encompassed such diverse areas as economics, law, and national history, and his published works, which were largely written in Portuguese, treated these subjects in considerable detail. Mariana's reference is to his *Primeira parte das chronicas dos reis de Portugal*, 2 vols. (Lisbon: Reimpresso por M. Coelho Amado, 1774). This work was originally published in Lisbon around 1600.

7. Ferdinand I of Portugal (1345–1383) succeeded to the throne in 1367. The wealthiest by far of the Portuguese monarchs to that time, Ferdinand did much to promote commerce and shipbuilding, and his economic legislation has justly been praised. The positive achievements during Ferdinand's reign have been obscured, however, by his three costly

and disastrous wars with Castile and by his marriage to the controversial Leonor Teles, who was already married to someone else at the time of her marriage to Ferdinand. (DMA, 10, 52, s.v. Portugal: 1279–1481)

8. Sebastian of Portugal (1554–1578) succeeded to the throne in 1557 following the death of Dom João III. Sebastian, a young child and grandson to Dom João III, now embodied all the hopes of the Avis dynasty. But Sebastian was chronically ill, both physically and mentally. Though he lived into adulthood, his weakness and unwillingness to leave an heir left considerable doubts about the dynasty's future. These doubts were realized in 1578 when Sebastian was killed in the battle of Alcacer Kebir (Qsar al-kabir), in an ill-conceived attempt to rekindle the Portuguese conquest in Morocco. His elderly great-uncle, Cardinal Dom Henrique, a caretaker king, proved unable to manage a smooth dynastic transition. A brief war of succession ensued in 1580, but Philip II of Spain met little resistance in laying claim to the throne of Portugal, which temporarily united Spain and Portugal. (EtR, 5, 135, s.v. Portugal)

9. Nicholas Sanders (1530–1581) was a controversial English historian and covert agent of the Roman Catholic Church during the reign of Queen Elizabeth I. He left England shortly after Elizabeth's accession to the throne and went to Rome where he obtained the doctor of divinity degree. He was present at various sessions of the Council of Trent and was a member of the theological faculty at the University of Louvain from 1565 to 1572. During his later years he tried to stimulate resistance to Elizabeth's government and was commissioned by the papacy to go to Ireland for the purpose of inciting the Irish chieftains to rebellion. The work of Sanders that Mariana references—*De origine ac progressu schismatis Anglicani libri tres: quibus historia continetur maximè ecclesiastica, annorum circiter sexaginta … ab anno 21. regni Henrici octaui … usque ad hunc vigesimum octauum Elisabethae …* (Ingolstadt: Ex officina typographica Wolfgangi Ederi, 1587)—remained incomplete at his death. Despite its unfinished state, however, the book became a repository of source material for many Roman Catholic accounts of the English Reformation. (NCE, XII, 1048–49, s.v. Sander, Nicholas [Sanders])

10. Henry VIII (1491–1547) succeeded to the throne in 1509. Known principally for his break with Rome over the divorce of his first wife, Catherine of Aragón, Henry has been described as "a man with grandiose plans, but without the energy and, perhaps, the skill to execute them…. Henry was no working monarch; for two long stretches of his reign (*c.* 1513–29 and *c.* 1532–40), first Cardinal Thomas Wolsey and then Thomas Cromwell held sway, and royal government was virtually shed by the King and placed upon the chief minister." Throughout his career Henry was hungry for glory and titles and viewed himself as a warrior king, which resulted in several skirmishes with France and Scotland, particularly during his latter years. Henry's wars with France and Scotland were costly and necessitated several debasements of the coinage to increase the royal treasury. Tragically, he was so preoccupied with Europe and his own domestic affairs that he showed no interest in the lucrative possibilities of the New World. "As a result, when England at last entered this field later in the century, it found itself generations behind the Spanish and Portuguese. But above all Henry had failed to turn to good use the vast new powers and the wealth that the Reformation had brought him." (NCE, VI, 1025–29, s.v. Henry VIII, King of England)

11. Edward VI of England (1537–1553) succeeded to the thrones of England and Ireland in 1547. Edward was born at Hampton Court Palace to Henry VIII and Jane Seymour, Henry's third wife. His reign, though brief, was auspicious, as it marked the official beginning of England's Protestant Reformation. Edward himself, however, played no part in making

royal policy. The authority to govern during his minor years lay with the sixteen executors of Henry VIII's will, the members of Edward's privy council. Edward Seymour, duke of Somerset, assumed power in March 1547 as lord protector of the realm and governor of the king's person. A zealous Protestant, he abolished the Mass and other "idolatries" and invaded Scotland in 1547. But war with Scotland brought war with France, which nearly bankrupted England. When rebellious peasants challenged his authority in 1549, a group of councillors led by John Dudley, earl of Warwick, abolished the protectorate in a blood-less coup. Dudley (the duke of Northumberland after October 1551) ruled from 1550 on. He made peace with France and restored royal finance. He respected Edward VI's desire for religious reform, thus giving Thomas Cranmer, archbishop of Canterbury, freedom to reform further the doctrines and liturgy of the Church of England and to develop the Book of Common Prayer. (EtR, 2, 254–56, s.v. Edward VI)

12. Mariana is likely making reference here to a passage by the Latin historian P. Cornelius Tacitus (c. 56-? A.D.) in his *Life of Agricola*, the biography of his father-in-law Cnaus Julius Agricola (40–93 A.D.), Roman governor of Britain for seven years from 77 (or 78) to 84 (or 85). After prevailing in a surprise night attack by the British, as Tacitus recounts, Agricola's Roman army "grew fierce and bold, presuming nothing could resist their Courage: They cried out, to be led into *Caledonia*, that by a continued Series of Victories, they might be brought to the utmost Limits of *Britain*." Tacitus observes, however, "the Romans returned, not fighting for Safety, but Glory and Honour" (XXVI, p. 24). Yet, due largely to Roman vainglory and arrogance, the counterattack resulted in a bloody stalemate. "This is the unjust Condition of War that all claim their Share in good Success, but bad is imputed but to one: The *Britains* supposing themselves defeated, not by the Courage of their Adversaries, but Conduct of their General, who had watched his Opportunity, abated nothing of their Arrogance, but lifted the stoutest Men they had, and carried their Wives and Children to Places of the greatest Security. The Cities confederated together, meeting frequently, and by Religious Rites, and offering up Sacrifices, confirmed their Association: And thus both Armies parted with equal Animosity" (XXVII, p. 25). *The Annals and History of Cornelius Tacitus: His Account of the Antient Germans and the Life of Agricola in Three Volumes*, Vol. I (London: Printed for Matthew Gillyflower at the Spread-Eagle in Westminster Hall, 1698). Tacitus' *Life of Agricola* was translated by John Potenger.

13. Philip IV of France (1268–1314), called the Fair, succeeded to the throne in 1285. After his father's death in the abortive Crusade against Aragón, a young Philip was forced to cope with a hopeless war and a heavy debt. Moreover, as the heir of crusaders, the grandson of a saint, and the ruler of the largest Roman Catholic country in Europe, Philip thought the French monarch was as necessary for human welfare as the Roman See. In an effort assert his sovereignty over territories he felt belonged to France, Philip engaged in costly warfare with England and Flanders. "These wars, fought with paid soldiers, were very expensive. Philip was always short of money; his greatest innovations and his greatest mistakes were due to the fact that he was near bankruptcy during most of his reign. He imposed the first general taxes in French history; he inflated currency; he expelled the Jews and confiscated their property; he abused judicial procedures to extort large fines from clergy, barons, and towns." (NCE, XI, 271–72, s.v. Philip IV, King of France)

14. Dante Alighieri (1265–1321), called "The Poet," is considered to be the father of Italian literature. He is reputed to have been the most learned laymen of his time and deeply versed in theology. His *Divine Comedy, Purgatory*, and *Inferno* place Dante in the highest eschalon of literary accomplishment in the western canon. His *De monarchia libri tres*,

though lesser known, presented an understanding of the "universal" monarch's sovereignty that epitomized political relations in the high Middles Ages. Dante made several critical jibes in relation to Philip IV, as seen from a casual perusal of the indexes to his major works. (DMA, 4, 94–105, s.v. Dante Alighieri)

15. Robert Gaguin (1433–1501), humanist rhetorician and general of the Maturin order, was employed as a diplomat/envoy in the service of several kings including Louis XI, Frederick III, Charles VIII, and Louis XII. He wrote several multivolume histories during his lifetime. Mariana is likely referring to his *Compendium suprà Francorum gestis à Pharamundo usque ad annum* (Paris: André Brocard, 1491). (BU, 16, 265–69, s.v. GAGUIN [Robert])

16. Louis X of France (1289–1316) succeeded to the throne in 1314. In 1314 leagues of nobles and towns were in rebellion against Philip IV's unpopular taxes for an abortive military campaign in Flanders, and the king's daughters-in-law had recently been involved in an adultery scandal. Louis attempted to defuse the political opposition, "mainly by issuing charters of reform to various regions. Historians have considered it significant that the French rebels (mostly nobles) did not demand or receive a national Magna Carta, but were content with specific charters addressed to the particular interests of their localities. Regional particularism remained a potent factor in France, placing limitations on the scope of opposition to the crown but also preventing the crown from establishing common, centralized policies or institutions. Despite the expansion of royal power and institutions of government in the preceding reigns, France lacked a sense of 'community of the realm.' Like his father, Louis X needed money to fight the Flemings and experimented with representative assemblies. Louis did not use the latter merely for propaganda but tried to have them endorse royal taxes. His early death cut short this effort." (DMA, 5, 181, s.v. France: 1314–1494)

17. Enguerrand de Marigny (1260–1315) was Philip IV's prime minister. After becoming royal chamberlain in 1304, Marigny increasingly gained the king's confidence. By 1311 he was an important figure and by 1313–14, the most influential adviser of the King. "He was prudent and skillful both as a diplomat and financial expert; he avoided unnecessary expenses and preferred negotiation to war. He helped to settle the difficulties arising out of the attack on Boniface VIII and tried to end the war with Flanders through a reasonable peace treaty." Charles of Valois, however, disliked Marigny's prudence and resented his influence. Thus, when Philip died, Charles brought false charges against Marigny, and succeeded in having him condemned to death. (NCE, IX, 221, s.v. Marigny, Enguerrand de; DMA, 5, 181–82, s.v. France: 1314–1494)

18. Charles IV of France (1294–1328), called the Fair, succeeded to the throne in 1322 and immediately faced problems over the uncertainty of succession, a need to devise a systematic form of taxation, and the requirement of living up to the traditional moral demands of French kingship. "Charles IV was particularly astute in making do with revenues of an extraordinary nature (seizures of the chattels of the returned Jews and of the profits of Italian bankers, for example). He was also successful in restoring a good deal of the moral image of the monarchy. Even in war—in Guienne and Flanders—he enjoyed temporary military successes without exciting, by his modest taxation, the rebellious opposition of his subjects. During peaceful interludes he refrained from exacting subsidies, obedient to the principle that when the cause of the subsidy ceases, the subsidy itself must cease. Below the surface, of course, historians can see unresolved major problems; but to the educated or influential Frenchman of 1328, the year of Charles's death, the monarchy strengthened by Philip Augustus, hallowed by Louis IX, and made conscious of its destiny by Philip the

Fair, seemed to have weathered the stormiest period in a century with little loss of prestige."
(DMA, 5, 172–73, s.v. France: 1223–1328)

19. This law concerns the crime of fraud.

20. Philip VI of France (1293–1350) succeeded to the throne in 1328. Early in 1328 Charles IV sickened and died, thereby opening the second phase of the royal succession crisis. Charles had no sons, and even before he died, the nobles decided that his first cousin, Philip of Valois, would be regent, becoming king if the pregnant queen did not bear a son. The problem with this arrangement was that Philip had no claim to Champagne or Navarre, strategic lands that were rich in latent revenue. Champagne and Navarre were supposed to pass to Joan, Louis X's daughter, who was married to her cousin, Philip of Évreux. But Philip and the Valois managed these lands so poorly that Joan and the Évreux family held a grudge. A second problem for Philip concerned Edward III of England, Charles IV's nephew and the nearest male relative of Charles IV. At the time of Charles' death, Edward was ruled by his unpopular mother and he now headed the Plantagenet family, France's ancient enemy. The nobles were concerned, in Edward's case especially but even more generally, to reserve the throne of France to the male line and thus eliminate future conflicting claims. Philip began his reign with a military victory over Flemish rebels in 1328, but relations with England steadily deteriorated in the 1330s. Philip was unsuccessful in pushing the people to abandon their historic hostility to taxation, an attitude that made collection of significant taxes impossible until outright fighting was in progress. This led many to think that the war with England was not a threat to their vital interests. However, after a series of defeats in 1340's, the Estates General of late 1347 authorized an extremely large tax to finance an effective army. But, as this was occurring, the Black Plague arrived in Europe and disrupted everything. (DMA, 5, 183–84, s.v. France: 1314–1494)

21. Peter Belluga (?–1468) was born in Valencia and worked as a jurist and counsellor to Alfonso V of Aragón (1416–1458). Alfonso V's costly efforts to maintain his family's interests in Castile were unpopular in the Crown of Aragón. From 1420 to 1423 he increased his power in the Mediterranean (Sardinia, Sicily, and Corsica). "In Naples he secured Queen Giovanna's recognition as her heir, then lost that fragile prospect to Louis III of Anjou, whose brother René finally succeeded her in 1435. After a time in Spain (1423–1432) Alfonso returned to Sicily, and through tortuous negotiation and fighting conquered Naples (1436–1443)." The original title of Belluga's work is: *Speculum principum ac iustitiae* (Paris, 1530). (DMA, 1, 417, s.v. Aragón, Crown of (1137–1479)

22. The special privileges of the people of Valencia had been fixed by the order and deposition of the kings through a general charter, the "Council of One Hundred," dating back to 1265. The 1265 charter was part of a larger move to institute the cortes system in Valencia as was the case already in Aragón and Catalonia. "In local government royal judges supplemented the vicars, who remained officers of justice, police, and muster in Catalonia. James I actively promoted urban life. A series of charters to Barcelona (1249–1274) attributed increasing administrative autonomy to the elected counselors and the assembly; the 'Council of One Hundred' dates from 1265. The commercial law of Barcelona was codified in the *Libre del consolat del mar* (Book of the Sea Consulate) one of a remarkable series of legal compilations in the mid thirteenth century that include the customs of Valencia, Aragón, and Lérida, and the *Commemorations* of Pere Albert." (DMA, 1, 413, s.v. Aragón, Crown of [1137–1479])

Chapter 11

1. When they met on the battlefield in the Trojan war, Glaucus exchanged his gold armor for Diomedes' bronze armor.

2. Tacitus enjoyed an uninterrupted career under the Emperors Vespasian, Titus, and Domitian, which brought him to the praetorship in 88 A.D., by which time he was also a member of the prestigious priesthood, the college of the *Quindecimviri sacris faciundis*. In 97 he was suffect consul and delivered the funeral oration upon L. Verginius Rufus. We know of no other office held by Tacitus, until senority brought him the proconsulship of Asia for 112–13. The date of his death is unknown, but is not likely to have been before 118. The *Annals* originally consisted of eighteen (or sixteen) books—six for Tiberius, six for Gaius and Claudius, six (or four) for Nero. Of these there are lost most of 5, all of 7–10, the first half of 11, and everything after the middle of 16. It is not known whether Tacitus completed the *Annals*; nor is the date of composition known with certainty, though scholars seem to think some passages are datable to 114 or 115. (OCD, 1469–71, s.v. Tacitus)

3. The Spanish text reads: "certainly exceed six million." Cf. Mariana, *Tratado y discurso sobre la moneda de vellón*.

4. Recall, by way of illustration, Mariana's earlier examples of John I of Castile (who depreciated the currency by 50 percent) and Henry II of Castile (who depreciated it by 66 percent).

5. This is a reference to the Hundred Years' War (1337–1453), which, as described by the *Dictionary of the Middle Ages*, "was actually a series of wars, continuing the succession of Anglo-French conflicts that had begun in 1294. The one significant difference between the wars that preceded 1337 and those that followed was the existence of the Plantagenet claim to the French throne. The English invoked the claim only sporadically, but it enabled them to attract the support of enough anti-Valois magnates to justify the argument that the whole struggle was essentially a civil war between competing factions of French princes. Recent English scholarship permits identification of three twenty-year periods of intense conflict: the Edwardian War of 1340–1360, the Caroline War of 1369–1389, and the Lancastrian War of 1415–1435. The first and third of these were marked by English victories." (DMA, 5, 184, s.v. France: 1314–1494)

6. Edward, Prince of Wales (1330–1376), called the "Black Prince," was the eldest son of Edward III (1312–1377) and Philippa of Hainault. He was created prince of Wales in 1343. As heir to the English crown, Edward was given honors and symbolic duties from an early age. His involvement with the Hundred Years' War began in 1345 when he led a troupe into France on a burning and pillaging rampage. He gained fame in 1356, at the Battle of Poitiers, where his archers dealt a fatal blow to the French charges. Unskilled as a ruler, however, Edward was never able to master the restless Gascon nobility. "When his Spanish expedition of 1367 led not just to the victory at Navarrete, but also to harse taxation to pay for it, their response was revolt and an appeal to the king of France. Charles V replied on 23 January 1369 by summoning the Black Prince to Paris." In 1370 he lead his last campaign and then returned to England in 1371, where he spent his final years leading the opposition to the Lancastrian party of his brother, John of Gaunt. (DMA, 4, 398–99, s.v. Edward the Black Prince)

7. Mariana is referring to Peter I of Castile and León (1334–1369). For more on Peter, see chapter 6, note 12.

8. Jean Froissart (1337–1410) wrote a four-volume chronicle of England, France, Spain, Portugal, Scotland, Brittany, Flanders, and adjoining countries, which treats extensively the notable events and persons in those countries from 1325–1400. The first volume, which Mariana references in the *Treatise*, covers the period from 1325 to 1378.

Chapter 12

1. That is, the Catholic Kings Ferdinand and Isabella of Castile.

2. The Spanish text reads *dineros*. Cf. Mariana, *Tratado y discurso sobre la moneda de vellón*.

3. Charles I of Hapsburg (1500–1558), later became Emperor Charles V of the Holy Roman Empire. As the son of Philip the Handsome, Duke of Burgundy, and Joanna, third child of Ferdinand of Aragón and Isabella of Castile, he was heir presumptive to an empire vaster than Charlemagne's, and over which the "sun never set." The empire included the Netherlands and claims to the Burgundian circle; it included Castile, Aragón, the conquered kingdoms of Navarre and Granada, Naples, Sicily, Sardinia, the conquests of the New World, and possessions in North Africa, all of which after the death of Ferdinand he ruled jointly with his mad mother; and it included the Hapsburg duchies of Austria with rights over Hungary and Bohemia, inherited from his paternal grandfather, Emperor Maximilian I. The main objective of his reign was not new conquest but the protection and consolidation of his inheritance, which he sought to accomplish through strategic matrimonial alliances. But, as it turns out, his reign would be plagued with international conflict that would eventually overcome him. The conflicts were exacerbated by the Lutheran Reformation in Germany. Shortly before his death, Charles' proposal of the succession of his son Philip to the imperial title was rejected at the Diet of Augsburg and that event, in conjunction with several other blows, led him to abdicate his office. He gave the governments of the Netherlands, Spain, and Sicily to Philip. To Ferdinand he handed over the Hapsburg Empire, but not the title of Emperor, which he retained until 1558. (NCE, III, 503–06, s.v. Charles V, Holy Roman Emperor)

4. The French humanist, philosopher, and philologist Guillaume Budé (1468–1540) developed a method of critical-historical analysis of texts. With his work, *De asse et partibus eius Libri quinque* (Paris: Vẹnundantur in ẹdibus Ascensianis, 1514), Budé combined archeology and philology and was, consequently, a founder of the science of numismatics (the study and collection of coins, medals, tokens, paper money, and other human artifacts). Mariana's *De ponderibus et mensuris* displays a similar historical-critical interest in numismatics to Budé's *De asse*.

5. *Dinero* is the standard for silver and is equivalent to 24 grains.

Chapter 13

1. Don Carlos (1545–1568), the Infante of Spain, was born of Philip's first wife Maria of Portugal who died in child birth. His second marriage to Mary Tudor was barren and devoid of love. His third marriage to Elizabeth of Valois was a diplomatic arrangement. Philip grew to love her and was heartbroken when she died in 1568, having borne him two surviving daughters. Elizabeth's death was preceded that same year by the death of Don Carlos, Philip's infirm son who was mentally and physically handicapped. Given Don Carlos' condition, Philip regarded him as permanently unfit to rule and so put him into confinement in January 1568. In 1579 Philip married his fourth and final wife, Anne of Austria, who bore

five children but only one of which survived and who later succeeded his father as Philip III. (NCE, XI, 273, s.v. Philip II, King of Spain)

2. Don Juan of Austria (1547–1578), the natural born son of Emperor Charles V and Barbara Blomberg and half-brother to Philip II of Spain, is remembered for leading the Christian fleet to victory at the Battle of Lepanto: an engagement fought between the Christian and Turkish fleets on October 7, 1571, and the last great naval battle under oars. (NCE, VIII, 665–66, s.v. Lepanto, Battle of)

3. Alfonso XII of Castile (?–1468) succeeded to the throne in 1465 after a revolt (of the nobility) the previous year deposed his brother Henry IV. Henry was forced to recognize his brother Alfonso as heir to the throne over his own daughter Juana. After Alfonso's death in 1467 the nobles turned to Henry's half-sister Isabella. "The princess, however, was of different mettle, and she disregarded the advances of the nobility. In the pact of Los Toros de Guisando (1468), Henry recognized Isabella as his successor as long as she was willing to accept his guidance on the selection of her husband. Their peaceful relations only lasted a short time. The next year Isabella married Ferdinand of Aragón, prince and heir of the neighboring kingdom, without her brother's consent. When Henry recognized his daughter Juana ... as his heir (1470) civil war broke out. After Henry's death in 1474, Isabella, with the support of the Castilian bourgeoisie and of her husband, was proclaimed queen of Castile." (DMA, 3, 138, s.v. Castile)

4. This sentence is not found in book 19 of Tacitus' *Annals*. The source of Mariana's citation is unknown.

5. Vittelius (15–69 A.D.), Roman emperor, who met a tragic fate. Already a consul in 48, he became proconsul of Africa, then served as legate to his brother in the same post. Galba appointed him governor of Lower Germany in November 68, perhaps thinking that his reputed indolence made him less of a political threat. Vittelius won over the disaffected soldiers in the province by an ostentatious display of generosity. On January 2, 69 Vittelius was proclaimed emperor by his troops, and quickly won the support of the legions of Upper Germany, which had refused allegiance to Galba the day before. After consolidating his support, he marched on Rome in July; made offerings to Nero; and had himself created consul in perpetuity. But he did nothing to appease troops that had been defeated in earlier battles. In July Vespasian becomes emperor and soon marches with troops from the east to invade Italy. Vittelius fails to block the Alpine passes and suffers defeat. Vespasian's forces attack Rome and overcome Vittelius' resistance. On December 20, 69 Vittelius was dragged through the streets, humiliated, tortured, and killed. (OCD, 1608–09, s.v. Vittelius, Aulus)

6. Robert de Sorbon (1201–1274), theologian and founder of the Sorbonne, first endowed college of the University of Paris. He became a master theologian (*c.* 1236), and as master regent taught at the University of Paris from 1254–1274. Robert was a contemporary and colleague of Thomas Aquinas, Bonaventure, Albert the Great, and Giles of Rome. Named chaplain of Cambrai (*c.* 1250) and in 1258 at Notre Dame de Paris, he belonged to the circle of friends of Louis IX, who regarded him as a man of great wisdom and chose him as his confessor. His renown stems from the initiative he took to found a college for "poor lay theology students." His project won the interest of Louis IX, the bishops, and even the Pope, and he opened the college in October 1257. After a well-organized search for suitable property, he bought almost all the houses in the neighborhood of Rue Coupe Gueule, a site still occupied by the Sorbonne. He gave the institution carefully planned statutes that provided for the recruitment, common life, and studies of the students who took up

residence there. Mariana studied for five years (1569–1574) at the Sorbonne. (NCE, XIII, 440, s.v. Sorbon, Robert de)

7. Louis IX of France (1214–1270) succeeded to the throne in 1226. He married Marguerite of Provence in 1234 and they had 10 children together. He is best remembered for his crusades and for the way he promoted peace and justice throughout his long reign. He drew up new ordinances to improve public administration, eradicate corruption, and improve the law of his dominions. (NCE, VIII, 1010–12, s.v. Louis IX, King of France, St.)

8. The forfeiture of the northern provinces of the Netherlands occurred in 1581.

9. The Jesuit Giovanni P. Maffei (1536–1603) wrote an "Indian History" (that is, a history of eastern peoples) in Latin. The original title was *Historiarum Indicarum libri XVI* (Florence, 1588). As a professor of rhetoric, he was educated in Latin, Greek, and Hebrew; his literary style was thought to be highly refined and, consequently, was emulated widely by later Jesuit writers.

10. Hadrian (76–138 A.D.) was adopted emperor in 117. His goal as emperor was to establish natural or man-made boundaries for the empire. He realized that the empire's extent had severely strained its capacity to maintain and protect itself. Consolidation was his policy, not expansion, and this brought him trouble in the early years, when Trajan's (53–117 A.D.) eastern conquests were abandoned. Hadrian's own military experience was extensive. He had served in provinces in the east, along the Danube, and along the Rhine. Soon after his arrival in Rome, he began several lengthy journeys that took him to nearly every province. He spent more than half his reign traveling abroad. (OCD, 662–63, s.v. Hadrian [Publius Aelius Hadrianus])

11. That is, Henry III of Castile (1390–1406).

12. Juan de Mariana, S.J., *Io. Marianae Hispani, e socie. Iesu, historiae de rebus Hispaniae, libri XXX ...* (Toledo: Thomae Gusmanii, 1595). This title is Mariana's first main work.

13. Ferdinand I of Aragón (1380–1416), also known as Ferdinand of Antequera, was chosen in 1412 by electors of parliaments in the peninsular realms to assume the Aragonese throne. Ferdinand was related both to Peter IV of Aragón and the king of Castile. James of Urgell, the other contender, rebelled, but was captured in 1413 and died in prison twenty years later. The election of Ferdinand was a fateful turning point for Aragón, "the dynastic ratification of Castile's demographic and military superiority. Ferdinand and his sons ruling after him were Castilians who married Castilians and appointed Castilians, and they were in real and constant danger of losing touch with their subjects." (DMA, 1, 417, s.v. Aragón, Crown of [1137–1479])

14. Marcus Aurelius Severus Alexander (209–235 A.D.), son of Iulia Avita Mamaea by her second husband, the procurator Gessius Marcianus of Arca Caesarea in Syria, was adopted emperor in 222. (OCD, 222, s.v. Aurelius Severus Alexander, Marcus)

15. Juan de Mariana, S.J., *De rege et regis institutione, libri III* (Mainz: Typis Balthasaris Lippii, impensis Heredum Andreae VVechelis, 1605). This title is Mariana's second main work. It was first published by a Toledo typesetter in 1599.

16. For more on Francis I, see chapter 2, note 3.

17. Henry II of France (1519–1559) succeeded to the throne in 1547. He was the second son of Francis I and Claude. When only seven years old he was sent by his father, with his brother the dauphin Francis, as a hostage to Spain in 1526, after peace was reached at Cambrai in 1530 they both returned home. In 1533 he was wed to Catherine de'Medici. In 1536 Henry, formerly duke of Orleans, became dauphin by the death of his older brother

Francis. From that time forward he was strongly influenced by two persons: Diane of Poitiers, his mistress, and Anne de Montmorency, his mentor. His younger brother, Charles of Orleans, was his father's favorite. Henry supported the constable Montmorency when he was disgraced in 1541; protested against the treaty of Crépy in 1544; and at the end of his reign held himself aloof. His accession in 1547 created quite a stir at court. Henry was a robust man, but had weak character and mediocre intelligence. He was cold, haughty, melancholy, and dull. During his reign the royal authority became more severe and absolute than ever. He showed no mercy to Protestants. He was injured in a jousting accident and died several days later. (EB, 13, 291, s.v. Henry II, King of France)

18. Charles IX of France (1550–1574) succeeded to the throne in 1560. He was the third son of Henry II and Catherine de'Medici. He was first known as the duke of Orleans, until the death of his brother Francis II in 1560, at which time he became king. Still a minor, the power was in the hands of the queen-mother, Catherine. Charles' weaknesses were his passionate nature and his imaginative pursuits. Hunting, violent exercise, and poetry were his undoing. He submitted easily to his mother's authority, which freed him to pursue his own interests. In 1570 he was wed to Elizabeth of Austria, daughter of Maximilian II. After the massacre of Saint Bartholomew, in which he displayed a weak and intemperate character, he became melancholy, severe, and taciturn. (EB, V, 921, s.v. Charles IX, King of France)

19. Maximilian I (1459–1519), "the last knight," German emperor from 1493 on, married his son Philip of Austria (i.e., Philip the Handsome) to Joanna the Mad, the daughter (third child) of Ferdinand and Isabella of Castile. (EtR, 4, 77, s.v. Maximilian I)

WORKS CITED

Primary Sources

Adrian VI. *In Quartum sententiarum*. Paris, 1530.

Albertanus of Brescia. "Genovese Sermon" (1243). Translated by Patrick T. Brannan, S.J. *Journal of Markets & Morality* 7, no. 2 (Fall 2004): 623–38.

Alexander, de Imola. *Commentaria in librum III Decretalium*. Bologna, 1480.

———. *Lectura super I et II parte Digesti Veteris*. Venice, 1488.

Ancharano, Petrum. *In quinque decretalium libros iacundissima commentaria*. Bologna, 1580.

Andreae, Ioannes. *In Decretalium Novella commentaria*. Venice, 1571.

Angelica. *Summa Angelica de casibus conscientiae*. Nürnberg, 1498.

Annanias, Ioannes (Giovanni d'Agnani). *Commentaria super prima et secunda parte libri V Decretalium*. Bologna, 1480.

Antonino (Antonio Niccolo de Pierzzo). *Summa theologicae*. Venice, 1503.

Aristotle. *Nicomachean Ethics*. Translated by Martin Ostwald. Indianapolis and New York: Bobbs-Merrill Company, 1962.

———. *The Politics of Aristotle*. Translated by Ernest Barker. Oxford: Clarendon Press, 1948.

Augustine. *De Trinitate libri XV*. Freiburg: Fischer, 1494.

Ayala, Pedro López de. *Crónica del rey don Pedro y del rey don Enrique, su hermano, hijos del rey don Alfonso onceno*. 2 vols. Edited by Germán Orduna. Buenos Aires: SECRIT: Ediciones INCIPIT, 1994–1997.

Azpilcueta, Martín de (Doctor Navarrus). "Apologetic Letter from Martín de Azpilcueta to don Gabriel de la Cueva, Duque de Alburquerque." In *Comentario Resolutorio de Cambios*, introducción y texto critico por Alberto Ullastres, José M. Perez Prendes y Luciano Pereña. Madrid: Consejo Superior de Investigaciones Cientificas, 1965.

———. *Comentario Resolutorio de Cambios*. Introducción y texto critico por Alberto Ullastres, José M. Perez Prendes y Luciano Pereña. Madrid: Consejo Superior de Investigaciones Cientificas, 1965.

————. *Comentario Resolutorio de Usuras*. Salamanca: Andrea de Portonarijs, 1556.

————. "Los escritos sobre el Doctor Navarrus." In *Estudios sobre el Doctor Navarrus: En el IV centenario de la muerte de Martín de Azpilcueta*, ed. Gobierno de Navarra. Pamplona: Universidad de Navarra, 1988.

————. *Manual de confesores y penitents*. Salamanca, 1556.

Baldo, de Ubaldis. *In V libros Decretalium*. Venice, 1570.

————. *Lectura super I–X libris Codicis*. Zürich, 1487.

————. *Lectura authenticorum*. Venice, 1485.

Bartolo, de Sassoferrato. *In secundan Codicis partem*. Lyons, 1581.

Belluga, Peter. *Speculum principum ac iustitiae*. Paris, 1530.

Biel, Gabriel. *Commentarii doctissimi in IV sententiarum libros*. Brescia, 1574.

Budé, Guillaume. *De asse et partibus eius Libri quinque*. Paris: Vęnundantur in ędibus Ascensianis, 1514.

Budel, René. *De Monetis et Re nummaria libri duos: his accesserunt tractatus varii atque utiles tam veterum quam neotericorum authorum*. Cologne, 1591.

Burgos, Antonio de. *De emptione et venditione*. Venice, 1575.

Cajetan, Tomás de Vio. *Summa Caietani*. Lyons, 1544.

————. *De cambiis* (Milan, 1499). In *Scripta philosophica: Opuscula oeconomico-socialia*, ed. P. P. Zammit, O.P. Rome: Ex Typographia Missionaria Dominicana, 1934.

————. *De monte pietatis* (1498). In *Scripta philosophica: Opuscula oeconomico-socialia*, ed. P. P. Zammit, O.P. Rome: Ex Typographia Missionaria Dominicana, 1934.

————. *Prima pars summe theologie Angelici Doctoris Sancti Thome Aquinatis*. Venice: Expensis . . . Luce Antonij de Giunta Florentini, 1522.

Calderini, Juan. *Consilia domini Iohannis Calderini et domini Gasparis e ius filii redacta*. Rome, 1472.

Calle, Luís Saravia de la. *Instrucción de mercaderes muy provechosa*. Medina del Compe: A. de Urveña, 1544.

Codex iustinianus. Lyons: Magistri Nicolai de Benedictis, 1506.

Compilatio Decretalium Gregorii IX. Venice: Ductu impensisque Bernardini de Tridino, 1486.

Covarrubias y Leyva, Diego de. *De collatione veterum nummismatum*. Venice, 1581.

————. *Opera omnia*. Venice, 1581.

————. *Variarum Resolutionum Liber Primus*. Salamanca, 1578.

Curcio, Francisco. *Tractatus de Monetis* (*Enchiridion tractatum iuris utriusque subscriptos completens tractatus cum singulorum tabulis*). Paris, 1522.

Decio, Felipe. *Commentaria nova et vetera in Codicem*. Lyons, 1527.

Decreto Gratiani. *Juris canonici h.e. ecclesiastici ejusque in Occidentali Ecclesia novi sive pontificii gemmulae theologicae: e vulgo sic dicto Decreto Gratiani in gratiam studiosae juventutis collectae / a Luca Friederico Reinharto . . . accesserunt similes gemmulae è glossa in illud Decretum erutae, cum aliquot indicibus*. Altdorf: Typis & impensis Henrici Meyeri . . . , 1682.

Durando, Porciano (Durandus, de Sancto Porciano, d. 1334). *Quolibeta Avenionensia tria, additis correctionibus Hervei Natalis supra dicta Durandi in primo Quolibet*. Cura P. T. Stella. Zürich: Pas-Verlag, 1965.

Felinus. *Felini Sandei Canonici Ferrarensis iurisconsultique clarissimi super prohemio decretalium*. Venice, 1589.

Firmio, Bartachino (Giovanni Bertachini). *Tractatus de Gabellis. Solēnis et bodierne practice q̄; cōmodissimus tractatus vectigalium gabellarūve casus etiam quotidianos decidens, per egregium juris vtriusq; lumē. d. Jo. Bertachinū de firmo editus: nuncq; primū summa rijs numeratun auctus: curaq; nō mediocri repurgatus bic babetur.* Lyons: Excudebat B. Bonnyn sumptibus V. de Portonarijs, 1533.

Froissart, Jean. *Here begynneth the first volum of sir Iohan Froyssart: of the cronycles of Englande, Fraunce, Spayne, Portyngale, Scotlande, Bretayne, Flau[n]ders: and other places adioynynge.* Translated out of French by Iohan Bourchier. London: In Fletestrete by Richarde Pynson, 1523.

Gaguin, Robert. *Compendium suprà Francorum gestis à Pharamundo usque ad annum.* Paris: André Brocard, 1491.

Gómez, Antonio. *Opus praeclarum et utilissimum super legibus Tauri.* Salamanca, 1567.

Gutiérrez. *Practicarum Quaestionum circa Leges Regias Hispaniae.* Salamanca, 1589.

Guzmán, Fernán Pérez de. *Crónica del serenissimo rey don Iuan.* Edited by Angus Mackay and Dorothy Sherman Severin. Exeter: University of Exeter Press, 1981.

Hostiensis (Enrique de Segusio). *Iur. utr. monarchae celeberrimi in V Decretalium commentaria.* Venice, 1581.

Iason, Federico. *Super Digestum.*

Justinian. *D. Justiniani sacratissimi principis institutionum, sive, Elementorum libri quatuor: notis perpetuis multo, quam hucusque, diligentius illustrati /* cura & studio Arnoldi Vinnii J.C. Leyden: Ex officina Francisci Hackii, 1646.

———. *The Digest of Justinian.* Latin text edited by Theodor Mommsen with the aid of Paul Krueger. English translation edited by Alan Watson. Philadelphia: University of Pennsylvania Press, 1985.

Lassarte, Ignacio de. *De decima venditionis et permutationis.* Madrid, 1599.

Lião, Duarte Nunez do. *Primeira parte das chronicas dos reis de Portugal.* 2 vols. Lisbon: Reimpresso por M. Coelho Amado, 1774.

Maffei, Giovanni P. *Historiarum Indicarum libri XVI.* Florence, 1588.

Major, John. *In quartum sententiarum quaestiones utilissimae.* Paris, 1521.

Mariana, Juan de, S.J. *De monetae mutatione. Tractatus VII.* Cologne, 1609.

———. *De monetae mutatione (MDCIX) = Über die Münzveränderung (1609).* Herausgegeben, übersetzt und mit Einzelerklärungen versehen von Josef Falzberger. Heidelberg: Manutius, 1996.

———. *De ponderibus et mensuris.* Toledo: apud T. Gusmanium, 1599.

———. *De rege et regis institutione, libri III.* Mainz: Typis Balthasaris Lippii, impensis Heredum Andreae VVechelis, 1605.

———. *Io. Marianae Hispani, e socie. Iesu, historiae de rebus Hispaniae, libri XXX.* Toledo: Thomae Gusmanii, 1595.

———. *History of Spain.* Translated by Captain John Stevens. London: Richard Sare, Francis Saunders, and Thomas Bennett, 1699.

———. *The King and the Education of the King.* Translated by G. A. Moore. Chevy Chase, Md.: Country Dollar Press, 1948.

———. *Tratado y discurso sobre la moneda de vellón.* Estudio introductorio por Lucas Beltrán. Madrid: Instituto de Estudios Fiscales, 1987.

Medina, Juan de. *Codex de Restitutione et Contractibus.* Compluti, 1546.

———. *De cambiis.* Salamanca, 1550.

Menchaca, F. Vázquez de. *Controversiarum usu frequentium libri tres.* Barcelona, 1563.

Menochio, Giacomo. *Consiliorum sive responsorum liber quartus.* Venice: apud Franciscum Zilettum, 1584.

Mercado, Tomás de. *Summa de tratos y contratos de mercaderes.* Seville: H. Diaz, 1571.

Molina, Ludovico (Luis de), S.J. *De iustitia et iure.* Cuenca, 1597.

———. *De iustitia et iure, tomus secundus de contractibus.* Mainz: Ex officina typographica Balthasari Lippii sumptibus Arnoldi Mylii, 1602.

———. *La teoría del justo precio.* Edición preparada por Francisco Gómez Camacho, S.J. Madrid: Editora Nacional, 1981.

———. *Tratado sobre los cambios.* Edición, introducción, y notas por Francisco Gómez Camacho, S.J. Madrid: Instituto de Estudios Fiscales, 1990.

Molinaeus (Charles du Moulin). *Tractatus commerciorum, Contractum, Redituumque pecunia constitutorum, et monetarum.* Paris, 1638.

Nueva recopilación de los fueros, privilegios, buenos usos y costumbres, leyes y ordenes de la muy noble y muy leal provincia de Guipuzcoa. Toledo: Bernardo de Vgarte, 1696.

Panormitanus (Nicolò de' Tudeschi). *Panormitani prima in primum quintum Decretalium.* Lyons, 1555–1559.

Parladorius (Yáñez Parladorio, Juan). *Ioannis Yañez Parladorii iurisperiti in regio Vallisoletano . . . Rerum quotidianarum libri duo: nam singulari, qui iam multos floret annos, accessit nunc alter, illo quidem priori & rerum pondere, & sermonis elegantia non inferior, volumine verò longè auctior. / Sed & ille prior nunc denuo ab autore ipson recognitus, praesentissimis est scholijs locupletatur.* Salamanca: Excudebat Michael Serranus de Vargas: Expensis Francisci Martini bibliopolae, 1595.

Partidas. *Las siete Partidas del Rey Don Alfonso el Sabio. Cotejadas con varios codices antiguos por la Real Academia de la Historia.* Madrid, 1807.

Pinel, Arias. *Ad rubricam et legem secundam C. de rescindenda venditione commentarii.* Salamanca, 1568.

Plato. *Plato's Republic.* Translated by G. M. A. Grube. Indianapolis: Hackett Publishing Company, 1974.

Ravena, Petrus. *Compendium iuris canonicis.* Paris, 1521.

Reales ordenes. Colección de ordenanzas, decretos, pragmaticos, y reales cedulas. 12 vols. Madrid, 1664–1799.

Rodulfo, Laurencio de. *Tractatus de usuries.*

Rosella. *Summa de casibus conscientiae.* Venice, 1516.

Saliceto, Bartolome. *Lectura super IX libris codicis.* Lyons, 1500.

Sanders, Nicholas. *De origine ac progressu schismatis Anglicani libri tres: quibus historia continetur maximè ecclesiastica, annorum circiter sexaginta . . . ab anno 21. regni Henrici octaui . . . usque ad hunc vigesimum octauum Elisabethae . . .* Ingolstadt: Ex officina typographica Wolfgangi Ederi, 1587.

Scotus, Johannes Duns. *Quaestiones in quattuor libros sententiarum.* Venice, 1490.

Silvestre, Prierias de. *Sylvestrina suma, qua summa summarum merito nuncupatur.* Lyons, 1555.

Soto, Domingo de. *De iustitia et iure, libri decem.* Salamanca, 1553.

Summenhart, Conrado de. *Opus septipartitum de contractibus.* Hannover, 1500.

Tacitus, P. Cornelius. *The Annals and History of Cornelius Tacitus: His Account of the Antient Germans and the Life of Agricola in Three Volumes.* Translated by John Potenger. London: Printed for Matthew Gillyflower at the Spread-Eagle in Westminster Hall, 1698.

Thomas Aquinas. *Aquinas: Selected Political Writings*. Edited by A. P. D'Entrèves. Translated by J. G. Dawson. Oxford: Basil Blackwell, 1974.

———. *De regimine principum ad regem cypri et de regimine judæorum ad ducissam brabantiæ, politica opuscula duo* / Divi Thomæ Aquinatis; ad fidem optimarum editonum diligenter recusa Joseph Mathis. Taurini: Petri Marietti, 1924.

———. *Sancti Thomae Aquinatis, doctoris angelici, Opera omnia* / *iussu impensaque Leonis XIII. P. M. edita*. Rome: Ex Typographia Polyglotta S. C. de Propaganda Fide, 1882–1918.

———. *Summa theologicae: accuratissime emendata ac annotationibus ex auctoribus probatis et Conciliorum Pontificumque definitionibus ad fidem et mores pertinentibus illustrata, tabulis ac synthetica synopsi instructa* / a quibusdam scholæ S. Thomæ discipulis. Paris: P. Lethielleux, 1887–1889.

Thucydides. *The History of the Peloponnesian War*. Translated, with Introduction, Notes, and Glossary by Steven Lattimore. Indianapolis: Hackett Publishing Company, 1998.

Secondary Sources

Abellán, José Luís. *Historia Crítica Del Pensamiento Español*. 5 vols. Madrid: Espasa-Calpe, 1979.

Acton, John Emerich Edward Dalberg. *The History of Freedom and Other Essays*. New York: Classics of Liberty Library, 1993.

———. *Lectures on Modern History*. London: Macmillan, 1929.

Alvey, James E. "A Short History of Economics as a Moral Science." *Journal of Markets & Morality* 2, no. 1 (Spring 1999): 53–73.

———. "The Secret, Natural Theological Foundation of Adam Smith's Work." *Journal of Markets & Morality* 7, no. 2 (Fall 2004): 335–61.

Ayres, Clarence Edwin. *The Theory of Economic Progress: A Study of the Fundamentals of Economic Development and Cultural Change*. Chapel Hill: North Carolina University Press, 1955.

Backhouse, Roger E. *The Ordinary Business of Life: A History of Economics from the Ancient World to the Twenty-First Century*. Princeton and Oxford: Princeton University Press, 2002.

Balmés, J. *European Civilization: Protestantism and Catholicity [sic] Compared*. 3d ed. London: Burns and Lambert, 1861.

Barchet, B. Aguilera. *Historia de la letra de cambio en España, seis siglos de práctica trayecticia*. Madrid: Tecnos, 1988.

Bavinck, Herman. *Reformed Dogmatics*. Vol. 1. *Prolegomena*. Edited by John Bolt. Translated by John Vriend. Grand Rapids, Mich.: Baker Academic, 2003.

Bettenson, Henry, ed. and trans. *The Early Christian Fathers: A Selection from the Writings of the Fathers from St. Clement of Rome to St. Athanasius*. London and New York: Oxford University Press, 1956.

Biographie Universelle, ancienne et moderne; ou Histoire, par ordre alphabétique, de la vie publique et privée de tous les hommes qui se sont fait remarquer par leurs écrits, leurs actions, leurs talents, leurs vertus our leurs crimes. Edited by J. Fr. Michaud and L. G. Michaud. 85 vols. Paris: Michaud freres [etc.], 1811–1862.

Black, Robert A. "What Did Adam Smith Say About Self-Love?" *Journal of Markets & Morality* 9, no. 1 (Spring 2006): 7–34.

Blackburn, Mark. "Money and Coinage." In *The New Cambridge Medieval History*. Vol. II, c. 700–c. 900. Edited by Rosamond McKitterick. Cambridge: Cambridge University Press, 1995.

Blaug, Mark. *Economic Theory in Retrospect*. 5th ed. Cambridge: Cambridge University Press, 1997.

Boettke, Peter J. "Is Economics a Moral Science? A Response to Ricardo F. Crespo." *Journal of Markets & Morality* 1, no. 2 (Fall 1998): 212–19.

Boyer, C. B. *The History of the Calculus and Its Conceptual Development*. New York: Dover, 1959.

Bredvold, Louis I. "The Meaning of the Concept of Right Reason in the Natural-Law Tradition." *University of Detroit Law Journal* 36 (December 1959): 120–29.

Brill's New Pauly: Encyclopaedia of the Ancient World. Mang. ed. English edition, Christine F. Salazar. 9 vols. Leiden: Brill, 2002–.

Burtt, Edwin Arthur. *The Metaphysical Foundations of Modern Science*. Garden City, N.J.: Doubleday Anchor Books, 1954.

Camacho, Francisco Gómez, S.J. *Economía y filosofía moral: la formación del pensameinto económico europeo en la Escolástica Española*. Madrid: Síntesis, 1998.

———. "El pensamiento económico de la Escolástica española a la Ilustración escocesa." In *El pensamiento económico en la Escuela de Salamanca*, ed. Francisco Gómez Camacho, S.J. and R. Robledo. Salamanca: Ediciones Universidad de Salamanca, 1998.

———. "El triángulo Glasgow, París, Salamanca y los orígenes de la ciencia económica." *Miscelánea Comillas* 48 (1990): 231–55.

———. "Later Scholastics: Spanish Economic Thought in the XVIth and XVIIth Centuries." In *Ancient and Medieval Economic Ideas and Concepts of Social Justice*, ed. S. Todd Lowry and Barry Gordon. Leiden and New York: Brill, 1998.

———. "Luis de Molina y la metodología de la ley natural." *Miscelánea Comillas* 43, no. 82 (January–June 1985): 155–94.

Carande, R. *Carlos V y sus banqueros: La vida económica en Castilla (1516–1556)*. Madrid: Sociedad de Estudios y Publicaciones, 1965.

Castelot, André. "Juan de Mariana, S.J." In *Palgrave's Dictionary of Political Economy*. London: Macmillan, 1926.

Catholic Encyclopedia: An International Work of Reference on the Constitution, Doctrine, Discipline, and History of the Catholic Church. Edited by Charles G. Herbermann et al. 17 vols. New York: The Encyclopedia Press, 1840–1916.

Chafuen, Alejandro A. *Faith and Liberty: The Economic Thought of the Late Scholastics*. Lanham and New York: Lexington Books, 2003.

Courtenay, William J. *Covenant and Causality in Medieval Thought: Studies in Philosophy, Theology, and Economic Practice*. London: Variorum Reprints, 1984.

Crespo, Ricardo F. "Is Economics a Moral Science?" *Journal of Markets & Morality* 1, no. 2 (Fall 1998): 201–11.

———. "Is Economics a Moral Science? A Response to Peter J. Boettke." *Journal of Markets & Morality* 1, no. 2 (Fall 1998): 220–25.

Crosby, A. W. *The Measure of Reality: Quantification and Western Society, 1250–1600*. Cambridge: Cambridge University Press, 1997.

de Roover, Raymond A. *Business, Banking, and Economic Thought in Late Medieval and Early Modern Europe: Selected Studies of Raymond de Roover*, ed. Julius Kirshner. Chicago and London: University of Chicago Press, 1974.

————. *Gresham on Foreign Exchange: An Essay on Early English Mercantilism with the Text of Sir Thomas Gresham's Memorandum: For the Understanding of the Exchange.* Cambridge, Mass.: Harvard University Press, 1949.

————. *La pensée économique des scholastiques: doctrines et méthodes.* Montréal: Institute for Medieval Studies, 1971.

————. *Leonardus Lessius als economist: De economische leerstellingen van de latere scholastiek in de Zuidelijke Nederlanden.* Brussels: Paleis de Academiën, 1969.

————. *Money, Banking and Credit in Mediaeval Bruges; Italian Merchant Bankers, Lombards and Money-Changers: A Study in the Origins of Banking.* Cambridge, Mass.: Mediaeval Academy of America, 1948.

————. *San Bernardino of Siena and Sant'Antonino of Florence: The Two Great Economic Thinkers of the Middle Ages.* Boston: Baker Library/Harvard Graduate School of Business Administration, 1967.

————. "Scholastic Economics: Survival and Lasting Influence from the Sixteenth Century to Adam Smith." In *Business, Banking, and Economic Thought in Late Medieval and Early Modern Europe: Selected Studies of Raymond de Roover*, ed. Julius Kirshner. Chicago and London: University of Chicago Press, 1974.

————. *The Rise and Decline of the Medici Bank, 1397–1494.* Cambridge, Mass.: Harvard University Press, 1963.

Dempsey, Bernard W., S.J. *Interest and Usury.* Washington, D.C.: American Council on Public Affairs, 1943.

————. "The Historical Emergence of Quantity Theory." *The Quarterly Journal of Economics* 50, no. 1 (November 1935): 174–84.

Der neue Pauly: Enzyklopadie der Antike. Edited by Hubert Cancik and Helmut Schneider. 16 vols. Stuttgart: J. B. Metzler, 1996–.

Dictionary of the Middle Ages. Edited by Joseph R. Strayer. 13 vols. New York: Scribner, 1982–1986.

Drakopoulos, S., and G. N. Gotsis. "A Meta-Theoretical Assessment of the Decline of Scholastic Economics." *History of Economics Review* 40 (Summer 2004): 19–45.

Drucker, Peter F. "Toward the Next Economics." In *The Crisis in Economic Theory*, ed. Daniel Bell and Irving Kristol. New York: Basic Books, 1981.

Dunoyer, E. *L'Enchiridion confessariorum del Navarrus: Dissertatio ad lauream in facultate S. Theologiae apud Pontificium Institutum "Angelicum" de Urbe.* Pamplona: Gurrea, 1957.

Ekelund, Robert B., Jr., and Robert F. Hebert. *A History of Economic Theory and Method.* New York: McGraw-Hill, Inc., 1975.

Encyclopaedia Brittannica: A Dictionary of Arts, Sciences, Literature, and General Information. 11th ed. Edited by Hugh Chisholm. 32 vols. New York: The Encyclopaedia Brittannica Company, 1910–1911.

Encyclopedia of Religion and Ethics. Edited by James Hastings. 13 vols. New York: Charles Scribner's Sons, Edinburgh: T. & T. Clark, 1911–1922.

Encyclopedia of the Renaissance. Edited by Paul F. Grendler. 6 vols. New York: Scribner's published in association with the Renaissance Society of America, 1999.

Endemann, Wilhelm. *Studien in der romanisch-kanonistischen Wirtschafts- und Rechtslehre: bis gegen Ende des siebenzehnten Jahrhunderts.* 2 vols. Berlin: J. Guttentag, 1874–1883.

Felice, Flavio. "Introduction to Albertanus of Brescia's *Genovese Sermon* (1243)." *Journal of Markets & Morality* 7, no. 2 (Fall 2004): 603–22.

Figgis, John Neville. *The Divine Right of Kings*. 2d ed. Cambridge: Cambridge University Press, 1922.

Finnis, John. *Natural Law and Natural Rights*. Oxford: Oxford University Press, 1993.

Freedman, Joseph S. "Aristotle and the Content of Philosophy Instruction at Central European Schools and Universities during the Reformation Era (1500–1650)." In *Proceedings of the American Philosophical Society* 137, no. 2 (1993): 213–53.

———. "Philosophy Instruction within the Institutional Framework of Central European Schools and Universities during the Reformation Era." *History of Universities* 5 (1985): 117–66.

Funkenstein, A. *Theology and the Scientific Imagination from the Middle Ages to the Seventeenth Century*. Princeton: Princeton University Press, 1986.

Gazier, Bernard, and Michele. *Or et monnaie chez Martín de Azpilcueta*. Paris: Economica, 1978.

Gordley, J. *The Philosophical Origins of Modern Contract Doctrine*. Oxford: Clarendon Press, 1992.

Gordon, Barry. *Economic Analysis before Adam Smith: Hesiod to Lessius*. New York: Macmillan, 1975.

Grabill, Stephen J. *Rediscovering the Natural Law in Reformed Theological Ethics*. Grand Rapids, Mich.: Wm. B. Eerdmans Publishing Company, 2006.

Gregg, Samuel. *The Commercial Society: Foundations and Challenges in a Global Age*. Lanham and New York: Lexington Books, 2007.

Grice-Hutchinson, Marjorie. *Aproximación al pensamiento económico en Andalucía: de Séneca a finales del siglo XVIII*. Málaga: Editorial Librería Agora, 1990.

———. *Early Economic Thought in Spain, 1177–1740*. London: G. Allen & Unwin, 1978.

———. *Economic Thought in Spain: Selected Essays of Marjorie Grice-Hutchinson*, ed. Laurence S. Moss and Christopher K. Ryan. Brookfield, Vt.: Edward Elgar Publishing Company, 1993.

———. "The Concept of the School of Salamanca: Its Origins and Development." In *Economic Thought in Spain: Selected Essays of Marjorie Grice-Hutchinson*, ed. Laurence S. Moss and Christopher K. Ryan. Brookfield, Vt.: Edward Elgar Publishing Company, 1993.

———. *The School of Salamanca: Readings in Spanish Monetary Theory, 1544–1605*. Oxford: Clarendon Press, 1952.

Gutiérrez, A. del Vigo. *Cambistas mercaderes y banqueros en el Siglo de Oro español*. Madrid: BAC, 1997.

Hallam, Henry. *View of the State of Europe during the Middle Ages*. 4th ed. London: Alex Murray and Son, 1868.

Hamilton, Earl J. *American Treasure and the Price Revolution in Spain, 1501–1650*. Cambridge, Mass.: Harvard University Press, 1934.

———. "Spanish Mercantilism Before 1700." In *Facts and Factors in Economic History: Articles by Former Students*, ed. E. F. Gay. Cambridge, Mass.: Harvard University Press, 1932.

Hayek, F. A. *The Counter-Revolution of Science: Studies on the Abuse of Reason*. Indianapolis: Liberty Fund, 1979.

Hicks, John. *Causality in Economics*. Oxford: Basil Blackwell, 1979.

———. *Critical Essays in Monetary Theory*. Oxford: Clarendon Press, 1965.

Huerta de Soto, Jesús. "New Light on the Prehistory of the Theory of Banking and the School of Salamanca." *The Review of Austrian Economics* 9, no. 2 (1996): 59–81.

Hutchinson, Terence. *Before Adam Smith: The Emergence of Political Economy, 1662–1776*. Oxford: Basil Blackwell, 1988.

Jàszi, Oscar, and John D. Lewis. *Against the Tyrant*. Glencoe, Ill.: Free Press, 1957.

Jefferson, Thomas. *Autobiography, Notes on the State of Virginia, Public and Private Papers, Addresses, Letters*. New York: Library of America, 1984.

Johnson, Herbert L. "Some Medieval Doctrines on Extrinsic Titles to Interest." In *An Etienne Gilson Tribute*, ed. C. J. O'Neil. Milwaukee: Marquette University Press, 1959.

Keynes, John Maynard. *The Treatise on Probability*. London: Macmillan, 1921.

———. *A Treatise on Money*. New York: AMS Press, 1976.

Kirshner, Julius. "Raymond de Roover on Scholastic Economic Thought." In *Business, Banking, and Economic Thought in Late Medieval and Early Modern Europe: Selected Studies of Raymond de Roover*, ed. Julius Kirshner. Chicago and London: University of Chicago Press, 1974.

Knight, Frank H. "Schumpeter's History of Economics." *Southern Economic Journal* 21, no. 3 (January 1955): 261–72.

Koyré, Alexandre. *From the Closed World to the Infinite Universe*. Baltimore and London: John Hopkins University Press, 1957.

Kristeller, Paul Oskar. "Renaissance Aristotelianism." *Greek, Roman, and Byzantine Studies* 6, no. 2 (1965): 157–174.

Langholm, Odd. *Economics in the Medieval Schools: Wealth, Exchange, Value, Money, and Usury According to the Paris Theological Tradition, 1200–1350*. Leiden and New York: Brill, 1992.

———. *Price and Value in the Aristotelian Tradition: A Study in Scholastic Economic Sources*. Bergen: Universitetsforlaget, 1979.

———. "Scholastic Economics." In *Pre-Classical Economic Thought: From the Greeks to the Scottish Enlightenment*, ed. S. Todd Lowry. Boston/Dordrecht/Lancaster: Kluwer Academic Publishers, 1987.

———. *The Aristotelian Analysis of Usury*. Bergen: Universitetsforlaget, 1984.

———. *The Legacy of Scholasticism in Economic Thought: Antecedents of Choice and Power*. Cambridge and New York: Cambridge University Press, 1998.

———. *The Merchant in the Confessional: Trade and Price in the Pre-Reformation Penitential Handbooks*. Leiden and New York: Brill, 2003.

———. *Wealth and Money in the Aristotelian Tradition: A Study in Scholastic Economic Sources*. Bergen: Universitetsforlaget, 1983.

Lapeyre, H. *Une famille de merchands: les Ruiz*. Paris: Colin, 1955.

Lasa, M. Arigita y. *El Doctor Navarrus Don Martin de Azpilcueta y sus obras: Estudio histórico-crítico*. Pamplona: J. Ezquerro, 1895.

Laures, John, S.J. *The Political Economy of Juan de Mariana*. New York: Fordham University Press, 1928.

Larraz, José. *La época del mercantilismo en Castilla, 1500–1700*. Madrid: Aguilar, 1943.

Lea, Henry Charles. "The Ecclesiastical Treatment of Usury." *Yale Review* II (February 1894): 375–85.

Le Bras, G. "Usure. II. La doctrine ecclésiastique de l'usure a l'époque clasique (XII–XV siecle)." *Dictionnaire de Théologie Catholique* 15, no. 2 (1950): 2336–72.

Lecky, William Edward Hartpole. *History of the Rise and Influence of the Spirit of Rationalism in Europe.* Rev. ed. 2 vols. London: Longmans, Green, & Co., 1887–1890.

Leijonhufvud, Axel. *Macroeconomic Instability and Coordination: Selected Essays of Axel Leijonhufvud.* Cheltenham, U.K.: Edward Elgar Publishing Limited, 2000.

Locke, John. *An Essay Concerning Human Understanding.* London: Awnsham, John Churchill, and Samuel Mansbip, 1690.

López, J. Larraz. *La época del mercantilismo en Castilla, 1500–1700.* Madrid: Atlas, 1943; Madrid, Aguilar, 1963.

Lowry, S. Todd. "Aristotle's Mathematical Analysis of Exchange." *History of Political Economy* 1 (1969): 44–66.

———. *The Archeology of Economic Ideas: The Classical Greek Tradition.* Durham, N.C.: Duke University Press, 1987.

Lowry, S. Todd, ed. *Pre-Classical Economic Thought: From the Greeks to the Scottish Enlightenment.* Boston/Dordrecht/Lancaster: Kluwer Academic Publishers, 1987.

Lowry, S. Todd, and Barry Gordon, ed. *Ancient and Medieval Economic Ideas and Concepts of Social Justice.* Leiden and New York: Brill, 1998.

Martín, F. Ruiz. "La banca en España hasta 1782." In *El Banco de España: Una historia económica,* ed. A. Moreno Redondo. Madrid: Banco de España, 1970.

McLaughlin, T. P. "The Teaching of the Canonist on Usury (XII, XIII, and XIV Centuries)." *Mediaeval Studies* 1 (1939): 81–147.

———. "The Teaching of the Canonist on Usury (XII, XIII, and XIV Centuries)." *Mediaeval Studies* 2 (1940): 1–22.

Millar, Moorhouse F. X., S.J., "Scholasticism and American Political Philosophy." In *Present-Day Thinkers and the New Scholasticism,* ed. John S. Zybura. St. Louis: Herder, 1927.

Milton, J. R. "John Locke and the Nominalist Tradition." In *John Locke: Symposium Wolfenbüttel 1979,* ed. Reinhard Brandt. Berlin and New York: Walter de Gruyter, 1981.

Mochrie, Robert I. "Justice in Exchange: The Economic Philosophy of John Duns Scotus." *Journal of Markets & Morality* 9, no. 1 (Spring 2006): 35–56.

Morgenstern, Oskar. "Perfect Foresight and Economic Equilibrium." Economic Research Program, Research Memorandum no. 55. Princeton, N.J.: Princeton University, 1963.

Moss, Laurence S. "Introduction." In *Economic Thought in Spain: Selected Essays of Marjorie Grice-Hutchinson,* ed. Laurence S. Moss and Christopher K. Ryan. Brookfield, Vt.: Edward Elgar Publishing Company, 1993.

Muller, Richard A. *After Calvin: Studies in the Development of a Theological Tradition.* New York: Oxford University Press, 2003.

———. *Post-Reformation Reformed Dogmatics: The Rise and Development of Reformed Orthodoxy, ca. 1520 to ca. 1725.* 4 vols. Grand Rapids, Mich.: Baker Academic, 2003.

———. "The Problem of Protestant Scholasticism—A Review and Definition." In *Reformation and Scholasticism: An Ecumenical Enterprise,* ed. Willem J. van Asselt and Eef Dekker. Grand Rapids, Mich.: Baker Book House, 2001.

————. *The Unaccommodated Calvin: Studies in the Foundation of a Theological Tradition.* New York: Oxford University Press, 2000.

Muñoz, Rodrigo, de Juana. *Moral y economía en la obra de Martín de Azpilcueta.* Pamplona: Ediciones Universidad de Navarra, 1998.

————. "Scholastic Morality and the Birth of Economics: The Thought of Martín de Azpilcueta." *Journal of Markets & Morality* 4, no. 1 (2001): 14–42.

New Catholic Encyclopedia. Prepared by an editorial staff at the Catholic University of America. 18 vols. New York: McGraw-Hill, 1967–1988.

New Century Italian Renaissance Encyclopedia. Edited by Catherine B. Avery. New York: Appleton-Century-Crofts, 1972.

Noonan, John T. *The Scholastic Analysis of Usury.* Cambridge, Mass.: Harvard University Press, 1957.

Nouvelle biographie générale depuis les temps les plus reculés jusqu'a nos jours, avec les renseignements bibliographiques et l'indication des sources a consulter; publiee par mm. Firmin Didot freres, sous la direction de m. le dr. Hoefer. Edited by M. Jean Chrétien Ferdinand Hoefer. 46 vols. Copenhagen: Rosenkilde et Bagger, 1963. Reprint of the 1857 edition.

Nuccio, Oscar. *Economisti italiani del XVII secolo: Ferdinando Galiani, Antonio Genovesi, Pietro Verri, Francesco Mengotti.* Rome: Mengotti, 1974.

————. *Epistemologia della "azione umana" e razionalismo economico nel Duecento italiano: Il caso Albertano da Brescia.* Torino: Effatà Editrice, 2005.

————. *Il pensiero economico italiano.* 5 vols. Sassari: Gallizzi, 1984–1991.

————. *Scrittori classici italiani di economia politica.* Rome: Bizzari, 1965.

Oakley, Francis. *Kingship: The Politics of Enchantment.* Oxford: Blackwell Publishing, 2006.

————. "Locke, Natural Law, and God: Again." In *Politics and Eternity: Studies in the History of Medieval and Early-Modern Political Thought.* Leiden: Brill, 1999.

————. *Natural Law, Laws of Nature, Natural Rights: Continuity and Discontinuity in the History of Ideas.* New York and London: Continuum International Publishing Group, 2005.

————. *Omnipotence, Covenant, and Order: An Excursion in the History of Ideas from Abelard to Leibniz.* Ithaca: Cornell University Press, 1984.

————. *Politics and Eternity: Studies in the History of Medieval and Early-Modern Political Thought.* Leiden: Brill, 1999.

Oller, J. Nadal. "La revolución de los precios españoles en el XVI: Estado actual de la cuestión." *Hispania* 19 (1959): 503–29.

Olóriz, H. De. *Nueva biografía del Doctor Navarrus D. Martín de Azpilcueta y enumeración de sus obras.* Pamplona: N. Aramburu, 1916.

Oxford Classical Dictionary. Edited by Simon Hornblower and Antony Spawforth. 3d ed. New York: Oxford University Press, 1996.

Pereña, L. "El comentario de cambios." In *Comentario Resolutorio de Cambios*, introducción y texto crítico por Alberto Ullastres, José M. Perez Prendes y Luciano Pereña. Madrid: Consejo Superior de Investigaciones Científicas, 1965.

Piedra, Alberto M. *Natural Law: The Foundation of an Orderly Economic System.* Lanham and New York: Lexington Books, 2004.

Pribram, Karl. *A History of Economic Reasoning.* Baltimore and London: Johns Hopkins University Press, 1983.

Reichenbach, H. *The Philosophy of Space and Time*. New York: Dover, 1958.

Robinson, J. *La segunda crisis del pensamiento económico*. Mexico City: Ed. Actual, 1973.

Rothbard, Murray N. *Economic Thought before Adam Smith: An Austrian Perspective on the History of Economic Thought*. Vol. 1. Brookfield, Vt.: Edward Elgar Publishing Company, 1995.

Russell, Bertrand. *An Essay on the Foundations of Geometry*. New York: Dover, 1956.

Schmitt, Charles B. *Aristotle and the Renaissance*. Cambridge, Mass.: Harvard University Press, 1983.

———. "Towards a Reassessment of Renaissance Aristotelianism." *History of Science* 11 (1973): 159–93.

Schumpeter, Joseph A. *History of Economic Analysis*, ed. Elizabeth Booty Schumpeter. Oxford: Oxford University Press, 1954.

Sirico, Robert A. "The Economics of the Late Scholastics." *Journal of Markets & Morality* 1, no. 2 (Fall 1998): 122–29.

Spufford, P. *Money and Its Use in Medieval Europe*. Cambridge: Cambridge University Press, 1989.

Stark, Rodney. *The Victory of Reason: How Christianity Led to Freedom, Capitalism, and Western Success*. New York: Random House, 2005.

Tallmadge, G. Kasten. "Juan de Mariana." In *Jesuit Thinkers of the Renaissance*, ed. Gerard Smith, S.J. Milwaukee: Marquette University Press, 1939.

Theiner, J. *Die Entwicklung der Moraltheologie zur eigenständigen Diszpilin*. Regensburg: F. Pustet, 1970.

Trueman, Carl R., and R. S. Clark, ed. *Protestant Scholasticism: Essays in Reassessment*. Carlisle, U.K.: Paternoster Press, 1999.

Ullastres, A. *Anales de Economia*. Madrid: Consejo Superior de Investigaciones Científicas, 1965.

———. "Martín de Azpiluceta y su comentario resolutorio de cambios: Las ideas económicas de un moralista español del siglo XVI." *Anales de Economía* 3–4 (1941): 375–409.

———. "Martín de Azpiluceta y su comentario resolutorio de cambios: Las ideas económicas de un moralista español del siglo XVI." *Anales de Economía* 5 (1942): 51–95.

van Asselt, Willem J., and Eef Dekker, ed. *Reformation and Scholasticism: An Ecumenical Enterprise*. Grand Rapids, Mich.: Baker Book House, 2001.

Van Steenberghen, Fernand. *Aristotle in the West: The Origins of Latin Aristotelianism*. Translated by Leonard Johnston. Louvain: E. Nauwelaerts, 1955.

Vansteenberge, E. "Molina." *Dictionnaire de Théologie Catholique* (1929), X.

Vereecke, L. *De Guillaume d'Ockham à Saint Alphonse de Liguori: études d'historie de la théologie morale moderne, 1300–1787*. Rome: Collegium St. Alfonsi de Urbe, 1986.

Vilar, Pierre. *A History of Gold and Money, 1450–1920*. Translated by Judith White. Atlantic Highlands, N.J.: Humanities Press, 1976.

Viner, Jacob. *Religious Thought and Economic Society: Four Chapters of an Unfinished Work by Jacob Viner*, ed. Jacques Melitz and Donald Winch. Durham, N.C.: Duke University Press, 1978.

White, Andrew Dickson. *A History of the Warfare of Science with Theology in Christendom*. 2 vols. New York and London: D. Appleton and Company, 1896.

Whitehead, Alfred North. *The Concept of Nature*. Cambridge: Cambridge University Press, 1964.

Widow, Juan Antonio. "The Economic Teachings of the Spanish Scholastics." In *Hispanic Philosophy in the Age of Discovery*, ed. Kevin White. Washington, D.C.: Catholic University of America Press, 1997.

Young, Jeffrey T. *Economics as a Moral Science: The Political Economy of Adam Smith.* Cheltenham, U.K.: Edward Elgar Publishing Limited, 1997.

Young, Jeffrey T., and Barry Gordon. "Economic Justice in the Natural Law Tradition: Thomas Aquinas to Francis Hutcheson." *Journal of the History of Economic Thought* 14 (Spring 1992): 1–17.

Yuengert, Andrew. *The Boundaries of Technique: Ordering Positive and Normative Concerns in Economic Research.* Lanham and New York: Lexington Books, 2004.

CONTRIBUTORS

PATRICK T. BRANNAN, S.J. has been a Jesuit for fifty-seven years. He has the A.B./ M.A. (*Cantab.*) in the Classical Tripos from Cambridge University in England and the Ph.D. in Classical Philology from Stanford University in California, as well as the ecclesiastical degrees Ph.L and S.T. L. in philosophy and theology. He has taught classical languages and some philosophy and theology (mainly in seminaries) and has done a good deal of translation. In Rome he was a translator at the Thirty-Fourth General Congregation of the Society of Jesus and also attended two Synods of Bishops in the Vatican as a translator of documents in French, German, Italian, Latin, Spanish, and English. He has published, among other things, a translation of A.-J. Festugiere O.P.'s *Liberte et civilisation chez les Grecques*, and is awaiting the publication of his translation of selected topics from Saint Robert Bellarmine, S.J.'s *Controversia* (with commentary of Professor Robert Fastiggi, Ph.D.), and has just finished translating from the German some of the indices of the forthcoming English version of *Denzinger's Enchiridion*. Currently, he continues his work as a translator for the *Journal of Markets & Morality* as he engages in pastoral work.

FRANCISCO GÓMEZ CAMACHO, S.J. is Professor of Economics at the Universidad Pontificia Comillas in Madrid. He earned a licentiate in philosophy from the Facultad Complu-tense de la Compañía de Jesus, a Ph.D. in theology from the Universidad Pontificia Comillas, and a Ph.D. in economics from the Universidad Pontificia Comillas. He has held visiting professorships at numerous universities including Universidad de Salamanca (1993–2005), Universidad del Pacífico (Lima, Peru), Universidad Católica de Santiago de Chili, and Universidad Internacional Menéndez Pelayo. He is an internationally recognized expert on Spanish economic thought in the sixteenth and seventeenth centuries and has prepared modern critical editions of several works by Luis de Molina, S.J. (1535–1600) on such topics as the just price, usury, and money (exchange). He is the author of *Economia y Filosofia Moral: Los* *orígenes del pensamiento económico europeo en la Escolástica española* (Síntesis, 1998), as well as numerous articles and chapters in edited collections.

ALEJANDRO A. CHAFUEN is President and Chief Executive Officer of the Atlas Economic Research Foundation. Born in Argentina, he was educated at Grove City College in Pennsylvania, and the Argentine Catholic University in Buenos Aires. He holds a Ph.D. in economics from International College in California. A member of the Mont Pelerin Society, he has written extensively in academic journals and other publications. He is one of the world's leading commentators on the economic thought of Thomistic and Late-Scholastic thinkers. He has taught at Universidad Francisco Marroquín in Guatemala; the National Hispanic University in Oakland, California; the University of Buenos Aires; and the Argentine Catholic University in Buenos Aires, among others. He has also been published in newspapers ranging from *La Nación* to the *Wall Street Journal*.

JEANNINE EMERY has a degree in Spanish Literature, and a master's in nonfiction writing. She works as editor and translator in both English and Spanish and is currently working on the Spanish translation of *Banking, Justice, and the Common Good* by Samuel Gregg. She lives in Buenos Aires, Argentina.

STEPHEN J. GRABILL is Research Scholar in Theology at the Acton Institute for the Study of Religion and Liberty and the founding editor of the *Journal of Markets & Morality*, a peer-reviewed, interdisciplinary journal that explores issues at the intersection of moral philosophy, economics, ethics, and theology. He earned his M.T.S., Th.M., and Ph.D. in systematic theology from Calvin Theological Seminary in Grand Rapids, Michigan. He is an expert on natural law in the Protestant Scholastic tradition and has read widely in the history of economics and Catholic social thought. He has published several popular and scholarly articles on these and other topics. He is the author of *Rediscovering the Natural Law in Reformed Theological Ethics* (Eerdmans, 2006) and the editor and a contributing author to the three-volume *Foundations of Economic Personalism* series (Lexington Books, 2002).

RODRIGO MUÑOZ DE JUANA is Professor of Moral and Spiritual Theology at the Universidad de Navarra in Pamplona, Spain. He earned a licentiate in law from the Universidad Complutense de Madrid, a licentiate in systematic and moral theology, and his Ph.D. in theology from the Universidad de Navarra. He is an editorial board member of *Scripta Theologica*, the theological journal published by the Universidad de Navarra. He is an expert on economic topics in sixteenth-century Spanish moral theology and has written numerous articles and reviews in this field of study. He is the author of a recent book on the thought of Martín de Azpilcueta titled, *Moral y economía en la obra de Martín de Azpilcueta* (Eunsa, 1998), as well as a contributing editor in two recent publications, *Bartolomé Carranza: Tratado sobre la virtud de la justicia (1540)* (Eunsa, 2003) and *Teología: misterio de Dios y saber del hombre, textos para una conmemoración* (Eunsa, 2000).

INDEX

Tacitus, 291, 300, 320n12, 325n4
Tertullian, Quintus, xxii, xxiii, xxiv
text interpretation of CRM, 21–28
  Annanias and, 25, 28
  Antonine and, 26
  Cajetan and, 22
  Gregory IX and, 21, 23, 24, 25, 26, 28,
    91–92n5
  Laurencio and, 64
  Major on, 22
  Medina and, 22
  Molinaeus and, 28
  Silvestre and, 22
  Soto and, 22
Titus Maccius Plautus, 268, 312n7
tradition of individual duty
  Christianity and, xxxiiN37
transference of money, 9, 10
Treatise on Money (Molina), 111–229.
  See also *specific Arguments*
  about, 111
  axiom of free divisibility and, 129–30
  causality and, 115–16, 134n26
  continuity and change of paradigm and,
    114–15
  contract of usury and, 129–30
  debasement of money by kings and,
    130–32
  description of businessmen, 112–13
  economic context of, 112–13
  financial innovation and excesses and,
    113–14
  fungibility, liquidity, and quantification
    of economic value in, 123, 124
  lucrum cessans (profit ceasing/
    foregone) and, 126, 128, 152
  mutuum (consumption) and, 113,
    129–30
  natural-law tradition and, 116–18
  nominalism, 118–19
  probabilism and, 116–18
  standard unit of measurement and,
    119–20
A Treatise on the Alteration of Money
  (Mariana), 241–322

  advantages and disadvantages from
    alteration of copper money and,
    271–72, 279–82
  alteration of money and, 267–69,
    289–93
  argument of, 249
  debasement of money by kings and,
    242, 243–44, 259–60
  described, 241
  different *maravedis* of varying values
    and, 273–77
  disadvantages from alteration of money
    and, 283–88
  gold money and, 295–97
  king's economic expenses and, 299–
    304
  king's ownership of subjects' goods
    and, 253–54
  money, weights, and measures as
    foundations of commerce and,
    98n31, 265–66
  silver money and, 289–93
  tributes to kings and, 255–58
  twofold value of money and, 261–63,
    310n2
Tribune of the Plebs, 267, 311–12n4
tributes to kings, 255–58
Tudeschi, Nicolò de', 91–92n5
twofold value of money, 261–63, 310n2

Ullastres, Alberto, 5, 124
Umayyad empire (Moors), 274, 316–
  17n5, 316n4
Urban V, 233–34n9, 308n5
usury theory. *See also* interest
  Aristotle and, xxix–xxxN11
  common estimation to determine just
    price and, xiv
  CRM and, 6–9
  cupidity and, xiv
  decline of scholastic economics and,
    xvi, xxxiN31
  just price and, xiv
  natural-law tradition and, xxix–xxxN11
  positivism and, xv